CLARENDON STUDIES IN THE HISTORY OF ART

General Editor: Dennis Farr

THE RELIGIOUS PAINTINGS OF

Giambattista Tiepolo

Piety and Tradition in Eighteenth-century Venice

WILLIAM L. BARCHAM

CLARENDON PRESS · OXFORD
1989

Oxford University Press, Walton Street, Oxford OX2 6DP
Oxford New York Toronto
Delhi Bombay Calcutta Madras Karachi
Petaling Jaya Singapore Hong Kong Tokyo
Nairobi Dar es Salaam Cape Town
Melbourne Auckland
and associated companies in
Berlin Ibadan

Oxford is a trade mark of Oxford University Press

Published in the United States
by Oxford University Press, New York

British Library Cataloguing in Publication Data
Barcham, William L.
The religious paintings of Giambattista
Tiepolo: Piety and tradition in
eighteenth-century Venice.—(Clarendon
studies in the history of art).
1. Italian painting. Tiepolo, Giovanni
Battista 1696–1770
I. Title
759.5
ISBN 0–19–817501–9

Library of Congress Cataloging-in-Publication Data
Barcham, William L.
The religious paintings of Giambattista Tiepolo: piety and
tradition in eighteenth-century Venice/William L. Barcham.
(The Clarendon studies in the history of art)
Bibliography. Includes index.
1. Tiepolo, Giovanni Battista, 1696–1770—Criticism and
interpretation. 2. Christian art and symbolism—Modern period,
1500—Italy—Venice. 3. Mary, Blessed Virgin, Saint—Art.
4. Christian saints in art. I. Tiepolo, Giovanni Battista,
1696–1770. II. Title. III. Series.
ND623.T5B37   1988   759.5—dc19   88–3996
ISBN 0–19–817501–9

Set and Printed in Great Britain by
Butler & Tanner Ltd, Frome and London

For My Father, Aaron Barcham
and to the Memory
of My Mother, Rose C. Barcham

GENERAL EDITOR'S PREFACE

The Clarendon Studies in the History of Art is a new series devoted primarily to the art and architecture of Western Europe from the medieval period to the present day. The series will publish the results of recent research in a readable and attractively illustrated form, either as monographs or as studies dealing with a particular aspect of art history. Established scholars will contribute, but it is also intended to give young scholars the opportunity to publish their first major work.

Dr William Barcham discusses Giambattista Tiepolo's religious painting of his Venetian period. He does this within a conventional art-historical framework, but combines sophisticated iconographical analysis with sensitive critical appraisal. I am delighted to introduce the Clarendon Studies with this pioneering work, which is the author's first book.

DENNIS FARR

ACKNOWLEDGEMENTS

STUDYING Tiepolo's religious themes and narratives has steered me into uncharted waters—but rarely alone. Although the subject-matter of the great painter's sacred imagery has been little considered, its beauty and individuality have been far from ignored. All lovers and students of Tiepolo's art must gratefully acknowledge the pioneering studies of Pompeo Molmenti, Giulio Lorenzetti, Edward Sack, Giuseppe Fiocco, and Antonio Morassi. Rodolfo Pallucchini and the late Anna Pallucchini have also significantly increased our understanding of Tiepolo; without constant reference to their work, the younger scholar would find his own severely weakened. Closer to home, I have enjoyed the generosity of George Knox, whose knowledge of 'matters Tiepolo' is without parallel, and of David Rosand, to whom I am indebted for his knowledge of the Serenissima and its history. I am deeply grateful to Donald Posner, who first encouraged my study of Venetian painting; he has always offered advice and support, and his scholarly example has been my constant model.

During my periods of study in Italy, many friends gave me special warmth and assistance. It is but little recompense to thank in print Adriana De Angelis, Franco Giacobelli, Franca Lolli, Giuliano Calligaris and, in particular, Luigina De Grandis. Special thanks are also due to Rona Goffen, Deborah Howard, Paul H. D. Kaplan, Rudolph Rooms, and Sarah Blake McHam. Without the collaboration of Ubaldo Vitali and the aid of his excellent drawings, several of my arguments would be weaker. Peter Dreyer and Erich Schleier at the Staatliche Museen, Berlin-Dahlem; Hannelore Nützmann at the Bode Museum, Berlin (DDR); Angelo Walther at the Gemäldegalerie, Dresden; Hugh Macandrew at the National Gallery of Scotland, Edinburgh; Christiane D. Andersson and Michael Maekt-Gerard at the Städtische Galerie, Frankfurt; Linda Horvitz Roth at the Wadsworth Atheneum, Hartford (Conn.); Scott Schaeffer at the Los Angeles County Museum; Michael Semff at the Staatsgalerie, Stuttgart; Maria Francesca Tiepolo at the Archivio di Stato, Venice; and Michael Levey at the National Gallery, London, all offered their kind assistance. Sir Michael's own *Giambattista Tiepolo* came out after my text was completed, too late unfortunately for me to take full advantage of some of his excellent discussions.

Generosity from other quarters must be acknowledged, too, and I would like to express my gratitude to Kathleen Weil-Garris Brandt, Penelope Brownell, Linda Carroll, Lucia Casanova, Enrico Colleoni, Piero Corsini, Becky Edwards, Mary W. Gibbons, Ann Sutherland Harris, Mary Jane Harris, Hans-Michael Herzog, Laurence Homolka, William Hood, C. Douglas Lewis, Lucilla Marino, Adriano Mariuz, Egidio Martini, Edward Muir, Michelangelo Muraro, Mons. Antonio Niero, Giuseppe Pavanello, Denise and Alfred Puglisi, W. R. Rearick, Pietro Scarpa, Joyce Seltzer, Suzanne Stratton, and—

finally—the *parroci* and *sacristani* of Este, Folzano, Noventa Vicentina, Piove di Sacco, Rampazzo, Rovetta, Somaglia, Thiene, and Verolanuova.

The ease and pleasure of producing this book are a result of the guidance and help of all those who were involved at Oxford University Press, among whom I want to single out Frances Whistler. In addition, I should like to mention Dennis Farr, General Editor of this series, whose support of this work has been of fundamental importance.

Research in Italy over the last few years has largely been possible through the generous support of the American Council of Learned Societies, the National Endowment for the Humanities, and the Gladys Krieble Delmas Foundation. The Delmas Foundation also generously aided the publication of this book. We *venezianisti* in the Anglo-Saxon world are especially grateful to it and to its founder, Mrs Delmas. In Rome, the staffs of the American Academy, the Biblioteca Apostolica Vaticana, and the Biblioteca Hertziana aided me in my work, and in Venice my way was eased at all times by those who work in the Archivio di Stato, the Biblioteca Municipale Correr, the Biblioteca Nazionale Marciana, and the Biblioteca della Fondazione Giorgio Cini.

The final name here, Catherine Puglisi, is far from being the least important. Fortunately for me, her contribution was not 'wifely' and directed towards the typescript or keeping *custodi* at bay. Instead, she sought to understand with me the meaning of Tiepolo's art; without her excellent eye and her sharp mind, this book would be poorer indeed.

W.L.B.

CONTENTS

LIST OF COLOUR PLATES

LIST OF BLACK AND WHITE PLATES

PHOTOGRAPHIC CREDITS

Athens: National Pinacothiki and Alexander Soutzos Museum, 49; Bergamo: Ing. Enrico Colleoni, 66; Berlin (DDR): Bode Museum, 75; Chicago: Art Institute, 76; Cologne: Wallraf-Richartz Museum, 25; Edinburgh: National Gallery of Scotland, 99; Florence: Scala, I, II; Frankfurt: Städelsches Kunstinstitut, VIII, 126; Hartford, CT: Wadsworth Atheneum, 20, 103; Innsbruck: Tirolerlandesmuseum Ferdinandeum, 11; London: Courtauld Institute Galleries, V, 96, 97; National Gallery, VII, 5, 46, 115, 117, 125; Victoria and Albert Museum, 26; Los Angeles, CA: Grunwald Center for the Graphic Arts, Wight Art Gallery, UCLA, 31; Milan: Musei Civici, 56; Museo Poldi-Pezzoli, VI; Soprintendenza per i Beni Artistici e Storici per Milano, 63, 110; Montreal: Musée des Beaux-Arts, 51–3; Graphische Sammlung, 102, 116; New York: Art Resource, 2, 14, 29, 34–45, 47, 65, 74, 81, 82–4, 86–9, 108, 111; Metropolitan Museum of Art, 128, 129; Private Collections, III, 100; Padua: Museo Civico, 123; Paris: Réunion des Musées Nationaux, IV, 107; Raleigh, NC: North Carolina Museum of Art, 1; San Diego, CA: San Diego Museum of Art, 22; Venice: Archivio Fotografico, Museo Correr, 10, 17, 23, 58, 105, 106; Archivio Fotografico, Palazzo Ducale, 64; Böhm, 7–9, 12, 13, 15, 16, 19, 21, 24, 27, 28, 32, 33, 48, 50, 54, 55, 59, 62, 67–73, 77–80, 85, 90–5, 98, 101, 104, 109, 113, 114, 118–21; Private Collection, 30; Soprintendenza per i Beni Artistici e Storici di Venezia, 6, 112; Soprintendenza per i Beni Ambientali e Architettonici di Venezia, 60; Verona: Soprintendenza per i Beni Artistici e Storici del Veneto, 61, 127, 130; Washington, DC: National Gallery of Art, 122; Zurich: Kunsthaus, 124

LIST OF FIGURES

ABBREVIATIONS

ASV	Archivio di Stato, Venice
b.	busta
BMC	Biblioteca Municipale Correr, Venice
BNM	Biblioteca Nazionale Marciana, Venice

INTRODUCTION

GIAMBATTISTA TIEPOLO was Italy's greatest painter in the eighteenth century and the last to present the themes of Christian redemption celebrating the veneration of saints, devotion to Mary, and adoration of Christ. These aspects of his art, however, have not been generally appreciated in our own century. Quite the contrary: the critic and historian Roberto Longhi even went so far as to accuse Tiepolo's religious art of both 'anachronistic rhetoric' and 'haughty scepticism', condemning it totally because, in his opinion, it fatally damaged the entire tradition of Italian painting![1] Longhi misinterpreted the Venetian painter entirely, of course, for there were few in the Italian pictorial tradition whose imagery was more sensitively attuned to both the message of eternal salvation and the doctrines of the Catholic Church than Tiepolo. Paradoxically, two Englishmen have remarked more sensitively on Tiepolo's serious attitude towards sacred subject-matter. Shortly after Longhi made his derogatory statements, James Byam Shaw noted that 'for all the worldly splendours of [the secular frescos at] Würzburg or Strà . . . [Tiepolo] remains essentially a religious artist'. And more recently writing about the exquisite oil-sketches for the Aranjuez altar-pieces, Christopher Brown remarked with surprise that there were still 'pockets of resistance' to the idea that Tiepolo was 'a profoundly serious painter of religious subjects . . .'.[2]

Why the seriousness of Tiepolo's sacred art has been held in question by so many intelligent observers until only recently is not easy to understand.[3] Especially because, while art lovers were ignoring his religious paintings—or if they considered them, they accused them of false sentiment—concert audiences were flocking to the oratorios of Antonio Vivaldi, to Bach's *St Matthew Passion*, Handel's *Messiah*, Haydn's *Creation*, and Mozart's *Requiem*. It would appear that the twentieth century can easily surmount its prevailing secularity to appreciate the great music of the eighteenth. Who, while attending a performance of the *Messiah*, has not been amazed to see thousands of non-believers rising to their feet during the 'Hallelujah Chorus'?

Tiepolo's religious art was as sincere an expression of spiritual fervour as Handel's famous chorus. And it was contemporaneous with the *musica sacra* of his two Venetian compatriots, Antonio Vivaldi (1678–1741) and Benedetto Marcello (1686–1739). Moreover, Tiepolo was just thirty-three when Leipzig heard the *St Matthew Passion*, and

---

[1] R. Longhi, 'Viatico per cinque secoli di pittura veneziana' [1946], *Ricerche sulla pittura veneta 1946–1969* (Florence, 1978), 32 ff.

[2] J. Byam Shaw, *Drawings and Etchings by Giovanni Battista and Giovanni Domenico Tiepolo* (Plaistow, 1955), 7; and C. Brown, review of H. Braham, *The Princes Gate Collection* (London, 1981), in *Burlington Magazine*, 123 (1981), 502.

[3] A dislike of Baroque religious art was fairly typical of late eighteenth- and nineteenth-century taste. Criticism of Tiepolo's painting has to some extent paralleled that, but appreciation of him has come more slowly than for Bernini, for example. Religious art of the Enlightenment has been slighted in most general studies of eighteenth-century art; it is now being remedied with, for instance, P. Conisbee's 'Religious Painting in the Age of Reason', in C. B. Bailey (ed.), *The First Painters of the King: French Royal Taste from Louis XIV to the Revolution* (exh. cat., Stair Sainty Matthiesen, New York, 1985 (London)), 20–30.

forty-six when Dublin witnessed the first performance of the *Messiah*. At the very end of the century, Haydn and Mozart composed some of the most sublime sacred music in the Western tradition. But, unlike the compositions that Bach, Handel, Haydn, and Mozart created for churches, Tiepolo's have been accused of hypocrisy.[4] Tiepolo's 'problem'—if it is his—is not that his religious imagery does *not* agree with the values of his epoch, but that it has too often been regarded without considering them at all. How can one then appreciate his painting?

The eighteenth century began with the fifty-seven-year-old Louis XIV on the throne of France, and concluded with John Adams as the second President of the United States of America. The numerous events that led to both the toppling of the French monarchy and to the creation of a constitutional democracy in the New World are too well known, and much too important, to bear facile repetition here. However, it must be remembered that the winds of social change that bore down on the Western political world also affected Catholic religious life. Even before Montesquieu published his *L'Esprit des lois* (1748), David Hume his *History of Religion* (1757), and Voltaire wrote: 'I conclude that all sensible men, all honest men must hold the Christian religion in dread', the Roman Church felt innovation rumbling from within.[5] There was, in particular, a movement to limit papal primacy and to return power to the Curia and the Council of Cardinals.[6] Many even thought that with the election of the enlightened Prospero Lambertini to the Throne of St Peter in 1740—he ruled as Benedict XIV—a real 'renewing and refreshening [of] ecclesiastical bodies and institutions . . .' was about to take place.[7] Unfortunately, age-old traditions and heavy bureaucracy prevented the papacy from doing more than only beginning an attempt at correction. But, the Holy See did seek to reorganize some of its affairs and rituals so that they would function more efficiently than before, and to control, too, outstanding abuses in the Church. Regarding the first matter, Benedict's revision of the breviary stands out, as does the *Magnum Bullarium Romanum*, the thirty-two-volume publication of pontifical letters covering the reigns from Leo I (d. 461) to Benedict (d. 1758). In the category of 'correction', one noteworthy act was Benedict's reduction of the excessive number of compulsory feast-days in the liturgical calendar.[8]

Despite these accomplishments, often backed by the Holy See's sincere wish to accommodate and modernize, the eighteenth century witnessed a sharp and decisive 'divorce between the religious world and the secularized' for the first time since the beginning of the Christian era.[9] But what to us might appear as a stark polarity in 1799 did not begin

[4] Some years ago, Terisio Pignatti wrote in an otherwise very useful article that Tiepolo's bright colour and pictorial rhetoric expressed a lack of sincerity: cf. his 'Religion and Eighteenth-century Venetian Painting', *Apollo*, 90 (1969), 20.

[5] Voltaire, 'Examen important de Milord Bolingbroke ou le tombeau du fanatisme' [1767], in *Œuvres complètes*, xxvi (Paris, 1879), 298: 'Je conclus que tout homme sensé, tout homme de bien, doit avoir la secte chrétienne en horreur.'

[6] A. C. Jemolo, *Stato e Chiesa negli scrittori politici italiani del Seicento e del Settecento* (Turin, 1914), 133 ff.

[7] M. Rosa, *Riformatori e ribelli nel '700 religioso italiano* (Bari, 1969), 54: 'I primi anni del pontificato lambertiniano sono segnati in effeti da uno slancio eccezionale, che indica in Benedetto XIV

la precisa volontà di rinvigorire e ringiovanire le strutture e le istituzioni ecclesiastiche, di recuperare rapidamente posizioni perdute, di creare possibilità nuove per la Chiesa romana.'

[8] For the breviary, see A. Vecchi, *Correnti religiose nel Sei-Settecento veneto* (Venice, 1962), 206. For Catholic reform, see E. Préclin and E. Jarry, *Le lotte politiche e dottrinali nei secoli XVII e XVIII (1648–1789)* (Turin, 1974) (*Storia della Chiesa dalle origini ai nostri giorni*, ed. L. Mezzadri), 65; and F. Venturi, *Settecento riformatore: Da Muratori a Beccaria* (Turin, 1969). For Benedict's reduction of feast-days, cf. Chap. 2, p. 140.

[9] A. Prandi, 'Spiritualità e sensibilità', in V. Branca (ed.), *Sensibilità e razionalità nel Settecento* (Venice, 1967), 65; see also Vecchi, *Correnti religiose*, p. 390.

as such in 1700. In fact, when Cardinal Giovanni Francesco Albani became Clement XI in that year, post-Tridentine Catholic fervour was still at its height.[10] The religious orders continued to serve the papacy faithfully throughout the Universal Church. The Jesuits were the most important of all, their influence growing with each succeeding decade.[11] Up until their fall (1773), they unfailingly supported papal policy, and they upheld the authoritarian privileges that for years had separated their membership from that of their brother orders. The Society of Jesus stood for traditional values, or at least for their public recognition.[12] One of the most important of these was devotion to the Mother of God. Exploiting their unique position within the inner circles of the Holy See, the Jesuits sought to elevate her figure by having the Immaculate Conception declared church dogma. Had the Jesuits been successful in their argument, their power would have escalated even further.[13] Devotion to the Virgin was, in any case, a popular form of eighteenth-century spirituality, and its popularity was reflected in the widespread success of Alfonso de' Liguori's publication, *Le glorie di Maria* (1750), and, as I shall argue, Tiepolo's four great Marian ceiling-paintings.[14]

The salient point is that for much of the eighteenth century religious issues were at the centre of European thought. The controversy over Jansenism, for instance, troubled some of Europe's best thinkers.[15] In his *Istoria teologica* (1742), Scipione Maffei remarked that everyone's attention in Paris was focused on this subject.[16] But less clamorous matters, too, caught public notice; because of the numerous publications in which ordinary men and women testified to visions of the Deity or the Virgin, mysticism became popular and even fashionable. This was particularly the case in Italy.[17] More 'prosaic' people who were denied the unique private moments of such personal visions could experience intense spiritual fervour through 'group happenings' organized by the Church. The *Via Crucis* was for the masses the equivalent of the visions sustained by individuals; the Stations of the Cross enjoyed enormous popularity in the eighteenth century, receiving their first spectacular 'performance' at the Colosseum in 1750, a Jubilee Year. This celebration was so successful that Rome could not offer hospitality to all the pilgrims who flocked there, and more than one-quarter of them had to camp outside the city.[18] Observing this, who would have said in 1750 that the Enlightenment was altering history, that times were changing?

[10] Préclin and Jarry, *Le lotte politiche*, p. 82.

[11] For the strength of the religious orders, see Vecchi, 'I modi della devozione', in Branca, *Sensibilità e razionalità*, p. 110. Of the 29 men and women canonized in the eighteenth century, 18 were members of religious orders: cf. O. Chadwick, *The Popes and European Revolution* (Oxford, 1981), 26. On Jesuit power, see E. Codignola, *Illuministi, Giansenisti e Giacobini nell'Italia del Settecento* (Florence, 1947), 187ff.; according to Vecchi, *Correnti religiose*, pp. 129–30, the Jesuits were particularly powerful in the Veneto, and some of the best families there sent their children to Jesuit colleges.

[12] The very closeness of the Jesuits to the papacy represented to many a 'spirito di resistenza onde Roma andava opponendosi alle novità': cf. Vecchi, *Correnti religiose*, p. 214.

[13] For the Immaculate Conception and the Church in the 1740s, cf. Chap. 2, pp. 158–9ff. Although the Order was disbanded in the 1770s, it was still strong during the pontificate of Clement XIII (1758–69) of the Venetian Rezzonico family; his Bull of 1765, *Apostolicum*, was meant to help the Jesuits against Louis XV of France.

[14] Alfonso was canonized in 1839 and declared a Doctor of the Church in 1871; for St Alfonse, see Chadwick, *The Popes*, pp. 231–2, and G. Cacciatore, *S. Alfonso de' Liguori e il Giansenismo: Le ultime fortune del moto giansenistico e la restituzione del pensiero cattolico nel secolo* XVIII (Florence, 1944). For a brief summary of the effect of the Marian cult on feast-days during the period, cf. Préclin and Jarry, *Le lotte politiche*, p. 78. See Chap. 2, pp. 136ff., for a short description of S. Alfonso's publication.

[15] For further discussion on Jansenism, see Chap. 2, pp. 130ff.

[16] S. Maffei, *Istoria teologica delle dottrine e delle opinioni corse ne' cinque primi secoli della Chiesa in proposito della divina grazia, del libero arbitrio, e della predestinazione* (Trent, 1742), pp. ixff., where Maffei explains his reasons for writing the book.

[17] Cf. Préclin and Jarry, *Le lotte politiche*, p. 101; and Prandi, 'Spiritualità e sensibilità', p. 87.

[18] Cf. Préclin and Jarry, *Le lotte politiche*, p. 57; Chadwick, *The Popes*, p. 164; and L. Pastor, *The History of the Popes*, xxxv (London, 1949), 325ff.

1. P. Batoni, *Triumph of Venice* (oil on canvas, 174·3 × 286 cm.)

Few important European cities were changing as little as Venice. Indeed, permanence is one of the prime sensations felt there, where urban existence is, paradoxically, so fragile. The immutability experienced in Venice can partly be accounted for by nature's eternal laws. The endless lapping of water against quays and building foundations is as convincing a justification of eternity as are the sands and ancient monuments along the Nile. Venice in the eighteenth century also sustained a perception of timelessness because the same institutions, the same structures, and the same ruling class had been governing the Serenissima, as the State referred to itself, for almost a millennium.[19] Venetians themselves subscribed to the precept that tradition conferred authority and to the myth that history was forever. This point of view was explicitly expressed by Pompeo Batoni in his *Triumph of Venice* (Pl. 1). Painted in 1737 for Marco Foscarini, Venice's official historiographer, this remarkable image was meant to recall the glorious period after the Cambrai wars (*c*.1510) when the State was restored to peace and prosperity.[20] Evoking the past was only the ostensible purpose of the painting, however. Foscarini commissioned it while in Rome as the Serenissima's ambassador to the Papal States, a diplomatic position just as sensitive in the eighteenth century as it had been during and after the reign of Julius II in the early sixteenth. In expressing himself through the brush of a Roman painter who 'made no concessions to Venetian taste', Foscarini spoke directly to the papacy at a time when some of Venice's most important ancient rights and traditions were being threatened by papal prerogative.[21] Batoni's image, in which abstract virtues and cultural achievements have been pictorially personified to form a machine-like apparatus of civic glorification, was conceived as much to vaunt contemporary Venetian political ambitions as it was to document past Venetian glory. But, like Gertrude reacting to the Player Queen in *Hamlet*, the more sceptical viewer looking at the painting knows that 'The lady doth protest too much . . .' (III. ii).[22]

Venetian patriotism in the eighteenth century rested not on the city's recent accomplishments but on its time-honoured traditions, the most special of which was that 'Venice [was] like a type of State-Church, almost a national church . . .'.[23] This belief provided one of the fundamental underpinnings for religious life there, and the organization of day-to-day ecclesiastical ritual to a large degree complemented the functioning of government. But precisely because the management of religion was a vital matter for the

[19] For a fundamental study of eighteenth-century Venice, see J. Georgelin, *Venise au siècle des lumières* (Paris, 1978). See, too, N. Jonard, *La vita a Venezia nel* XVIII *secolo* (Milan, 1967), 145 ff.; G. Torcellan, 'Un problema aperto: Politica e cultura nella Venezia del '700', in *Settecento Veneto e altri scritti storici* (Turin, 1969), 303–21; and M. Brusatin, *Venezia nel Settecento* (Turin, 1980).

[20] Cf. A. Clark and E. P. Bowron, *Pompeo Batoni: A Complete Catalogue* (New York, 1985), 213, with relevant bibliography; and F. Haskell, *Patrons and Painters: Art and Society in Baroque Italy* (New Haven and London, 1980), 259.

[21] Haskell, *Patrons and Painters*, p. 259. The issue at hand was the Patriarchy of Aquileia: cf. Chap. 1, pp. 56 ff.

[22] Many astute citizens were aware at the time that Venice's star had fallen. When Foscarini commissioned Batoni, Maffei wrote his *Consiglio politico . . . presentato al governo Veneto nell'anno 1736* (Venice, 1797), in which he described 'our present weakness'

(p. 10). See also L. Einaudi, 'L'economia pubblica veneziana dal 1736 al 1755', *La riforma sociale*, 14 (1904), 177–96, 261–82, 429 50, and 509–37; and C. Semenzato, 'Venezia religiosa nell' arte del Seicento', *Studi veneziani*, 14 (1972), 185–93.

[23] S. Caponetto, 'Origini e caratteri della riforma in Sicilia', *Rinascimento*, 7 (1956), 304. This belief—which was based on two historical events, the 'translatio' of St Mark's body to Venice in 828, and the meeting in Venice in 1177 of Doge Sebastiano Ziani with Pope Alexander III and Emperor Frederick I Barbarossa—was, of course, hardly new in the settecento: cf. O. Demus, *The Church of San Marco in Venice* (Washington, DC, 1960), 7; and S. Sinding-Larsen, *Christ in the Council Hall: Studies in the Religious Iconography of the Venetian Republic* (Acta ad Archaeologiam et Artium Historiam Pertinentia, 5; Institutum Romanum Norvegiae, Rome, 1974), *passim*.

State, Venice did not have much trust in the papacy: indeed, '. . . for the Venetian establishment, the Roman Church and the Catholic religion were completely different things . . .'.[24] Mistrust for the one was so great that no member of the Roman hierarchy could hold public office in the Republic.[25] No papal bull could be published within the Republic without the signature of a Venetian official. As a result, antagonism between the Senate and the Curia rose to a point at which Benedict XIV felt that 'the Venetians [were] mortal enemies of the pontifical State . . .'.[26] In 1751, eight years after writing the above, Benedict deprived the Serenissima of its ancient Patriarchy of Aquileia! The situation was aggravated even further in 1754 when the Senate issued a decree prohibiting all citizens from applying to Rome for dispensations or pardons without authority from the Republic.[27] Rome saw this as Venetian high-handedness and—worse still—as interference in ecclesiastical affairs.[28] Tensions between the two states, already historically pained, grew more acute. A last blow to Venetian–Roman relations was the law of 1767 forbidding mortmain—that is, the willing of goods into ecclesiastical hands—unless first approved by the Senate.[29] In sum, religion in eighteenth-century Venice remained, as before, under the direct control of the Venetian State.

The daily and public administration of this control lay largely in the hands of the *tre savii all'eresia*, three noblemen chosen from the Council of Ten, the government's most powerful committee, and the Councillors of the Doge. Although these lay ministers often constituted the State Inquisition together with clerics of papal appointment, they could also sit alone if matters before them touched specifically on 'Venetian orthodoxy'.[30] And such work never ceased to occupy the *savii* throughout the settecento. Their responsibilities during an era when Protestant heresy no longer threatened the State ranged from punishing blasphemy against Christ to disciplining men who made shameless comments about women in front of a church.[31] Often acting without directives from the Council of Ten, the *savii* sent their spies all over the city, seeking to maintain a firm grasp on the citizenry's thoughts and behaviour in order, as Haskell has noted, to preserve the status quo.[32]

Indeed, in eighteenth-century Venice the seams linking the present to the millennial

[24] Cf. M. Berengo, *La società veneta alla fine del Settecento: Ricerche storiche* (Florence, 1956), 226, 242: '. . . per la classe dirigente veneziana, Chiesa di Roma e religione cattolica erano cose del tutto diverse . . .'. And, furthermore: '[to the government and its State Inquisitors] la religione appariva anzitutto come il più sicuro puntello d'un potere indisturbato ed indiscusso . . .'.

[25] A. Sagredo, 'Leggi venete intorno agli ecclesiastici sino al secolo XVIII', *Archivio storico italiano*, 3/2 (1865), 95 ff.

[26] This was written on 9 Aug. 1743 to Cardinal De Tencin: cf. E. Morelli (ed.), *Le lettere di Benedetto XIV al Card. De Tencin (1740–47)*, i (Rome, 1955), 99–100; see also L.-P. Raybaud, *Papauté et pouvoir temporel sous les pontificats de Clément XII et Benoît XIV 1730–1758* (Paris, 1963), 121; and M. Petrocchi, *Il tramonto della repubblica di Venezia e l'assolutismo illuminato* (Venice, 1950), 9 n. 1.

[27] A. Stella, *Chiesa e Stato nelle relazioni dei nunzi pontifici a Venezia: Ricerche sul giurisdizionalismo veneziano dal XVI al XVIII secolo* (Vatican City, 1964), 84; and B. Cecchetti, *La repubblica di Venezia e la corte di Roma* (Venice, 1874), 367 ff.

[28] A. M. Bettanini, *Benedetto XIV e la repubblica di Venezia:*

Storia delle trattative diplomatiche per la difesa dei diritti giurisdizionali ecclesiastici (Milan, 1931), 9 ff.

[29] The fundamental text for explaining this Venetian decision is A. Montegnacco's *Ragionamento intorno a' beni temporali posseduti dalle Chiese, dagli ecclesiastici . . .* (Venice, 1766). See also G. Tabacco, *Andrea Tron (1712–1785) e la crisi dell'aristocrazia senatoria a Venezia* (Trieste, 1957), 123; and Chadwick, *The Popes*, p. 247: 'France passed a law on mortmain (1749), Tuscany two years later. The flood of laws limiting bequests to church charities and monasteries came in 1761–7: Spain, Portugal, Austria, Bavaria, the Palatinate, Lombardy, Genoa, Modena, Lucca, Parma, Mantua, and finally Venice.'

[30] Cf. Stella, *Chiesa e Stato*, pp. 277 ff., for Alberto Bolognetti's late sixteenth-century description of the Holy Office's workings.

[31] Cf. G. Comisso, *Les Agents secrets de Venise au xviii᷉ siècle (1705–1797)* (Paris, 1944), 51, for examples of informers' accusations. And for a specific case of state spies moving against patricians, cf. Haskell, *Patrons and Painters*, p. 245 n. 2.

[32] Haskell, *Patrons and Painters*, p. 246.

past were imperceptibly woven. Governmental functions, for example, continued to run smoothly, so much so that foreigners flocked there to study and understand the State. Although Montesquieu came away entirely disenchanted, Voltaire praised Venetian liberty.[33] Liberty did exist in the city during its last hundred years of independent political life, but mostly in the gaming houses, for which Venice enjoyed inordinate contemporary renown. That reputation has descended to us undiminished, overwhelming our appreciation for all other aspects of late Venetian civilization.[34] But Venice's self-esteem towards the end of its existence was not built upon its fame for debauchery; it rested instead on its sense of itself as a Christian city, and on its pride in its political machinery. Twentieth-century historians, however, have not given the Republic much credit for piety. But dare one gauge the depth of people's beliefs two hundred years after the event?

One must remember that consecrated altars in Venice vastly outnumbered betting tables. Moreover, in terms of the number of new churches and their generally high artistic level, no city on the continent could compete with eighteenth-century Venice. To get a superficial idea of where Venetian monies and energies were being directed at the time, one need only glance down Douglas Lewis's long list of contemporary ecclesiastical architectural projects.[35] Façades were added to churches already built, and interiors were finished in buildings already standing, but most impressive of all is the array of completely new churches. If the numbers of gambling houses are to be read as an indication of corruption, then the numbers of churches must likewise be read as signs of piety.[36]

The city also enjoyed an extraordinary ratio of clergy to citizenry, perhaps the highest in Europe.[37] To objections that these priests were the poor sons of impoverished patricians with no other choice of career before them, that as spiritual caretakers they were not very concerned for their parishioners' well-being, and that statistics reveal nothing of inner sentiment, one can only respond that church services were, nevertheless, well attended. Of course, people often went to church in Italy in the eighteenth century just to pass the time, but sermons in Venice were an important public function.[38] The grandiloquent language of some of the contemporary preachers may account for the turn-out, but more

---

[33] Montesquieu, 'Voyages', in *Œuvres complètes de Montesquieu*, ii (Paris, 1950), 992; and Voltaire, 'Venise, et, par occasion, de la liberté', in *Œuvres complètes*, xx (Paris, 1879), 553.

[34] Voltaire used carnival in Venice as the setting for Candide's search for Cunegunde in chaps. 24–6 of *Candide* (1759), and emphasized the madness and oblivion there at holiday time by telling of four kings who went to vacation in the city after having lost their states in war. On this all too overstated image of Venice, see P. Sohm's recent 'Pietro Longhi and Carlo Goldoni: Relations between Painting and Theatre', *Zeitschrift für Kunstgeschichte*, 45 (1982), 258 and n. 8.

[35] C. Douglas Lewis, *The Late Baroque Churches of Venice* (New York and London, 1979), 8 ff.; see also E. Bassi, *Architettura del Sei e Settecento a Venezia* (Naples, 1962).

[36] For the *casini*, see Georgelin, *Venise*, pp. 733–4.

[37] All authorities agree on this point, although their exact figures contradict each other. In 1753, according to C. Tivaroni, *L'Italia prima della rivoluzione francese 1753–1789* (Turin and Naples, 1888), 32–3, there was a religious population of 37,910 out of a total of 139,095. Préclin and Jarry, *Le lotte politiche*, p. 85, write that in the Veneto in 1766 there were 22,307 priests out of a

total citizenry of 2,334,972, a little more than 100 people to 1 clergyman. Georgelin, *Venise*, p. 740, reports instead that in the same year Venice had 1 priest for every 54 inhabitants. This last is confirmed by L.-J. Rogier, G. de Bertier de Sauvigny, and J. Hajjar in *Secolo dei lumi, rivoluzioni, restaurazioni* (Turin, 1976), 92, who state that in the Veneto at mid-century there was a religious community of 40,797 (they add all the members of the religious orders to the number of priests, 22,307) in a population of 2,354,922, or 1 for about every 58 lay people. For the allegiance of the ordinary clergy in the Veneto to Catholic dogma, cf. Berengo, *La società veneta*, pp. 241 ff.

[38] F. Zanotto, *Storia della predicazione nei secoli della letteratura italiana* (Modena, 1899), 322. On p. 337, he mentions two important preachers of the time, Antonio Bassani (d. 1747) and Girolamo Tornielli (d. 1752): for the latter, see Chap. 1, p. 78 n. 132. Daniele Concina of the Gesuati was one of Italy's greatest sermonizers during the century: for more on him, see Chap. 2, p. 134 n. 92. The literature does not provide numbers for church attendance in Italian cities, but the general consensus seems to be that crowds were large in Venice.

[39] On the importance of sermons, see L. A. Muratori's *Dei*

likely it was the direct appeal of dramatic stories from the Old Testament.[39] Venice's distinction in public discourse in church may also be accounted for by its pre-eminence, at least through the first half of the century, as Italy's centre for the printing of sermons.[40] Local preachers were thus able to keep abreast of recent publications.

Venice's leading position for printing in general was such that many books, treatises, tracts, and panegyrics dealing with religious information and spiritual guidance were published there. As well as short works on specific subjects often Venetian in emphasis, there were also more extensive writings in which fundamental Christian issues were raised. One very important publication of this type was Antonino Valsecchi's *Dei fondamenti della religione e dei fonti dell'empietà*, in which God's very existence was questioned (at least in a rhetorical mode), along with a long discussion of the nature of Mosaic law.[41] The Jansenist controversy, too, played a large role in Venetian printing; indeed, the debate spread through Italy because of Venice's presses.[42] But the grandest editorial undertaking in religious subject-matter was the publication of the complete works of Jacques Bossuet (1627–1704). Lavishly presented in ten volumes by Giambattista Albrizzi, the writings of the 'eagle of Meaux' on Catholicism versus Protestantism and monarchy versus individualism appeared during the 1730s, 1740s, and 1750s, and were accompanied by illustrations based on drawings by Giambattista Piazzetta.[43]

Taken together, this general information produces a picture of a city with an active spiritual life. Venice gave every sign of being a deeply pious city.[44] The State was deeply committed to Christian belief; and all classes of citizens, led by a concerned religious community, contributed to the building of new churches and to the restoration of old ones, where willing listeners attended the preaching of sermons. At home, the literate could devote their private moments to reading about theology and piety. One such prominent figure was the writer Apostolo Zeno, who not only composed librettos for religious oratorios but also had an important library on religious subject-matter.[45] The twentieth century can only conclude that along with the seemingly rampant licentiousness of many aspects of public life and the hard-headed business acumen of the merchant class, eighteenth-century Venice was an observant city: religion played a large part in its daily affairs, and its citizenry went to church.

---

[39] On the importance of sermons, see L. A. Muratori's *Dei pregi dell'eloquenza popolare* (Venice, 1750), *passim*; he differentiates between 'sublime' and 'popolare' on pp. 17ff. See also P. Metodio Da Nembro, OFM Cap., 'Note sulla sacra predicazione in Italia nel Settecento', *L'Italia francescana*, 33 (1958), 117–30. It should be recalled, too, that attendance at sermons was helped in the eighteenth century by the new practice of bringing in chairs and benches: cf. Préclin and Jarry, *Le lotte politiche*, p. 76.

[40] For some relevant publications, see Zanotto, *Storia della predicazione*, pp. 355–63.

[41] Valsecchi was a Dominican and Professor of Theology in Padua. The book is in three volumes; it was approved by Rome in 1757, and was published in Venice in 1764 and in Padua in 1767. A number of chapters in vol. i are concerned with concepts such as liberty, consent, and rights. For other tracts and panegyrics, see Chaps. 1 and 2 of this work, pp. 78 and 148 respectively.

[42] A. C. Jemolo, *Il Giansenismo in Italia prima della rivoluzione* (Bari, 1928), 126; and Chap. 2, p. 131.

[43] See A. Mariuz, *L'opera completa del Piazzetta* (Milan, 1982), 134ff.; and M. Richter, 'Piazzetta e le opere del Bossuet', in *G. B. Piazzetta* (exh. cat., Fondazione Giorgio Cini, Venice, 1983 (Vicenza)), 63–6. Piazzetta had already contributed the preparatory drawing for the frontispiece to Antonio da Venezia's *La chiesa di Gesù Cristo vendicata* (Venice, 1724).

[44] And this is hardly my conclusion alone: cf. Vecchi, *Correnti religiose*, p. 384.

[45] Zeno's house was along the Zattere, and he left his library, which filled more than 200 crates, to the nearby Dominican church of the Gesuati: cf. F. Negri, *La vita di Apostolo Zeno* (Venice, 1816), 370ff. The Dominican brothers' sense of loss at Zeno's death can be read in Valsecchi's *Orazione in morte di Apostolo Zeno* (Venice, 1750), *passim*.

Piety is revealed just as much through the making of sacred imagery as through the building of churches, the preaching of sermons, and the publication of ecclesiastical tracts. And in settecento Venice, Giambattista Tiepolo's art was the most impressive pictorial revelation of religious sentiment. Even relying on numbers alone, the length of his career and the size of his production overwhelm those of his colleagues. For about forty-six years, from 1716 when he was twenty and exhibited his first religious subject, to 1762 when he left home for Spain never to return, he executed numerous paintings and frescos for the churches of Venice and the Veneto. These works reflected the spiritual needs of the State and expressed popular religious fervour in a pictorial variety not encountered in the art of any of his contemporaries.[46] Moreover, Tiepolo served a wide-ranging spectrum of patrons: he worked for small confraternities and large ones (the Suffragio della Beata Vergine del Carmine in S. Apollinare and the Scuola Grande dei Carmini); he painted altar-pieces for very old churches (S. Salvador) and for brand new ones (S. Maria della Fava), for parish churches (S. Polo) and for the churches of religious orders (the Scalzi); he portrayed saints from the earliest history of Christianity (St Augustine) to some just recently canonized (St John Nepomuk); his art manifested devotion to familiar figures like St Lucy, but also to the less well-known like St Oswald of Northumbria; and he narrated epic events from Mosaic history (the *Brazen Serpent*) as well as intimate moments from saintly visions (*The Virgin Appearing to S. Gaetano di Thiene*). Lastly, he, better than anyone else, knew how to paint a church ceiling not just to ornament its surface but to create a convincing re-enactment of a holy event. While praying to Heaven, the faithful could 'witness' the miraculous for themselves, in the Gesuati and the Scalzi, the Scuola dei Carmini, and the Pietà.

Tiepolo's fame as a painter of religious subject-matter suffered after his death, however, continuing to decline in the nineteenth century. In the twentieth, as I indicated above, it was soundly condemned by Longhi. This was partly due to a reaction against not only Tiepolo's painting but Italian Baroque religious art in general. Condemnation of Tiepolo went hand in hand with that of Bernini. The late eighteenth-century historian and connoisseur Francesco Milizia wrote that while Tiepolo's work was 'happy in composition, and in the female heads, in the rest [it was] false'.[47] In 1864, the writer Hyppolite Taine condemned the Gesuati ceiling *tout court* as being 'a pretty painting *de boudoir*, with slender, nude, pink legs; in short, a cold sumptuousness, a display of expensive daintiness. Italian eighteenth-century [painting] is even worse than ours.'[48] But such condemnations were in reality few, and they only partially explain the disdain with which Tiepolo's sacred imagery has been viewed.

Changes in taste from one epoch to another and the accusations of moral depravity so

---

[46] One caveat must be mentioned, however, but it applies to the work of most Venetian painters of the era: Tiepolo painted very few images showing Christ's life. As this study makes clear, eighteenth-century religious art in the Serenissima was traditionally post-Tridentine and Venetian in character, celebrating Mary and the saints more often than it did the Saviour. The first serious attempt to discuss the differing aspects of Tiepolo's religious art was A. Pallucchini's 'Aggiunte e precisazioni al catalogo delle opere del Tiepolo', *Atti del Congresso Internazionale*

di Studi sul Tiepolo (Venice, 1972), 101–4.

[47] F. Milizia, *Dizionario delle belle arti del disegno*, ii (Bassano, 1797), 271: 'Felice nella composizione, e nelle teste muliebri, nel resto falso'.

[48] H. Taine, *Voyage en Italie* [*1864*] (Paris, 1902), 291: '. . . au plafond, une jolie peinture de boudoir, de fines jambes nues et roses;—bref, un luxe froid, un étalage de mignardises coûteuses. Le dix-huitième siècle italien est encore pire que le nôtre.'

often thrown at settecento Venice are certainly a hindrance to our appreciation of Tiepolo's altar-pieces and church frescos; but so is the death of his State in 1797. Every tradition that nourished Tiepolo's art was killed when Napoleon crossed the lagoon and undid the Republic: the aristocracy that commissioned Tiepolo was disbanded, and several of the ecclesiastical organizations for which he worked were suppressed. Venetian history became a closed book.[49] In addition, our own century's prevailing lack of faith has not helped us to understand religious art, particularly that of the eighteenth century, which we continue to look at for its nascent secularity rather than for its traditional piety. But if we seriously take into account the themes and narratives held dear by devout Venetians during the Serenissima's final century of life, then Tiepolo's religious art emerges as the Western world's last great artistic expression of traditional Christian piety.

[49] Berengo, *La società veneta*, p. 228: 'Quando la persuasione che il regime aristocratico sia ormai molto lontano dalle massime evangeliche, si sarà fatta comune, la Repubblica di Venezia avrà persa la sua ultima ragione di vita.'

1

THE YOUNG TIEPOLO

GIAMBATTISTA TIEPOLO has been largely appreciated for his brightly coloured paintings and frescos of historical narrative *alla* Veronese, and for his sumptuous apotheoses of aristocratic families seeking imperishable glory. Yet, Tiepolo's earliest art was quite different. During his first decade of professional activity, from 1716 to 1726, Tiepolo produced many sombre scenes of biblical narrative. His imagery often shows dramatic confrontations distinguished by threatening gestures, and his compositions are unsettling and staccato in their rhythms. Vincenzo Da Canal, his master's biographer, defined Tiepolo's youthful style as 'fiery' and 'decisive' in its pictorial manner, and he characterized the young artist's mind as both 'fertile' and 'bizarre'.[1] This keen intelligence allowed Tiepolo not only to follow those artistic ideas current in early eighteenth-century Venetian painting, but also to expand upon others that had been popular a century or so earlier. More than any other of his contemporaries, Tiepolo had an understanding of the pictorial traditions that had existed in Venice since the sixteenth century. So well did he practise their high conventions and popular forms—with seriousness where needed and with wit when it would delight—that one may see his art as the fitting conclusion to the entire history of Venetian painting.

The young Tiepolo studied in the workshop of Gregorio Lazzarini. His apprenticeship there could have begun as early as 1710, when he was fourteen, and it must have been completed by 1717, by which time he was working as an independent artist. During the years 1710–17, Lazzarini was one of Venice's most successful artists.[2] Indeed, one could almost describe him as a court painter for the Serenissima. At the end of the seventeenth century, Lazzarini had participated in the decoration of the presbytery of S. Pietro di Castello, the seat of Venice's Patriarch and the site of the most important artistic commissions then available in Venice.[3] Lazzarini's *Almsgiving of S. Lorenzo Giustinian* hangs on the left lateral wall there. The painting was modelled on the old masters of Venetian art (Pl. 2). The reclining *coulisse* figures direct our glance towards the painting's centre, reminding us of the pictorial devices of Padovanino, Palma Giovane, and, above all, of the canonical source for such groupings in Venice, Jacopo Tintoretto. The figure of S. Lorenzo recalls Tintoretto's *Christ before Pilate* in the Scuola Grande di S. Rocco. Like Christ, S. Lorenzo is still and in white; he is alone in his own space but encircled by active

[1] V. Da Canal, *Vita di Gregorio Lazzarini* (Venice, 1809), pp. xxxi–xxxii: Tiepolo was 'tutto spirito e foco . . . abbracciò una [maniera] spedita e risoluta', and: 'Egli è fecondissimo d'ingegno'; his works show 'bizzarrie di pensieri'.

[2] Ibid.; and P. A. Orlandi, *Abecedario pittorico . . .* (Venice, 1753), 282: Tiepolo 'fu alla scuola di Gregorio Lazarini, che

in quel tempo era il miglior Pittore di Venezia'. For general information on artistic apprenticeships in Venice, cf. A. Binion, *Antonio and Francesco Guardi: Their Life and Milieu* (New York and London, 1976), 44–5.

[3] Cf. G. M. Pilo, *Lorenzo Giustiniani* (Pordenone, 1982).

2. G. Lazzarini, *Almsgiving of S. Lorenzo Giustinian* (oil on canvas)

forms that kneel, twist, and surge forward on a lower level. Lazzarini was also influenced by Veronese, as the painting's architectural setting shows. It was these obvious ties to the Venetian pictorial tradition that made the *Almsgiving of S. Lorenzo Giustinian* so especially appreciated. Da Canal noted that the work was: 'after those of Paolo [Veronese] both the most correct and the best of our school', adding, moreover, that when he saw the painting for the first time, he found in it 'every pleasure in the beauty of both the robust as well as in the delicate nudes'.[4]

In his biography of Lazzarini, published only two years after the old painter's death, Da Canal astutely commented that his style was different from that of his Venetian contemporaries. Because of its highly finished surfaces and elegant forms, it seemed more Bolognese in manner than Venetian. Lazzarini thus seemed a unique figure in his own city, and as a result his fame spread. No less an authority than the Roman Carlo Maratta considered him praiseworthy.[5] The Venetian government, too, recognized Lazzarini's special gifts; in 1694 he was commissioned to paint the canvases set into the commemorative Arco Morosini in the Sala dello Scrutinio of the Ducal Palace. Lazzarini produced six paintings for the Arco, in all of which the figures' forms, their stately bearing, and the highly keyed tonalities of colour confirm an allegiance to Emilian rather than Venetian tradition. This broad knowledge of different pictorial styles made Lazzarini an excellent artistic pedagogue.

Lazzarini's qualifications for teaching were not solely limited to his public achievements. Da Canal listed what the teacher had to offer someone anxious to learn the craft of painting: 'perspective, architecture, reflections, cast shadows, and other erudite things'. Also of importance was the fact that Lazzarini was able to talk about his art, as Da Canal himself experienced in personal discussions with the artist. Lazzarini's 'kind attitude towards his disciples' must have been particularly attractive, and, finally, the master worked slowly, laboriously in fact, so that his works would be 'finished and correct'.[6] Thus, by listening and observing attentively, Tiepolo could learn from Lazzarini how a painting developed from its first drawings through to its eventual completion on canvas.

One would have expected the master to have moulded the young student into an obedient follower who, like his teacher, painted with 'a most correct manner'.[7] Strangely, however, this did not happen, and what emerged from Lazzarini's studio was not a dutiful follower at all. Rather, Giambattista was a kind of artistic maverick whose earliest works seek purposefully to display a style completely unlike that of his master. If Lazzarini's works are 'finished' and 'exact', Tiepolo's seem 'hurried' and 'unreserved'; whereas the master's style is 'studied', the student's is 'fanciful' or 'bizarre'. One wonders what the young artist learned from Lazzarini, or, putting the question in a more telling form, why did Tiepolo study with Lazzarini? Da Canal supplies the answer: 'Meanwhile the young who desired to get ahead in the pictorial arts chose Lazzarini as their master, as it was he who was then enjoying the highest degree of fame.'[8]

[4] Da Canal, *Vita*, p. xlii.
[5] Ibid., p. xxx.
[6] Ibid., p. xxiv: 'prospettive, architettura, riflessi, sbattimenti ed altre erudizioni'; p. lxix: 'Ei fu di soave natura verso a' suoi discepoli . . .'; and p. xxii: 'finite e corrette'.

[7] Ibid., p. xx: 'una maniera correttissima'.
[8] Ibid., p. xxxi: 'Intanto i giovani vogliosi di avanzare nella pittoric'arte sceglievano a loro maestro il Lazzarini, siccome quello, che allora godeva della più nobil fama.'

Whether the decision to enter Lazzarini's workshop was made by the teenage Giambattista himself or by someone else acting for him, the young apprentice soon found himself in a place where he could not only learn the basic skills of his craft but could also forge important professional links. The doors that Lazzarini could open to the Venetian art-buying public must have been opportune. To make a name in his atelier surely meant that prestigious commissions would come one's way.[9]

Tiepolo's two earliest known public works, both mentioned by Da Canal in his biography of Lazzarini, are religious in subject-matter. Of the first, Da Canal wrote that the young artist painted '. . . Apostles . . . at age nineteen . . . over the niches in the Church of the Ospedaletto'.[10] During the last half-century, *tiepolisti* have debated about this commission a great deal, speculating on which of the apostles were actually executed by the young painter and which can be attributed to others, such as Giambattista Pittoni and Nicola Grassi. Bernard Aikema has recently studied the knotty problem and has argued convincingly that Tiepolo's hand can be seen in the prophet Daniel and in St Matthew, as well as in SS Thomas and John, who have traditionally been ascribed to the nineteen-year-old painter.[11] Apart from stylistic questions, however, the Ospedaletto commission tells us little about the young Tiepolo. His early artistic success and his remarkable ability to present religious subject-matter in potently dramatic form are more immediately understood by focusing instead on his *Crossing of the Red Sea*, a painting exhibited on 16 August 1716 (Pls. 3, 4).

It is Da Canal again who informs us of this event: 'At age twenty and in competition with other painters [Tiepolo] executed a canvas showing the *Faraone sommerso* [the *Crossing of the Red Sea*], a work much applauded on the day of St Roch, when it was exhibited.'[12] Every year on 16 August, the feast of St Roch, an outdoor art exhibition was held in Venice in the *campo* in front of the church and the Scuola Grande dedicated to that saint.[13] Paintings were hung on the Scuola's façade and on those directly adjacent to it towards the left. It was understood that artists risked general criticism by exhibiting in such a public space, but, of course, they also stood to gain universal admiration and applause, since the Fiera di S. Rocco was visited by the Doge and the government, and by those foreign ambassadors who attended Mass at the Church of S. Rocco. The festival aspect of the event is captured in a view of it by Antonio Canaletto, datable to *c.*1735 (Pl. 5). This painting and a print of 1741 by Michele Marieschi also tell us that the works exhibited at S. Rocco ranged in size from small to enormous canvases.[14]

[9] For example, the young Tiepolo began working from the very beginning for the Cornaro and Pisani families: cf. ibid., p. xxxii.

[10] Ibid., p. xxxii: 'Ciò appare negli Appostoli, che in età d'anni diciannove dipinse sopra le nicchie nella chiesa dell'Ospedaletto.' His birth-date was 5 Mar. 1696, so that to have painted the apostles at age 19 Tiepolo would have had to work in the Ospedaletto between Mar. 1715 and late Feb. 1716. The date 1716 can, in fact, be seen painted in the lunette with the figure of St Peter.

[11] B. Aikema, 'Early Tiepolo Studies, 1. The Ospedaletto Problem', *Mitteilungen des Kunsthistorischen Institutes in Florenz*, 26 (1982), 340–82; the reader is referred there and to F. Zava

Boccazzi, *Pittoni* (Venice, 1979), 167–70, for relevant bibliography. Aikema's iconographical conclusions on the Ospedaletto's pictorial complex are less convincing than his stylistic analyses.

[12] Da Canal, *Vita*, p. xxxii: 'D'anni venti in concorrenza d'altri pittori [Tiepolo] esegui in tela *Faraone sommerso*, opera applaudita il giorno di S. Rocco, in cui venne esposto.'

[13] F. Haskell and M. Levey, 'Art Exhibitions in 18th-century Venice', *Arte veneta*, 12 (1958), 179–85.

[14] Marieschi's print can be seen in D. Succi (ed.), *Da Carlevarijs ai Tiepolo: Incisori veneti e friulani del Settecento* (exh. cat., Museo Correr, Venice, 1983), fig. 293.

Just how ambitious a work Tiepolo's *Faraone sommerso* was, however, is unclear; what has come down to us today is a painting measuring 75 by 37 centimetres. Its present whereabouts are unknown to this author, but its appearance in published photographs suggests that the work was prepared as a *bozzetto* or preparatory sketch.[15] Is this the canvas seen by Da Canal and others attending the Fiera in 1716, or did they see a finished, larger painting? Da Canal noted that the *Faraone sommerso* was painted as part of a competition; I shall argue later that Tiepolo probably submitted the small canvas that has survived as a competition piece for a cycle of paintings on Mosaic subject-matter for the Church of SS Cosmas and Damian on the Giudecca Island.[16]

The *Faraone sommerso* retells the story of the Hebrews' miraculous salvation from the pursuing Egyptians recounted in Exodus 14: 27–8:

And Moses stretched forth his hand over the sea, and the sea returned to its strength when the morning appeared; and the Egyptians fled against it; and the Lord overthrew the Egyptians in the midst of the sea. And the waters returned, and covered the chariots, and the horsemen, and all the host of the Pharaoh that came into the sea after them; there remained not so much as one of them.

In Tiepolo's painting, Moses stretches out his wand, the Hebrews gathered behind him, on a height to the left, while the Egyptian army drowns on the right.

From its very first look at the *Crossing of the Red Sea*, the Venetian public of 1716 must have realized that, although the work had been painted by a young man barely out of his teens whose name was most likely not yet known to them, its bold pictorial style demanded attention. It must have been evident to the art critic of the time, as it has been to everyone since, that the young Tiepolo had rejected Lazzarini's dry interpretations of cinquecento and mid-seicento painting. In place of the luministic clarity and porcelain-like surfaces that his master offered, Tiepolo chose harsh, raking shadows and choppy brushwork. Instead of rounded contours, he opted for angular forms and awkward displacement of shapes. Pockets and planes of shadow alternate with brightly lit surfaces; forms within the same spatial zone shift abruptly from dark to sun-filled areas. Lazzarini also insisted upon strong contrasts, but he did so in order to separate groups, not to fragment forms. The teacher conceived of light and shadow as tools for the construction of easily legible compositions, but the student saw them as a means of achieving dramatic intensification.

The extent to which Tiepolo refused Lazzarini's Bolognese manner can best be appreciated by examining the *Crossing of the Red Sea* alongside the latter's *Healing of the Paralytic*, an almost contemporary work of 1719 also involving many figures (Pl. 6). Lazzarini tied the figural groups together, linking them through gesture and an architectural surround, but Tiepolo burst the elements asunder. Of course, the subject-matter demanded an arrangement of antithetical forces, but the young Giambattista did not merely separate

---

[15] The canvas was first mentioned by E. Martini, *La pittura veneziana del Settecento* (Venice, 1964), 203. A. Pallucchini published a photograph of the work in 'Nota tiepolesca', in *Studi di storia dell'arte in onore di Antonio Morassi* (Venice, 1971), 303–7, and again in 'Aggiunte e precisazioni al catalogo delle opere del

Tiepolo', *Atti del Congresso Internazionale di Studi sul Tiepolo* (Venice, 1972), 102; it has since appeared in Martini's *La pittura del Settecento veneto* (Udine, 1982), figs. 134 and 584.

[16] See below, pp. 94 ff.

3. G. B. Tiepolo, *Crossing of the Red Sea* (oil on canvas, 75 × 37 cm.)

4. Detail of Pl. 3

5. A. Canaletto, *Feast-day of St Roch* (oil on canvas, 147 × 199 cm.)

6. G. Lazzarini, *Healing of the Paralytic* (oil on canvas, 345 × 660 cm.)

the Hebrews from the Egyptians, as a number of other artists had when depicting the same event; he placed Moses on the top of a precipice, creating a vertical as well as a horizontal break and thereby emphasizing Moses' victory over his former captors. A series of jagged angles characterize the Jewish leader, who looms high in space and peers down on to the enemy below. The Hebrews and the drowning Egyptians squirm and writhe in reaction to the unexpected miracle; there is not one form that creates smoothly flowing rhythms. A tree on the upper left breaks towards the sky and creates another series of broken angles, and a light, surely of divine origin, descends obliquely on to God's 'Chosen People'. The anguished faces, the tense limbs, and the generally dark tonality of the *bozzetto* serve to reinforce the dramatic confrontation the artist sought. Clearly he wanted to avoid his teacher's classicizing style at all costs.

Instead, Tiepolo looked to a style current among other young painters of the period. It has long been maintained that his first phase reveals influences of the art of Giambattista Piazzetta and Federico Bencovich.[17] And, indeed, Tiepolo's dark palette and intense shadows, certainly as seen in the *Faraone sommerso* of 1716, are similar to the sombre tonalities and luministic contrasts of these older artists. But the tenebrist tradition was a strong one in Venetian art and a number of older artists besides Piazzetta and Bencovich were also working in this style. Giulia Lama, born in 1681 and two years older than Piazzetta, completed the altar-piece for S. Maria Formosa about 1723.[18] Although the work corresponds to the style of both Bencovich and Piazzetta, the importance of the commission and Lama's age by 1723—forty-two—lead one to conclude that her style must have been formulated several years earlier, perhaps even by 1710, and that its success by 1720 was already well established. Giambattista Pittoni was also painting in a dark manner during the second decade of the century.

By choosing to associate himself with a new generation of *tenebrosi*, the young Tiepolo emphasized his rejection of Lazzarini's officially approved art. But Tiepolo's writhing figures and angular gestures differ, too, from the pictorial solutions of Bencovich, Lama, Piazzetta, and Pittoni. It would seem that he did not follow either the example of his 'establishment teacher' or that offered by any other young artist of the period. A decade younger than Pittoni, approximately fifteen years younger than both Lama and Piazzetta, and twenty years younger than Bencovich, the twenty-year-old Tiepolo transformed their early eighteenth-century tenebrism into a more fiery and dynamic aesthetic.

The ultimate source in Venetian art for many aspects of Giambattista's *Faraone sommerso* is Jacopo Tintoretto's three large paintings of Mosaic subject-matter on the ceiling of the upper hall in the Scuola Grande di S. Rocco: *Moses Striking Water from the Rock of Horeb*; the *Brazen Serpent*; and the *Fall of Manna* (Pls. 7–9). It is not surprising that Tiepolo should have turned to these works, given the subject-matter's common source in Exodus. His decision to place Moses on top of a precipice so that the viewer is forced to look up at him may have been determined by Tintoretto's solutions for the first two S. Rocco

---

[17] One of the most recent assertions to this effect is P. Rosenberg's in his *Catalogue de la donation Othon Kaufmann et François Schlageter au Département des Peintures, Musée du Louvre* (Paris, 1984), 122.

[18] G. Bortolan, 'Per una "più completa" conoscenza di Giulia Lama', *Ateneo veneto*, 11 (1973), 187.

paintings.[19] Revealing, too, is Tiepolo's conception of a dramatically gesturing Moses backed by a towering vertical element and supported beneath by twisting figures, a compositional unit found in Tintoretto's *Moses Striking Water from the Rock of Horeb* and the *Brazen Serpent*.[20] Although there is no one form carried over from the canvases in the Scuola di S. Rocco into the *Faraone sommerso*, the viewer can recognize the twenty-year-old artist's debt to Tintoretto in the complicated juxtapositioning of figures, the angularity of both limbs and torsos, the expressive faces, and, above all, in the light rippling over the figures' musculature.[21]

It may seem paradoxical, but it was Lazzarini who helped Giambattista to understand the formulation of heroic figures. Da Canal tells us that Lazzarini studied for two years with Francesco Rosa, a painter who worked in Venice during the 1670s and who died in Rome in 1687.[22] Rosa was influenced by Giambattista Langetti and Luca Giordano. Beginning in the 1650s, the latter had introduced into Venice a neo-Riberesque style whose essential elements were a bold, almost crude naturalism and a dramatic chiaroscuro. Emphasis fell particularly on tautly stretched male figures hit by raking lights. This first phase of Venetian tenebrism enjoyed immense popularity during the 1660s and 1670s, exactly when Lazzarini was training with Rosa. The tortured bodies that appear again and again in the paintings of Giambattista Langetti, the muscular torsion emphasized in the art of Carl Loth, and the dramatically lit nudes repeated from one work to another by Antonio Zanchi, were in fact Lazzarini's artistic foundations, aspects of which can indeed be found in his own work. This late seicento style, created by grafting Neapolitan Caravaggism on to the pictorial heritage of Tintoretto, significantly increased the stylistic possibilities open to Venetian artists. Tiepolo's youthful dramatic art was the ultimate offspring of this tenebrist tradition.

The Venetians who passed through Campo S. Rocco on 16 August 1716, on what must have been a very warm summer day, were certainly struck by the dramatic confrontation and bold style they saw in Tiepolo's *Faraone sommerso*; Da Canal remembered more than fifteen years later that the work had been much applauded. The painting's notable success was not purely based on its appearance, however. In viewing the miraculous salvation of the Hebrews and the drowning of the pursuing Egyptians, Tiepolo's fellow citizens must also have recognized the all too obvious parallels between the biblical narrative facing them and the terrible situation surrounding them. It was in fact to the dire political events of 1716 that Tiepolo's *Faraone sommerso* responded.

The subject of the *Crossing of the Red Sea* is a traditional one in Christian art. The story has been presented on sarcophagi, in manuscript painting, and in the decoration of Roman churches, as for instance in the mosaics of S. Maria Maggiore and on the wooden

[19] This positioning of the Hebrew leader could also be seen in other Mosaic scenes in Venetian art, both earlier and later than Tintoretto's: I am thinking of Jacopo Salviati's ceiling tondo of the *Fall of Manna* in S. Maria della Salute, Giannantonio Pellegrini's *Brazen Serpent* (Pl. 16), and Niccolò Bambini's *Crossing of the Red Sea*, the latter two in the choir of S. Moisè and painted about a decade before Tiepolo's *Crossing*.
[20] Lazzarini also did two versions of this same subject: see Da

Canal, *Vita*, pp. xxxix and liii. Michael Levey mentions this in his *Painting in XVIII Century Venice* (London, 1980), 195, and I am grateful to him for reminding me of this.
[21] On this important aspect in Tintoretto's art, cf. E. M. A. Banks, 'Tintoretto's Religious Imagery of the 1560s', Ph.D. diss. (Princeton, 1978), 154.
[22] Da Canal, *Vita*, p. xx; and R. Pallucchini, *La pittura veneziana del Seicento* (Milan, 1981), i. 376.

7. J. Tintoretto, *Moses Striking Water from the Rock at Horeb* (oil on canvas, 550 × 520 cm.)

8. J. Tintoretto, *Brazen Serpent* (oil on canvas, 840 × 520 cm.)

9. J. Tintoretto, *The Fall of Manna* (oil on canvas, 550 × 520 cm.)

doors of S. Sabina.[23] The narrative was used in early Christian art as an Old Testament typology for baptism or for the freeing of souls from limbo. It served, in addition, as a metaphor for liberation from a hated enemy.[24] The subject carried with it, therefore, a double meaning of deliverance towards a new life.

In the late fifteenth century, the *Crossing of the Red Sea* appeared in monumental form in the Sistine Chapel, as part of the cycle of frescos retelling events from the life of Moses. In explaining these paintings in terms of Pope Sixtus IV's leadership of the Church against the Conciliar movement of the period, Leopold Ettlinger has shown how Cosimo Rosselli's *Crossing* represented a complex interweaving of religious salvation and political independence.[25]

The *Faraone sommerso* first appeared in Venetian art approximately thirty years after the Sistine frescos—as a giant wood-block designed by Titian. David Rosand and Michelangelo Muraro were the first to relate the print's subject to the aftermath of the Battle of Agnadello, where on 14 May 1509 the Serenissima's army suffered a devastating defeat at the hands of the assembled forces of the League of Cambrai.[26] Having overpowered the Venetians, the Imperial armies swept eastwards from Agnadello, near Milan, towards Venice. They were stopped at Padua, and, like the ancient Egyptians, the Germans never made it across the waters. Rosand and Muraro underscore the relationship between that political situation and Titian's print, pointing out the sixteenth-century armour worn by the Pharaoh's army as well as the non-Italian architecture of the distant city. The Hebrews safe on the shore-line may be taken to represent the Venetian people rescued from destruction by divine intervention.[27]

The subject was depicted again in sixteenth-century Venice, once by Andrea Previtali and once by Palma Giovane. Previtali's painting, formerly attributed to Titian, dates from the early part of the century, close in time to the Battle of Agnadello and perhaps a reference to it.[28] Palma's version is in the old sacristy of S. Giacomo dall'Orio, along

[23] Cf. O. Schmitt (ed.), *Reallexikon für deutschen Kunstgeschichte*, 4 (Stuttgart, 1958), 612ff.; E. Kirschbaum (ed.), *Lexikon der christlichen Ikonographie*, i (Freiburg, 1968), 554–8; E. Le Blant, *Étude sur les sarcophages chrétiens antiques de la ville d'Arles* (Paris, 1878), 14ff.; J. Lassus, 'Quelques représentations du "passage de la mer rouge" dans l'art chrétien d'Orient et dans d'Occident', *Mélanges d'archéologie et d'histoire*, 46 (1929), 159–81; F. Benoit, *Sarcophages paléochrétiens d'Arles et de Marseilles* (Paris, 1954), 22ff.; and H. Rosenau, 'Problems of Jewish Iconography', *Gazette des Beaux-Arts*, 56 (1960), 4–18. For the Roman mosaics and wood sculpture, cf. C. Cecchelli, *I mosaici della basilica di S. Maria Maggiore* (Turin, 1956), 157; and M. Petrassi, 'La porta lignea di Sta. Sabina', *Capitolium*, 48 (1973), 19ff. Another, and much later, pictorial 'crossing of the waters' with patriotic meaning is Leutze's *Washington Crossing the Delaware*.

[24] Lassus, 'Quelques représentations', p. 161. Ridolfi mentions the subject in terms of baptism: cf. *Le maraviglie dell'arte . . .* (Venice, 1648), ed. D. von Hadeln (Berlin, 1914), ii. 174.

[25] Cf. L. D. Ettlinger, *The Sistine Chapel before Michelangelo* (Oxford, 1965), 63ff.; and R. Goffen, 'Friar Sixtus and the Sistine Chapel', *Renaissance Quarterly*, 39 (1986), 247–51, where the author explains Rosselli's *Crossing* in terms of Franciscan history.

[26] D. Rosand and M. Muraro, *Titian and the Venetian Woodcut* (exh. cat., National Gallery of Art, Washington, DC, 1976), 72–

3; this was voiced again by L. Olivato, 'La submersione di Pharaone', *Tiziano e Venezia* (Convegno Internazionale di Studi, Venice, 1976 (Verona, 1980)), 529–37. See also M. Catelli Isola (ed.), *Immagini da Tiziano* (exh. cat., Villa Farnesina, Rome, 1976); and M. A. Chiari, *Incisioni da Tiziano* (Venice, 1982), 37ff. The woodcut's execution was attributed to Andrea Schiavone by C. Karpinski, 'Some Woodcuts after Early Designs of Titian', *Zeitschrift für Kunstgeschichte*, 39 (1976), 272, but refuted by F. L. Richardson, *Andrea Schiavone* (Oxford, 1980), 106.

[27] The dog defecating below Moses' outstretched arm must also be read as Titian's own scatological insult hurled at the pursuing army. For more on the trauma suffered in Venice after Agnadello, cf. D. Howard, 'Giorgione's *Tempesta* and Titian's *Assunta* in the Context of the Cambrai Wars', *Art History*, 8 (1985), 271–89; and P. H. D. Kaplan, 'The Storm of War: The Heraldic Key to Giorgione's *Tempesta*', Abstract for a Talk Delivered at the Meeting of the College Art Association, New York, 1986; 'The Storm of War: the Padman Key to Giorgione's *Tempesta*', *Art History*, 9 (1986), 405–27.

[28] S. Moschini Marconi, *Gallerie dell'Accademia di Venezia: Opere d'arte del secolo XVI* (Rome, 1962), 179, fig. 299. There is also a *Faraone sommerso* of the mid-sixteenth century in the sacristy of S. Sebastiano, Venice, and one in mosaic, after a seventeenth-century cartoon by Pietro della Vecchia, in the atrium of S. Marco.

with the *Brazen Serpent*. The traditional eucharistic meaning of the pairing of these two Old Testament narratives has been commented upon by Maurice E. Cope, Antonio Niero, and Stefania Mason Rinaldi.[29] Don Niero suggests that Palma's *Crossing* refers to the Venetian victory over the Turks at Lepanto in 1571. He notes the proximity in date between that famous naval battle and the painting in S. Giacomo, and he also points out that Palma, unlike Titian, dressed the Pharaoh as a Turk and not as a European.[30]

It is not surprising that the crossing of the Red Sea functioned as a metaphor for patriotism in Venice. The Old Testament narrative responded to time-honoured traditions in the city as well as to the Venetians' deeply felt convictions about who they were. One of the legends of the founding of Venice tells the story of mainland refugees fleeing from Attila the Hun towards the tiny islands in the Adriatic Sea's north-west lagoon.[31] An obvious parallel exists with the Hebrews' race from the terrible Pharaoh of Egypt. Going beyond this association, writers of local history attributed further meaning to the link between the ancient Hebrews and the first Venetians by referring to the Christian significance of the crossing of the Red Sea: they interpreted their ancestors' flight from barbarians as a passage from darkness into light. They stated that divine aid had guided the settlers and had helped them found a new land where the true religion would reign. Their city was founded as a Christian establishment untainted by pagan temples; in effect, the Venetians were a 'Chosen People'.[32]

Other ties between local patriotic spirit and Hebraic traditions stem from the figure of Moses. The great leader stands as a reminder of Venice's unique physical origins. The Bible narrates (Exodus 2: 3–10) that his mother had placed him in an 'ark of bulrushes . . . daubed . . . with slime and with pitch', an image that reminds us of the lagoon's first settlements. Then, Moses was saved from the waters like the first Venetians; according to the Pharaoh's daughter, his very name was chosen 'because I drew him out of the water'. The Serenissima had, of course, risen from the sea, and just as Moses owed his survival to the Egyptian Princess, so Venice had become powerful, it was believed, under the protection of the Virgin Mary. A suggestive parallel also exists between Moses' role in Jewish history and St Mark's place in Venetian history: the former did not survive to settle in Israel but viewed it from afar, and Mark left the lagoon even as he foresaw Venice's future establishment there.[33]

One must consider, too, the Byzantine heritage enjoyed by Venice. In his *Book of Ceremonies*, written in the tenth century and summing up long-established rituals and

[29] M. Cope, *The Venetian Chapel of the Sacrament in the Sixteenth Century: A Study in the Iconography of the Early Counter-Reformation* (New York, 1979), 176 and 241 ff.; A. Niero, *Chiesa di S. Giacomo dall'Orio, Venezia* (Venice, 1979), 82 ff.; and S. Mason Rinaldi, *Palma il Giovane* (Milan, 1984), 121–2.

[30] For Bronzino's *Crossing* in the Palazzo Vecchio, Florence, see J. Cox-Rearick, 'Bronzino's *Crossing of the Red Sea and Moses Appointing Joshua*: Prolegomena to the Chapel of Eleonora di Toledo', *Art Bulletin*, 69 (1987), 45–67. Poussin also painted a *Crossing* (Melbourne, National Gallery) for Amedeo dal Pozzo in Turin: cf. A. Blunt, *The Paintings of Nicolas Poussin* (London, 1966), 17–18.

[31] On this story and its relationship with Venice's founding, see E. Muir, *Civic Ritual in Renaissance Venice* (Princeton, 1981),

68; and W. Dorigo, *Venezia origini* (Milan, 1983), i. 223. For a more general discussion on the story of Exodus and its political significance of national independence, see M. Walzer, *Exodus and Revolution* (New York, 1985).

[32] Cf. A. Carile, 'Le origini di Venezia nella tradizione storiografica', in *Storia della cultura veneta dalle origini al Trecento* (Vicenza, 1976), i. 135–66; and Muir, *Civic Ritual*, pp. 16 and 23 ff.

[33] For the associations between Moses and the Venetian Doge, see S. Sinding-Larsen, *Christ in the Council Hall: Studies in the Religious Iconography of the Venetian Republic* (*Acta ad Archaelogiam et Artium Historiam Pertinentia*, 5; Institutum Romanum Norvegiae, Rome, 1974), 141.

practices, Constantine VII Porphyrogenetos records how the story of the crossing of the Red Sea was read and celebrated at Court during times of naval victories.[34] While I know of no parallel in Venice, the popularity of the subject in the Venetian pictorial tradition might well be a reflection of that old court custom. Byzantium's impact on Venice was felt in a myriad of ways.[35] All these associations and historical traditions deep in the city's collective consciousness may well have provided the basis for the profound emotions which Exodus 14 still called forth in the eighteenth century.

Venetian patriotism was being sorely tested during the summer that the young Tiepolo showed his canvas in Campo S. Rocco. Beginning in early July 1716, Corfu, which had been in Venetian hands since 1386, fell under Turkish bombardment.[36] Because possession of this strategically situated outpost had given the Serenissima complete mastery of the Adriatic, Corfu became the keystone of the State's maritime defence system. Located opposite the tip of Italy's heel, and functioning therefore as the gateway to Venice's sea, it eventually housed the headquarters of the Venetian naval command. Every ship, whether military or mercantile, whether travelling east to Turkey or west to Gibraltar and then north to Flanders, stopped at Corfu. A large part of Venetian wealth and power was realized through dominion over its waters. The Republic came to regard the Adriatic Sea as its very own and called it 'il golfo nostro'—'our gulf'. For Venetians the loss of Corfu was unthinkable: shipping would come to a halt and the State's economy would face collapse.[37] But far worse would be a Turkish conquest of the island, followed by Ottoman penetration of the Adriatic, the Turkish flotilla's sailing north towards Venice, and the certain death of the thousand-year-old Venetian State.

Such an event almost came to pass. In 1714, a Venetian galley in the Mediterranean was forcibly boarded by Turks. At the time, the mishap seemed to be simply another instance of the traditional enmity between the two empires, each seeking hegemony in the same sea. But, taking advantage of its naval and military superiority over Venice as well as the latter's unreadiness for any type of confrontation, Istanbul made lightning advances towards the west. By the late summer of 1715, the Turks had taken all of Venice's possessions in Greece apart from the island of Corfu. The Republic's decision to make its military stand there rather than to exhaust its navy in further fighting over the Morea (the Peloponnese) eventually brought the Turkish navy to the Gulf of Corfu on

[34] Constantine VII Porphyrogenetos, *De Cerimoniis Aulae* (Patrologia Graeca, vol. 112), ii. 19, ed. J.-P. Migne (Paris, 1897), col. 1138. I am grateful to Ioli Kalavrezou for this information. It should also be recalled that in his life of Constantine, Eusebius likened the Christian Emperor to Moses after the defeat of Maxentius at the Milvian Bridge in 312: see A. Grabar, *L'Empereur dans l'art byzantin* (London, 1936), 237; and M. Shapiro, 'The Place of the Joshua Roll in Byzantine History', *Gazette des Beaux-Arts*, 35 (1949), 171–2. An amusing reversal of this in more modern times was the recarving of the Pharaoh's face on the doors of S. Sabina to capture the likeness of Napoleon: cf. D. G. Cavallero (ed.), *Guide rionali di Roma: Rione XII—Ripa*, ii (Rome, 1978), 70.

[35] Sinding-Larsen, *Christ in the Council Hall*, p. 252: 'some features concerning San Marco and the [Ducal] Palace bear a striking resemblance to Byzantine practice ...'; p. 253: 'As regards the post-Iconoclast Imperial Palace at Constantinople, Constantine Porphyrogenetes' *Ceremony Book* contains information

that might suggest a parallel or even a direct borrowing on the part of Venice [in terms of "functional] affinity between the rooms of the Golden Triclinium" and some in the Ducal Palace].'

[36] The Corfu bibliography is immense, but see M. Nani-Mocenigo, *Storia della marina veneziana da Lepanto alla caduta della repubblica* (Rome, 1935), 313ff.; and his 'Corfù, sentinella dell'Adriatico', Abstract from *Rivista di cultura marinara* (1941), 3–14; R. Cessi, *La repubblica di Venezia e il problema Adriatico* (Naples, 1953), 127ff.; and id., *Storia della repubblica di Venezia* (Florence, 1981), 599ff.; and H. Jervis-White Jervis, *History of the Island of Corfu and of the Republic of the Ionian Islands* (Amsterdam, 1970), 133ff.

[37] This became immediately apparent during the war in Corfu, 1715–16: cf. J. Georgelin, *Venise au siècle des lumières* (Paris, 1978), 73 nn. 127 and 128, with the following contemporary citations: '... le commerce s'anéantit ...', and: 'La navigation diminue journellement ... depuis la déclaration de la guerre contre les Turcs.' Cf. also Cessi, *Storia della repubblica*, p. 656.

5 July 1716. Only one month before, Venice had strengthened its militia at the island's old fortress and had appointed the famous German Field Marshal, Matthais Johannes Schulemburg, as General. Schulemburg and Antonio Loredan, Governor-General of Corfu, led the Venetian campaign, while the Ottoman navy began a terrible forty-two-day siege of the island. The Turks took possession of the hills overlooking the fortifications, and bombardment from above inflicted severe losses on the Venetians. In early August the Turkish commander, feeling quite sure of an imminent victory, invited Loredan to surrender. The offer was rejected, and the battle raged on.[38]

All Venetians must have known what was happening in Corfu from one week to the next because ships sailing from the island to Venice took, on average, only fifteen days.[39] The Turkish flotilla's arrival at the fortress on 5 July might have been known in Venice as early as the third week of that very same month. At times of crisis the voyage up the entire length of the Adriatic could be accomplished in as little as seven days, so the Turkish call on 5 August for the Venetian Governor-General to surrender may well have been known in Venice by 12 or 13 August. It is perfectly reasonable to assume that the situation facing the Republic was publicly known just as Tiepolo was finishing the *Faraone sommerso* in mid-August.

Study of his *bozzetto* confirms this possibility. The Hebrews cower while viewing the destruction of the Egyptians, who are pointedly dressed as Turks. Although God's celestial light shines down upon the 'Chosen People', they recoil in torment, their bodies contort in anguish, and their faces fill with fear. Neither Titian's print, nor Palma's painting, nor any other representation of the subject that I know of would have suggested such an interpretation to Tiepolo. Indeed, Titian and Palma celebrated the salvation that followed the Battle of Agnadello in one case, and that of Lepanto in the other. Tiepolo's *Crossing of the Red Sea* mirrors another emotional and physical reality altogether: during July and early August 1716, the Venetians were hoping that God would intervene on their behalf just as in the past. Giambattista's painting appeared to those attending the Fiera di S. Rocco as a desperate prayer for survival.

Tiepolo's *Faraone sommerso* was not the only work of art to respond to the war in Corfu. A week after the Fiera, Antonio Vivaldi presented his *Juditha Triumphans* in the state church of the Pietà.[40] This oratorio also relates an Old Testament story in which divine intervention miraculously aids God's Chosen People against a fearful enemy, and its libretto likens Judith to Venice and Holofernes to the Turkish Sultan. A stirring battle chorus, accompanied by horns, opens the piece, while at its conclusion a group of maidens

[38] See S. Romanin, *Storia documentata di Venezia* (Venice, 1915), viii. 49ff.; A. Battistella, *La repubblica di Venezia* (Venice, 1921), 755ff.; N. Stamatopoulos, *Old Corfu: History and Culture* (Corfu, 1978), 30ff.; and BNM, MSS It. Cl. VII–MDCXIX (1619), 8412 ('Diaria relazione dell'attacco della Piazza di Corfù formato dalle Armi Ottomane L'Anno 1716'); BMC, MS Cicogna 3640 ('Journal De L'Année 1716, pendant laquelle arrive le siege de Corfu, & l'heureuse Delivrance de Cette Place', perhaps written by Schulemburg himself).

[39] P. Sardella, *Nouvelles et spéculations à Venise au début du XVIe siècle* (Paris, 1948); and F. Braudel, *La Méditerranée et le monde méditerranéen à l'époque de Philippe II* (Paris, 1966), i. 113ff.

and 330ff.

[40] Cf. M. Talbot, *Vivaldi* (London, 1978), 59–60. In 1714, Vivaldi composed the *Moyses Deus Pharaonis*, also for the Pietà, but its music has been lost. For the role of music in the State, see E. Rosand, 'Music in the Myth of Venice', *Renaissance Quarterly*, 30 (1977), 511–37; and Howard, 'Giorgione's *Tempesta*', p. 283. For Venice's 'riaffermazione della mitologia politica internazionale', c.1715–20, cf. P. Del Negro, 'Proposte illuminate e conservazione nel dibattito sulla teoria e la prassi dello Stato', in G. Arnaldi and M. Pastore Stocchi (eds.), *Il Settecento (Storia della cultura veneta*, v²) (Vicenza, 1985), 127.

celebrate Judith's victory in a stanza that reads: 'May the Queen of the Sea triumph. . . . Long live Adria, and may she reign in peace.'[41]

In that third week of August 1716 neither Vivaldi nor Tiepolo knew that the battle at Corfu would go well; luckily for them, it did. On 17 August the Turks made a general assault on the Venetian encampments, but during the night of 18 August there was torrential rain and, as at Waterloo almost one hundred years later, the course of history was changed by a storm.[42] The Turks were bogged down in the mud, and with only eight hundred men Schulemburg attacked and won the day. The Ottoman navy retreated on 21 August. The Serenissima justifiably saw in these events the victory of divine intervention over earthly might. Although Corfu had 'always been looked upon with envy by the Ottoman emperors . . . God Himself had protected the fortress, which was sustained with great strength by the Republic'.[43]

Tiepolo painted the *Faraone sommerso* during a period of national crisis, when the very future of the Venetian State seemed to be hanging by a thread. In applauding the work, the public must have understood its contemporary relevance. Da Canal and his fellow Venetians may also have recognized the genius of the youthful painter; with the *Crossing of the Red Sea* the twenty-year-old Giambattista had boldly seized the attention of all Venice.

Tiepolo's artistic independence was established by 1717, but his professional ties with Lazzarini and his circle seem to have continued none the less. In 1720 he collaborated with two other young men trained in the same studio, Silvestro Manaigo and Giuseppe Camerata, to illustrate Domenico Lovisa's publication, *Il gran teatro di Venezia ovvero raccolta delle principali vedute e pitture che in essi si contengono*. Tiepolo's part in the production was to make drawings after Francesco Bassano's *Rout of the Imperial Troops by Giorgio Cornaro and Bartolomeo d'Alviano* in the Sala del Maggior Consiglio of the Ducal Palace (Pl. 10), Salviati's *Fall of Manna* in the choir of S. Maria della Salute, and Tintoretto's *Beheading of St Christopher* in S. Maria dell'Orto and his *Assumption of the Virgin* in the Gesuiti.[44] Along with others by Manaigo and Camerata, these drawings were made into engravings for Lovisa's two volumes by the print-maker Andrea Zucchi. Tiepolo's designs follow the originals very closely, although the proportions of the figures have been changed slightly.

[41] 'Triumphatrix sit Maris Regina . . . Adria vivat, et regnet in pace.' It is noted on the back of the original libretto that Judith is Venice, and Holofernes the Sultan. For a pictorial representation of Venice/Adria, cf. Tintoretto's painting in the centre of the Sala del Senato's ceiling in the Ducal Palace: cf. W. Wolters, *Der Bilderschmuck des Dogenpalastes* (Wiesbaden, 1983), 269 ff.

[42] For dates, cf. R. Morozzo della Rocca and M. F. Tiepolo, 'Cronologia veneziana dal 1600 al 1866', in V. Branca (ed.), *Storia della civiltà veneziana*, iii (Florence, 1979), 445–6; Romanin, *Storia documentata*, p. 51; Nani-Mocenigo, 'Corfù, sentinella dell'Adriatico', p. 8; and Jervis, *History of the Island of Corfu*, p. 140. L. Pastor, *History of the Popes*, xxxiii (London, 1949), 128, gives 20 Aug. as the date for the storm.

[43] For a contemporary recounting of these 'miraculous events', see V. Coronelli, *La galleria di Minerva*, vii (Venice, 1717), 283–

4: 'Con quanto di gelosia però [Corfu] fù sempre mai custodita dalla Repubblica, con altrettanto d'invidia fù altresì sempre rimirata da gl'Imperatori Ottomani . . .', and Corfu was: 'una Piazza tanto protetta da Dio, e sostenuto con tanto vigore dalla Repubblica'. Venice commissioned Antonio Corradini to sculpt a statue of Schulemburg, which is now on Corfu just outside the old fortress. Schulemburg himself received a lifetime pension from Venice and retired to that city. In Corfu's Cathedral, a silver lamp was dedicated to S. Spiridione, the island's patron saint. In Venice itself, Niccolò Bambini completed a votive painting in which Doge Giovanni Cornaro humbly thanks the Virgin Mary, the Christ-child, and S. Spiridione (Venice, Ducal Palace; (Pl. 64).

[44] Bassano's painting recorded the heroic events of Giorgio Cornaro, for whose family Tiepolo had worked *c.*1716. He was to paint for them again: see Chap. 3, pp. 202 ff.

12. G. B. Tiepolo, *Crucifixion* (oil on canvas, 250 × 400 cm.)

10. Opposite, above: A. Zucchi, engraving of the *Rout of the Imperial Troops by Giorgio Cornaro*, based on a drawing by G. B. Tiepolo and after the painting by F. Bassano (from D. Lovisa's *Il gran teatro delle pitture e prospettive di Venezia*)

11. Opposite, below: G. B. Tiepolo, Drawing for the *Crucifixion* (pen and brown wash with pencil on white paper, 385 × 537 mm.)

The small heads and the very supple forms, as well as the somewhat fleshy decorative details, betray an aesthetic quite different from that of the cinquecento.

Although the Lovisa commission was useful to Tiepolo for the prestige that it conferred and the historic associations that it implied, it was the wealth of pictorial ideas that he learned while drawing on the spot that was more meaningful still for the twenty-four-year-old painter. This experience of copying sixteenth-century art was a direct influence, I suggest, on the *Crucifixion* he painted for the Church of S. Martino on the island of Burano (Pl. 12). The painting merits serious study because of its monumental challenge to the young artist (the canvas is over eight feet in height and thirteen in width), its many complex figural groupings, and because it tells us a great deal about his development and early sources. A comparison of the *Crucifixion* with its preparatory drawing (Pl. 11) in the Tiroler Landesmuseum, Innsbruck, as well as with Zucchi's print based on Bassano's *Rout of the Imperial Troops*, whose original drawing is no longer extant, allows some of Tiepolo's early artistic decisions to be followed.[45] For example, the thief being tied to the cross in the painting's centre left is not a repetition of the drawing but a restatement of Bassano's fallen soldier. Tiepolo reproduced exactly that torso's sharp foreshortening and head, and, moreover, the contortion of the original figure's shoulder and chin; only the limbs have been altered. This same combination of a head viewed *di sotto in sù* and a severely wrenched shoulder was also used by Tiepolo for the right thief, another change from the preparatory drawing as well.

The viewer will no doubt be struck by the influence of Tintoretto's art on the *Crucifixion*. Several ideas from his *Cain and Abel* (Pl. 13), which, like Bassano's battle scene, was included in Lovisa's *Il gran teatro*, can be seen in the Burano painting but not in the drawing. Tiepolo turned the kneeling soldier who is tying up the left thief so that the arching of his back is more visible than it was in the drawing, and he lifted the soldier's right arm and fully extended it so that the figure looms over the thief more dramatically; Tintoretto's Cain is the source of these changes. I would suggest, too, that the remarkable tilting angle of the right thief, who looks as if he is about to fall over backwards, comes from Tintoretto's Abel, whom Tiepolo has spun around on a 180-degree axis. Tiepolo's purpose in making these changes, as the painting clearly shows, is to emphasize the contrast between the thieves' unreadiness to die and Christ's calm acceptance of his mission.[46]

In the past, the date of the *Crucifixion* has been shifted back and forth within the period 1718 to 1725.[47] But the figural links between the finished canvas on Burano and Lovisa's

---

[45] Two other drawings may also be associated with the Burano *Crucifixion*: a sheet in a private collection dated *c.*1726 by G. Knox, in *Tiepolo: A Bicentenary Exhibition 1770–1970* (exh. cat., Fogg Art Museum, Harvard University, Cambridge, 1970), no. 5; and a drawing, early in date, in the Staatliche Graphische Sammlung, Munich, no. 1980: 46.

[46] Tiepolo's positioning and, indeed, the actual grouping of the three mourning women, the fixed upward gaze of St John, the figure of the horseman acting as a coulisse, and the overall dramatic presentation of the narrative are all hallmarks of Tintoretto's versions of the same subject in the Scuola di S. Rocco and the Museo Civico, Padua.

[47] Knox first dated the *Crucifixion* to *c.*1722 (*Tiepolo: A Bicentenary Exhibition*, no. 5), and then to 1718 ('Giambattista Tiepolo: Queen Zenobia and Ca' Zenobio: "una delle prime sue fatture"', *Burlington Magazine*, 121 (1979), 414). A. Morassi and R. and A. Pallucchini all put it in the 1720s: cf. A. Morassi, *A Complete Catalogue of the Paintings of G. B. Tiepolo* (London, 1962), 8, *c.*1720–2; R. Pallucchini, 'Nota per Giambattista Tiepolo', *Emporium*, 50 (1944), 4, *c.*1721–5; and A. Pallucchini, *L'opera completa del Tiepolo* (Milan, 1968), no. 31, 1724–5. A. Rizzi, *Mostra del Tiepolo: Dipinti* (exh. cat., Udine, 1971 (Milan)), no. 9, places it towards *c.*1722–3.

publication of 1720 strongly suggest that Tiepolo's painting dates to 1719–20. In copying the dramatic movement and the complex and strange figural juxtapositions of Bassano's *Rout of the Imperial Troops* and Tintoretto's *Cain and Abel*, the brilliant young draughtsman must soon have mastered their difficulties. Then, understanding the aptness of these examples to the pictorial problems imposed by the *Crucifixion*, Tiepolo altered his original ideas to create in the finished painting the thieves' dramatic and even violent resistance to physical coercion.[48]

Besides the figural ties between the Burano *Crucifixion* and several of the prints in Lovisa's volumes, there are two other reasons for dating the painting before 1720. The very ambitiousness of the scene, at once dense with action but unhappily splintered in its parts, reveals the hand of a painter not yet totally in charge of his resources, unable to orchestrate his many motifs into one composition. Each figure or group functions as its own drama; one observes in turn the haloed Christ on the cross, the psychological isolation of the portly man on the right, the agony of the thief above him, Mary's collapse and the care given to her by her two companions, St John's bewildered grief, and the beseeching thief on the ground each as a separate unit. Tiepolo's inability to sacrifice the independence of the individual element for the benefit of the whole can be said to characterize his *Crucifixion*. Painted at a moment when Tiepolo was still unable to co-ordinate a myriad of elements successfully, the *Crucifixion* is not the work of the great impresario of dramatic narrative, which Tiepolo was soon to become when he painted the *Martyrdom of St Bartholomew* (Pl. 24) in 1722–3.

A final reason for believing that the *Crucifixion* pre-dates *c*.1720 is the oval portrait of the patron, thought to be a pharmacist from Burano, seen in the painting's bottom left-hand corner.[49] The practice of including the commissioner's portrait in a painting can be traced back to the late sixteenth- and early seventeenth-century custom of presenting the patron so that he seems to be looking out at the spectator from a space near to or identical with that of the scene's actual participants. Among the notable examples from the Venetian tradition is Pietro della Vecchia's *Crucifixion*, painted in 1633 for the Church of S. Lio (Pl. 14). There, three members of a confraternity offer themselves as intermediaries to the viewer before the spectacle of Christ's death.[50]

Isolating a patron within the work he commissioned seems to have become a popular practice in Venetian art during the second half of the seventeenth century. Such a pictorial device must have appealed to the wealthy as efficacious for the achievement of personal salvation and public recognition. In Francesco Cassana's *Resurrection of Christ*, painted in 1656, the patron beckons the viewer to meditate upon the scene behind him, and he

[48] The face of the mounted centurion on the left of the *Crucifixion* is very similar to the seated nude youth in the drawing belonging to the Staatsgalerie in Stuttgart: cf. G. Knox and C. Thiem, *Tiepolo: Zeichnungen von Giambattista, Domenico und Lorenzo Tiepolo aus der graphischen Sammlung der Staatsgalerie Stuttgart, aus württembergischem Privatbesitz und dem Martin von Wagner Museum der Universität Würzburg* (exh. cat., Staatsgalerie, Stuttgart, 1970), no. 1.

[49] It was Rizzi who identified the patron as a pharmacist: cf. *Mostra del Tiepolo*, no. 9.

[50] The practice can be traced back in Venetian art to the portraits of the Pesaro family in Titian's altar-piece in the Frari. For information on the figures in S. Lio, cf. *Venezia e la peste* (exh. cat., Venice, 1979), 268–9, no. 243. There are other elements in della Vecchia's painting that also appear in the Burano *Crucifixion*: note in both paintings the pyramidal groupings of the three Marys, the cloaked figures of the observing St Johns, the portly bystanders on one side, the soldiers arriving with their spears in the far distance, and even the appearance of Christ himself. For another work of the same type, see Aliense's *Virgin and Child with St Francis and Federico Contarini*, in R. Pallucchini's *La pittura veneziana del Seicento*, ii, fig. 99.

14. P. della Vecchia, *Crucifixion* (oil on canvas, 450 × 440 cm.)

13. J. Tintoretto, *Cain and Abel*, detail (oil on canvas, 149 × 196 cm.)

16. G. Pellegrini, *Brazen Serpent*, detail (oil on canvas)

15. A. Zanchi, *Martyrdom of S. Zulian*, detail (oil on canvas)

commemorates his offering of the painting to the church with an inscribed cartouche held next to him by an angel.[51] Another example of a painting in which a patron is included in a similar fashion is Zanchi's *Martyrdom of St Zulian* (Pl. 15), dated 1674 and executed for the right wall of the presbytery of the Church of S. Zulian in Venice. Zanchi isolated the patron completely by enclosing him within an oval frame, thus embellishing the dramatic narrative with an elegant medallion.[52] This same decorative solution appears again in the Venetian tradition and within an identical format in Pellegrini's *Brazen Serpent* (Venice, S. Moisè; Pl. 16, bottom right-hand corner). But, unlike Tiepolo, Zanchi and Pellegrini depict their patrons as being unaware of the violent dramas enacted next to them. Tiepolo's 'pharmacist' from Burano, although not a participant in the *Crucifixion*, presents it to us for our thoughtful consideration and as tangible proof of his personal devotion. With the same gesture seen in Cassana's *Resurrection*, he asks us to meditate upon salvation through Christ.

By framing his periwigged patron with an ornate gilt border, Tiepolo certainly fashioned a portrait that befitted a gentleman of means. But in so doing, the young artist broke into the drama of the scene, sacrificing in part the narrative of the two soldiers who are throwing dice for Christ's robe. No other artist of Tiepolo's generation ever disrupted the integrity of a dramatic situation in this way. The only possible explanation for Tiepolo's old-fashioned oval portrait was that he had been ordered to include it. Although enrolled in the guild of painters, Tiepolo was perhaps not sufficiently established in his dealings with a patron for the contract's final terms to reflect his dictates rather than the commissioner's. The obvious implication of the donor's portrait is that Tiepolo's artistic control was still quite limited while he was working on this painting. This, along with the painting's stylistic immaturities and its close ties with specific elements in Lovisa's prints of 1720, confirm that the Burano canvas was executed midway between the *Faraone sommerso* of 1716 and the *Martyrdom of St Bartholomew* of 1722–3, namely 1719–20.

Soon after his completion of the large *Crucifixion*, Tiepolo received a commission to paint a still grander canvas, a *Madonna del Carmelo* for the Church of Sant'Apollinare, or Sant'Aponal (Pls. 17, 18; Pl. I).[53] The painting, whose iconography is discussed in Chapter 2, depicts the Virgin Mary and Christ bestowing scapulars on three figures in adoration— the Patriarch Albert of Jerusalem, St Theresa, and Simon Stock; at the far right, the prophet Elijah appears shrouded in darkness. At the left an angel gesturing towards Mary and Christ reminds penitent souls in purgatory that their eternal salvation can be attained by means of the Virgin's intercession, specifically through her gift of the scapular. In the painting's centre, a procession of hooded devotees led by an angel approaches Mary and Christ.

The *Madonna del Carmelo* was commissioned for Sant'Aponal's Chapel of the Carmine, which was to the left of the church's presbytery.[54] The chapel also contained Palma

[51] For Cassana's work, cf. R. Pallucchini, *La pittura veneziana del Seicento*, ii, fig. 774.

[52] Ibid., fig. 825.

[53] The Sant'Aponal canvas measures 210 by 650 cm., and the *Crucifixion* 250 by 400 cm.

[54] A. M. Zanetti, *Descrizione di tutte le pubbliche pitture della città di Venezia* ... (Venice, 1733), 268, identified the place as the 'cappella alla destra dell'altar maggiore, ora del Carmine'. His description of the church begins with its left flank, and his directions for the altar end of the building are given from the position of an officiating priest, not that of a parishioner.

Giovane's *Heavenly Father, SS John the Evangelist and Charles Borromeo* and Giambattista Mariotti's *Birth of Mary*, the latter work facing the *Madonna del Carmelo*.[55] Two guidebooks of 1724 and 1744 published under the name of Vincenzo Coronelli inform us that the chapel belonged to the Molin family and that in 1710 its altar was adorned with 'the suffrage of the Dead under the protection of the B.V. [Beata Vergine] of the Carmine'.[56] This suffrage enjoyed important ecclesiastical privileges, for it was tied to a similar one in S. Giovanni in Laterano in Rome, with which it shared the same indulgences. The *Madonna del Carmelo* hung on the Carmine Chapel's left wall, exactly between the springing of the vault and the dado, so the altar on which the Christ-child stands was very close to the chapel's real altar.[57] Moreover, the light shining on the Saviour and his mother, as well as on the three saints, could be identified with that entering through the chapel's windows in the wall behind the altar. Because Sant'Aponal is oriented, it is a morning light that filters in, and this accorded well with the liturgical rites carried out at the Carmine altar. Coronelli recorded that 'every Wednesday in the morning . . . there is a Prayer and other Devotions'.[58] The prayers, offered by a confraternity providing burial for its dead brethren, were to free souls from their pains of purgatory so that they could ascend to heaven in everlasting union with God.[59]

In 1751, Charles-Nicolas Cochin stood before the *Madonna del Carmelo* and judged it 'well done, with a broad manner, and a rather good tone'.[60] The figures are in fact conceived on a grand scale, and the dark hues mirror perfectly the work's sombre theme. The colours of the nude souls range from muddy browns to tawny beiges and darkly golden yellows, and they are set against deep blues. The messenger-angel is the brightest figure in this section of the work; his wings are slate grey highlighted with white, and his swirling drapery is painted an olive green. Immediately to the right is a forlorn world of grey inhabited by figures carrying torches; their hoods are embroidered with skulls and

---

[55] Ridolfi, *Le maraviglie dell'arte*, ii. 186, notes that there was another *Birth of Mary* in the chapel before Mariotti's: 'Nascita di Nostra Signora nell'Altare de' Farinari molto ben condotta . . .'. Mason Rinaldi, *Palma il Giovane*, p. 86, cat. no. 109, suggests that the work may be identified with Palma's version of that subject now in the collection of Bob Jones University. Before it belonged to the Scuola del Carmine, the chapel in Sant'Aponal was in the hands of the 'scuola de' Fontegari, ò farinari sotto titolo della Natività della B.V.': cf. P. A. Pacifico, *Cronica veneta: Sacra e profana* (Venice, 1697), 365. A. Zorzi, *Venezia scomparsa* (Milan, 1977), ii. 489, correctly identifies Mariotti's painting as the *Natività di Maria*; for Palma's *Heavenly Father, SS John the Evangelist and Charles Borromeo*, cf. Mason Rinaldi, *Palma il Giovane*, p. 182. A. M. Zanetti, *Della pittura veneziana e delle opere pubbliche* (Venice, 1771), notes the presence in the chapel of the works by Palma, Mariotti, and Tiepolo on pp. 317, 436, and 467 respectively; see also P. Cecchetti, *Notizie storiche intorno all'antica e moderna chiesa di Santo Apollinare* (Venice, 1851), 19 and 28.

[56] V. Coronelli, *Guida de' forestieri . . . per la città di Venezia* (Venice, 1724), 307, (1744), 275. In the *Dizionario di erudizione storico-ecclesiastica* (Venice, 1855), lxxi. 33, the term 'suffragio' is defined as a 'preghiera che i Santi fanno a Dio'. See also J. Le Goff's *The Birth of Purgatory*, trans. A. Goldhammer (Chicago, 1984), 11 ff.

[57] The *Madonna del Carmelo* remained in Sant'Aponal until the church was deconsecrated at the time of the Napoleonic suppressions, when the canvas was sent to France and cut into

two. Both pieces were bought by the Brera in 1925 and were then sewn back together.

[58] Coronelli, *Guida de' forestieri* (1724), p. 307.

[59] This was the goal of all Venetian *scuole*: cf. P. Humfrey and R. Mackenney, 'The Venetian Trade Guilds as Patrons of Art in the Renaissance', *Burlington Magazine*, 128 (1986), 317–30. The Scuola del Carmine of Sant'Aponal made a hole in their chapel's floor in 1712, two years after the creation of the original suffrage, into which the ashes of their dead brothers were placed: BMC, MS Gradenigo 201 ('Iscrizione sepolcrali, ed altre, nelle Chiese di Venezia, iii'), fo. 32ᵛ; the same inscription is reprinted by E. Cicogna, *Delle iscrizioni veneziane*, iii (Venice, 1830), 275. For documentation on the confraternity, see ASV, 'Scuole Piccole', b. 118: 'Libro di Cassa. Suffragio della B.V. del Carmine in S. Apollinare. 1780 Fin . . . [1806]'. Unfortunately, there is no mention of Tiepolo's painting amongst these papers; indeed, there are no documents there at all for the Scuola's early period. For the release of souls from purgatory, cf. Le Goff, *The Birth of Purgatory*, pp. 214 and 229; and M. Warner, *Alone of All Her Sex* (New York, 1983), 318: '. . . the prayers of the saints to God, besought by the living on behalf of the dead, can commute the sentence or even pluck a soul from purgatory and transfer it to eternal bliss.'

[60] C.-N. Cochin, *Voyage d'Italie . . . (1758)*, ed. M. Gault de Saint-Germain and M. Guyot de Fère (Geneva, 1972), 135: 'Ce tableau est fort bien, d'une manière large & d'assez bon ton.'

17. Above: G. B. Tiepolo, *Madonna del Carmelo* (oil on canvas, 210 × 650 cm.)

18. Opposite: Elijah, detail of Pl. 17

19. Titian, *Madonna and Saints*, detail (oil on canvas, 485 × 270 cm.)

their robes are stitched with the special insignia of a confraternity. On the far right Elijah hovers over a midnight-blue landscape. Tiepolo thus employed dark, muddy, and grey areas to denote those not yet saved, or, as with Elijah, someone not blessed with Christian understanding. In contrast, from behind Christ there shines a divine halo, and a bright light illuminates the grey/white habits of Theresa and Simon Stock, Mary's face and her red and blue robes, and Christ's stomach and swaddling drapery. This light, pouring across the broad canvas and appearing to emanate from the chapel's real altar, unites the angel, the atoning soul, and the gathering of the saintly and the divine.

A broad canvas such as this (twenty-one feet in width) conformed to the Venetian pictorial tradition of *scuola* or confraternal commissions.[61] One thinks back to the cycles of paintings executed in the late fifteenth and early sixteenth centuries for the Scuola Grande di S. Giovanni Evangelista and the Scuola di S. Giorgio degli Schiavoni, where miraculous and saintly stories were presented as a continuous narrative from one canvas to another. Tiepolo's painting, commissioned by a *scuola di devozione*, belongs to that tradition—but only in part, for the *Madonna del Carmelo* does not tell a story or belong to a larger cycle of works. Further, Tiepolo did not create a composition with a constant rhythmical accent across its entire span, as one usually finds in confraternal narratives. Instead, he emphasized the holy gathering on one side as the canvas's fitting pictorial culmination.

Tiepolo's sources for the holy group lie in devotional paintings like Veronese's Pala di S. Zaccaria (Venice, Accademia) and Pala Marogna (Verona, S. Paolo), in which the Madonna and Child are placed next to a column and adored by saints below. But the painting of most use to the young Giambattista in formulating his holy group was probably Titian's Pesaro altar-piece in the Frari (Pl. 19).[62] Striking points of comparison exist between the two. For instance, the glances with which Tiepolo links both Mary and Christ to the saints below are identical to the way in which Titian tied figures together in the Pesaro altar-piece; Mary's relationship with Simon Stock is similar to that of Titian's Christ-child with St Francis; and Tiepolo's Christ and St Theresa depend upon Titian's Mary and Jacopo Pesaro.[63] Moreover, Tiepolo's Blessed Albert is a twin brother to Titian's St Peter. But the most telling element in the comparison is the crosier-bearing angel in the *Madonna del Carmelo*'s centre who isolates the celestial sphere from both earth and purgatory. This figure plays a similar compositional role to the flag-bearing soldier

[61] There is evidence, however, that Tiepolo might have begun the painting differently. Three drawings now in Gdansk and all datable to the early 1720s when the Brera work was done, suggest that other devotions were perhaps once considered: M. Mrozinska, *Disegni veneti in Polonia* (exh. cat., Fondazione Cini, Venice, 1958), figs. 40–2. St Michael's presence in one drawing hints that perhaps St Gregory, whose vision of St Michael is famous, had been considered. In another drawing, the Angel Gabriel is holding a flower and gesturing to figures very like the 'souls' in the *Madonna del Carmelo*; this Gabriel could certainly have been drawn with an Annunciation in mind. The third drawing shows what has been identified as a Capuchin saint with a heretic.

[62] M. Levey, *Giambattista Tiepolo* (New Haven and London, 1986), 16, has also seen the link with Titian's Pesaro altar-piece. For Veronese, cf. T. Pignatti, *Veronese* (Venice, 1976), ii, figs. 370 and 382. The formula was often repeated by Veronese's followers,

and works such as Battista del Moro's *Virgin and Child, with SS Mark and John the Baptist* provide points of easy comparison with Tiepolo's painting: cf. *Da Tiziano a El Greco* (exh. cat., Ducal Palace, Venice, 1981 (Milan), no. 70.

[63] Tiepolo's Mary is standing, of course, and follows a very traditional form in Italian art: cf. Andrea del Sarto's Virgin in the *Madonna of the Harpies* (Florence, Uffizi), Annibale Carracci's *St Catherine* (Rome, S. Caterina dei Funari), and his 'Virtue' in *The Choice of Hercules* (Naples, Capodimonte). One suspects as well that Tiepolo might have turned to an ancient source, such as the 'Victory' of Brescia (discovered only in 1826). There is also a tie between Mary and Solimena's Rebecca (*Rebecca at the Well*: Venice, Accademia; Pl. 28), a work that Tiepolo knew well and was using at this time, 1722–3, for the *Martyrdom of St Bartholomew* in S. Stae.

in Titian's *pala*, who also, let it be noted, separates figures on the left from the enthroned Madonna and Christ.

The *Madonna del Carmelo* is a compositionally sophisticated work, with no sign of the overcrowding and awkwardnesses of the Burano *Crucifixion*. Mannered figures are still present, but they have been used to express dramatic purpose, and they are integral to the painting's meaning. For example, the exaggerated extension of the flying angel's arm and, directly below, the muscularity of the supine soul's back may appear unnatural and overworked, but they are appropriate, for they point the faithful to Mary and her scapular, and to Christ and salvation. Tiepolo specialists have usually agreed that the painting dates from the early 1720s, Knox even specifying the year 1722; Lino Moretti has recently uncovered a document stating that the canvas was commissioned in December 1721, but was not completed ('ridotto a perfetione') until mid-1727.[64] One is left with many questions about when the painting was begun and which part was still incomplete in 1727. But the *Madonna del Carmelo* is almost completely consistent stylistically. I would hazard a guess that, apart from Elijah and his shadowy landscape on the right, the entire work can still be dated to 1722; for the figures are consonant both in type and execution with Tiepolo's style of those early years. Moreover, 1722 was the four hundredth anniversary of the Sabbatine Bull promulgated by Pope John XXII and promising liberation from purgatory for all who wore the scapular, as well as the centenary of Theresa of Avila's canonization.[65] It is more than likely that Tiepolo was pressed into having the painting ready for Carmelite celebrations at that time but that, perhaps for reasons of professional over-commitment, he was simply unable to finish it.

Having established a plausible, albeit tentative, chronology for both the *Crucifixion* and the *Madonna del Carmelo*, one may plot a course for Tiepolo's stylistic maturation between 1719–20 and 1722–3. Similar to the *Crucifixion* in its crowded composition, its conflicting areas of dramatic tension, its overwrought emotionalism, and its darting and fragmenting lighting is the *Healing of the Paralytic* (Venice, Accademia; Pl. 21).[66] Tiepolo has, as it were, over-directed the scene; contorted and dramatically lit figures tend to pull the viewer's glance away from a very passive-looking Christ, just as in S. Martino the two struggling thieves on the right and left and Mary's bright red gown in the foreground almost overpower the crucified Christ in the centre.

Religious works which are closer in style to the *Madonna del Carmelo*, that is to its beginnings in 1722, are *Susannah and the Elders* in the Wadsworth Atheneum, Hartford (Pl. 20), the *Rest on the Flight* in the San Diego Museum of Art (Pl. 23), and the *Expulsion of Hagar* in the Rasini Collection, Milan (Pl. 22). The exaggerated extension of Susannah's curving form finds an echo in St Theresa in the Brera. Another link between the two paintings is the similar physiognomies of the two elders leering at Susannah, and of Albert

[64] Cf. L. Moretti, 'Notizie e appunti su G. B. Piazzetta: Alcuni piazzetteschi e G. B. Tiepolo', *Atti dell'Istituto Veneto di Scienze, Lettere, ed Arti*, 143 (1984–5), 379. For previous assessments, cf. Morassi, *A Complete Catalogue*, p. 24; R. Pallucchini, 'Nota per Giambattista', p. 4; id., *La pittura veneziana del Settecento* (Venice, 1960), 67, and 'Un Tiepolo in più, un Bencovich in meno', in *Studi in onore di Giulio Carlo Argan* (Rome, 1984), 368; Rizzi, *Mostra*

del Tiepolo, no. 5; and Knox, 'Giambattista Tiepolo', p. 417.
[65] Cf. Chap. 2, p. 146.
[66] A. Pallucchini, *L'opera completa*, no. 14, dates it to 1720, and Morassi, *A Complete Catalogue*, p. 54, to *c*.1718–20, i.e., contemporary with Lazzarini's version of the same subject (Pl. 6). Cf. also G. Fogolari, 'Dipinti giovanili di G. B. Tiepolo', *Bollettino d'arte*, 3 (1923), 49–64.

20. Above, left: G. B. Tiepolo, *Susannah and the Elders* (oil on canvas, 56 × 43 cm.)

21. Above, right: G. B. Tiepolo, *Healing of the Paralytic* (oil on canvas, 63 × 46 cm.)

22. G. B. Tiepolo, *Rest on the Flight into Egypt* (oil on canvas, 60 × 50 cm.)

23. G. B. Tiepolo, *Expulsion of Hagar* (oil on canvas, 96 × 136 cm.)

and Simon Stock. Looking at the jewelled chain on Susannah's breast and the sparkling embroidery on the band of Albert's robe, one notes the same handling of paint. Those features which indicate that the Hartford work is the earlier of the two are, I believe, its more sketchy technique, its crowded and very busy composition, and the nervous insistence with which the young Tiepolo sought to dramatize even still forms, namely, the fountain, the draperies, and the flowers.

The San Diego *Rest on the Flight* and the Rasini *Expulsion of Hagar* show a change in Tiepolo's attitude towards the placement of figures. Space opens up, figures turn and gesticulate more broadly than before, and background landscape is given a new importance.[67] One notes, too, links to both *Susannah and the Elders* and the *Madonna del Carmelo*. For example, the pose of the Virgin in the *Rest on the Flight* is the same as Susannah's, but with less tension and in a somewhat more natural way of course, and the Virgin's sharply oblique position *vis-à-vis* St Joseph and the angel repeats the distinction made between St Theresa and those around her in the right half of the *Madonna del Carmelo*. The angel visiting the holy family in the San Diego canvas is younger and less muscular but a relative none the less of the one flying above the souls in purgatory.

The *Expulsion of Hagar* is also close to the *Madonna del Carmelo*.[68] Abraham's gesture reappears on the angel pointing to the right, the patriarch looks like the Blessed Albert, Hagar's position is that of the recumbent 'soul', and the serving woman looking towards us is the same face that peers out from purgatory. Hagar's and St Theresa's draperies have been conceived with exactly the same chiaroscuro, and the space in the Rasini painting opens on a diagonal towards a landscape, as in the Brera painting and the *Rest on the Flight*. What is most impressive about the *Expulsion of Hagar* is the sharp confrontation between Abraham and Hagar, which is brilliantly realized through the latter's attitude of self-abasement that moves contrapuntally against the former's gesture and hanging cloak.

The step in development from the *Madonna del Carmelo* and the *Expulsion of Hagar*, to the *Martyrdom of St Bartholomew* in S. Stae (Pl. 24) and the competition sketch for the ceiling of the Cappella di S. Domenico in SS Giovanni e Paolo, both dated 1722–3, is a very small one.[69] Many of the dramatic elements in the *Martyrdom*, in particular, are already present in the Brera and Rasini paintings. The movement of Bartholomew's left arm comes from the pointing arms of the angel and Abraham, and the open gesture of the martyred saint's right hand can be seen in the angel's own right hand as well as in the serving woman's hand reaching through the light towards the recumbent Hagar. Finally, Bartholomew's executioner is physiognomically the male counterpart to Hagar, and their noses cut forward from shadow in a similar fashion.

---

[67] These two works must be contemporary with Tiepolo's four mythological landscape-paintings in the Accademia.

[68] The painting has usually been dated to either 1717 or 1719 because of an inscription on the stick in the bottom right-hand corner; but although the first two digits are clearly 17, the last two are indecipherable. Morassi, *A Complete Catalogue*, p. 28, dated the work to either 1717 or 1719; A. Pallucchini, *L'opera completa*, no. 13, dated it to 1719; Knox, 'Giambattista Tiepolo', p. 414, placed it in 1719; R. Pallucchini, 'Nota per Giambattista Tiepolo', p. 4, put it to *c*.1719, directly before the Brera work (Pallucchini repeats this date in 'Un Tiepolo in più', p. 368); and in

the *Mostra del Tiepolo*, no. 3, Rizzi notes only the inscription's illegibility. Aikema, 'Early Tiepolo Studies, 1.', p. 367 (fig. 25), believes that the Rasini painting represents a mythological subject rather than Hagar's expulsion. This may be so, but it should be noted that Pietro da Cortona painted a work now called *The Return of Hagar to Abraham* in which there is the same cast of characters as appears in Tiepolo's work: cf. G. Briganti, *Pietro da Cortona* (Florence, 1962), fig. 179.

[69] For the dating of S. Stae, cf. note 71, below. For the dating of the S. Domenico sketch recovered from a newly found document, cf. Moretti, 'Notizie e appunti', pp. 375 ff.

The custom by which a painter uses, reuses, and then elaborates on motifs from one work of art to another is common in modern Western painting. Tiepolo's early practice of reworking poses and studying them from many angles is evident in a drawing in the Wallraf-Richartz Museum in Cologne (Pl. 25), in which one male nude is examined seventeen times in a variety of related movements.[70] But the most surprising of the young Tiepolo's reformulations is the one in which the angel flying above purgatory in the *Madonna del Carmelo* has been transformed into St Bartholomew in the *Martyrdom*; the back leg was brought forward and the head changed (Pl. 26). None the less, the dramatic urgency that Tiepolo created in the magnificent figure of St Bartholomew can be found already in both the *Expulsion of Hagar* and the *Madonna del Carmelo*.

The *Martyrdom of St Bartholomew* (Pl. 24) was painted as part of a cycle of twelve works for the Church of S. Stae (Venetian dialect for Sant'Eustachio, or St Eustace); each canvas was assigned to a different artist and each was to portray an apostle of Christ. Moretti has published the documentation for the project, showing that in April 1722 Andrea Stazio left some money to pay for the paintings, which were to be placed on the twelve pilasters in S. Stae's nave.[71] The *Martyrdom of St Bartholomew* is without doubt the most successful of the twelve. Neither Lazzarini's classicism, nor Bambini's rhetoric, nor Ricci's and Pellegrini's painterly brushwork, nor even Piazzetta's invigorated mixture of Venetian–Bolognese elements can compete with Tiepolo's spirited drama. He achieved this in part by lifting elements from other paintings, all of which borrowings are well known: from Piazzetta's *Arrest of St James* (Pl. 27), also one of the S. Stae cycle, Tiepolo took the device of placing a spectator in the bottom left-hand corner, both to monumentalize the martyrdom in the foreground and to create a strong luministic contrast; and Bartholomew's gaoler in the bottom right-hand corner is based to some extent on a reversal of the servant holding Eliezer's camel in Francesco Solimena's *Rebecca at the Well* (Pl. 28). But it was not from either Piazzetta's or Solimena's composition that Tiepolo borrowed the abrupt, angular movements and the staccato-like rhythms that make the *Martyrdom of St Bartholomew* one of the most forceful paintings produced in Venice in the first quarter of the eighteenth century. A work that could have helped Tiepolo in devising his composition was Luca Giordano's *Crucifixion of St Peter*, which the artist had left in Venice (Pl. 29).[72] Giordano's painting showed the young Giambattista how to create visual power and muscular tension out of a bold zigzag, one in which straining limbs pull vigorously away from each other in a three-dimensional space.

Tiepolo's success as a young painter depended to a considerable extent on his understanding of and experimentation with a variety of pictorial styles. His art developed quickly because he responded with feverish intensity to many different sources, something

[70] The Cologne drawing can be dated anywhere between 1719–20 and 1725. A similar sheet, worked on both recto and verso, is in the Prado, Madrid: cf. E. Feinblatt, 'More Early Drawings by Giovanni Battista Tiepolo', *Master Drawings*, 5 (1967), pls. 34–5.

[71] L. Moretti, 'La data degli apostoli della chiesa di San Stae', *Arte veneta*, 27 (1973), 318ff. The other painters were Ricci, Lazzarini, Pellegrini, Piazzetta, Balestra, Pittoni, Bambini, Mariotti, Manaigo, Pietro Uberti, and Angelo Trevisani.

[72] Cf. O. Ferrari and G. Scavizzi, *Luca Giordano* (Naples, 1966), ii. 47, dated c.1659; and S. Moschini Marconi, *Gallerie dell'Accademia di Venezia: Opere d'arte dei secoli XVII, XVIII, XIX* (Rome, 1970), 142. Note the relationship between Giordano's muscular figure in the bottom right-hand corner and Tiepolo's own impressive gaoler.

24. G. B. Tiepolo, *Martyrdom of St Bartholomew* (oil on canvas, 167 × 139 cm.)

25. G. B. Tiepolo, *Figure Studies* (pen and black ink on white paper, 220 × 335 mm.)

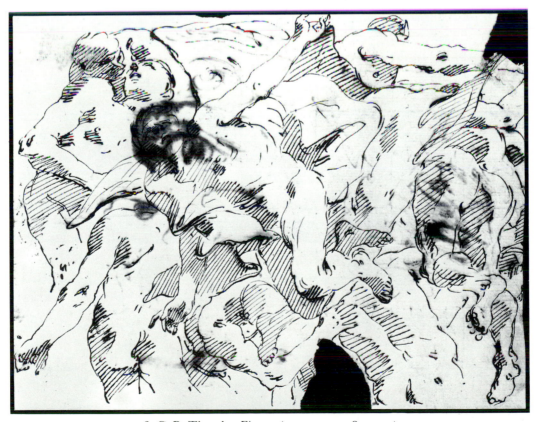

26. G. B. Tiepolo, *Figures* (pen, 144 × 185 mm.)

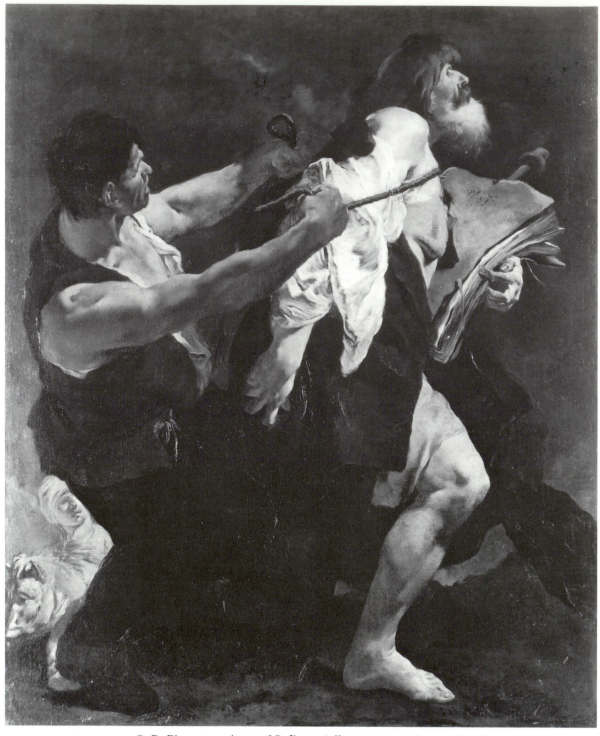

27. G. B. Piazzetta, *Arrest of St James* (oil on canvas, 165 × 138 cm.)

28. Opposite, above: F. Solimena, *Rebecca at the Well*
(oil on canvas, 202 × 150 cm.)

29. Opposite, below: L. Giordano, *Crucifixion of St
Peter* (oil on canvas, 196 × 258 cm.)

which was recognized even by his contemporaries. His friend and admirer Francesco Algarotti, a sophisticated man whose cultural and intellectual pretensions were at ease at several royal Courts, wrote extensively and perceptively about Tiepolo's reactions to artistic stimuli: 'In some of my sketches of things copied in Verona and Mantua from San Micheli, Cataneo, Leon Battista Alberti, Giulio Romano, and Bertano, he [Tiepolo] understood what was good even though I myself hadn't been able to catch it. He was enchanted above all by the proportions, the loveliness and the harmony of Palladio, and he made them his own.'[73] Tiepolo's remarkable ability to assimilate resulted from his insistence on elaborating upon what he saw. Algarotti continues: 'If you give him a design [un pensiero]; he will examine it, and consider it from all angles; he will work it in ten different ways, and reshape it into better forms, nor can he stop until he has found the best possible solution.'[74]

Writing this in 1760, Algarotti was amazed to note the enthusiasm and readiness with which the elderly Tiepolo attacked such artistic challenges: 'Open a path before him; and he will be like a tartar ['barbaro'] who has run and won the pallium.'[75] This spontaneity burst from a sixty-four-year-old; one can imagine with what intensity the same man must have worked at the age of twenty-four. Although 'born a painter', Tiepolo sought to master the pictorial tradition that preceded him, to absorb two centuries of Venetian art.[76]

There are four principal aspects of Tiepolo's early work that reveal his sources. First, the heroic nude that fills much of his youthful *œuvre*; secondly, an intense emotional sentiment; thirdly, his first works are dark in tonality and, as has often been noted, continue the Venetian tenebrist tradition; and, lastly, he sought pictorial refinement through decorative details and figural elegance.

In every large public painting that Tiepolo executed on a religious theme before 1725, the youthful, muscular, male nude plays a significant role in the narrative's unfolding. Whether the subject was drawn from the Old Testament, as in the *Faraone sommerso*, the New Testament, as in the *Crucifixion*, traditional Christian writings, as in the *Martyrdom of St Bartholomew*, or was a devotional work responding to a specific cult, as in the *Madonna del Carmelo*, Tiepolo developed the dramatic action through the physical presence and the exertions of the classical ideal of male beauty. Two types dominate his early art. The most frequent is the figure in exaggerated contortion. Such a form is characterized by its vigorous struggles against forces more powerful than itself: in the *Faraone sommerso*, the Hebrews fight fear and fatigue and the Egyptians the swelling waters; the thieves in the

[73] F. Algarotti, 'Lettere sopra la pittura', *Opere* (Venice, 1792), viii. 104 (dated 12 Feb. 1760 and written to Prospero Pesci): 'In alcuni miei schizzi di cose copiate a Verona e a Mantova dal San Micheli, dal Cataneo, da Leon Battista Alberti, da Giulio Romano, e dal Bertano, ci sapea vedere quel buono che io non ci ho saputo mettere. Le proporzioni sopra tutto, la venustà e l'armonico del Palladio lo incanta, e se le ha fatte sue.'

[74] Ibid.: 'se gli dia un pensiero; egli lo esamina, lo considera da tutti i lati; lo tratta in dieci maniere, lo modula nelle migliori forme, nè sa quietarsi ch'egli non abbia trovato l'ottimo'.

[75] Ibid.: 'Apritegli una strada; ed egli è un barbaro che ha corso e vinto il pallio . . .'.

[76] Ibid.: 'Grande ingegno veramente ha egli sortito da natura . . .', an opinion repeated by A. Longhi in *Compendio delle vite de' pittori veneziani istorici più rinomati del presente secolo . . .* (Venice, 1762), 17.

Crucifixion fight their bonds; and St Bartholomew pulls against his tormentors. The second type of heroic male is diametrically opposed to the first, for he does not combat his fate but willingly submits to it: the prostrate form on the left in the *Madonna del Carmelo* awaits salvation through the Virgin Mary's intercession; and Christ on the cross in the Burano painting yields to the divine plan. All of these heroic figures, whether resisting or submitting, are creatures confronting God's will and were adopted by the young Giambattista as metaphors of powerlessness before divine omnipotence.

Tiepolo was not the first painter to depict robust muscularity to signify man's inability to contradict supernatural will, but he was the first in Venice to make this pictorial metaphor meaningful and forceful after the death of Jacopo Tintoretto in the late sixteenth century.[77] More than sixty years ago, Gino Fogolari noted that the young Giambattista had studied Tintoretto's paintings, but he did not cite specific examples or explain why Tiepolo's art resembled that of Tintoretto.[78] In working with Lazzarini, the young Giambattista would have encountered Tintorettesque motifs dozens of times; Lazzarini's *Almsgiving of S. Lorenzo Giustinian* is full of figures taken from the canvases painted for the Scuola Grande di S. Rocco. But if Tiepolo had studied only Lazzarini's interpretation of Tintoretto's art, he would not have understood the importance of the heroic nude, because Lazzarini's figures—no matter how closely they follow their originals in stance or gesture— are almost always enervated. Their torsion appears without purpose, and their musculature is dramatically meaningless.

Tiepolo's appreciation of the spiritual force that Tintoretto achieved with powerful figures is apparent in a series of drawings illustrating the *Brazen Serpent*.[79] Two of them (Pls. 30, 31) show several men falling backwards towards the viewer, and they call to mind similar forms by Tintoretto (cf. Pl. 13). On another sheet, in a private collection in Paris, a figure in the bottom right-hand corner restates the brightly lit nude on the top of the middle heap in Tintoretto's the *Brazen Serpent* (Pl. 8).[80] Borrowing another nude from the same painting, the one seen directly under God's left arm and darkly shadowed, Tiepolo then turned it ninety degrees in space on a drawing now in the Victoria and Albert Museum (Pl. 26). Here, Giambattista reduced the figure's extension but compensated for it by accentuating the limbs' angular positioning and movement; the figure eventually became St Bartholomew in the canvas painted for S. Stae. Tiepolo's aim in using such physical imbalance and instability was to create, like Tintoretto, a race of heroic men vulnerable before the Deity.

The second of Tiepolo's important sources was the work of Titian. I have already remarked on how Tiepolo used the Pesaro altar-piece for the *Madonna del Carmelo*, but Titian served Tiepolo's religious art in an even more important way, in the creation of intense emotion. Looking again at the *Madonna del Carmelo*, one notes that the soul in purgatory repeats the eloquent gesture of yearning of Titian's *David and Goliath* (Pl. 32).

[77] For Tintoretto, cf. Banks, 'Tintoretto's Religious Imagery', pp. 154–5. Michelangelo's *Last Judgement* in the Sistine Chapel stands out as the greatest example of this conceit in Italian art.

[78] Fogolari, 'Dipinti giovanili', p. 50.

[79] Cf. Mrozinska, *Disegni veneti in Polonia*, no. 40ᵛ; Feinblatt, 'More Early Drawings', pls. 36–7; and H. Voss, 'Un taccuino di disegni del Tiepolo giovane', *Saggi e memorie di storia dell'arte*, ii (1958–9), figs. 1, 3, 5, 7, 9. For the drawings in Pls. 30, 31, cf. *Finarte*, 15 Apr. 1985, no. 203; and A. Moir, *Old Master Drawings from the Feitelson Collection* (exh. cat., University Art Museum, Santa Barbara, California, 1983), no. 63.

[80] Cf. Voss, 'Un taccuino', fig. 7.

30. G. B. Tiepolo, *Figure Studies* (pen and brown wash on white paper, 143 × 201 mm.)

31. G. B. Tiepolo, *The People of Israel and the Fiery Serpents* (pen and brown wash on white paper, 146 × 205 mm.)

But the *Martyrdom of St Bartholomew* provides the best illustration of what the young Giambattista sought from Titian. Bartholomew's ecstatic incandescence recalls the saintly beatitude that characterizes two of Titian's greatest Venetian altar-pieces, the lost *Martyrdom of St Peter Martyr*, formerly in the Church of SS Giovanni e Paolo, and the *Martyrdom of St Lawrence*, commissioned for the Chiesa dei Crociferi but now in the Gesuiti.[81]

Although it may seem surprising that Giambattista came to understand both Tintoretto and Titian through his apprenticeship with Lazzarini, the value of his training with this master can best be appreciated by considering Piazzetta's art, in which rhetorical figures play almost no role at all. One must suppose that, leaving aside considerations of personal temperament, Piazzetta's study with Antonio Molinari and Giuseppe Maria Crespi did not prepare him for the heroic style.[82] Lazzarini's workshop, on the other hand, instilled in the young Tiepolo the fundamentals of monumental painting. A valid objection, of course, would be that Tiepolo was the only one of Lazzarini's students to succeed in following upon Venice's grand tradition: witness the lack-lustre paintings and careers of Silvestro Manaigo and Giuseppe Camerata. But Tiepolo's particular gift was to understand the artistic substance upon which his teacher's art was based and to move directly towards it, to the physical and emotional drama found in the paintings of both Tintoretto and Titian.

The third source of influence for the young Tiepolo was, as I have noted above, the late seicento tenebrism of Francesco Rosa, Giambattista Langetti, and Antonio Zanchi.[83] Zanchi's art, in particular, proved useful to Tiepolo. I have already shown how the type of donor portrait found in Zanchi's *Martyrdom of S. Zulian* was repeated by Giambattista in the *Crucifixion*, and how Zanchi's *Last Judgement* in the Scuola Grande di S. Fantin provided Tiepolo with a 'modern' example of Tintoretto's version of the same subject; the tumbling figures entwined about one another in the drawings for the *Brazen Serpent* may have been influenced by Zanchi's work.[84] Zanchi's grandest painting was *The Plague in Venice*, painted in 1666 to commemorate the terrible epidemic of 1630 (Pl. 33); the two-piece canvas in the stair-well of the Scuola di S. Rocco still creates an impression on any visitor willing to pause in his climb towards Tintoretto's more famous paintings above. *The Plague in Venice* must have appeared to Tiepolo as it does today, as a link in the Venetian tradition between Tintoretto's art and Lazzarini's *Almsgiving of S. Lorenzo Giustinian*. Zanchi's muscular figures dramatized by violently cutting shadows would have appealed to the young Tiepolo. And specific gestures like that of the man to the left of the bridge would have attracted him, too; indeed, this motif appears in both the *Expulsion of Hagar* and the *Madonna del Carmelo*.

Tiepolo's debt to Piazzetta's dark and sombre manner is now a commonplace in

[81] Cf. H. Wethey, *Titian: The Religious Paintings* (London, 1969–70), nos. 133 and 114.

[82] For the tradition that Piazzetta did study with Crespi in 1703–4, cf. Mariuz, *L'opera completa*, p. 67. Knox refuses this possibility: cf. his review of the exhibition *Giambattista Piazzetta: Il suo tempo, la sua scuola*, in *Burlington Magazine*, 125 (1983), 510; and cf. Moretti, 'Notizie e appunti', pp. 361–2.

[83] Cf. above, pp. 19ff. Aikema, 'Early Tiepolo Studies, 1.', p. 365, has come to the same conclusions regarding these early tenebrist sources. Zanchi would have had special standing among native Venetian painters, for he was the first local artist to achieve success using the tenebrist style. He lived until 1722, and through his teacher, Matteo Ponzone, he was able to offer contemporary painters a direct link back to late sixteenth- and early seventeenth-century art.

[84] Zanchi painted this work in the 1670s; it is reminiscent of Tintoretto's own *Last Judgement* in S. Maria dell'Orto and of the *Brazen Serpent* in the Scuola di S. Rocco.

32. Titian, *David and Goliath*, detail (oil on canvas, 292 × 282 cm.)

33. A. Zanchi, *The Plague in Venice*, detail (oil on canvas)

historical studies of eighteenth-century Venetian art.[85] The small pockets of shadow on the faces of the woman sustaining the Virgin in the Burano *Crucifixion*, the serving lady in profile in the *Expulsion of Hagar*, and Isaac in the *Sacrifice of Isaac* in the Ospedaletto, repeat almost exactly Piazzetta's treatment of the Virgin in the Pala Sagredo of *c*.1717, where the crisp juxtaposition of light and shade emphasizes the eye's bulbous protrusion within the socket's bony structure.[86] Tiepolo's use of this device called attention specifically to dramatic glances, such as Isaac's towards Abraham's dagger. However, if the young Tiepolo is to be considered a tenebrist painter *alla* Piazzetta, it must be with two important reservations. First, Tiepolo's colour spectrum is wider than that of his older colleague; his early works are certainly dominated by warm browns and areas of creamy whites moving into greys, but these zones are always contrasted with large blocks of bright colour. In the *Expulsion of Hagar*, Hagar and Abraham are presented as two major fields of white/grey and gold/brown, but directly behind them vivid reds create a warm blush. In the *Crucifixion* on Burano, Mary is picked out from the rest of the scene by her lobster-red gown, and her ashen face is contrasted against a surrounding field of the same red together with forest green, lemon yellow, sapphire blue, and snowy white. In the *Madonna del Carmelo*, the colouristic neutrality of the saint's robes on the right exalts the Virgin who is dressed in vivid red and blue. In the *Healing of the Paralytic* and the *Rest on the Flight*, different greens and blues stand out from the general darkness, and red drapery dominates the centre of *Susannah and the Elders*.

The second reservation regarding Tiepolo's dependence upon Piazzetta concerns the type of experience that each of the two painters asked the devout to undergo before a religious image. In Piazzetta's Pala Sagredo, the figures are enveloped by an insulating atmosphere; they exist in their own world. Tiepolo, however, propelled the drama into the spectator's world. The thieves in the Burano *Crucifixion*, the healed paralytic, St Bartholomew, and Isaac all have a physical presence that is consistently directed towards the picture plane. Moreover, the characters often face us and imply that they are concerned for our involvement: for example, the portrait in the *Crucifixion*, the attendants in the *Expulsion of Hagar*, and the young 'soul' in the bottom left-hand corner of the *Madonna del Carmelo*.

The extent to which Tiepolo was indebted to Piazzetta can be understood by examining the *Martyrdom of St Bartholomew* (Pl. 24). Creating a composition based on a diagonal zigzag was certainly not Piazzetta's invention; as I have already indicated Giordano's *Crucifixion of St Peter* was an earlier example of the type (Pl. 29). In addition, Bartholomew is a product of Tiepolo's study of Tintoretto, and the muscular gaoler in the bottom right-hand corner is a combination of figural ideas from both Solimena's *Rebecca at the Well* and Giordano's *Crucifixion of St Peter*. Neither the composition nor any of the major figures in the *Martyrdom of St Bartholomew* owe their existence to Piazzetta's art.

What Tiepolo did learn from Piazzetta's *Arrest of St James*, however, was how to monumentalize a dramatic action; he filled the canvas to its borders with muscular figures and juxtaposed them with an onlooker who appears to be on a different ground level.

[85] This opinion was put very well by R. Pallucchini in *La pittura veneziana del Settecento*, p. 66.

[86] For the Pala Sagredo and Tiepolo's *Sacrifice of Isaac*, cf. ibid., figs. 149 and 178.

But Tiepolo's conception of dramatic narrative differs radically from Piazzetta's. Piazzetta's figures turn away from the viewer; their facial expressions play only a small role in the terrible drama. Hands either express very little or are cloaked in shadow; St James is even composed enough to hold his pilgrimage staff and a book. Tiepolo's Bartholomew has another force altogether: he is both physically desperate and spiritually ecstatic; his brilliantly lit hands seek divine assistance despite his bound body; the hands of his tormentors, although in shadow, are powerful and prominently displayed; and, finally, his unstably positioned feet contrast with the firm stance of the knife-wielding executioner. Even in the Piazzettesque bystander in the bottom left-hand corner one sees Tiepolo's sense of drama at work, for this figure, unlike Piazzetta's, grimaces and then gestures with a sudden movement of the hand: the ghastly act is about to take place.

Sebastiano Ricci and Giannantonio Pellegrini were the last important influences on Tiepolo. It is significant that both of these painters returned to Venice from journeys to the north in the years before 1720, and that Tiepolo appears to have modified his youthful, dramatic style *c.*1720–1. This change can be seen by comparing the *Crucifixion* with both the *Expulsion of Hagar* and the *Madonna del Carmelo*. In the first work, Tiepolo emphasized the story's horror through the straining bodies of the two thieves, the swinging ropes, and the Virgin Mary's pallid face. In the two paintings in Milan, he modulated the drama through curvilinear forms and a refined figural style. For instance, the potent gesture of Abraham and the rupture between his figure and that of Hagar are softened by the curves of the urn in the bottom right-hand corner and the ornamental frieze on the wall behind. This blend of drama and elegance must stem from Ricci, whose *Dream of Æsculapius*, which Daniels dated to *c.*1719–20, also has an ornamental urn with a reclining figure nearby.[87] Even if in this case Tiepolo's ideas preceded Ricci's, such charming details as the altar cushion and its tassel hanging near the turning pages of a book in the *Madonna del Carmelo* have to be thought of in terms of Ricci's altar-piece for S. Giorgio Maggiore, dated 1708.

Ricci's influence on Tiepolo can also be seen in the figures of Hagar and Susannah, in the angels in the *Madonna del Carmelo* and the *Education of the Virgin* in Dijon (Pl. 105), and in a soldier on a sheet in a private collection in Paris.[88] These forms, only seen in Tiepolo's figural canon after 1720, are elongated rather than heavy, and their heads are invariably small in relation to their bodies. Ricci did not invent this type but, having absorbed ideas from Luca Giordano and Alessandro Magnasco, he began around 1700 to elongate his male nudes and to accentuate the curves of his females. His purpose was to create pictorial refinement and elegance. Tiepolo, on the other hand, used such figures for dramatic contrast: for example, Hagar versus Abraham, or the angel above purgatory against the muscular 'soul' below.

Tiepolo also modernized his style by adapting aspects of Pellegrini's art, impressed by the way in which the latter's bravura brushwork creates a pictorial vitality quite independent of the object or form it is meant to describe. Moreover, Pellegrini's loose handling of paint is usually coupled with such highly pitched colour that forms seem to levitate

[87] Cf. J. Daniels, *Sebastiano Ricci* (Hove, 1976), fig. 333.   [88] Voss, 'Un taccuino', fig. 4.

from the canvas. Tiepolo sought an altogether different form of intensity for his own art, but the drapery around Susannah in the Hartford painting and in the angels' wings in the works in Dijon and San Diego has a creaminess of texture that can only be compared with Pellegrini's.

Tiepolo's great achievement by the mid-1720s was to have created a new heroic style in Venetian painting. He had mastered the grand tradition of the sixteenth century, as well as the more recent artists of the seventeenth and the moderns of his own day, and he had accomplished this before he was thirty, younger than either Piazzetta or Ricci were when they had established their careers. Moreover, Tiepolo had not left Venice in all this time, unlike Piazzetta who had gone to Bologna for study, and Ricci who had travelled abroad to achieve success. In other words, he was Venetian through and through.

As Da Canal stated in his tract, 'Della maniera del dipingere moderno', Tiepolo's art reflected 'the best modern taste', an evaluation which is found within the author's discussion of the pictorial characteristics needed to create a properly modern style of painting and of the qualities that, in Da Canal's opinion, departed from the accepted canons of the Venetian tradition.[89] Among the latter are techniques that do 'not have naturalism particularly in religious imagery'. Recalling how in the late sixteenth century pictorial imagery had closely followed nature, Da Canal lamented the contemporary pursuit of 'grazia' for its own sake: 'in our day, a flying drapery that is turned ['rivolto'] with majesty is found more pleasing than one that is compact and natural.'[90]

Da Canal thought that 'the clever painter' was of less consequence than one with 'wise judgement'; and this could be weighed by the pictorial choices that a painter made. Tiepolo's intelligence must have ranked at the highest level, therefore, for his models were the very artists whom Da Canal had praised. For example, Da Canal mentioned 'Tintoretto's nudes and [their] movements'; he singled out Zanchi for his 'quick and free manner', 'the strong effect of [his] chiaroscuro', 'the power of [his] best works', and his 'good draughtsmanship'. Pellegrini's handling of paint was extolled, too, as were Ricci's nudes.[91]

Lauding Tiepolo for his draughtsmanship, for his 'pictorial freedom and ease', and for his 'new ideas', Da Canal recognized him as one of the supermen of modern art, noting also that the young painter justifiably aroused more professional jealousy among his contemporaries than any other artist.[92] But one of the young Tiepolo's greatest achievements within the context of Da Canal's writings, and very probably within the thinking of most of their contemporaries, was his perpetuation of the golden tradition of Venice's artistic past; his monumental figural style was able to convey deep seriousness and gravity, responding to the sacred themes of his Christian world.

Following immediately after his first tenebrist successes, Tiepolo turned his attention to

[89] V. Da Canal, 'Della maniera del dipingere moderno', in *Mercurio filosofico, letterario, e poetico* (Venice, 1810), 15: 'Giambattista Tiepolo . . . dà gelosia a quanti pittori possono lavorare col più buon gusto moderno.'

[90] Ibid., p. 18: 'non à naturalezza spezialmente nelle immagine pie'; and p. 17: 'A di nostri, più piacque un drappo volante rivolto con maestà che uno succinto e naturale.'

[91] Ibid., pp. 6–7, and 19–20: 'maniera franca, spedita', 'buon disegno', and 'lo sforzo del chiaroscuro'; and 'i nudi del Tintoretto con i suoi movimenti', and 'la forza nelle opere buone del Zanchi'. For Ricci, see p. 20: 'le sagome de' nudi del Rizzi con la sua nobil maniera'; but in his *Vita*, p. xvii, Da Canal censures Ricci's nudes.

[92] Da Canal, 'Della maniera', pp. 15, 17, and 20; and *Vita*, p. xxxiii.

another pictorial mode. Beginning in the middle of the 1720s, he studied Veronese's art and used it as the basis for a style of high rhetoric in a series of biblical scenes for the Archbishop's Palace in Udine (Pls. 34–41; Pl. II). This fresco commission, the grandest to come the young Tiepolo's way, was to demonstrate the breadth of his capabilities and his unique gifts as a decorative painter. The project's importance and the challenge it imposed on him cannot be overestimated: its importance lay in the patron's rank, and its challenge in its grand scale. The patron, a member of one of Venice's oldest families, was Dionisio Dolfin, who ruled as Patriarch of Aquileia from 1699 to 1734. The commission called for almost a dozen, large, Old Testament narratives and an equal number of smaller, subsidiary scenes in the palace's Gallery and on the ceilings of both the stairwell and the Ecclesiastical Tribunal.[93]

Tiepolo's reputation as an accomplished frescoist was already established before he began his work in Udine; his *Glory of St Theresa* in the Scalzi (S. Maria di Nazareth) and the ceiling of the *salone* in Palazzo Sandi, both of which have survived, can be dated to *c.*1722–3 and *c.*1724–5 respectively. He had also worked in fresco in a villa in Vascon, in the Palazzo Baglioni (Massanzago) and in the Church of S. Maria Assunta in Biadene.[94] Thus, when Dolfin chose Tiepolo for the Udine cycle he was hiring an accomplished technician. But what the Patriarch could not have foreseen was that this young frescoist had such a delicate pictorial sensibility; nor could he have predicted how brilliantly Tiepolo would realize the commission's political programme. Tiepolo's paintings in the Archbishop's Palace are, in equal measure, both beautiful images and convincing political arguments; the two components function in perfect unison.

The historical background to Dolfin's project is quickly explained.[95] It stemmed from a conflict between Venice and Vienna over the political control of the Patriarchy of Aquileia, the historical seat of the Church of Venice. The patriarchy had been founded in the third century on the Adriatic coastline where St Mark had supposedly stopped during his travels from Rome.[96] During the Middle Ages, the patriarchy was moved from Aquileia, its original seat, to Udine. From there, the patriarchal succession held temporal power over the region of Friuli until the Venetian State usurped that power in 1420. A little later in the century, the childless Count of Gorizia promised Maximilian of Austria that Friuli would pass to the Austrian Crown. These unexpected dynastic complications caused Venice to propose to the papacy that a Venetian aristocrat, Domenico Grimani, should be named Patriarch of Aquileia to counterbalance the changing political sov-

[93] For a biography of the Dolfin, see B. G. Dolfin, *I Dolfin: Patrizii veneziani nella storia di Venezia dall'anno 452 al 1910* (Belluno, 1912), 154 ff. Along with the prestigious Cornaro and the Pisani, the Dolfin seem to have been the only ancient Venetian house to have turned to Tiepolo during this early period of his career. Tiepolo did work for other important Venetian families, however; Da Canal mentions in his *Vita*, pp. xxxii–xxxv, that the young painter received commissions from the Baglioni, Nani, Sandi, and Zenobio families. Tiepolo also worked for the Dolfin in Ca' Dolfin at S. Pantaleon, where he did a series of Roman stories for the Sala Maggiore, and in Palazzo Dolfin on the Terraglio, the stretch of countryside between Mestre and Treviso.

[94] Cf. Da Canal, *Vita*, p. xxxii; for Vascon (1722–3) and Biadene, cf. the recent discoveries of Moretti, 'Notizie e appunti',

pp. 379–80; and for Biadene and Palazzo Baglioni at Massanzago (not at S. Cassiano, Venice, as Da Canal mistakenly notes), cf. the important article by A. Mariuz and G. Pavanello, 'I primi affreschi di Giambattista Tiepolo', *Arte veneta*, 39 (1985), 101–13.

[95] See this author's 'Patriarchy and Politics: Tiepolo's "Galleria Patriarcale" in Udine Revisited', in D. Rosand (ed.), *Interpretazioni veneziane: Studi di storia dell'arte in onore di Michelangelo Muraro* (Venice, 1984), 427–38; and M. Muraro, 'Ricerche su Tiepolo giovane', *Atti dell'Accademia di Scienze, Lettere ed Arti di Udine*, 9 (1970–2), 5–64.

[96] For a brief summary of the situation, cf. S. Tavani, 'La fine del patriarcato di Aquileia', in *Maria Teresa e il Settecento goriziano* (exh. cat., Palazzo Attems, Gorizia, 1982), 189 ff.

ereignty of Friuli. These discussions were a fortunate precaution, for after the War of Cambrai (*c.*1510) the Hapsburg Court insisted upon its rights in Friuli. When the Treaties of Cambrai were finally signed in the mid-1520s, the eastern and southern areas of the patriarchal territory, including Aquileia itself, fell completely under Austrian jurisdiction, but because of the earlier Venetian–papal negotiations, it was agreed that the Patriarch of Aquileia, despite his residence in Austrian Friuli, would continue to be chosen from among the Venetian nobility.[97]

During the course of the sixteenth and seventeenth centuries Austria repeatedly tried to diminish Venice's influence in Friuli. In the 1580s Vienna asked Pope Sixtus V to create a new bishopric at Gorizia; and about fifty years later it appealed to Urban VIII for the right to nominate the new Patriarch. Both times the papacy refused. In the meantime, Venice, alert to the extremely delicate nature of the situation, entered into a secret pact with the papacy that they would not allow the Patriarchy of Aquileia to fall into non-Venetian hands.[98] Finally, in 1719, frustrated by almost two hundred years of unsuccessful pleading before the papal court, Vienna took the matter into its own hands: the Austrian Emperor Charles VI promulgated the Edict of Graz, forbidding his citizens in Friuli to obey any official of the Venetian State. Charles followed this in 1721 by confiscating patriarchal possessions in German-speaking dioceses and encouraged Bishop Colonitz of Vienna to propose a plan that would increase the importance of his own seat at the expense of the Patriarch's at Udine. And two years later, in 1723, German-speaking seminarians were prohibited from receiving their holy orders from Patriarch Dolfin, who had assumed his office in 1699.

It was against the background of this long and bitter feud, based on conflicting rights of inheritance, secret negotiations, and virulent rivalry, that Tiepolo was asked by Patriarch Dolfin to fresco in the Patriarchal Palace. For a number of reasons, the commission must have originated in late 1724 or in 1725. Tiepolo himself would not have been free to tackle the project until then, for he was probably occupied with work in the Palazzo Sandi in Venice; the palace's staircase was not completed until 1725; and 15 December 1724 marked the bicentennial of Patriarch Marino Grimani's proclamation that Udine was the 'New Aquileia'—such a politically pertinent event would not have been lost on Dolfin.[99] Substantiating the date 1724–5, too, is the praise Tiepolo received in a contract offered to him in June 1726 by Udine's Confraternity of the Holy Sacrament, which referred to him as a 'celebrated painter'. The confraternal brothers probably used such language because of the artist's local reputation.[100]

Patriarch Dolfin's commission was part of an old Italian tradition whereby wealthy

[97] For this complicated series of events, cf. G. Biasutti, *Storia e guida del Palazzo Arcivescovile di Udine* (Udine, 1958), 7–8; P. Paschini, *Storia del Friuli* (Udine, 1954), ii. 337; id., 'Breve storia del patriarcato', in *La basilica di Aquileia* (Bologna, 1933), 3–36, and 'La nomina del patriarca di Aquileia e la repubblica di Venezia nel secolo XVI', in *Rivista di storia della Chiesa in Italia*, ii (1948), 61–76.

[98] B. Cecchetti, *La repubblica di Venezia e la corte di Roma* (Venice, 1874), p. 365; and Paschini, *Storia del Friuli*, ii. 375ff., and 'La nomina del patriarca', p. 70.

[99] Morassi, *A Complete Catalogue*, p. 53, says the staircase and the Gallery were painted in 1725 or 1726, and the Tribunal, or Sala Rossa, in 1727–8. A. Pallucchini, *L'opera completa*, no. 50, agrees with the date 1726–8 for the entire cycle. Muraro, 'Ricerche su Tiepolo', p. 31, suggested that Tiepolo may have painted the frescos as early as 1718, but the plaque on the palace's exterior giving the year 1718 does not refer at all to the interior decoration; 1718 can only function as a *terminus post quem*.

[100] The document is reprinted in Morassi, *A Complete Catalogue*, p. 230.

aristocrats lavishly decorated the walls of their villas and palaces with fresco cycles. A few obvious examples are the Villa Farnesina and the Palazzo Farnese in Rome, and the Villa Medici at Poggio a Caiano outside Florence. But Dolfin's Palace in Udine was not only a home; it was also the official residence of the Patriarchs of Aquileia. Following a precedent as eminent as that of Leo X's *logge* in the Vatican Palace, Dolfin chose to illustrate a cycle of Old Testament narratives and thus affirm his patriarchal dignity.[101] And because he needed a pictorial 'text' that would respond to the Austrian challenge to his sacramental and political authority, Dolfin chose for the ceilings over the stair-well and the Ecclesiastical Tribunal the *Fall of the Rebel Angels* and the *Judgement of Solomon*, scenes that demonstrate the punishment of usurpers and the magistracy of princes. Then, in the Gallery, he had Tiepolo paint narratives from the lives of Abraham, Isaac, and Jacob—the Old Testament's three great patriarchs—showing Rachel and Laban, Jacob and Esau, Isaac and Ishmael, and Sarah and Hagar: all pairs of rivals claiming either their own or their offspring's rights of inheritance.

All of the biblical narratives that Tiepolo painted for Dolfin are seen by visitors to the Archbishop's Palace, or Arcivescovado, in exactly the same order as they appear in the Bible itself, and to appreciate their force as politico-ecclesiastical statements they must be read in that very same sequence. To begin: climbing the stairway one sees the *Fall of the Rebel Angels* painted overhead as if it were taking place in the heavens (Pl. 34). The story of the Archangel Michael striking those who dare to question God's authority is not actually in the Old Testament, but it is none the less part of the Judeo-Christian tradition of Creation.[102] Surrounding the *Fall of the Rebel Angels* and within its decorative borders, are eight scenes painted as monochromes which tell the story of Adam and Eve from the *Creation of Adam* to the *Expulsion of Adam and Eve from Paradise*.[103] God's punishment of those who defy his strictures is demonstrated twice, therefore: the angels are thrown from heaven, and Adam and Eve are cast out from the Garden of Eden. This pictorial complex was surely meant to remind those ascending the stairs to the Archbishop's Throne Room that rejection from grace awaits all who challenge God's power or even dare to question his established order. The relevance of the imagery to the Patriarch of Aquileia and his time-honoured ecclesiastical authority is made specific by the numerous motifs that decorate the stories' enframement: a crosier, a pastoral staff, a sceptre, a cardinal's hat, an archbishop's mitre, swords, and scales.

Arriving on the second-floor landing, one enters the Throne Room, or Sala del Trono, in which rows of portraits on the walls emphasize the patriarchal succession (Fig. 1). The visitor would then walk to the Patriarchal Gallery, whose iconographical programme I have already explained elsewhere.[104] Its main ideas can be quickly summarized, however.

[101] Cf. N. Dacos, *Le logge di Raffaello* (Rome, 1977), 59–60.

[102] Revelations 12: 7–9.

[103] The stories are (1) the creation of Adam; (2) the creation of Eve; (3) the serpent offering the fruit to Eve; (4) Eve's temptation of Adam; (5) their shame; (6) Adam and Eve hiding from God as he walks through Paradise; (7) God's chastisement of Adam and Eve; and finally (8) the expulsion. For a photograph of the complete ceiling, cf. Morassi, *A Complete Catalogue*, fig. 2.

[104] Barcham, 'Patriarchy and Politics', *passim*. A number of drawings in one of two sketch-books in the Drawing Cabinet of the Staatliche Museen, Berlin-Dahlem, can be related to the frescos in Udine: cf. vol. i, fo. 47ᵛ, for *Jacob and Esau*; fo. 48ᵛ, for the falling figures in the *Fall of the Rebel Angels*; and fo. 58ʳ, for *Sarah and the Angel*. See G. Knox, 'Francesco Guardi as an Apprentice in the Studio of Giambattista Tiepolo', in R. C. Rosbottom (ed.), *Studies in Eighteenth-century Culture*, v (Madison, 1976), 29–39; and Knox and Thiem, *Tiepolo*, no. 4ʳ ᵛ, for the *Judgement of Solomon*.

34. G. B. Tiepolo, *Fall of the Rebel Angels* (fresco, 420 × 180 cm.)

a = Stairwell
b = Sala del Trono (Throne Room)
c = Gallery
d = Sala Rossa (Ecclesiastical
      Tribunal)
× = Position of figure entering
      Ecclesiastical Tribunal

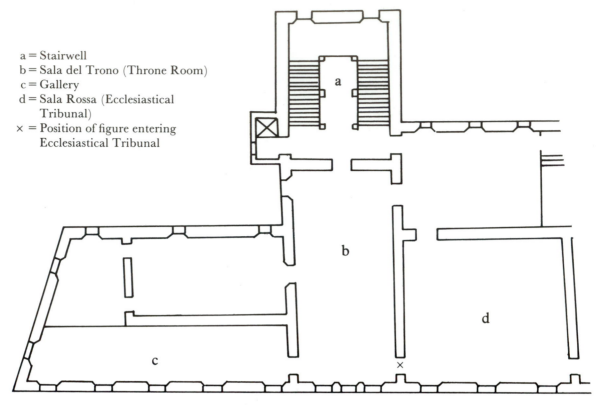

FIG. 1. Plan of second floor of Archbishop's Palace, Udine

The first three scenes of *Abraham and the Three Angels*, the *Dream of Jacob*, and *Jacob's Struggle with the Angel* show (1) the patriarch Abraham receiving the Lord's promise of an heir; (2) the offering of land to Jacob; and (3) Jacob's renaming by the angel (Pls. 35, 36). The significance of these stories in terms of Udine's political situation is clear. Abraham symbolizes the old Patriarchy of Aquileia and Isaac its new capital in Udine. The *Dream of Jacob* fulfils the promised gift of new land. And Jacob's renaming recalls. Marino Grimani's proclamation in 1524 that Udine was the 'New Aquileia'.

In the centre of the Gallery's long wall, the story of *Rachel Hiding the Idols of Laban* is used to underline the themes of succession and patriarchal inheritance (Pl. 37). The event itself is concerned with primogeniture, and at the painting's very heart Rachel's child, surely her first-born son Joseph, reminds us that Christ descended from this patriarchal lineage, ensuring mankind's salvation through the Church and its hierarchy. On the Gallery's ceiling, the *Sacrifice of Isaac* represents patriarchal submission to divine will; the golden light radiating down upon the patriarchs Abraham and Isaac and upon Jacob and Joseph on the wall-fresco below, symbolizes God's protection of his chosen servants (Pl. 38). Facing *Rachel Hiding the Idols of Laban* and below the *Sacrifice of Isaac* is a portrait of Dionisio Dolfin, the positioning of which associates him with the biblical patriarchs.

At the Gallery's far end are the scenes of *Jacob's Meeting with Esau, Hagar and Ishmael Lost in the Wilderness*, and *Sarah and the Angel* (Pls. 39, 40). The first painting is a portrayal

35. G. B. Tiepolo, *Abraham and the Angels* (fresco, 200 × 400 cm.)

36. Below: G. B. Tiepolo, *Dream of Jacob* (fresco)

37. G. B. Tiepolo, *Rachel Hiding the Idols of Laban* (fresco, 400 × 500 cm.)

38. G. B. Tiepolo, *Sacrifice of Isaac* (fresco, 400 × 500 cm.)

39. Above: G. B. Tiepolo, *Hagar and Ishmael Lost in the Wilderness* (fresco)

40. G. B. Tiepolo, *Sarah and the Angel* (fresco, 200 × 400 cm.)

of fraternal reconciliation; the ceiling-painting of Hagar and Ishmael has survival as its subject-matter; and the last scene shows God promising a son to the aged Sarah and thereby securing her line's future. If one concludes that the first two-thirds of the Gallery's programme refer to God's gift of Udine to the Patriarchs of Aquileia and to its earthly legitimacy and divine sanction, then the last three paintings acknowledge reconciliation, salvation, and survival as gifts that come directly from God.[105]

Returning to the Throne Room and passing beyond it, the visitor enters the Ecclesiastical Tribunal, or the Sala Rossa (see Fig. 1), on whose ceiling Tiepolo painted the *Judgement of Solomon* and the prophets Isaiah, Jeremiah, Ezekiel, and Daniel (Pls. 41–5; Pl. II). The story of King Solomon and the baby is traditionally associated in Christian art with the theme of justice: for example, in Raphael's fresco in the Stanza della Segnatura in the Vatican Palace, or on the sculpted ensemble in the north-west corner of the Ducal Palace in Venice.[106] The *Judgement of Solomon* is a fitting narrative for an ecclesiastical court of law like that of the Archbishop's Sala Rossa, for it promised petitioners that they could expect wisdom and equity at Dolfin's hands. Most importantly, in portraying a noble mother protecting her child from a jealous party, the story dramatically illustrated Venice's situation *vis-à-vis* Vienna, implying that division into two was as unjust a resolution for the Patriarchy of Aquileia as it was for the biblical baby.

When composing the *Judgement of Solomon*, Tiepolo took into account the fact that visitors would enter the almost square-shaped Tribunal through a corner doorway leading from the Throne Room (Fig. 2). The first view of the ceiling was, and still is, oblique, and Tiepolo wisely placed Solomon so that he sits on one of the composition's diagonal axes. Upon entering, the visitor comes face to face with Solomon and associates him with the enthroned Patriarch below. As a result, Dolfin was a part of the majesty of the Solomonic scene and was flanked, as it were, with monumental statues and honoured with a cloth of gold. The astute visitor to the Tribunal quickly appreciated this parallelism, of course, and realized too that the *Judgement of Solomon* reiterated the theme of justice first seen in the stair-well. The cycle began with angelic retribution and concludes with royal punishment: the Patriarch's historic right to sit on the judge's cathedra is affirmed, and his responsibility to castigate those who dare to question and seek to overturn God's will is well defined.

Tiepolo's positioning on the ceiling of Isaiah, Jeremiah, Ezekiel, and Daniel follows the correct biblical sequence of the prophets' books. Over the doorway leading into the Sala Rossa, Isaiah receives a coal from one of God's seraphim (Pl. 42); the story is told in Isaiah 6: 6–7: 'Then flew one of the seraphim to me, having in his hand a burning coal which he had taken with tongs from the altar. And he touched my mouth, and said:

[105] Those who question Tiepolo's seriousness in showing the aged Sarah grinning at the angel should turn to Genesis 18: 12: 'So Sarah laughed to herself, saying, "After I have grown old, and my husband is old, shall I have pleasure?"'; and to v. 15: 'But Sarah denied [laughing], saying, "I did not laugh", for she was afraid. He [the angel] said, "No, but you did laugh".' For the six 'prophetesses' painted in the Gallery, see Barcham, 'Patriarchy and Politics', p. 434.

[106] For an explicit reference to the Solomonic story in Venetian

political thought, cf. L. Puppi, '"Rex sum justicie": Note per una storia metaforica del Palazzo dei Dogi', in G. Benzoni (ed.), *I Dogi* (Milan, 1982), 192. See also M. Hirst's discussion of Sebastiano del Piombo's painting in *Sebastiano del Piombo* (Oxford, 1981), 18ff.; and Howard, 'Giorgione's *Tempesta*', p. 273. The Sala Rossa also contains four other scenes, in stucco, of Old Testament justice: Jael and Sisara; Judith and Holofernes; Joseph and Potiphar's Wife; and Susannah and the Elders.

FIG. 2. Axonometric rendering of the Tribunal (Sala Rossa),
Archbishop's Palace, Udine (see Pls. 41–5)

a = Isaiah; b = Jeremiah; c = Ezekiel; d = Daniel

"Behold, this has touched your lips; your guilt is taken away, and your sin forgiven."'
The Lord directs the prophet to speak to the people, but they will refuse to understand
the divine message. Deafness to God's will is deplored.

Looking to the left, to the nearest corner on the coved vault, the visitor then sees
Jeremiah lamenting Jerusalem's destruction, a reference, I believe, to the abandoned
Aquileia (Pl. 43). The third prophet, Ezekiel, was placed diagonally across the Sala Rossa
(Pl. 44); he is being offered a scroll by a hand in heaven. Ezekiel 2: 9–10 reads: 'And
when I looked, behold, a hand was stretched out to me, and, lo, a written scroll was in
it; and he spread it before me; and it had written on the front and on the back, and there
were written on it words of lamentation and mourning and woe.' Ezekiel is then told to
eat the scroll and to say: '"Thus says the Lord God", whether they hear or refuse to
hear.' His presence sustains the sorrow evoked by Jeremiah and exhorts mankind to follow
God's laws.

The painting of the fourth prophet, Daniel, is over the doorway directly opposite the
Tribunal's entrance and consists of a scene taken from a dream (Pl. 45) that is recounted
in Daniel 7: 3: 'And four great beasts came up out of the sea, different from one another.
The first was like *a lion and had eagles' wings* [my italics].' The reader need not follow
Daniel's dream any further, and Tiepolo did not even bother to depict all of the four
beasts.

To recapitulate: the four prophets speak of a people deaf to understanding (Isaiah); of
lamentation over a city's loss (Jeremiah); of insistent exhortation (Ezekiel); and finally,
and explicitly, of Venetian suzerainty (Daniel's lion).[107] The Old Testament cycle that
had begun over the stair-well with the *Fall of the Rebel Angels* and the *Expulsion of Adam
and Eve from Paradise*, and that had continued through the stories of Abraham, Isaac, and
Jacob in the Gallery, reaches its culmination in Solomon's magisterial power and in the
four surrounding prophets. In sum, Tiepolo's narrative states that Venice's possession of
the Patriarchy of Aquileia is legitimate because it was God-given; offered in perpetuity,
Venetian dominion will be protected against those who attempt to usurp it.

Having to explain such varied points from several rooms was a complex task, and it is
unlikely that Tiepolo handled the iconography by himself. In his study of the cycle,
Muraro suggested that Niccolò Madrisio, a Udinese man of letters, was mainly responsible
for the programme.[108] Madrisio's pamphlet entitled *Apologia per l'antico stato e condizione
della famosa Aquileia . . .*, published in 1721 and dedicated to Dolfin himself, would indeed
seem to be relevant to the cycle's meaning. The pamphlet urges that the Patriarch of
Aquileia's seat should be respected both for its antiquity and its international position
and that Udine should be accepted as its proper successor.

Madrisio's courtly phrases and elegant locutions had their pictorial equivalence in the
elegant mouldings and ornate designs that surround the various scenes of the frescos. This
decorative work was probably done by an assistant, perhaps by Girolamo Mengozzi-

[107] For another instance of the political use of Daniel's dream, see R. C. Aiken, 'Romae de Dacia Triumphantis: Roma and Captives at the Capitoline Hill', *Art Bulletin*, 62 (1980), 583–97. These same four prophets also appear in the pendentives of the Abraham cupola in S. Marco's atrium.

[108] Muraro, 'Ricerche su Tiepolo', pp. 51 ff.; and Barcham, 'Patriarchy and Politics', pp. 435–6.

41. G. B. Tiepolo, *Judgement of Solomon* (fresco, 350 × 650 cm.)

42. G. B. Tiepolo, *Isaiah* (fresco, 200 × 250 cm.)

43. G. B. Tiepolo, *Jeremiah* (fresco, 200 × 250 cm.)

44. G. B. Tiepolo, *Ezekiel* (fresco, 200 × 250 cm.)

45. G. B. Tiepolo, *Daniel* (fresco, 200 × 250 cm.)

Colonna who was Tiepolo's collaborator in later commissions.[109] If it was Colonna, then it was his Bolognese specialization in architectural illusionism that enabled him to develop such splendid devices as the dizzying perspective seen in the *Judgement of Solomon*, the broken pediments over the doorways on the two short walls of the Gallery, and the feigned spiral columns that 'support' those pediments. These columns are particularly brilliant contrivances, not only for their elegance and refinement of course, but also because they imply that the authority of the Patriarch of Aquileia was equal to that of the Pope, and that Udine was as ancient a See as that of Rome. The motif is based on the spiral columns in St Peter's, which were thought to have come from Solomon's Temple in Jerusalem.[110]

Elegance and refinement were also brought to the patriarchal frescos by Tiepolo's melodic designs. Prior to the commission in Udine, the painter had articulated his figures with limbs that departed at right angles from the torso's principal axis, as, for example, in the flying angel in the *Madonna del Carmelo* (Pl. 17). But the angel visiting Sarah in the Gallery in Udine was very differently conceived (Pl. 40); the white on the right wing flows lyrically into the gown's neckline, which is painted in contrasting black, while the left wing frames the angel's profile and follows its gentle rhythms. In *Abraham and the Three Angels* the heavenly messengers have been drawn so that the bare leg on the left, which belongs to the angel in apple green, replicates that of the group's leader in the centre, and the rhythms of the two great wings at the heart of the painting are given melodic variation by the smaller ones at the sides. Finally, the curves of the draperies make swelling bell-shapes across the triad of elongated forms.

The sources for Tiepolo's new pictorial grace and refinement can be found in the art of Pellegrini and Ricci, as mentioned above. And one must remember as well that while he was painting in the Palazzo Arcivescovile Tiepolo would have had the opportunity of looking daily at the frescos of Bambini and Louis Dorigny (executed *c.*1710). The richness of the different traditions incorporated in their styles is remarkable: Pietro da Cortona and Luca Giordano in the former's, and Charles Le Brun, Annibale Carracci, and Giulio Carpioni in the latter's. Through such varied sources, Bambini and Dorigny created new pictorial conceptions of space, air, colour, and light, and their bright tonalities, elegant shapes, and lavish ornamental surrounds helped to lay the groundwork for Tiepolo's own decorative fresco painting.

There was another figure from the Venetian pictorial tradition of even greater importance to Tiepolo's work at Udine. Tiepolo's debt to Paolo Veronese is mentioned frequently but never discussed at length.[111] Strangely, Tiepolo's contemporaries in Venice were not very concerned with the link; it was not until after 1750 that any one of them characterized Tiepolo's art in print in terms of Veronese's. It was a visitor to the city who first noted

[109] Da Canal, *Vita*, p. xxxiii: 'Nella architettura ebbe un compagno'.

[110] The viewer should recall the 'presence' of these columns in the Gallery when he looks at the *Judgement of Solomon* in the Sala Rossa. Veronese had also remembered the Solomonic columns in the execution of the *Triumph of Venice* in the Sala del Maggior Consiglio of the Ducal Palace: cf. Howard, 'Giorgione's *Tempesta*',

p. 289 n. 75.

[111] For two discussions, cf. R. Cooke, 'The Development of Veronese's Critical Reputation', *Arte veneta*, 34 (1980), 96–111; and M. Piai, 'Il "Veronese Revival" nella pittura veneziana del Settecento', *Atti dell'Istituto Veneto di Scienze, Lettere, ed Arti*, 133 (1974–5), 295–312. There are also references to Veronese's art throughout the Tiepolo literature.

that Tiepolo was a 'follower ['sectataire'] of Paolo Veronese',[112] and it was only after Tiepolo completed his major ceiling-frescos in Venice that Venetians began to describe his art as *paolesca*. In 1750, Algarotti wrote that the *Banquet of Antony and Cleopatra*, which Tiepolo had painted for Augustus III of Poland, was 'truly *paolesca*'; three years later, Padre Orlandi noted that the more Tiepolo moved away from Lazzarini's manner, the closer he moved to Cagliari's; and finally, in 1762, Alessandro Longhi categorized Tiepolo's style as having 'una maniera Paolesca'.[113]

But Tiepolo had looked to Veronese for help much earlier than this, having used various illusionistic devices *alla Veronese* in the Archbishop's Palace. The *Fall of the Rebel Angels* in the stair-well is based on Paolo's *Jupiter Expelling the Vices* from the Hall of the Council of Ten in the Ducal Palace; and the *Judgement of Solomon* has as its antecedent the scene of *Esther Crowned by Ahasuerus* from the ceiling of S. Sebastiano. In the *Judgement of Solomon*, too, as in several scenes in the Gallery, Tiepolo clothed his figures in fabrics patterned *alla Veronese*. There is not much else that can be identified as a specific debt that Tiepolo owed to Paolo, and yet Veronese's presence is felt everywhere in the cycle in Udine. There are two reasons for this: the stage-like presentation of a dramatic event; and the relationship between narrative and colour.

It is well known that Veronese often treated his religious and historical narratives as theatre pieces, organizing his figures as if 'directing' a cast of actors: leading men and women, *comprimari*, and onlookers. These figures are usually grouped in front of architectural ensembles that resemble, or borrow elements from, the Renaissance theatre.[114] It is this theatrical organization, in which each figure plays a precise scenic role, that Tiepolo learned to control at Udine. One need only compare the Burano *Crucifixion* with *Rachel Hiding the Idols of Laban* to note the change in Tiepolo's handling of a narrative; each character's size, position, and gesture are now evidence of his importance within the drama. To appreciate this, it is useful to compare *Rachel Hiding the Idols of Laban* with Veronese's *Family of Darius before Alexander*, which remained in Venice until 1857 (Pl. 46). Tiepolo's central group reflects the principal actors in Veronese's canvas: the bearded Laban, framed by two tall trees and gesticulating towards Rachel, repeats in type and gesture the bearded man behind Darius' women; in the figure of Rachel, Tiepolo borrowed some of the rich drapery and pearl jewellery as well as the sudden hand movements of these same women. On both the far right and the far left there are figures who, as in Veronese's painting, watch quietly from the sides, and in the corners Tiepolo placed children and animals in order to monumentalize the stage centre; a young girl and dog on the right correspond to Veronese's similarly situated page and hound. The result is a narrative with dramatic clarity.

The colours that Tiepolo used in the Arcivescovado, particularly in the Gallery, offer a chromatic splendour very special in Venetian eighteenth-century painting, and they

[112] The foreigner was Count Tessin, who was looking for someone to paint in the Royal Palace in Stockholm: cf. O. Sirèn, *Dessins et tableaux de la Renaissance italienne dans les collections de Suède* (Stockholm, 1902), 107–8. A few years later, in 1740, Tiepolo was identified as '. . . celebre pittore veneto/ immitatore/ di Paolo Veronese . . .'. This appears in a poem praising his frescos in the Palazzo Clerici in Milan: cf. BNM, Misc. 118.

[113] Algarotti's statement was in a letter dated 13 Feb. 1751 and sent from Potsdam to Jean Mariette in Paris: cf. 'Lettere sopra la pittura', p. 15; P. A. Orlandi, *Abecedario pittorico* (Florence, 1776; written in 1753), 666; R. Longhi, 'Viatico per cinque secoli', p. 17.

[114] D. Rosand, *Painting in Cinquecento Venice* (New Haven and London, 1982), 145 ff.

make the biblical scenes gorgeously effective as pure decoration. Apricot, melon, and cinnamon sit alongside lavender; and deep wines are placed near apple greens. The hues help both to unify and juxtapose the forms. For instance, in *Sarah and the Angel* Tiepolo gave each figure an outer cloak of golden orange in order to link the two, but dressed the aged Sarah in a complementary blue as a way of comparing her earth-bound position with the winged and youthful messenger dressed in brilliant white. The greyish clouds and the cold grey/blue tree-trunk behind provide even more contrast, so that the angel does indeed seem to be a celestial radiance. Tiepolo's use of colour in the corresponding scene of Abraham is identical in concept; the old patriarch is dressed in dark purple and muddy brown, while the angels are in brighter tones; and the central angel in white stands between complementary fields of green and wine and in front of lavender-like clouds.

Tiepolo's palette is definitely not based upon Veronese's, but the concept underlying its use is. Using the latter's three splendid paintings in the chancel of S. Sebastiano as examples, one notes how in *SS Mark and Marcellianus Encouraged towards Martyrdom by St Sebastian* Veronese runs through a range of pinks, silvers, and golds. In the facing *Martyrdom of St Sebastian*, the three primaries are contrasted with the greys, whites, and neutral tones of flesh and architecture. In the altar-piece flanked by these two narratives, Veronese used pinks, golden yellows, and cold blues as well as dull whites and greys, thus fusing the two sets of colours. The pictorial ensemble offers chromatic brilliance, superseding the figures' naturalism to project a heightened intensity fitting to scenes of martyrdom, exaltation, and Christian devotion.

This same coupling of ornament and meaning characterizes Tiepolo's use of colour in the Patriarchal Gallery. His spectrum of fruity apricot, peach, cherry, and grape pitted against cold blues, greens, and dark earth colours creates a luxurious rainbow effect, which builds up towards a brilliant intensification in the hallway's centre. In *Rachel Hiding the Idols of Laban*, which depicts the theme of patriarchal succession, Tiepolo reiterated the melon and wine tones that he had used elsewhere in the Gallery's wall-frescos. In the *Sacrifice of Isaac*, where a divine light shines down upon the Bible's first two patriarchs, Tiepolo combined cold blues and hot tones of cherry red with radiant whites and yellows, the same colours he used in the ceiling's two other paintings, the *Dream of Jacob* and *Hagar and Ishmael Lost in the Wilderness*. This manipulation of colour for both decorative purposes and thematic emphasis represents the young Tiepolo's most important debt to Veronese's art.

Two decades before Tiepolo worked in Udine, Sebastiano Ricci had already looked to Veronese for pictorial ideas. In S. Marziale, for example, Ricci's roundel of the *Miraculous Arrival of the Statue of the Madonna* clearly shows his study of Veronese's art.[115] From then on, Ricci turned to him again and again, copying his perspectival viewpoints, architectural ensembles, and compositional solutions. But in spite of the mastery with which he could confect a Veronese-like altar-piece, as in S. Giorgio Maggiore (Pl. 47), Ricci's paintings lack the serious thoughtfulness of Veronese's art. Two examples are enough to prove my

---

[115] The S. Marziale roundels are usually dated to *c.*1703–4: cf. Daniels, *Sebastiano Ricci*, figs. 305–9. Ricci had previously worked in the choir-vault in S. Sebastiano, where he had come into direct contact with Veronese's art.

46. P. Veronese, *Family of Darius before Alexander* (oil on canvas, 93 × 187 cm.)

47. S. Ricci, *Virgin and Child with Saints* (oil on canvas, 406 × 208 cm.)

48. S. Ricci, *Glorification of the Arts and Sciences* (oil on canvas, 800 × 400 cm.)

point. In Ricci's *Glorification of the Arts and Sciences* in the Patriarchal Seminary in Venice (Pl. 48), the classical columns and cornice are based on those in Veronese's *Triumph of Mordecai*, but while the latter artist used them to monumentalize his composition and to create a convincing space, Ricci's architectural apparatus only serves to fill one quadrant of the oval canvas.[116] In the altar-piece in S. Giorgio Maggiore mentioned above, Ricci repeated the composition of Veronese's *Mystic Marriage of St Catherine*, but could not match the power of the latter's draped columns and the slow rhythms that move from the sandalled foot in the bottom left-hand corner to the Christ-child and Mary above.[117]

Tiepolo understood and re-created the high seriousness that characterizes Veronese's art. In the *Judgement of Solomon* (Pl. II), the sweeping curve of the cloth of gold, broken at two points by the King's turbaned head and gesturing hand, cuts down and across the composition towards the false and jealous mother, who is picked out by a telling green robe and two intersecting spears, the end of one of which has been wittingly broken off. A broad, white entablature encases this woman with the executioner, whose arm is raised to the same level as the enthroned Solomon, and with the true mother who is dressed in pure white and noble blue and who faces the royal judge. The entire scene is enacted on a great platform that is painted dark brown, brightening in colour towards the white and yellow-gold brocade carpet under Solomon's throne. Finally, between Solomon's youthful majesty and the executioner's terrible sword, a pink and white cloud rises to cover one that is dark and threatening.

Tiepolo had studied Veronese's art for reasons that were very different from those of Ricci. The latter had arrived at his neo-Veronesian style after his neo-Carraccesque style, which had been eclipsed by his neo-Cortonesque style, which, in turn, had been superseded by his neo-Giordanesque style. For Tiepolo, Veronesianism was not simply a matter of stylistic fashion, and his use of it in Udine had a special purpose: it was meant to re-create, I believe, Venice's artistic past, to recall the Serenissima's glory. Indeed, viewed in this way, Tiepolo's Veronesianism endorses local pictorial tradition in the same way as the iconography does for the Venetian State and the authority of the Patriarch of Aquileia. The painterly mode that Tiepolo chose for his frescos had as significant a voice in reasserting Venetian power as the frescos' political argument did.

Tiepolo's neo-Veronesianism must stand with contemporary Palladianism as a revival style with political overtones.[118] Neo-Palladianism was imbued not only with ancient Roman appeal, of course, but also with local patriotism, for it reminded eighteenth-century Venetians of the wealth and power that had once belonged to their State. The Churches of S. Giorgio Maggiore and the Redentore form a part of the monumental image of the city, as did the ensemble of the Ducal Palace, the Library, the Mint, and the State Granaries on the Riva degli Schiavoni. With their classical dignity and quiet

[116] For the painting in S. Sebastiano, cf. J. Schulz, *Venetian Painted Ceilings of the Renaissance* (Berkeley, 1968), pl. 51.

[117] For the *Mystic Marriage of St Catherine*, cf. Pignatti, *Veronese*, ii, fig. 475.

[118] Such revivals took place several times in Venice's past: see D. Pincus, 'Christian Relics and the Body Politic: A Thirteenth-century Relief Plaque in the Church of San Marco', in Rosand (ed.), *Interpretazioni veneziane*, p. 53 n. 10; M. Muraro, *La vita nelle*

pietre (Venice, 1985), 23; and H.-M. Herzog, *Untersuchungen zur Plastik der venezianischen 'Protorenaissance'* (Munich, 1986), chaps. 9 and 10. Cf. Piai, 'Il "Veronese Revival"', pp. 295–312, who explains why the Venetian ruling class, closed to new ideas, sought traditional values in art; she also suggests why the paintings of Giorgione, Titian, and Tintoretto did not meet the Establishment's needs.

majesty, Palladio's two churches overwhelm anyone approaching the city by water. When Andrea Tirali and Giorgio Massari re-created a Palladian style in Venice in the early settecento, they visually restored to their contemporaries a sense of the city's venerable authority and sovereignty.

Neo-Veronesianism was the pictorial equivalent of the Palladian revival.[119] Both styles are rich in coloration and magnificent in material display, yet they are also serious and profoundly sober. The dignity of Veronese's paintings and Palladio's architecture conveys the ceremony and ritual that the Venetian State wished to display to those watching it. In the early settecento, Venice could not do otherwise but try to convince its international audience that the State's former soundness, reliability, and vigour were undiminished. The styles of neo-Palladianism—solid and antique-looking—and neo-Veronesianism—rich and formalized—fulfilled these political needs in the eighteenth century as the originals had done in the sixteenth. Ricci's version of Veronese's art, although faithful and attractive, could not meet such serious demands. But Tiepolo seems to have understood how Veronese's lofty rhetoric and ornamental splendour could together satisfy the pictorial requirements of a patron who was both a prince of the Church and a member of the Venetian nobility. Recasting Veronese's dramatic but dignified language, Tiepolo's Udine frescos responded to the political pressures of a foreign state, speaking with reproof in the *Fall of the Rebel Angels*, with persuasiveness in the Gallery's patriarchal narratives, and with forewarning in the *Judgement of Solomon*.

Tiepolo's first decade of artistic activity both began and ended with paintings of Old Testament stories that were greatly praised during his lifetime.[120] In 1716, the young artist had been stimulated by the publicity and artistic rivalry surrounding the showing of the *Crossing of the Red Sea*, and in 1725–6 the official status of the Arcivescovado commission urged Tiepolo on towards excellence. In both situations, however, there was also another influence at work: in each case a defence was propounded for Venetian survival and Venetian autonomy. It is significant that these ideas were pictorially realized through Old Testament narrative.

As I have explained above, Venetians identified themselves with the Chosen People. Not only did they link their settlement to the story of the Hebrews fleeing across the waters, but they also saw a parallel in the connection between Church and State in Venice and organized religion and nationhood in biblical Israel. Venetian political theory interpreted the Serenissima as a direct gift from the Creator, an idea expressed in the eighteenth century as it had been earlier.[121] Such a belief carried with it the assertion that

---

[119] This parallel, without its political meaning, has already been drawn: cf. C. Semenzato, 'Problemi di architettura veneta: Giorgio Massari', *Arte veneta*, 11 (1959), 152–61.

[120] Cf. Da Canal, *Vita*, p. xxxii, for the *Crossing of the Red Sea*, and p. xxxiii for the frescos in Udine: '. . . opera delle più belle in tutti i numeri sì di bravura che d'intelligenza, la qual non invidia il fresco di pittori più singolari antichi'.

[121] A. Montegnacco, *Ragionamento intorno a' beni temporali posseduti dalle Chiese, dagli ecclesiastici* . . . (Venice, 1766), pp. xcviiff., wrote, for example, that authority '. . . ci è stata libera [Potestà], ed assolutamente concessa da Dio, al quale dobbiamo render conto del nostro Governo'. Cf. also Sinding-Larsen, *Christ in the Council Hall*, p. 55; and his 'L'immagine della repubblica di Venezia', in *Architettura e utopia nella Venezia del Cinquecento* (exh. cat., Ducal Palace, Venice, 1980 (Milan)), 40; and S. Caponetto, 'Origini e caratteri della riforma in Sicilia', *Rinascimento*, 7 (1956), 304, who defines Venice '. . . come un tipo di Stato-Chiesa, quasi una chiesa nazionale, dove verticalmente scende la grazia di Dio senza dover di necessità passare attraverso la dispensazione della Curia romana'. It should be kept in mind that the 'Stato-Chiesa' was a distinguishing aspect of Byzantine political theory.

the State alone had the right to control the clergy. Venice's defence of this right is so well known that it hardly needs comment here.[122] The State's conception of its hierarchic structure, one in which the government's authority exceeded that of any family or dynastic power and contained within it para-ecclesiastical functions, was similar to that of the ancient Hebrews.[123] In sum, narratives from the Old Testament were an easily under-standable, metaphorical language for the Venetians, at least since the sixteenth century.

Italian art abounds with stories and figures from the Jewish Bible, but it is worth noting that Renaissance Venice could boast of four great pictorial cycles in which Old Testament heroes and heroines play a central role. Early in the sixteenth century, Giorgione and his pupil Titian painted the figure of a seated woman brandishing a sword and resting one foot on a gigantic, severed head, on the façade of the Fondaco dei Tedeschi in the centre of the city. Although now regarded primarily as a personification of Justice, this figure was thought to represent Judith well into the eighteenth century.[124] The figure assumed deeper significance at the end of the sixteenth century because of the sculptures that were then added to the nearby Rialto Bridge: the Archangel Gabriel and the Virgin Mary were attached to the 'downstream' side, while SS Mark and Theodore, Venice's two patron saints, look at the Fondaco from 'upstream'. It is more than likely that within this setting of patriotic imagery, Judith was seen as an emblem for Venice.

Following upon the Fondaco frescos, Titian, Veronese, and Tintoretto painted series of Old Testament narratives, each centred on a great Jewish figure, and each decorating the ceiling of an important Renaissance building. In the 1540s Titian executed a group of paintings that includes three large canvases showing the *Sacrifice of Isaac, Cain Killing Abel*, and *David and Goliath*.[125] It has been suggested that these should be understood in terms of contemporary Venetian–Turkish hostilities, an idea supported by the works' original location in S. Spirito in Isola, a church 'behind' the Giudecca Island and on the main sea lane between the Porto di Lido and the Porto di Malamocco. Those ships that were on their way to battle with the Turks, and entered from or left for the Adriatic, would almost certainly have passed the church.[126]

In 1556 Veronese painted a series of ceiling-canvases for S. Sebastiano, including *Vashti Banished* (formerly identified as *Esther Led to Ahasuerus*), *Esther Crowned by Ahasuerus*, and the *Triumph of Mordecai*; small surrounding roundels present four allegorical figures. It should not be forgotten that Esther's coronation would have had particular meaning in

[122] For Paul V's excommunication of the city in the early seventeenth century, see Cessi, *Storia della repubblica di Venezia*, pp. 588ff.; and F. Lane, *Venice: A Maritime Republic* (Baltimore, 1973), 396ff.

[123] This belief found official expression in *Venice Distributing Ecclesiastical and Other Offices*, a ceiling-painting attributed to Veronese in the Sala dell'Anticollegio in the Ducal Palace. On this subject, cf. Sinding-Larsen, *Christ in the Council Hall*, p. 258, and his 'Titian's Triumph of Faith, and the Medieval Tradition of the Glory of Christ', *Institutum Romanum Novegiae: Acta*, 6 (1975), 316; and cf. Walzer, *Exodus and Revolution*, pp. 126ff., for kingship among the Israelites in Exodus.

[124] Zanetti, *Descrizione*, p. 192; and cf. *Giorgione a Venezia* (exh. cat., Accademia, Venice, 1978 (Milan)), 130ff.

[125] There are also eight small *tondi* representing the four Evangelists and the four Fathers of the Church. Executed between

1542 and 1544 for S. Spirito in Isola, the group was transferred to the sacristy of S. Maria della Salute in 1675.

[126] The presence of the sword in all three paintings is consonant with this interpretation of the cycle: cf. M. Kahr, 'Titian's Old Testament Cycle', *Journal of the Warburg and Courtauld Institutes*, 29 (1966), 193–205. Of course, the paintings could also serve as prototypes for events described in Christian Scripture. Schulz, *Venetian Painted Ceilings*, pp. 77ff., suggests that they are associated with sin, atonement, and redemption. Jacopo Salviati also painted Old Testament scenes for S. Spirito, and they too were transferred to the Salute, where they were placed in the ceiling above the choir; they are *Elijah and the Angel, The Fall of Manna*, and *Habakkuk and Daniel*: cf. Schulz, *Venetian Painted Ceilings*, no. 21, p. 79. Tiepolo engraved the second of Salviati's paintings for Lovisa's publication of 1720.

I. G. B. Tiepolo, *Madonna del Carmelo*, (oil on canvas)

II. G. B. Tiepolo, *Judgement of Solomon*, (fresco)

a city whose pictorial tradition granted the Virgin's own coronation such an important place.[127]

Another of the great Venetian pictorial cycles showing figures and events from Hebrew Scripture is Tintoretto's in the upper hall of the Scuola Grande di S. Rocco.[128] In the centre of the coffered ceiling are the three stories of *Moses Striking Water from the Rock of Horeb,* the *Brazen Serpent,* and the *Fall of Manna* (Pls. 7–9). They represent Baptism, Sacrifice, and Eucharist, the ceiling's principal themes, but they also illuminate in particular the figure of Moses. As I have suggested earlier, Moses was a powerful symbol for the city; his birth points to Venice's founding and his view of Israel parallels Mark's vision of the lagoon.[129]

Although these three cycles by Titian, Veronese, and Tintoretto are vastly different in meaning and appearance, they have one important feature in common: they are all ceiling-paintings. And within the context of Venetian Renaissance art, this must be of special significance, for only three types of subject-matter appear to have been considered suitable for ceilings in public spaces. In governmental buildings like the Ducal Palace and the Library, the State was lauded through allegorical representation. Such subjects suggest universal, even eternal, themes and values.[130] In ecclesiastical ceilings of the same period, Marian and Hebraic imagery appears to have been very popular. Mary's importance to the Christian mysteries is obvious and her significance to the Church during the Counter-Reformation is crucial, but it is surely her role as Venice's sainted patroness that gives meaning to such works as Veronese's *Coronation of the Virgin* or his *Assumption.*[131] It would seem reasonable to conclude that, like their Marian counterparts, Hebraic stories used on Venetian ceilings would also have had allegorical meaning. They, too, spoke a language symbolic of Venetian civic tradition. Venetian citizens would have understood them as conveying more than messages of Christian salvation. Paintings of Old Testament narrative inserted into elaborately carved coffered ceilings were intended, like allegories of the State, to support sacrosanct beliefs regarding Venice's heritage.

During Tiepolo's lifetime, stories from Hebrew Scripture continued to carry the same allegorical weight, as shown by contemporary Venetian tracts in which traditional parallels are drawn, for example, between the Virgin Mary and Jewish heroines like

---

[127] The most important of the many in Venice was Guariento's in the Sala del Maggior Consiglio of the Ducal Palace; it was destroyed by fire in the 1580s. Esther's coronation, her superseding of Vashti, and Mordecai's crushing of Haman represent the Church destroying evil; but see M. Kahr, 'The Meaning of Veronese's Paintings in the Church of San Sebastiano in Venice', *Journal of the Warburg and Courtauld Institutes,* 33 (1970), 235–47; Schulz, *Venetian Painted Ceilings,* pp. 76–7, no. 19; and T. Pignatti, *Le pitture di Paolo Veronese nella chiesa di S. Sebastiano a Venezia* (Milan, 1966). For the possible association between Queen Esther and Venice's Dogaressa, see G. Fasoli, 'Liturgia e cerimoniale ducale', in A. Perusi (ed.), *Venezia e il Levante fino al secolo XV,* i² (Florence, 1973), 289.

[128] The canvases were finished by 1578: see Schulz, *Venetian Painted Ceilings,* pp. 87–91, no. 29.

[129] Cf. p. 24. On Moses as an analogue for the Doge, see

Sinding-Larsen, *Christ in the Council Hall,* p. 141 n. 2.

[130] Historical scenes about the State's past are also found on ceilings, but usually because the cycle had 'spilled' over from the walls, as in the Sala del Maggior Consiglio in the Ducal Palace; narrative was more properly situated on a wall because it could then be read from left to right. Sometimes allegory and history were married, as in Tintoretto's great canvas in the ceiling of the Sala del Maggior Consiglio, *Doge Niccolò da Ponte Receiving the Palm and the Laurel from Venice as Diverse States Render their Spontaneous Submission to the Signoria.* The advantages of a union in which myth and fact merge are clear enough.

[131] The former is in the sacristy of S. Sebastiano, and the latter, now in the Chapel of the Rosary in SS Giovanni e Paolo, was in S. Maria dell'Umiltà: cf. Schulz, *Venetian Painted Ceilings,* pp. 71–2, no. 14. For the cult of Mary in Venice, see Muir, *Civic Ritual,* pp. 139 ff.; and Chap. 2 of this work, pp. 102 ff.

Esther, Judith, Susannah, and Rebecca.[132] Esther had been raised to glory and a crown like Mary, and she interceded with Ahasuerus as Mary does with God himself; such an analogue served as the basis for sermons in the eighteenth century.[133] Judith was considered the very presager and prefiguration of the Virgin; like Mary, Judith '. . . destroyed the infernal Monster, and, still more, is the consolation of the righteous, and the glory of the Christian as well as of the Venetian People'.[134] Susannah, of course, is the emblem of chastity and was therefore considered by the Venetians, who were proud of their city's inviolate territory, to represent the encapsulation of virginity itself.[135]

Rebecca, Isaac's wife, was painted by Tiepolo in at least two works, both of which are roughly contemporaneous with the Hartford *Susannah*. A small *Rebecca at the Well*, probably a study, is in a New York private collection, and a more finished canvas belongs to the Museum of Fine Arts, Athens; the two are almost identical in composition (Pl. 49; Pl. III).[136] Rebecca, holding a vase, stands on the right leaning against the well, while Abraham's servant approaches from the left to offer a gift of jewellery. Surrounding Rebecca are 'the daughters of the men of the city . . . coming out to draw water', and following behind the servant is a retinue of men who perhaps accompanied him on his journey. Abraham's camels stand directly behind Rebecca and the well. Genesis 24: 22 narrates how, after the servant and the camels had all drunk their fill, the servant rewarded Rebecca with a gold ring and two gold bracelets, realizing that he had found his way to the home of Abraham's kinsmen and to the woman that Isaac will marry.

This moment is only one of several that have been depicted in artistic representations of the story of Rebecca. The Vienna Genesis shows Rebecca's arrival at the well, as well

---

[132] In several of these literary endeavours the frontispieces show allegories of Venice: cf. Padre Girolamo Tornielli, *Raccolta di canzoni in aria marinaresca sopra le festività di Maria sempre Vergine Madre di Dio* (Venice, 1786), where a female figure wearing the ducal mantle, with a lion and ducal crown at her feet, kneels in adoration before Mary and Christ. On p. 20, while explaining the feast of Mary's birth, Tornielli writes: 'Oh forte, oh bella, Giuditta, e Rachele! / Oh ombre liete del vecchio Israele! / Oh Sara madre, o Ester regina, / Già vi conosce la bella bambina [Mary].' See also F. Haskell, *Patrons and Painters: Art and Society in Baroque Italy* (New Haven and London, 1980), 274.

[133] See F. Zucconi, *Lezioni sacre sopra la divina scrittura . . .* (Venice, 1714), vii. 71 ff. (Lezione 222 in particular). For more on Esther, see P. Sarnelli, *Lezioni scritturali alla mente, ed al cuore sopra l'uno, e l'altro Testamento* (Venice, 1744), 739 ff. G. Zanetti, 'Memorie per servire all'istoria della inclita città di Venezia', ed. F. Stefani, *Archivio veneto*, 29 (1885), 110: on 25 March 1743 (the feast of the Annunciation), a Jesuit priest in S. Lorenzo gave a sermon for the Doge: '. . . e fece un bel panegirico della B.V. paragonandola ingegnosamente ad Ester . . .'; Haskell, *Patrons and Painters*, p. 274, also cites this event.

[134] Zucconi, *Lezioni sacre*, vi. 300 ff. (Lezione 223); and O. Battistella, *Della vita e delle opere di Gaetano Gherardo Zompini* (Nervesa, 1916), pp. 42–3. See also Sarnelli, *Lezioni scritturali*, p. 22.

[135] See Zucconi, *Lezioni sacre*, vii. 63 ff. (Lezione 221), where Esther, Judith, and Susannah are grouped together as three exemplars. André Grabar defines Susannah as a paradigm of deliverance as well: cf. *Christian Iconography: A Study of its Origins*

(Princeton, 1968), 137. For the ubiquitous appearance of Susannah in Venetian art during the second half of the sixteenth century, see W. R. Rearick, 'Jacopo Bassano and Changing Religious Imagery in the Mid-Cinquecento', in S. Bertelli and G. Ramakus (eds.), *Essays Presented to Myron P. Gilmore* (Florence, 1978), 331–43; Rearick suggests that contemporary patrons were interested in the story of Susannah's sensuality as a reaction to the Council of Trent's moralizing of biblical themes. I would also suggest that the subject's appearance in Venetian art fits in neatly with Susannah's symbolic meaning of Mary/Venice at a time when the State often faced Turkish aggression. Tiepolo painted all three heroines: for *Susannah and the Elders*, cf. Pl. 20. His *Esther and Ahasuerus* and its pendant, *David and Abigail*, are dated c.1751–3: cf. Morassi, *A Complete Catalogue*, pp. 13 and 31; and A. Pallucchini, *L'opera completa*, nos. 207–8. *Judith Showing the Head of Holofernes*, a scene of public triumph, is usually dated to the early 1730s and is in the Rossello Collection, Milan: cf. Morassi, *A Complete Catalogue*, p. 28; and A. Pallucchini, *L'opera completa*, no. 98.

[136] The small sketch measures 28 by 38.7 cm. The version in Athens is 146 by 197 cm. Some of its figures seem untypical of Tiepolo's work, and it may be a later copy of a lost painting for which the NY sketch served as a preliminary study. Morassi, *A Complete Catalogue*, p. 36, fig. 10, mentions another *Rebecca at the Well*, but it is not autograph; it is no. 701b in the Frick Art Reference Library Photographic Collection. Still another version of the subject linked with Tiepolo's name, although surely not by him, is that reproduced by P. Molmenti, *Tiepolo: La Vie et l'oeuvre du peintre* (Paris, 1911), pl. 146.

49. G. B. Tiepolo, *Rebecca at the Well* (oil on canvas, 146 × 197 cm.)

50. *Annunciation to the Virgin*, S. Marco, Venice (mosaic)

as her offering of water to the servant.[137] Two versions that are much closer in time to Tiepolo's are Poussin's, one of which shows Rebecca giving water, the other Eliezer offering jewels.[138] It is this last episode that appeared time and time again in Venetian representations of the subject of the late seventeenth and early eighteenth centuries. Among the many artists in Venice who painted the story were Loth, della Vecchia, Lazzarini, Bellucci, Molinari, Solimena, Sebastiano Ricci, Pellegrini, Amigoni, Pittoni, Grassi, Piazzetta, and Gaspare Diziani.[139] Almost all of their works can be dated between 1675 and *c.*1750, and, like Tiepolo's, they place pictorial emphasis on Rebecca's vase and on the pearls she receives from Abraham's servant. I suggest that these two objects, each in the hand of one of the protagonists, identify the story as a metaphor for the Annunciation, transforming Rebecca herself into an analogue of the Virgin Mary.

The biblical narrative specifies that Abraham's gift to Rebecca was a gold ring and bracelets. The substitution of pearls for gold cannot be either accidental or capricious. In his *Iconologia*, Ripa shows a woman wearing pearls at her neck as 'Gratia'; he explains that pearls were a gift of nature 'that shine and please . . . like grace itself, which in mankind ['uomini'] is like a special loveliness that carries their minds to love . . .'.[140] Extending the simile one step further, pearls may be likened to Christ himself, for just as flawless opalescence is formed and separated from its birthplace without harm either to itself or to its maternal shell, so too Christ was born in perfection, leaving Mary inviolate.[141] In Tiepolo's painting of *Rebecca at the Well*, and others like it which use the same imagery, the present that Abraham sends with his servant to give to his son's future bride signifies the unique preciousness of the gift that God the Father offers Mary through his messenger Gabriel.[142]

Rebecca's vase, too, plays an important role in endowing this Jewish scene of annunciation with a Christian meaning. With camels nearby, the vase tells us that the thirst of both Eliezer and his animals has already been quenched. Two eighteenth-century sources mention that this offering of water to both man and beast likens Rebecca to

[137] For the Vienna Genesis, cf. H. Gerstinger, *Die Wiener Genesis* (Vienna, n.d.), fos. 13–14. The same scene is shown in mosaics in the Cappella Palatina in Palermo and in the cathedral at Monreale.

[138] For the identification of Abraham's servant, see Genesis 15: 2. For Poussin, see Blunt, *The Paintings of Nicolas Poussin*, pp. 10–11, nos. 8 (Louvre, Paris), and 9 (formerly Blunt Collection, London). The second work was still in Rome during the first part of the eighteenth century (cf. C. De Brosses, *Lettres familières écrites d'Italie en 1739 et 1740*, ed. Y. Bézard (Paris, 1931), ii. 456), and a print of it had been produced; Tiepolo may well have taken the motif of the woman balancing an ancient jug on her head from this work or from a School of Fontainebleau print of the subject. See D. Mahon, 'The Dossier of a Picture: Nicolas Poussin's "Rebecca al Pozzo"', *Apollo*, 81 (1965), 196–205.

[139] The following list is selective: Loth, two versions: cf. R. Pallucchini, *La pittura veneziana del Seicento*, figs. 855 and 859; della Vecchia: *Arte veneta*, 15 (1961), p. 137; Lazzarini: Pallucchini, *La pittura veneziana del Seicento*, fig. 1221; Bellucci: Pallucchini, *La pittura veneziana del Seicento*, fig. 1207; Molinari, two versions: Pallucchini, *La pittura veneziana del Seicento*, fig. 1258, and *Arte veneta*, 33 (1979), p. 61, fig. 3; Ricci, four versions: Pallucchini, *La pittura*

veneziana del Seicento, pl. XXXI, and Daniels, *Sebastiano Ricci*, figs. 310, 337, 440*b*; Pittoni: Zava Boccazzi, *Pittoni*, fig. 93; Pellegrini: Pallucchini, *La pittura veneziana del Settecento*, fig. 38; Amigoni: Pallucchini, *La pittura veneziana del Settecento*, fig. 63; Piazzetta: Pallucchini, *La pittura veneziana del Settecento*, fig. 168; Grassi: Pallucchini, *La pittura veneziana del Settecento*, fig. 315; and Diziani: A. P. Zugni-Tauro, *Gaspare Diziani* (Venice, 1971), figs. 196 and 204.

[140] C. Ripa, *Iconologia* (Siena, 1613), i. 302: '. . . le perle, le quali risplendono, & piacciono, per singolare, & occulto dono della natura, come le gratie, che è negli huomini una certa venusta particolare, che muove, e rapisce gl'animi all'amore, & genera occultamente obbligo, e benevolenza'.

[141] H. Leclercq, 'Perle', in *Dictionnaire d'archéologie chrétienne et de liturgie*, ed. F. Cabrol and H. Leclercq (Paris, 1939), xiv. 379.

[142] It should be pointed out that the NY sketch and the Athens painting are slightly different regarding the pearls. In the latter, the pearl strands are clearly visible in the canvas's very centre. In the sketch, Rebecca is already wearing the pearls like Ripa's 'Gratia'; Eliezer offers her several strands of jewellery with his left hand and, with his right, he signals to a jewel case in which one can definitely discern several pearl-like beads.

Mary: '. . . liberal in Her Gifts, not only with the Righteous, but with Sinners as well'.[143] The traditional, Middle Byzantine pictorial representation of the Annunciation establishes a further link between Rebecca and the Virgin. In St Sophia in Kiev, in Daphne, Monreale, Palermo, and at the Karye Çami in Istanbul, the Annunciate Mary is shown alongside a well, even drawing water from it. Tiepolo was familiar with this Byzantine image, for it figures in the north transept of St Mark's in one of the greatest Marian cycles in Western art (Pl. 50).[144] Within the context of this tradition, Tiepolo's *Rebecca at the Well* must be read as a typology of the Annunciation, whose feast-day (25 March) was celebrated each year in Venice along with the city's founding.

One Old Testament narrative in particular featured prominently in Tiepolo's early career: the story of Moses and the Brazen Serpent (Numbers 21: 6–9), which he dealt with four, possibly five, times. A very early drawing, recorded by Sack in 1910 but now lost, illustrates the story (Pl. 57), and so does a group of about ten drawings usually dated to the early 1720s (Pls. 30, 31).[145] The Brazen Serpent appears again in the background of two different versions of *Apelles Painting the Portrait of Campaspe*, one in the Museum of Fine Arts, Montreal (Pl. 51), the other in a private collection in London; both can be dated to the 1720s.[146] Finally, there is the large horizontal canvas, now in the Accademia in Venice, that hung in the Church of SS Cosmas and Damian on the Giudecca Island until the early nineteenth century; this work has usually been dated to *c*.1735 (Pl. 54).[147]

Painting the Brazen Serpent offered the young Tiepolo what he most desired artistically: the opportunity to create within one scene a complex series of forms in pictorial opposition. The early *Crossing of the Red Sea*, where the figures contort and twist in mutually opposing arrangements, is an example of his taste for this kind of challenge. Algarotti's statement of 1760 returns to mind here: Tiepolo, he wrote, 'will work [an idea] in different ways, and reshape it into better forms, nor can he stop until he has found the best possible solution'.[148] Relevant, too, is Zanetti's remark: 'His [Tiepolo's] distinct merit is his ready

[143] Cf. Battistella, *Della vita*, p. 42; and Zucconi, *Lezioni sacre*, pp. 519–20. For other interpretations of a vase pertinent to this painting, see G. Schiller, *Iconography of Christian Art* (London, 1971), i. 40, where a vase is read as the Fountain of Life; and E. Cropper, 'On Beautiful Women, Parmigianino, *Petrarchismo*, and the Vernacular Style', *Art Bulletin*, 58 (1976), 381, where the relationship between the Virgin and the vase of balsam in the Song of Songs is made.

[144] Cf. 'Annunciation', in Schiller, *Iconography*, i. 33ff. The scene in St Mark's dates from the early thirteenth century: cf. O. Demus, *The Mosaics of San Marco in Venice* (Chicago, 1984), i. 132–42. And cf. J. Schulz, 'Tintoretto and the First Competition for the Ducal Palace "Paradise"', *Arte veneta*, 34 (1980), 112–26.

[145] E. Sack, *Giambattista und Domenico Tiepolo: Ihr Leben und Ihre Werke* (Hamburg, 1910), fig. 51a. The drawing, formerly in Leipzig, measured 3.75 by 5.15cm. It became part of the Dan Fellows Platt Collection, Princeton, NJ, in 1920, but its present whereabouts are unknown: cf. Knox's reference to it in *Tiepolo: A Bicentenary Exhibition*, no. 4.

[146] For the Montreal painting, see T. Pignatti, 'Clues to Tiepolo's Youth', *M*, 3 (1971), 6–11; and B. Hannegan's discussion

in *Painting in Italy in the Eighteenth Century: Rococo to Romanticism* (exh. cat., Art Institute, Chicago, 1970), no. 40. For the London version, on loan to the National Gallery in the 1960s, see Morassi, 'Un Nouveau Tiepolo pour la National Gallery de Londres', *Connaissance des Arts*, 150 (1964), 32–9. A painting absolutely identical to the London canvas is catalogued in the Instituto Amatller de Arte Spanico in Barcelona (neg. *Gudiol 60.347*) as belonging to the Várez Collection in San Sebastian, Guipuzcoa.

[147] See below, p. 87, for its dating. Sack published a photograph, fig. 50 in his book, of an oil-sketch (formerly in the Beyerlen Collection, Stuttgart) that appears to be related to the painting for SS Cosmas and Damian. G. Fiocco, 'Aggiunte di Francesco Maria Tassis alla guida di Venezia di Antonio Maria Zanetti', *Rivista di Venezia*, 6 (1927), 167, fig. 28, published the same sketch; see also Morassi, *A Complete Catalogue*, fig. 16. The sketch, which measures 17 by 69 cm., was later acquired by the Drey Collection, Munich, but has since appeared on the art market: cf. Sotheby's (London) sale catalogue dated 25 June 1969, no. 15.

[148] Quoted from a letter to Prospero Pesci dated 12 Feb. 1760, 'Lettere sopra la pittura', p. 104.

ability to invent and, while doing this, to distinguish and resolve at one and the same time a quantity of figures with originality and multiplicity of invention . . .'.[149]

Tiepolo's continuing enthusiasm for portraying the heroic male nude in dramatic action is evident in all of his different versions of the *Brazen Serpent*—in the Leipzig drawing now lost, in those dispersed to collections in Gdansk (Danzig), Paris, Venice, and Los Angeles, and in the paintings in Montreal, London, and Venice. It is interesting to note that there is one type of action common to all of these images that is rarely found in other painters' interpretations of the Brazen Serpent. Michelangelo's fresco on the Sistine Chapel ceiling, Bronzino's in the Eleonora Chapel in the Palazzo Vecchio, and Tintoretto's in the ceiling of the Scuola di S. Rocco's upper floor (Pl. 8)—to mention only three of the most famous versions—all show numerous figures in contorted movement, overcome by God's wrath, who invariably yield to the scourge of serpents until they view Moses' bronze replica. The biblical narrative (Numbers 21: 6, 9) is quite specific: 'Then the Lord sent fiery serpents among the people, and they bit the people, so that many people of Israel died.' Three verses later it continues: 'So Moses made a bronze serpent, and set it on a pole; and if a serpent bit any man, he would look at the bronze serpent and live.'

Michelangelo, Bronzino, and Tintoretto present only the healed as being able to raise their arms; all the others struggle futilely and succumb. Pellegrini's version of the subject contains the same contrast (Pl. 16); two figures in the middle distance collapse after fighting the serpents, while in the left foreground a kneeling figure views Moses' miraculous serpent and raises his arms to it in adoration. In Tiepolo's interpretation of the theme, the afflicted heroically cast their arms up towards heaven as well. This motif dominates the right half of the lost Leipzig drawing, it is present in six of the dozen or so drawings of the 1720s, it is visible in the Montreal and London canvases, and it appears twice in the painted frieze from SS Cosmas and Damian.[150]

The Accademia canvas is the only one of Tiepolo's several *Brazen Serpents* to come from a particular church, but each of his versions can, I think, be associated with a specific commission. The earliest of the group, the lost drawing from Leipzig, may be dated to the very first phase of Tiepolo's career, close in time, as Knox has posited, to the *Crossing of the Red Sea*. The figural style is similar in both, and the two compositions are almost identical: Moses stands to the left, one arm is outstretched so that the rod is silhouetted against the sky, and on the right, below a broad and open expanse, figures hurtle themselves against each other. This very closeness in composition, however, makes it unlikely that the two works were conceived of as pendants. None the less, Knox's suggestion that they are contemporaneous is convincing for iconographic as well as stylistic reasons.[151] It is reasonable to hypothesize that at around 1716 Tiepolo decided to paint a *Brazen Serpent*; I shall return to this problem later.

[149] Zanetti, *Descrizione*, p. 62: 'Suo distinto pregio è il pronto carattere d'inventare, e inventando distinguere e risolvere ad uno stesso tempo quantità di figure con novità di ritrovati, con moltiplicità . . .'.

[150] That arm conveys, I believe, something that both Da Canal and Zanetti noted about Tiepolo and his art: Da Canal, *Vita*, p. xxxii, hailed the painter's style as 'tutto spirito e fuoco'; and

Zanetti, *Descrizione*, p. 62, complimented him for having a 'vivacissimo spirito'. Although they were writing in the early 1730s, the comments of these two contemporaries reflect a quality that must have distinguished Tiepolo's personality since his youth.

[151] For the pairing of the *Crossing* and the *Brazen Serpent*, cf. Cope, *The Venetian Chapel of the Sacrament*, p. 242.

Both the Montreal and London versions of *Apelles Painting the Portrait of Campaspe* (see Pls. 51–3) contain a canvas standing against the studio's rear wall that shows a completed *Brazen Serpent*. Taking up Pignatti's idea that Apelles' workshop represents Tiepolo's own and that Campaspe is Cecilia, Tiepolo's young wife, one wonders whether the 'paintings' in the painting were meant to signify actual works.[152] Does one have the right to read Tiepolo's *Apelles Painting the Portrait of Campaspe* as an autobiographical image? Comparing Tiepolo's self-portrait at the age of fifty-seven with Apelles, and a portrait of the elderly Cecilia with Campaspe, as Pignatti has done, does not help to answer such a question. Still, there is some indication in the Montreal painting, if not in that in London, that Apelles' studio should be taken to represent Tiepolo's own, and that it is indeed Cecilia whose portrait is being painted. If this is correct, then one can assume that the *Brazen Serpent* directly behind Apelles also had a real equivalent.

The key to the entire problem lies in the second 'canvas' in Apelles' studio. From what can be seen, it depicts a man half fallen to the ground, his back turned towards us, who is gazing up at an angel holding a tablet or document in his left arm and a military helmet in his right. This 'canvas', I suggest, relates to one mentioned by Da Canal as having been painted by Tiepolo for the Church of S. Martino, '*Santa Cecilia con sposo e con angioli scherzanti*'.[153] What we see on the 'canvas' accords with a fragmented representation of this subject—a divine messenger descending before Cecilia's military 'sposo'.[154] And objection that this proposal ignores the absence of St Cecilia herself should take into account Tiepolo's wry detail that the left side of the 'canvas', where Cecilia should appear, is hidden by an unfinished female portrait. In other words, the two partially complete works must be read together. The juxtaposition of the missing figure with the image that begins to take shape directly in front of it, and the fact that the saint and Tiepolo's wife share the same name, are such charming and winning ideas that they cannot be accidental. Also providing confirmation of Campaspe's identity as Cecilia Guardi Tiepolo is the intimate relationship between the painter and his sitter; while Apelles is staring at the 'real' Campaspe, his brush is painting her nipple, the most delightful of artistic details. To conclude: Tiepolo falls violently in love with Cecilia just as Apelles did with Campaspe.[155]

It is reasonable to assume that the *Brazen Serpent* visually conjoined with Apelles,

[152] The story of Apelles painting Campaspe and then falling in love with her is recounted by Pliny, *Natural History*, ix (The Loeb Classical Library; Cambridge, 1952), bk. xxxv, chap. 36, vs. 85 ff., p. 325.

[153] Da Canal, *Vita*, p. xxxv. Molmenti, *Tiepolo*, p. 207, proposed a story of Venus and Aeneas, which may be correct for the London canvas. Although Da Canal was the only one to mention Tiepolo's *Santa Cecilia con sposo & angeli scherzanti* in the old literature, there is every good reason to believe him. The feast-day of Cecilia, the patron saint of music, was actually celebrated in S. Martino, where an altar was created in her honour as early as 1662. A special devotion or 'sovegno' was held there in late Nov., on St Cecilia's Day, throughout Tiepolo's active career; the holiday and its musical celebrations are mentioned in sources as early as 1724 and as late as 1755 (Coronelli, *Guida de' forestieri* (1724), p. 68, (1744), p. 85; and L. Livan (ed.), *Notizie d'arte tratte dai notatori e dagli annali del N. H. Pietro Gradenigo* (Venice, 1942), 19).

[154] See Reni's *Coronation of SS Cecilia and Valerian* in St Cecilia in Trastevere, Rome, reproduced, in D. S. Pepper, *Guido Reni* (Oxford, 1984), fig. 13; Domenichino's in S. Luigi dei Francesi, Rome, in R. E. Spear, *Domenichino* (New Haven and London, 1982), fig. 146; and Orazio Gentileschi's in the Museo del Brera, Milan, in R. W. Bissell, *Orazio Gentileschi* (University Park and London, 1981), fig. 92.

[155] In 1719 the young man asked the patriarchal office in Venice for dispensation to marry secretly his *fidanzata*, Cecilia Guardi. His parents were against the marriage, and if the bans were made public, they would stand in his way; he would have to abandon Cecilia and, as a result, she would remain unmarried all her life. Tiepolo asked the Curia to register the union secretly, hoping that in the meantime he would overcome his family's opposition. He promised that the marriage would then be published normally: cf. G. Bortolan, 'Asterischi d'archivio per il '700 veneziano', *Notizie da Palazzo Albani*, 2 (1973), 49–53. Tiepolo and Cecilia were married on 21 Nov. 1719; for the relevant document, cf. P. Molmenti, *Acque-Forti dei Tiepolo* (Venice, 1896), p. xiv.

51. Above: G. B. Tiepolo, *Apelles Painting the Portrait of Campaspe, c.* 1730 (oil on canvas, 54 × 74 cm.)

52 and 53. Details of Pl. 51

Campaspe, and *Santa Cecilia con sposo e con angioli scherzanti* would have had, like them, a real counterpart. But a question about Apelles' two paintings immediately leaps to mind. Why is the ancient Greek artist depicting Jewish and Christian stories? Surely Tiepolo could have furnished the studio with more historically correct subject-matter? The answer must be that in presenting three very different types of painting—a portrait, the marriage of a Christian saint, and a Hebrew narrative—Tiepolo is confronting the traditional challenges of Italian painting: he, Tiepolo, is successful as a portraitist, a painter of Christian subject-matter, and an artist of biblical narrative. Other elements in the painting confirm and enrich this interpretation: the black servant dressed in Veronesian costume and the distant loggia set the scene in Venice; and the Farnese Hercules forges links between Tiepolo and ancient art.[156] In presenting himself as a court painter by means of Pliny's story about Apelles, the young Giambattista is proudly boasting of his own remarkable professional success.[157]

The *Brazen Serpent* must have been a work with which the artist was very pleased. I think that the dozen or so drawings on the same subject, now divided among public and private collections in Los Angeles, Paris, Gdansk, and Venice, may well have been preparatory sketches for it. Several of the sheets show figures similar to those on the canvas in Tiepolo's studio in both the London and Montreal paintings, in which three Hebrews appear on a line that descends diagonally to the left of Moses and the Brazen Serpent above. The lowest of the figures, who is kneeling to his right with his arms crossed over his chest in an attitude of submission, corresponds to a form on the far right of one of the sheets in Los Angeles (Pl. 31). Over Apelles' turned head in the Montreal version, is a figure with his back towards us who is analagous to studies in Paris and Gdansk.[158] The close similarities between this figure and the souls in purgatory in the *Madonna del Carmelo* suggest that *c*.1720–2 might be the date for the Los Angeles, Paris, Gdansk, and Venice drawings, allowing one to postulate that the lost *Brazen Serpent* may have been executed immediately prior to both the Brera canvas and the *Martyrdom of St Bartholomew* in S. Stae.

The last of Tiepolo's *Brazen Serpents* is the large painted frieze now in the Accademia (Pl. 54). It is an imposing work, with its dramatic figures boldly gesticulating from within an ornamental framework of flowering elegance, and it appeals simultaneously for its human tragedy and extravagant decoration. Although we know its provenance, the work poses almost as many historical questions as Tiepolo's other versions of the subject do. Indeed, had the immense canvas not survived the maltreatment it received at the time of the Napoleonic suppressions—and given the painting's terribly abraded surface, its survival was indeed fortunate—one would be forced to speculate on its appearance.[159]

[156] Black servants were obviously signs of rank and importance: for example, Titian's *Diana and Actaeon* in the National Gallery of Scotland, Edinburgh; and Ricci's own *Apelles Painting the Portrait of Campaspe*, in the Galleria Nazionale, Parma.

[157] Knox has suggested to me that the Montreal painting could be dated to *c*.1720 when Doge Giovanni Cornaro was still alive (d. 1722). The Montreal canvas may bear out this 'court' connection, and 1720–2 could be a reasonable date for both the Montreal and London paintings. On the other hand, the usual date of *c*.1726–7 for the Montreal work is not without foundation,

both in terms of its style and for the connection between Tiepolo and the Dolfin family, whose princely position in Udine has already been discussed. I would like to think, too, that the detail of Apelles' brush touching Campaspe's breast relates to a personal event involving Giambattista and Cecilia—Giandomenico's birth in 1727. The Montreal painting would suit such an occasion.

[158] Cf. Mrozinska, *Disegni veneti in Polonia*, fig. 40ᵛ; and Voss, 'Un taccuino', fig. 1.

[159] The painting was rolled up and thus damaged: cf. Moschini Marconi, *Gallerie dell'Accademia*, p. 110.

Two eighteenth-century sources briefly mention this *Brazen Serpent*. The 1735–6 edition of Pacifico's *Cronica veneta* notes that 'the story of the serpents of Tiepoletti' was in the Church of SS Cosmas and Damian on the Giudecca Island, and Zanetti's 1771 *Della pittura veneziana* places the painting there 'under the choir'.[160] No other writer of the century mentions it at all. The exact date of the Accademia painting, its enormous size and strange shape, and its existence in a church along with other immense canvases, most of them on Old Testament themes, give occasion to inquire into its history.

The painting is usually dated to *c*.1734–5. Zanetti's 1733 edition of Boschini's *Ricche minere* does not mention the work, but, as I have noted above, the 1735–6 revision of Fra Pacifico's *Cronica veneta* does. Zanetti's lacuna does not necessarily mean that the canvas had not been completed, for guidebooks may fail to include items as well as report them incorrectly. And the 1733 date is not even an exact *terminus post quem*: the book was dedicated to Zanetti by its printer on 1 January of that year, but it was signed by the 'Riformatori di Padova' on 10 August and 7 September 1732. It is conceivable, therefore, that Tiepolo's *Brazen Serpent* was in place in SS Cosmas and Damian by the summer of 1732, after the guidebook was compiled and just as it was sent to Padua for its *nihil obstat*. It is even possible, of course, that the work had been finished somewhat earlier and sat for a short period in Tiepolo's studio.

Arslan dated the painting as early as 1728, and Knox also seems to believe that it dates from before the mid-1730s.[161] My own opinion is that it was painted *c*.1731–2, close in time to the frescos in the Palazzo Dugnani, Milan, to the *Adoration of the Christ-child* that was shown in S. Zulian in 1732, and to the lunettes in the Colleoni Chapel in Bergamo, which were begun in late 1732 and finished in 1733. Features which help to link the *Brazen Serpent* to the Dugnani paintings are the decorative swags of fruits and flowers and the feigned stuccoed mouldings (Pls. 55, 56), which in both commissions have the same fleshy forms and are made to curve and convolve in an identical manner. If these two sets of ornament, gargantuan in size and tuberous in vitality, are compared to the droopy swags of fruit and the undernourished leafy fronds above *Rachel Hiding the Idols from Laban* (Pl. 37), *c*.1726–7, a distinct change in style becomes noticeable, suggesting that the *Brazen Serpent* was executed at least two or three years after the Udine scene.[162]

The figures in the *Brazen Serpent* express tension and feverish drama and create complex rhythms that surge back and forth across the entire width of the frieze. Such dramatic tension and tightly knit compositions are also found in the *Adoration of the Christ-child* (Pl. 108), exhibited in S. Zulian at Christmas 1732, in the *Education of the Virgin* already in S. Maria della Fava in 1733 (Pl. 104), and in the *Beheading of St John the Baptist* frescoed

[160] Pacifico, *Cronica veneta*, p. 453; and Zanetti, *Della pittura veneziana*, p. 468: Tiepolo 'dipinse il gastigo de' serpenti sotto il coro'. The canvas measures 164 by 1,356 cm. For its probable sketch, cf. above, p. 81 n. 147; there is a free copy after the frieze by Cesare Ligari (1740), now in the Pinacoteca Ambrosiana, Milan.

[161] W. Arslan, 'Studi sulla pittura del primo Settecento veneziano', *Critica d'arte*, 1 (1935–6), 241; and Knox, *Tiepolo: A Bicentenary Exhibition*, no. 4: 'Even if one accepts this late date [1733–5] for the painting [in the Accademia] . . .'.

[162] The idea of decorative garlands surrounding a scene, as in the *Brazen Serpent*, could be found in both painting and sculpture. There are two small painted friezes with similar fronds in the chapel to the right of the presbytery in S. Moisè; the sculpted decoration on the attic level of the Library is another possible source. Work by Dorigny, such as his frescos with Old Testament subjects and roundels with elaborate wreaths in the Villa Turriani, might also have been familiar to Tiepolo: cf. F. Dal Forno, 'Un ciclo inedito di Affreschi di Ludovico Dorigny', *Antichità viva*, 17 (1979), 21–4.

54. G. B. Tiepolo, *Brazen Serpent* (oil on canvas, 164 × 1356 cm.)

55. G. B. Tiepolo, *Brazen Serpent*, detail of Pl. 54

57. G. B. Tiepolo, *Brazen Serpent*

56. G. B. Tiepolo, *Scipio and the Slave* (fresco, 520 × 450 cm.)

in the Colleoni Chapel in Bergamo in 1732–3. Its style is so markedly different from the still somewhat doughy *Triumph of Marius*, which dates from 1729, that the *Brazen Serpent* must have been begun a bit later: I suggest that it was just after Zanetti's revision of the *Ricche minere* went before the 'Riformatori di Padova' in the summer of 1732, and before the 1733 *terminus ante quem* of the Colleoni frescos in Bergamo.[163]

The *Brazen Serpent* was one of an important and little-studied group of late seventeenth- and early eighteenth-century paintings decorating the interior of SS Cosmas and Damian and depicting events from the Old and New Testaments. By discussing the entire cycle I hope to clarify the meaning of Tiepolo's work, to explain the importance of its size and shape, and to throw some light on the still vexing problem of the lost Leipzig drawing. Settecento guides tell us a good deal about what the interior of SS Cosmas and Damian must have looked like, and most of the paintings that hung there can still be identified. The biblical canvases have been scattered to five buildings in three different cities, and the church's space is now divided transversally into several floors for use as a factory, but one can still re-create the original ambience of SS Cosmas and Damian and imagine its effect upon contemporary Venetians.[164]

The church was founded in the late fifteenth century and served a community of Benedictine nuns until its suppression in 1810.[165] From what one can now surmise of its structure, the interior was a simple hall with a domed chancel on the south-west side, deep but narrow and flanked by small chapels (Pl. 60). The church's entire width is approximately forty-eight to fifty feet, and its length, from the entrance wall to the triumphal arch leading into the chancel, is about one hundred feet. Light originally entered the church through large lunette-shaped windows that were cut into the two sides. The church's façade is a typical Venetian Renaissance elevation, and two of its original lunette windows can still be seen in a late nineteenth-century photograph (Pl. 58). When the interior was broken up into several floors, other windows were opened on the front, and the lunettes have now been completely bricked in. Paintings of the late Renaissance decorated four of the church's altars: a *Crucifixion* by Tintoretto, a *Virgin and Child with Saints* by Marescalco and another by Palma Giovane, and a *Marriage of St Catherine* by Padovanino. In the late seventeenth century, Girolamo Pellegrini painted a fresco in the chancel's dome which shows the Virgin in heaven with various female saints, among whom can be recognized Agnes, Lucy, Mary Magdalene, Giustina, Margaret, and Agatha. A fitting subject for a convent of nuns, the fresco is still extant *in situ* and is typical of Pellegrini's style.[166]

[163] For the dating of the painting in the Metropolitan Museum, cf. F. Zeri, *Italian Paintings: A Catalogue of the Collection of the Metropolitan Museum of Art* (Greenwich, CT, 1973), 60ff.; the *Brazen Serpent* cannot post-date the Colleoni frescos, for it is quite different from the fresco cycle in the Villa Loschi, securely dated as 1734. Another comparison to be drawn is between the sleeve of the angel in the *Adoration of the Christ-child* with that of the woman on the far left in the *Brazen Serpent*. Only one figure in the Accademia *Brazen Serpent*, the supine male on the far right, really repeats an earlier motif from Tiepolo's other versions of the subject.

[164] I would like to thank the owner and administrator of the Maglificio Herion for permitting me to visit the former church in 1982, and again in 1985. George Knox's presence the second time was invaluable to this study.

[165] F. Corner, *Notizie storiche delle chiese e monasteri di Venezia* (Padua, 1758), 531 ff.; U. Franzoi and D. di Stefano, *Le chiese di Venezia* (Venice, 1976), 281–2; and Zorzi, *Venezia scomparsa*, ii. 496–7. There is no mention of the establishment in G. Perocco and A. Salvadori, 'I conventi benedettini nella laguna', in *Civiltà di Venezia* (Venice, 1977), i. 71–91; but see G. Mazzucco, *Monasteri benedettini nella laguna veneziana* (Venice, 1983), no. 76.

[166] Cf. F. Sansovino, *Venetia città nobilissima et singolare*, ed. G. Martinioni (Venice, 1663), 254–5, and Zorzi, *Venezia scomparsa*, ii. 496–7.

58. Ex-Church of SS Cosmas and Damian, façade

59. S. Michele in Isola, interior

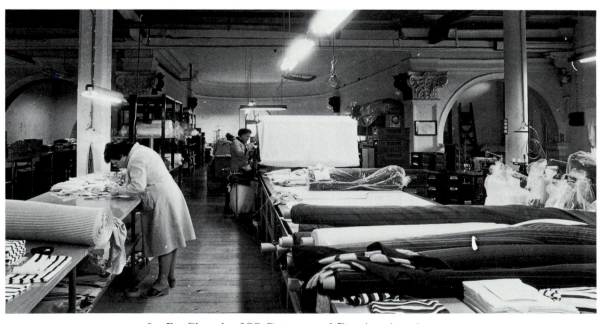

60. Ex-Church of SS Cosmas and Damian, interior

Roughly contemporary with Pellegrini's fresco are four paintings of Old Testament subject-matter by Zanchi. Mentioned by Boschini in 1674, these works seem to have been the first in a series of thirteen biblical narratives painted for the church. Zanchi depicted *David Presenting the Head of Goliath to Saul, David and Abigail*, and two prophets.[167] These four works have not survived, or have not been found, but Alberto Riccoboni has identified a drawing for the first of them. It shows a large hallway, with David standing on the right against the opening of a distant arch and holding Goliath's head up to Saul, who sits enthroned on a podium to the left.[168] The scene comes from 1 Samuel 17: 57–8, when David identifies himself to Saul as the son of Jesse after Goliath's death. *David and Abigail* narrated the event told in 1 Samuel 25: 23–35: Abigail apologizes for her husband's insulting behaviour to David's messengers.[169] David responds with thanks for having been 'kept . . . this day from bloodguilt and from avenging myself with my own hand'. Seen together, Zanchi's two works imply that God's grace has fallen on David as both a hero and a leader.

Late in the seventeenth century, Antonio Molinari painted a *Sacrifice of Saul* for SS Cosmas and Damian. Measuring 512 by 771 centimetres, the canvas hung on the chancel's left wall between two pilasters articulating the wall's surface and just below Zanchi's *David Presenting the Head of Goliath to Saul*; Molinari's painting has not been seen for decades, although two drawings for it have been identified.[170] The sacrifice depicted is that related in 1 Samuel 11: 14–15, where the Hebrews give thanks for their victory over the Ammonites; Saul is made 'king before the Lord', and he 'and all the men of Israel rejoiced greatly'. The story is important in Jewish history, for it tells of the Hebrew tribes' unification into a great nation after their victory over a hated enemy.[171]

By 1700, SS Cosmas and Damian contained five canvases of biblical subject-matter, and all of them were in the chancel. Within the next generation, eight more paintings were executed, and they were displayed throughout the church. However, the series was not continued until around *c.*1716–17 when three giant canvases by Sebastiano Ricci entered the church.[172] Zanetti tells us in 1733 that 'the first painting that he [Ricci] made

---

[167] Boschini, *Le ricche minere*, p. 75: 'Sopra la cornice, alla destra dell'Altar Maggiore [that is, on the left facing the altar] Davide vittorioso porta la testa del gigante innanzi al re Saulle con molto seguito; alla sinistra Davide viene incontrato da Abigail, che gli presenta molti regali.' Pacifico, *Cronica veneta*, pp. 449–50, cites them also. Coronelli, writing about the life and works of Zanchi in *La galleria di Minerva*, ii. 63ff., makes no mention of paintings by him in SS Cosmas and Damian.

[168] A. Riccoboni, 'Novità zanchiane', in *Studi di storia dell'arte in onore di Antonio Morassi*, 262–71, fig. 14; if both Boschini's placement of the painting and Riccobini's identification are correct, then David faced the church's congregation.

[169] Pacifico called the work 'David in contrasto d'Abigail'.

[170] Zanetti, *Della pittura veneziana*, p. 409: 'all'altar maggiore alla destra [again, on the left while facing the altar] . . . un sagrifizio della legge antica'. Cf. Moschini Marconi, *Gallerie dell' Accademia*, p. 88. The work was damaged earlier this century and is now in storage (Rullo A) in the Ducal Palace; its negative number in the Soprintendenza per i Beni Artistici e Storici, Venice, is 6043. See R. C. Green, 'Molinari Drawings in Düsseldorf', *Master Drawings*, 22 (1984), 198, nos. 10a and b; I am

grateful to Mr Green for help concerning the Molinari painting. Cf. L. Moretti, 'Antonio Molinari rivisitato', *Arte veneta*, 33 (1979), 69, no. 98. Given that Boschini does not mention Molinari's work, it must post-date Zanchi's four; Molinari died in 1704. One puzzling note must be added here: N. Melchiori, *Notizie di pittori e altri scritti*, ed. G. B. Favero (Venice–Rome, 1964), 126, does not mention the *Sacrifice of Saul*, but writes instead that the same painter's 'gran Quadro . . . con la Profanazione, e saccheggio del Tempio di Gerusaleme fatto dalle genti di Nabucodonosor Re di Babilonia' was in SS Cosmas and Damian.

[171] In the episodes both before and after this scene of sacrifice, much is made of the Hebrews' transition from tribal life to nationhood, and of Samuel's anointing of Saul as King: cf. 1 Samuel 10–12. It is more than possible that the choice of subject reflects Venice's several victories over the Turks in the late 1690s.

[172] Daniels, *Sebastiano Ricci*, nos. 408, 464, and 520, dates the three works 1716–20. Martini, *La pittura del settecento Veneto*, p. 479, states that one of the three, the *Transportation of the Ark*, is signed and dated 1729 and the other two, therefore, must be contemporary with it. However, the figural style of the works does not completely support this last conclusion.

here . . . in the chancel [shows] King Solomon speaking to his people in the Temple [i.e., *Solomon Speaking to the People at the Dedication of the Temple*]' (Pl. 61).[173] This brightly coloured work, a fine example of Ricci's capacity to create a monumental composition with a myriad of anecdotal detail, now hangs on the right wall of the chancel in the Duomo in Thiene, copying its original position in SS Cosmas and Damian, where it faced Molinari's *Sacrifice of Saul*. Continuing the narrative of that work, Ricci's painting draws from 1 Kings 8 (and 3 Chronicles 6 and 7): King Solomon gathers the leaders of his people into the temple, a cloud wafts in, and Solomon asks God to keep his covenant, to take care of Israel, to protect it against sickness, and to help the nation fight its enemies.

Zanetti states that Ricci's second work for SS Cosmas and Damian was *Moses Striking Water from the Rock at Horeb*, and that the third was the *Transportation of the Holy Ark* (Pls. 62, 63).[174] The former, done in collaboration with Marco Ricci, hung on the church's left wall just inside the entrance; the latter was placed on the same side but closer to the chancel, after the altar with Tintoretto's *Virgin and Child with SS Cecilia, Theodore, Marina, Cosmas, and Damian*. Ricci's two paintings brought the story of the Hebrews' search for nationhood into the nave. In *Moses Striking the Rock at Horeb* (Exodus 17: 1–7), the Jewish leader guides his people out of bondage, assuages their grievances, and cares for their wants. The *Transportation of the Holy Ark* (2 Samuel 6: 3–5, or 1 Chronicles 13: 1–3) emphasizes once again the unity of the Jewish nation and its covenant with God.

The subjects of Ricci's paintings follow the principal theme of the late seventeenth-century biblical works in SS Cosmas and Damian: like Zanchi's stories of David and Molinari's of Saul, Ricci's narratives present Solomon, Moses, and King David as Israelite leaders. These episodes recall, too, the Hebrews' liberation, unification, and finally the fulfilment of their covenant with God. Moreover, in emphasizing the relationship between a leader and his people, the paintings express the concept of nationhood. The probable date of *c*.1717–20 for Ricci's three works is, to say the least, provocative, because it suggests that their themes, like that of Tiepolo's contemporary *Crossing of the Red Sea*, reflect Venice's dire experiences during the war in Corfu.

The contemporaneity of Ricci's three canvases with Tiepolo's hints at another intriguing connection besides that of the victory at Corfu. Da Canal, who tells us that Tiepolo painted his *Faraone sommerso* 'in rivalry with other painters', does not indicate that the competition of the Fiera di S. Rocco specified the crossing of the Red Sea as a subject. One may wonder, therefore, whether Tiepolo's work responded to a general call from SS Cosmas and Damian for Old Testament and/or Mosaic subject-matter.[175] That Tiepolo's *bozzetto* could indeed have been conceived for SS Cosmas and Damian is supported, I believe, by Ricci's *Moses Striking the Rock at Horeb*. The two narratives are

[173] Zanetti, *Descrizione*, pp. 372 ff. Ricci's work now measures 354 by 656 cm., but it used to be approximately 410 by 750 cm. Cf. Daniels, *Sebastiano Ricci*, no. 520; and Moschini Marconi, *Gallerie dell' Accademia*, no. 188.

[174] See Daniels, *Sebastiano Ricci*, nos. 464 and 408. The first painting, now in the Cini Foundation, measures 530 by 830 cm.; the second, belonging to the Brera but on loan to the church in Somaglia, is 450 by 800 cm.

[175] Such descriptions are not unknown in Italian art. For instance, Malvasia twice mentions competitions in Bologna in which painters fought for artistic supremacy as they each executed a different subject: cf. *Felsina pittrice*, ed. G. Zanotti (Bologna, 1841), iv. 151: 'In tal guisa gareggiavasi tra di loro con l'opre . . .'; and his *Le pitture di Bologna*, ed. A. Emiliani (Bologna, 1969), 77–8: 'Sopra nell'Oratorio, tutti gli freschi attorno della passione del nostro amorosissimo Signore, sono similmente una gloriosa gara de' non anche provetti discepoli Carracceschi . . .'.

linked in the Bible, and at both the Red Sea and Horeb Moses' rod magically affects the water, sending it away in the first instance and bringing it forth in the second. A further proposal would be that the Leipzig drawing of the *Brazen Serpent*, in which Moses' rod again operates with divine assistance, was also executed with SS Cosmas and Damian in mind. Besides the chronological suitability and thematic relationship of such a possibility, the drawing's horizontal format fits in well with those of Tiepolo's sketch and Ricci's painting.

If one accepts that Tiepolo's *Crossing of the Red Sea* and early *Brazen Serpent* were executed for a competition organized by SS Cosmas and Damian, there are still two questions that need answering. The first is, why did Tiepolo lose to Ricci? The answer is easy: Ricci returned to Venice from London and Paris in late 1716 or early 1717; the public advantages he enjoyed as an internationally known painter were great and would have superseded whatever applause the talented—but unknown—Tiepolo received on 16 August 1716. And the second is, why was *Moses Striking the Rock at Horeb* chosen rather than the *Crossing of the Red Sea* or the *Brazen Serpent*? The latter two stories emphasize the Jewish people's confrontation with death and destruction. While they might aptly reflect the fearful struggle with the Turks during 1715–16, they would hardly be appealing subjects to the Venetians in 1717–18, or later, after the real dangers of Corfu had been overcome. The episode at Horeb, on the other hand, shows Moses' power as a healer; he allayed his people's worries, he quenched their thirst, and he cared for their needs. The relevance of these events to a church dedicated to two early Christian doctors is unmistakable.

After taking delivery of Ricci's three paintings, the authorities at SS Cosmas and Damian could have looked at their church's chancel with satisfaction, for it was magnificently decorated, but they would have noted with discomfort that both *Moses Striking the Rock at Horeb* and the *Transportation of the Holy Ark* were without pendants, that their nave's right wall was bare. When plans to resolve this situation and complete the cycle came to fruition, perhaps in the second half of the 1720s, it was the thaumaturgical aspect of the Bible's narrative of salvation that was emphasized. Furthermore, the historical context was shifted from the Old Testament to the New. Placed opposite Ricci's *Moses Striking the Rock at Horeb* was Pittoni's *Multiplication of the Loaves and Fishes*, in which Christ feeding the hungry provides a parallel to Moses quenching the thirsty.[176] In the Christian story (Matthew 15: 30–1), the theme of healing is underscored; the crowds to whom Christ ministered were '. . . the lame, the maimed, the blind, the dumb, and many others, and they put them at his feet, and he healed them, so that the throng wondered, when they saw the dumb speaking, the maimed whole, the lame walking, and the blind seeing; and they glorified the God of Israel'. Opposite Ricci's *Transportation of the Holy Ark*, was hung Angelo Trevisani's *Cleansing of the Temple* (John 2: 13–16); here the theme of Christ's restorative powers merged with that of Jewish nationhood. Both these paintings are now in the church in Somaglia.[177]

Tiepolo's great *Brazen Serpent* must have been placed in SS Cosmas and Damian in the

---

[176] Cf. Zava Boccazzi, *Pittoni*, no. 215, dated *c*.1725–6; the painting belongs to the Accademia but is in the Cini Foundation.

[177] The negative number of Trevisani's painting in the Soprintendenza per i Beni Artistici e Storici, Milan, is 9797/L.

63. S. Ricci, *Transportation of the Holy Ark* (oil on canvas, 450 × 800 cm.)

61. Opposite, above: S. Ricci, *Solomon Speaking to the People* (oil on canvas, 354 × 656 cm.)

62. Opposite, below: S. Ricci, Oil-sketch for *Moses Striking Water from the Rock at Horeb* (oil on canvas, 102 × 132 cm.)

early 1730s. Zanetti's remark that the frieze was 'under the choir', and the old photographs that show the painting in an elegantly carved wooden frame leave little doubt that the canvas decorated a *barco*, or choir-loft, a traditional piece of church furniture in Venetian monastic churches. Such constructions can still be seen: for example, over the inside of the entrance into S. Michele in Isola, which was built for a community of Camaldolese hermits (Pl. 59). The *barco* in SS Cosmas and Damian would have been in a similar position, and one can assume that the *Brazen Serpent* was hung on the inner wall of the church's façade, probably across the width of the church, and facing the high altar, i.e. above the central doorway. The sharp foreshortening of Tiepolo's figures confirms such a height. One can visualize this interior placement by looking at an old photograph of the church front (Pl. 58), noting in particular the area above the doorway's pediment and between the two pilasters.[178]

The *Brazen Serpent*'s position opposite the high altar of SS Cosmas and Damian was similar to that of several other Italian representations of the story. Bronzino's in the Chapel of Eleonora of Toledo in the Palazzo Vecchio in Florence is next to a consecrated altar, Michelangelo's on the Sistine Chapel's ceiling is above one, and Tintoretto's in the ceiling of the Scuola di S. Rocco's upper floor is, like Tiepolo's frieze, on a direct axis with one. Such an association points to the Christian interpretation of the Brazen Serpent as a prefiguration of Christ's crucifixion.[179] The *Brazen Serpent* also calls to mind the Christian paintings of Pittoni and Trevisani which show a leader healing his people. In sum, Tiepolo's painting functioned on many levels: its elegant framework ornamented the nuns' choir; the depiction of a divine cure for human illness reaffirmed the church's dedication to two saintly doctors; and the subject reminded the pious of Christ's sacrifice for their salvation. Finally, the image of Moses leading the Hebrews to freedom reasserted SS Cosmas and Damian's larger pictorial theme of the Chosen People's search for national unity.

A final word should be said about two other paintings which were part of this extensive biblical cycle, although they are not known today, and, as far as I know, they have never before been mentioned in association with it. In 1927, Fiocco published Francesco Maria Tassis's additions to Zanetti's guide, in which Tassis noted that under the choir in SS Cosmas and Damian there were not only 'the punishment of the serpents of G. B. Tiepolo' (a reference missing in Zanetti), but also: 'two paintings, one with the finding of Moses in the Nile by Gio. Batta Crosato. The other with the centurion before Christ of Giac.° Brusaferro.'[180]

---

[178] Relevant perhaps to both the dating of Tiepolo's painting and its placement in the choir-loft was the gift of money to buy an organ for SS Cosmas and Damian on 1 July 1732: cf. ASV, 'Ss. Cosma e Damiano', b. 23. Tiepolo's canvas measures 1,356 by 164 cm. If one assumes that the *barco*'s parapet was articulated by a gentle undulation, as several choir-lofts of the period were, then the painting would have covered much less than its 44-foot width. The two feigned consoles of the frieze that separate the narrative into three compartments confirm that the canvas had a curving form. These ornamental divisions suggest that Tiepolo had to cover a surface that shifted from concave to convex and back again, perhaps, and that he used such decorative elements

to deal artfully both with those areas where the curves were most accentuated and with the parapet's real consoles.

[179] John 3: 14–15: '"And as Moses lifted up the serpent in the wilderness, so must the Son of Man be lifted up, that whoever believes in him may have eternal life."' Cf. C. De Tolnay, 'L'interpretazione dei cicli pittorici del Tintoretto nella Scuola di San Rocco', *Critica d'arte*, 8 (1960), 341–76.

[180] Fiocco, 'Aggiunte di Francesco Maria Tassis', p. 170: 'Entrando in Chiesa sotto il coro vi sono due quadri uno con la trovata di Mosè nel Nilo di Gio. Batta Crosato. L'altro col centurione avanti a Cristo di Giac.° Brusaferro; e altri due quadri alle parti della porta di Francesco Polazzo.' A *Finding of Moses*

The *Finding of Moses* was, of course, an appropriate subject for the church's iconographic plan, and, as I explained earlier, it could be read in terms of Venice's founding. The pendant, *Christ and the Centurion*, relates the story of the centurion who approached Christ at Capernaum to ask him to cure his paralysed servant (Matthew 8: 5–13). It repeated the curative theme seen elsewhere in the nave and, like the pairs of paintings by Ricci and Pittoni and Ricci and Trevisani, it formed a link between the Old and New Testaments.

The thirteen biblical paintings hanging in SS Cosmas and Damian must have been an impressive sight, not only because they covered much of the church's interior, but also because of their consistently high artistic standard. Several contemporaries admired their quality. Charles De Brosses praised Ricci's, Pittoni's, and Trevisani's works, and Cochin also complimented Ricci's paintings.[181] Coronelli noted simply in his 1724 guide that 'there are very many paintings [in SS Cosmas and Damian]', but amplified this in the 1744 edition, by which time the series must have been complete, to read: 'Here there can be seen very many Paintings all by famous Artists, and these paintings deserve to be seen, and admired.'[182] Not one of these authors, however, mentioned the works' thematic unity.

Old Testament subject-matter served to link the Venetians to the ancient Hebrews, who had confronted numerous foes in their search for nationhood. These biblical themes were as relevant to the Serenissima in the eighteenth century as they had been in the sixteenth, since the State still found itself facing considerable challenges—from the Porte Sublime in Istanbul, the Holy See in Rome, and Charles VI in Vienna. The seventy-three-year period from 1645 to 1718 saw Venice fight three wars, and its economy suffered as a result. The foreign territories of Crete, Negroponte, and the Pelopponese, together with a number of other outposts, had been lost, and the threat to Corfu, upon which the State's very life depended, must have shaken Venetians to the core. Tiepolo's youthful paintings of Old Testament subjects were animated by the city's sense that its existence was under threat, and they express the nation's self-identification as a 'Chosen People'. The *Faraone sommerso* and the *Brazen Serpent* are both, to a great extent, statements of Venetian patriotism. Resonant and dramatic images, they seem to reflect the young artist's own love for Venice. A similar spirit motivates much of his later religious art, too, but in a more jubilant and triumphant key.

by Crosato does exist in the Museo Civico of Palazzo Madama in Turin; it measures 57 by 104 cm. See N. S. Harrison, 'The Paintings of Giovanni Battista Crosato', Ph.D. diss. (Georgia, 1983), 110; P. Zampetti, *Dal Ricci al Tiepolo: I pittori di figura del Settecento a Venezia* (exh. cat., Ducal Palace, Venice, 1969), no. 86; and R. Pallucchini, 'I "Figuristi" del Settecento a Palazzo Ducale', *Arte veneta*, 23 (1969), 291–2, who mentions another *Finding of Moses* in the Pushkin Museum, Moscow, and attributes it to Crosato.

[181] C. De Brosses, *Viaggio in Italia* (Rome, 1973), 141; and Cochin, *Voyage d'Italie*, p. 145; neither writer mentioned Tiepolo, however.

[182] Coronelli, *Guida de' forestieri* (1724), 391, and (1744), 334: 'Quivi veggonsi moltissime Pitture tutte di Autori, le quali meritano d'essere vedute, ed ammirate.'

2

MARIAN CEILING-PAINTING AND MARIAN DEVOTIONS

BY the time he turned forty in 1736, Tiepolo was already a famous painter and he had frescoed the first large-scale secular decorations of his career in the *palazzi* Archinto and Dugnani in Milan in 1731–2.[1] Recognition for his brilliance in this field followed in 1734, when he was commissioned to fresco in the Villa Loschi near Vicenza, the first of almost a dozen decorative projects for villas in the Veneto. Foreign patrons also sought after him avidly for such work; in 1736 he was invited to paint in the Royal Palace in Stockholm.[2] If he had accepted this offer, and had left Venice in 1736–7, he would probably not have created his first great ecclesiastical ceiling for S. Maria del Rosario in 1738–9. This monumental fresco cycle, together with the painted ceilings in the Scalzi, the Carmini, and the Pietà, and their relation to the eighteenth century's celebration of the Marian cult, are the principal topics of this chapter.

Tiepolo's ceiling in the Gesuati, S. Maria del Rosario's popular name, honours the mother of Christ as both Queen and intercessor (Pl. 70). Exaltation of the Virgin and her special role in redemption was not a new subject in Tiepolo's art; he had already painted a number of altar-pieces dedicated to this theme before the Gesuati commission came along. Two such works from the early 1730s are the *Education of the Virgin*, in S. Maria della Fava (Pl. 104), and the *Adoration of the Christ-child*, now in the Sacristy of the Canons in S. Marco but originally in S. Zulian (Pl. 108). In the first, the young Mary is dressed in immaculate white and stands on a small but ornate stool so that her feet do not touch the ground; angels and seraphim encircle her. She holds the Bible in one hand, mystically sharing its weight with the cloud-filled glory before her, and with the other points to the holy book, which is also painted a pure white. The painting venerates the Virgin's immaculacy as much as it describes her reading lesson with Anne. In the *Adoration of the Christ-child*, Mary is turning to gaze reverently towards heaven, a divine presence illuminating her face. In contrast, Joseph is looking down, his face in almost total darkness. Christ is cradled in a shroud-like drapery suggestive of the sacrifice he will endure for mankind's redemption. The painting implies that although Joseph recognizes and adores the Saviour, the Blessed Virgin fully comprehends the divine plan of redemption.[3] Two other altar-pieces of the early 1730s that celebrate Mary's special privileges are the

---

[1] P. L. Sohm, 'Giambattista Tiepolo at the Palazzo Archinto in Milan', *Arte lombarda*, 68–9 (1984), 70–8.

[2] O. Sirèn, *Dessins et tableaux de la Renaissance italienne dans les collections de Suède* (Stockholm, 1902), 103–13.

[3] The Immaculate Virgin in seventeenth- and eighteenth-century art is characterized in part by her white dress. This has become canonical in Catholic art: cf. Don Emmanuele Caronti, OSB, 'Come raffigurare l'Immacolata Concezione', *Fede e arte*, 2 (1954), 367. For Joseph in shadow as a symbol of the Old Testament, cf. H. Hibbard, *Poussin: The Holy Family on the Steps* (New York, 1974), 67.

Madonna and Child with SS Hyacinth and Dominic, in the Art Institute of Chicago, and the *Immaculate Conception*, in the Museo Civico in Vicenza.[4] In the first, a cloud encloses the Virgin and the Christ-child. Mary's feet rest on a brocaded cloth into which the mysteries of the Rosary have been woven; the worshipper approaches Christ through veneration of his mother and her Rosary. In the *Immaculate Conception*, the elongated figure of the Virgin standing on the globe assumes iconic eminence before mankind. Tiepolo did not invent any of these pictorial elements; all of them already existed in Marian imagery. But his use of them here, and in a number of other contemporary altar-pieces, which will be discussed in Chapter Three, demonstrates his sanction of one of the eighteenth century's major spiritual themes, the universal triumph of Christ's mother.

Mary's symbolic value for Venice has been commented upon in Chapter One: the Virgin protected Venice, and the city's historic inviolability proved Mary's special powers.[5] This analogue of Venice/Virgin continued well into the seventeenth and eighteenth centuries. Religious panegyrics and sermons issuing from local presses extolled Venetians and their city for enjoying unique ties with the Virgin Mary. In 1746, Francesco Antonio da Ferrara, a Franciscan from the province of Bologna, dedicated an *Orazione panegirica della protezione della Santissima Vergine sopra la città di Venezia* to Marco Antonio Giustiniani, Procurator of S. Marco, celebrating the loving and filial links which united the Mother of God to her children of Venice: 'You are the most fortunate among all Nations because . . . the Virgin chose you as her people and your city ['questa Dominante'] as hers; you with unique and exemplary devotion elected Maria as your Mother, and she likewise elected you as her children.'[6]

The most important aspect of this analogy continued to rest in the association between Venice's inviolability and Mary's virginity. Fra' Francesco asked: 'What never-conquered city can boast of Virginity as its richness? No other but Venice.'[7] Another author wrote: 'Only Venice, after more than thirteen centuries, enjoys the beautiful privilege of the same liberty in which it was born, to preserve itself integral, never subject to a tyrannical yoke, never dominated as a city, but *Dominante* and always *Vergine*.'[8] Venice's virginity

---

[4] A. Morassi, *A Complete Catalogue of the Paintings of G. B. Tiepolo* (London, 1962), 8, and 64, dates them to 1730–5 and *c*.1734–6: cf. figs. 66 and 96. A. Pallucchini, *L'opera completa del Tiepolo*, (Milan, 1968), nos. 105 and 108, puts them in *c*.1735 and 1734–6.

[5] Siena as well as several other Italian cities also claimed Mary's special protection. For Venice in particular, cf. R. Goffen, *Piety and Patronage in Renaissance Venice* (New Haven, 1986), 138–54; and for the origins of the association, cf. G. Musolino, 'Culto mariano', in S. Tramontin (ed.), *Culto dei santi a Venezia* (Venice, 1965), 241 ff.; see also S. Sinding-Larsen, *Christ in the Council Hall* (Acta ad Archaelogiam et Artium Historiam Pertinentia, 5; Institutum Romanum Norvegiae, Rome, 1974), 243; id., 'L'immagine della repubblica di Venezia', and Mason Rinaldi's 'Storia e mito nei cicli pittorici di Palazzo Ducale', both in *Architettura e utopia nella Venezia del Cinquecento* (exh. cat., Ducal Palace, Venice, 1980 (Milan), 40ff., 8off. Also cf. D. Rosand, 'Venetia Figurata: The Iconography of a Myth' in *Interpretazioni veneziane: Studi di storia dell'arte in onore di Michelangelo Muraro* (Venice, 1984), 177–96. For the myth's continuation into our own century, see F. Marchiori, *Maria e Venezia* (Venice, 1929), *passim*; Marchiori even went so

far as to link Venice's condition in the twentieth century to a lessening in Marian devotion: 'Oh beata Venezia! se avesse saputo conservarsi fedele alle tradizioni religiose dei suoi padri, e mantenere sempre viva la primitiva devozione alla Madonna: non ne avrebbe allora subito l'umiliante castigo!'

[6] Francesco Antonio da Ferrara, *Orazione panegirica della protezione della Santissima Vergine sopra la città di Venezia recitata il giorno delli 17. marzo* (Venice, 1746), 7. The entire statement reads: 'Sì sì popolo mio dilletissimo di Venezia, Voi, Voi solo siete frà tutte le Nazioni il più fortunato, perchè Voi solo frà tutte le Genti con particolare distinta amorosa inclinazione trascelse la Vergine, elleggendo Voi per suo Popolo, e questa Dominante per sua Cittade, se Voi con singolarissima esemplar divozione eleggeste Maria per Madre, Ella elesse altressi Voi per suoi Figli.'

[7] Ibid., p. 12: 'Qual Città non mai violata da Nimiche forze vanta la Verginità per suo fasto? Ah non altre se non se Venezia.'

[8] Padre d'Udine, 'Panegirico dell'Immacolata Concezione di Maria Vergine', in *Raccolta di panegirici sopra tutte le festività di nostro signore, di Maria Vergine, e de' santi, recitati da più celebri oratori del nostro secolo*, i (Venice, 1760), 10ff. (and repeated in v. 14ff.)

was so strongly sustained by its political theory that when new merchant families were admitted into the patriciate in the seventeenth century in order to fill the State's coffers, the act was criticized for its prostitution of the 'unstained Virgin'.[9]

The explanation for Venice's unique privilege lay, of course, in the tradition that the city was founded on the feast of the Incarnation (Annunciation), an event still glorified in the eighteenth century. As one anonymous author of the period wrote, Venetians should reflect upon and recognize '. . . with what great commitment the beloved Mother of God affectionately wished to distinguish Venice from all other cities, for it [Venice] had the glory of having been born Mary's daughter on the same day on which God's only born Son took on human flesh in the Mother's virginal uterus.'[10] But the supposed concordance in date between Christ's conception and Venice's founding, and the weighty historical evidence that Venice had actually remained *sempre vergine*, only provide a priori proof of the millennial association between the city and Mary *after the fact*; they do not explain the intent lying behind it.

In ancient Greece and Rome, the worship of both Athena and Minerva as virgin goddesses linked their strength and wisdom to their chastity. A pure woman was thought to be greater than any other of her sex, superior even to a mortal man. In the Christian world, Mary's virginity signified that she had not been possessed, and it also implied that no man could or would ever own her.[11] But through the Annunciation and Incarnation Mary achieved motherhood, a status that eventually brought believers to seek protection and safety under her aegis. For the Venetians, living in a physical world that was so vulnerable to the elements, the ancient and Christian resonances of virginity must have been enthralling. By embracing Mary within the myth of the State, Venice achieved muscle power, political acumen, and, finally, its ensured existence in the natural and man-made world surrounding it. One cannot marvel, therefore, that even as late as 1746 Fra' Francesco could write:

O great Virgin, look down upon this City, which you have elected here on Earth as the principal object of your Maternal Love. These are your States, your Provinces, your Government . . . Yours, too, are these People and this Lofty, Most August Senate, and therefore, you as the mystical Tree of Jesse will crown it [People and Senate] with Flowers, with Innocence, and with glory.[12]

Pictorial representations of the Virgin in Venetian art of the settecento suggest royal authority; they even trumpet forth a note of triumph. But the Republic's weakened international position after the Peace of Carlowitz in 1699 and Passarowitz in 1718 did not offer the State a concrete political basis for the perpetuation of the type of victorious

[9] See J. C. Davis, *The Decline of the Venetian Nobility as a Ruling Class* (Baltimore, 1962), 127; Davis gives no source.

[10] *Venezia favorita da Maria: Relazione delle immagini miracolose di Maria conservate in Venezia* (Padua, 1758), 3: 'con quanto impegno l'amabilissima Madre di Dio abbia voluto fra le altre Città distinguer affettuosamente Venezia, che si gloria d'esser nata figlia di Maria nel giorno stesso in cui, nel purissimo Virginal suo utero prese carne umana l'Unigenito Figlio dell'Eterno Padre.'

[11] Cf. M. Warner, *Alone of All Her Sex* (New York, 1983), 34–49.

[12] Fra' Francesco, *Orazione panegirica*, p. 14: 'Rimirate pertanto o gran Vergine cotesta Cittade, che Voi elegeste qui in Terra per principale oggetto del vostro Materno Amore. Vostri sono questi Stati, queste Province, questo Governo . . . Vostro perfine è questo Popolo, e questo Eccelso Augustissimo Senato, e perciò Voi come mistica Verga di Jesse lo avete a coronare co' Fiori, e d'Innocenza e di gloria.'

female imagery that filled, for example, the sixteenth-century ceiling-paintings of the Ducal Palace's Sala del Maggior Consiglio (Pls. 78–80). However, Tiepolo's exaltation of Mary can be explained, and three phenomena, I think, elicited it. The first is the almost total disappearance from seventeenth- and eighteenth-century art of the figure of St Mark, the nation's traditional symbol of patriotic spirit; the second is the contemporary glorification of Christ's mother within the Catholic world; and the last is the Republic's veneration of the icon of the *Nicopeia*.

The story of the Evangelist Mark, his legendary dream (or 'Sogno'), and the miracles that linked him to Venice are too well known to bear repetition here.[13] The importance of Mark's imagery in the history of Venetian art cannot be overestimated: four of the apse mosaics on the exterior of S. Marco retell his story; the *Sogno* itself sits above the very centre of the church's middle portal; Mark is present throughout the Ducal Palace; and the lion, his apocalyptic symbol, is the most frequent image in both the Piazza and the Piazzetta. Numerous altars in the city were adorned during the fifteenth and sixteenth centuries with paintings honouring St Mark, and a major cycle of works dedicated to his life and death occupied the patronage of the Scuola Grande di S. Marco, Venice's largest confraternity, for much of the third quarter of the sixteenth century.[14]

Then, after 1575, Mark began to disappear from the pictorial arts of the State. While many other saints, some of them not very well known, grew in popularity during the last two hundred years of the Republic's life, Mark receded in importance. Not one cycle was commissioned to honour him within the city after that of the Scuola Grande di S. Marco.[15] In the seventeenth century, he no longer even appeared in votive works concerning the State: he is missing from Giuseppe Heintz's painting for the Church of S. Fantin, in which SS John the Baptist, Theodore, and Roch intercede with the Virgin for the cessation of the plague of 1630; and he is also absent from Bellucci's monumental canvas for S. Pietro di Castello, where the Doge pleads with S. Lorenzo Giustinian, the city's first Patriarch, for alleviation of the same scourge.[16] One must conclude that the figure of St Mark no longer communicated either the idea of the mighty Venetian body politic or the power of its quasi-independent national Church.[17]

Mark and his lion do not appear very often in eighteenth-century Venetian art, and when they do it is usually within an evangelistic cycle.[18] There are exceptions to this general rule, however: works which either refer to territorial possessions or which were

[13] Cf. S. Tramontin, 'San Marco', in *Culto dei santi a Venezia* (Venice, 1965), 43 ff.

[14] For Tintoretto's paintings, cf. R. Pallucchini and P. Rossi, *Tintoretto: Le opere sacre e profane* (Milan, 1982), nos. 243–5, dated 1562–6.

[15] Giambattista Crosato painted a fresco cycle in 1748 that retells the 'translatio': cf. S. Kaufman, 'A Saint Mark Cycle of Frescoes by G. B. Crosato in Ponte di Brenta', Abstract for a Talk delivered at the College Art Association Meeting, New York, 1986.

[16] Cf. R. Pallucchini, *La pittura veneziana del Seicento* (Milan, 1981), ii, figs. 435–6 and 1193.

[17] The explanation for this lies in the fact that the *culto marciano* itself had diminished in importance: G. Musolino, 'I santi nel folklore', in A. Niero, G. Musolino, and S. Tramontin (eds.), *Santità a Venezia* (Venice, 1972), 184: 'La festa della Traslazione delle reliquie [of St Mark], prima celebrata con molta solennità, era ormai in decadenza verso la fine del secolo XV. A quel tempo infatti non veniva più osservata l'astensione dal lavoro e solo i pubblici uffici rimanevano chiusi.'

[18] Tiepolo's grisaille evangelistic symbols in the pendentives over the Gesuati's altar are a case in point, as are his evangelists on the pendentives in the Sagredo Chapel in S. Francesco della Vigna: cf. W. Barcham, 'The Cappella Sagredo in San Francesco della Vigna', *Artibus et Historiae*, 4 (1983), 101–24. Another evangelistic cycle associated with Tiepolo but never realized was that for the Colegiata de la Granja, Madrid; drawings now in the Biblioteca Nacional, Madrid, of SS Matthew, Mark, and John may have been done with that commission in mind: see M. B. Meña Marques, *Dibujos italianos de los siglos XVII y XVIII en la Biblioteca Nacional* (Madrid, 1984), nos. 191–4.

actually executed for the provinces. Niccolò Bambini's scene of thanksgiving (Venice, Ducal Palace; Pl. 64) for the 1716 victory of Corfu is a rare example of the first type; Mark sits in the heavens with his Gospel, while his lion crouches below, next to the cushion on which Doge Giovanni Cornaro is kneeling. And two examples will suffice for the second type: the winged lion in the Tribunal in the Arcivescovado in Udine is a symbol of Venetian authority;[19] and in Crespano del Grappa, a town that enjoyed an economic boom in the seicento owing to the wool industry, Molinari painted *The Arrival in Venice of the Body of St Mark*.[20]

The eighteenth century's most significant image of Mark and his lion is Tiepolo's fresco in the Colleoni Chapel in Bergamo, datable to 1732–3 (Pl. 66).[21] Tiepolo represents the saint as an elderly gentleman comfortably seated at a writing table. Mark shows none of the muscular vitality typical of earlier Venetian images of the figure; Venice's military might during the second quarter of the eighteenth century did not call for such a representation. Mark's lion, too, seems to have been tamed by Tiepolo into a domestic animal, hardly a likely descendant of the stalking beast of Carpaccio's *Lion of St Mark* of 1516.[22]

A fruitful comparison can also be made of Carpaccio's *Lion of St Mark* and Tiepolo's *Neptune Offering Gifts to Venice* (Pl. 65), *c.*1750, in which the lion is merely a warm cushion for the figure of Venice to rest upon. Tiepolo's emphasis is on Venice's opulence rather than on its physical strength, and the lion's body disappears to give way to beautiful draperies and a cornucopia of wealth. Judging from this officially commissioned painting, the State appears to have had little interest in the eighteenth century in advertising threatening defiance. Instead, the city sought to project an image of female warmth and secure guardianship, concepts eloquently communicated by Christ's mother and brilliantly projected by Tiepolo on the Gesuati, Scalzi, Carmini, and Pietà ceilings, where Mary reigns as a triumphant Queen.

Tiepolo's celebration of Mary as an icon of victory can be explained, in part, by the post-Tridentine glorification of Christ's mother. I would suggest, however, that along with the disappearance of Mark from Venetian iconography, it was the continued veneration in eighteenth-century Venice of the *Nicopeia* that so exalted the Marian cult. Writing in his diary on 8 December 1742, the feast of the Immaculate Conception, Girolamo Zanetti recorded how the *Madonna Nicopeia* was carried forth from the Ducal Basilica of S. Marco '. . . to implore the end of the overabundant rains and floods. Soon after it [the *Nicopeia*] was exhibited, the weather became serene. Similar processions with the same purpose were held by public order throughout the city's neighbourhoods.'[23]

[19] Cf. above, p. 66.

[20] Cf. R. Pallucchini, *La pittura veneziana del Seicento*, i, fig. 1263; and A. Mariuz, 'La "Traslazione del Corpo di San Marco" di Antonio Molinari e il suo modelletto', *Arte veneta*, 36 (1982), 222 ff. The painting has been dated to the end of Molinari's activity (d. 1704).

[21] Reminding us of Bartolomeo Colleoni's allegiance to the Venetian State, the lunette is paired with an image of St Bartholomew, the great *condottiere*'s own saintly patron: cf. A. Pallucchini, *L'opera completa*, nos. 81 E, F.

[22] Cf. *The Genius of Venice, 1500–1600* (exh. cat., Royal Academy of Arts, London, 1983), 50–1.

[23] G. Zanetti, 'Memorie per servire all'istoria della inclita città di Venezia', ed. F. Stefani, *Archivio veneto*, 29 (1885), 108: '. . . per impetrare la cessazione delle sovrabbondanti pioggie ed innondazioni. Poco dopo esposto, il tempo cominciò a serenarsi. Si fecero per lo stesso ogetto, le processioni per tutte le contrade della città, d'ordine publico.' The feast of the Immaculate Conception had been established in Venice in 1697 as a special day of prayer devoted to the *Nicopeia*: see L. Picchini, 'La repubblica

64. N. Bambini, *Virgin and Christ-child with Saints and Doge Giovanni II Cornaro* (oil on canvas)

65. G. B. Tiepolo, *Neptune Offering Gifts to Venice* (oil on canvas, 135 × 275 cm.)

66. G. B. Tiepolo, *St Mark* (fresco, 150 × 350 cm.)

The *Virgin Nicopeia*, or *Bearer of Victories*, is the Marian icon reportedly painted by St Luke and brought to Venice from Constantinople in 1204, when it was housed in St Mark's sacristy. A frame and sumptuous altar were created for it in the Basilica's left transept in 1618.[24] Although the icon had been shown publicly before that date, it was only after the construction of its new and lavish setting that the painting became, for all practical purposes, a symbol of all that was Venice. This was true to such an extent that in 1797, when the Republic collapsed, the image was held up for public adoration for fifteen days. The *Nicopeia* had assumed its status as an icon of State during the patriarchy of Giovanni Tiepolo, who ruled from 1619 to 1631.[25] In 1618, the year of the *Nicopeia*'s new altar and just shortly before Tiepolo was elected, he published his *Trattato dell'immagine della gloriosa Vergine dipinta da San Luca*, in which he stressed the *Nicopeia*'s ties to Venice.

Was it not right, Patriarch Tiepolo asked, that the *Nicopeia*, Mary's favourite image, should come to Venice, Mary's favoured city; and was it not right, too, that she should reside in 'our Ducal Church'?[26] Emphasizing Venice's 'virginity', the Patriarch reminded his readers that the city was born, had grown, and had endured as a Christian settlement. Moreover, he introduced a line of argument about the *Nicopeia* which was to become the most politically resounding support for its public acclaim during the seventeenth and eighteenth centuries:

. . . this heavenly treasure was obtained by our Ancestors by divine plan, so that at the time that the Image passed from the Greek to the Latin camp, there passed from them to us the protection and support of the great Mother of God. Thus, Venice has had the promise of the Virgin Mary's intercession with everything that can come from divine *misericordia*, and omnipotence. For Venice is no less great than the city of Byzantium rebuilt by Constantine; she [Venice] has not just been built but consecrated in honor of the Virgin, in honor of the Mother of God, because the Lord wished Venice to begin on the very same day in which Mary began to be the Mother of the Son of God.[27]

In other words, Patriarch Tiepolo saw the *Nicopeia* as tangible proof that Venice was heir to Imperial Constantinople and its Byzantine traditions.[28]

Later publications continued to glorify the *Nicopeia*. In 1645, Carlo Querini conjured up a remarkable scene of the holy image trying to leave Constantinople in 1204 in order

di Venezia e l'Immacolata', *Mater Dei: Rivista mariana*, 5 (1934), 263.

[24] Musolino, 'Culto mariano', pp. 245–6.

[25] A. Niero, *I patriarchi di Venezia* (Venice, 1961), 117–20. See also R. Goffen, 'Icon and Vision: Giovanni Bellini's Half-Length Madonnas', *Art Bulletin*, 58 (1975), 508–9, where the *Nicopeia*'s fifteenth-century importance is discussed.

[26] Giovanni Tiepolo, *Trattato dell'immagine della gloriosa Vergine dipinta da San Luca* (Venice, 1618), 29. Don Niero has confirmed to me that it was because of Patriarch Tiepolo that iconic devotion intensified in Venice.

[27] Ibid., p. 20: 'Tali sono le testificationi del conquisto di questo celeste Thesoro, ottenuto dagli Avi nostri per divina dispositione, acciò come all'hora col passare di quell'Imagine dal campo Greco al campo Latino, ne trapassò da essi à noi la protettione, & appoggio della gran Madre di Dio, così havesse d'indi Vinegia a promettersi con l'intercessioni di M. V. tutto ciò, che può venire dalla divina misericordia, & omnipotenza, sendo stata ella non meno, che la città di Bisantio da Costantino riedificata, in honore della Vergine non pure edificata, ma consecrata in honore di essa Madre di Dio, havendo voluto il Signore, che ricevesse il suo principio nel istesso giorno, nel quale incominciò Maria ad esser Madre del figliuolo di Dio.'

[28] Mary had been Byzantium's special protectress: see N. H. Baynes, 'The Supernatural Defenders of Constantinople', *Analecta Bollandiana*, 67 (1949), 165 ff.; and D. J. Geanakoplos, *Byzantine East and Latin West: Two Worlds of Christendom in the Middle Ages and Renaissance* (Oxford, 1966), 45.

III. G. B. Tiepolo, *Rebecca at the Well* (oil on canvas, 28 × 38.7 cm.).

IV. G. B. Tiepolo, Oil-sketch for the *Virgin of the Carmine and Christ-child Appearing to Simon Stock*
(oil on canvas, 65 × 41 cm.)

V. G. B. Tiepolo, *Glory of S. Luigi Gonzaga* (oil on canvas, 58 × 44.7 cm.)

VII. G. B. Tiepolo, Oil-sketch for the destroyed altar-piece in S. Salvador of *SS Augustine, John the Evangelist, Magno, and Louis of France* (oil on canvas, 58.1 × 33 cm.)

VI. G. B. Tiepolo, Oil-sketch for the *Virgin in Glory with Apostles and Saints* (oil on canvas, 47 × 29 cm.)

to travel west. Using zodiacal terminology, Querini explained why the icon chose Venice rather than any other Latin city: 'It is reasonable to understand that the Virgin, who is called the Sun, would be brought to live in the House of the Lion [Venice], for there She is inclined [in such a position] to shine her burning rays which bear her Grace and her favours.'[29] Several years later, at the end of the seventeenth century, the State issued a decree praising the *Nicopeia* as the reason for Mary's intercession in the wars against the Turks.[30]

The *Nicopeia* was still lovingly and publicly adored in the mid-eighteenth century, as Zanetti's remarks, referred to above, clearly demonstrate; likewise Flaminio Corner's encomium of 1761 carrying the icon's complete history.[31] Corner describes the *Nicopeia*'s journey from its first home in Ephesus to its years under Byzantine possession, and, finally, to its arrival in S. Marco, from whence—Corner asserts—the icon protects the Venetian Republic. Recounting stories of how the Byzantines achieved their early victories through ownership of the icon, Corner explains that it eventually became 'an insuperable companion in battles, with the Greek name "Nicopeja", which means vanquisher'.[32] When the Byzantines foolishly fought the Latins in 1204, Corner writes, the *Nicopeia* had no choice but to defect to the rightful camp, denying victory to the Greeks and seeking the protection of Doge Enrico Dandolo, General of the Venetian Forces. Sent on to Venice, the image wrought many miracles, both private and public.

Venice's traditional Marian veneration was intensified through the public outpouring of affection for the *Nicopeia*, and the cult of the Virgin was raised to a greater spiritual pinnacle than ever before. By the mid-settecento, St Mark was no longer a viable metaphor for Venetian patriotism: Mary was the city's sole, visible, saintly patron, and her person was transformed into what the *Nicopeia* had been in ancient Byzantium, the State's palladium.[33]

The *Institution of the Rosary* in S. Maria del Rosario was the first of Tiepolo's great ceilings to exalt the Virgin Mary and her cult. Completed in 1739, the fresco is part of an extensive ecclesiastical ensemble decorating Venice's most elegant eighteenth-century church (Pls. 67–70, 72–4). The Gesuati was built and dedicated in the 1720s, approximately a decade before Tiepolo worked there, but the Dominicans had lived on the Zattere since 1669, when the Reformed Congregation of the Blessed Jacopo Salomonio bought the Convent and Church of S. Maria della Visitazione. This sixteenth-century building complex had formerly belonged to the Order of the Gesuati, founded in the fourteenth century in Siena by Giovanni Colombini but suppressed in 1668 by Pope Clement IX.[34]

---

[29] C. Querini, *Relatione dell'imagine Nicopeia* (Venice, 1645), 27–8: 'Ben anco fù raggionevole, che la Vergine, che viene chiamata Sole, fosse condotta ad habitare nella stanza del Leone già, ch'ella è inclinata à diffondere sempre più cocenti i raggi delle sue gratie e de suoi favori.'

[30] Picchini, 'La repubblica', pp. 264–5.

[31] F. Corner, *Notizie storiche delle apparizioni, e delle immagini più celebri di Maria Vergine Santissima nella città, e dominio di Venezia* (Venice, 1761), 2–9.

[32] Ibid., pp. 2–3: 'Compagna insuperabile nelle battaglie, e

con Greco vocabolo 'Nicopeja', che significa vincitrice.'

[33] The *Nicopeia* appears to have enjoyed the same distinction in Venice as the Virgin's robe held in Constantinople: for the Byzantine Palladium, see Baynes, 'The Supernatural Defenders', p. 174. For other Eastern icons in Venice, see U. Fugagnollo, *Bisanzio e l'Oriente a Venezia* (Trieste, 1974), 107ff.

[34] For the history of Colombini's Order, see A. Bosisio, *La chiesa di S. Maria del Rosario o dei Gesuati* (Venice, 1943), 7–14; the reader shoud be warned that Bosisio is incorrect on a number of points later in the book concerning the feast of the Rosary and its history.

The Dominicans bought S. Maria della Visitazione at a public auction, the proceeds of which went to the State to finance the wars against the Turks. After about twenty years, the Reformed Congregation allowed several laymen to erect a *suffragio* in the church to honour the Virgin of the Rosary; this altar was only one of many in Venice to bear such a consecration.[35]

At the beginning of the eighteenth century, the Dominicans on the Zattere decided to replace the old S. Maria della Visitazione with a new building, and they approached the architect Andrea Musalo, but he died before any work was begun. The project then fell to Giorgio Massari, who completed his plans and model for the church by the early 1720s. The first stone was laid in 1726, but the new church's dedication had already been decided upon two years earlier: Coronelli noted that the establishment of the 'PP. Dom. Osservanti is now called SS. Rosario'.[36] Coronelli also mentioned a little-known confraternity that met at the church: 'It is commonly called the hour of the *Agonizzanti*, and it consists of a union of devout persons who are obliged to recite an entire Rosary, on certain days and at pre-determined hours, and to apportion them in such a way that they continue day and night . . .'[37] During the years in which this local confraternity gathered, two events of larger scope occurred that almost obliged the Reformed Congregation to dedicate their new church, then under construction, to the Virgin of the Rosary: first, Clement XI elevated the feast of the Rosary to universality within the Church; and, secondly, a Dominican friar, Vincenzo Maria Orsini, who had spent his novitiate in Venice, was elected to the Throne of St Peter.

The Rosary, central to Dominican spirituality, first received public attention in the late fifteenth century when a confraternity was formed in its honour in Cologne.[38] The cult's popularity grew enormously, particularly after 1571 when Pope Pius V, instituting the feast of the *Commemoratio B. Mariae V. de Victoria*, named the Rosary and its litany of prayers as the reason for the Christian victory over the heathen Turks at Lepanto.[39] His successor, Gregory XIII, subsequently established the actual feast of the Rosary on 7 October, the anniversary of the Battle of Lepanto. The feast was mainly celebrated by Dominicans, because legend held that the devotion had been created by the Virgin Mary

[35] For the numerous *scuole* dedicated to the *Madonna del Rosario*, cf. S. Tramontin, 'Il culto dei santi nelle confraternite', in *Santità a Venezia*, pp. 37–79.

[36] For the church's beginnings and construction, see ASV, 'Mani Morte, Convento Dei PP. Domenicani ai Gesuati', b. 59; A. Massari, *Giorgio Massari* (Vicenza, 1971), 42 ff.; and A. Niero, *Tre artisti per un tempio: S. Maria del Rosario—Gesuati, Venezia* (Padua, 1979), *passim*.

[37] V. Coronelli, *Guida de' forestieri: . . . per la città di Venezia* (Venice, 1724), 367: 've' un'altra specie di confraternità, detta volgarmente l'ora degli'Agonizzanti, la quale consiste nell'unione di persone divote, che l'obbligano di recitare un Rosario intero, in giorni ed in ore determinate, distribuite di tal maniera, che continuamente giorno, e notte . . .'.

[38] For some of the Rosary's history, see Warner, *Alone of All Her Sex*, pp. 305–6, and S. Orlandi, OP, *Libro del Rosario della gloriosa Vergine Maria* (Rome, 1965), 39. For general literature on the subject, see G. G. Meersseman, OP, 'Le origini della Confraternita del Rosario e della sua iconografia in Italia', *Memorie della Accademia Patavina di SS. LL. AA: Classe di Scienze*

Morali, Lettere ed Arti, 76 (1963–4), 223–328; A. Niero, 'La Mariegola della più antica scuola del Rosario di Venezia', *Rivista di storia della Chiesa in Italia*, 15 (1961), 324 ff.; id., 'Ancora sull'origine del Rosario', *Rivista di storia della Chiesa in Italia*, 28 (1974), 465–78; and P. L. Rambaldi, *La chiesa dei SS Gio. e Paolo e la cappella del Rosario in Venezia* (Venice, 1913). See also W. A. Hinnenbusch, OP, *Dominican Spirituality* (Thomist Press, 1965), 13: 'the Rosary in a sense epitomizes Dominican spirituality . . . The Rosary is a way of proclaiming the truths of faith expressed in the form of praise.'

[39] G. Löw, 'Festa del Rosario', *Enciclopedia italiana*, x (Rome, 1953), cols. 1351–4. Pius V, a Dominican devoted to the Rosary, had in part organized the Holy League that fought against the Turks at Lepanto: see H. Jedin, 'Pio V', *Enciclopedia italiana*, ix (Rome, 1952), cols. 1498–1500. For the history of the feast, see P. Bianchi dei Predicatori, 'Il Rosario e i Papi', *Mater Dei: Rivista mariana*, 5 (1934), 203–6; L. Berra, 'San Pio e la lega contro il Turco', in *Vita e cultura a Mondovì nell'età del Vescovo Michele Ghislieri (S. Pio V)* (Turin, 1967).

when she handed a string of wooden beads to St Dominic, the Order's founder, as an *aide-mémoire*. The association between the Dominicans and the Rosary deepened to such an extent that by 1582 they were given the secondary name of 'Confratelli del Rosario'. In the 1670s, Queen Maria of Spain obtained the feast's extension to all countries under the Spanish Crown. Then, on 3 October 1714, Pope Clement XI elevated the feast of the Rosary to the Universal Church. He had been urged to do so by Charles VI, Emperor of Austria, as a sign of thanksgiving for three Christian victories over the Turks—at Vienna in 1683, and at Pietrovaradino and Corfu in 1716—in which Austrian forces and money had played a substantial part. Clement's acquiescence to the Emperor's request followed the 1712 canonization of Pius V, who had been the first to recognize the Rosary's efficacy on earth.[40]

In 1724, Massari handed over his finished drawings for the new Dominican church on the Zattere. And, in that same year, Vincenzo Maria Orsini, a Dominican trained at S. Domenico di Castello in Venice, was elected to the papacy as Benedict XIII. One of Benedict's first acts was to call on the Sacred Congregation of Rites to refine and elaborate upon the feast of the Rosary. In 1726, Benedict published the notice that the Virgin Mary 'had been given the task to exterminate all heresy . . . to which end the Rosary was the highest remedy to error and vice'.[41] And the Dominicans laid the first stone of their new church, including in the foundations a medal designed by Massari which showed on one side the arms of Benedict XIII, and on the other the building's dedication to the *Vergine del Rosario*. In sum, the building's consecration was a response to the contemporaneity of two important Dominican events: Clement XI's promotion of the feast of the Rosary to the Universal Church; and Benedict XIII's ascension to papal power.

The Gesuati is a hall church, its nave flanked on both sides by three chapels, whose giant archways rise up to the height of the nave entablature (Pl. 67). A window is opened above each archway, and between them there are pairs of attached columns supporting a vaulting system that springs from above the cornice. Massari's design for the building was based on local tradition, above all on Andrea Palladio's Redentore, which stands across from it and slightly to the east on the Giudecca Island.[42] The Palladian type did not present the fresco painter with architectural forms that were easy to handle. For example, Tiepolo would have found that S. Maria del Rosario's nave vault contained areas that were both irregular in shape and varied in width. And the centre oblong, the one continuous expanse that the painter had at his disposal, did not offer a pictorial field of elegant proportions. The question of light, too, was one that Tiepolo must have had occasion to ponder. The Gesuati towers over its neighbouring buildings, so that its nave's six windows—three facing directly east and three west—transmit the Giudecca Canal's intense, very bright atmosphere. Brilliant light rather than a soft, diffused glow spreads across the church ceiling both in the early morning and in the late afternoon. In sum, Massari's architecture and the site's idiosyncratic lighting produced a set of conditions

---

[40] For the feast and Clement XI, cf. L. Pastor, *History of the Popes*, xxxiii (London, 1949), 342–3.

[41] Löw, 'Festa del Rosario', p. 1352; and Bianchi dei Predicatori, 'Il Rosario e i Papi', p. 205.

[42] In the Redentore, Palladio used thermal windows, whereas there are only single openings in the Gesuati. It must be added that the Gesuati's vaulting, unlike that of the Redentore, is structurally fake. The Fava and the Gesuiti were also important sources for Massari: see C. D. Lewis, *The Late Baroque Churches of Venice* (New York and London, 1979), 86ff.

67. S. Maria del Rosario, interior

68. Above: G. B. Tiepolo,
Vision of Pius V (fresco)

69. G. B. Tiepolo, *David
Playing the Harp* and *Four
Prophets* (fresco, diam.
260 cm.)

that would have severely hampered most artists. Yet, the church's frescos seem to respond perfectly to Massari's building.

Giambattista worked in the Gesuati just after the building's fabric was completed, executing forty paintings there in the twelve-month period beginning September 1738.[43] In the nave, the largest work is the *Institution of the Rosary* (Pl. 74); the scene below it is the *Glory of St Dominic* (Pl. 72), and the one above envisions the *Virgin Appearing to St Dominic and the Glory of the Dominican Order* (Pl. 73). Sixteen grisailles surround these three large fields, fifteen of which portray the mysteries of the Rosary. The sixteenth, over the principal doorway, shows cherubs carrying the Rosary, roses, and symbols of Dominic. Below, directly over the door, is a grisaille roundel in which Pope Pius V (1566–72) kneels before an altar; an angel overhead points to a scene of naval warfare in the far distance that alludes to the Battle of Lepanto (Pl. 68).[44] Also in the nave are sixteen smaller frescos, two around each window, which show eucharistic, papal, Dominican, and rosarian symbols.[45]

Over the Gesuati's high altar, Tiepolo painted the four symbols of the Evangelists in grisaille (Pl. 69); over the central bay of the choir, he frescoed a roundel of *David Playing the Harp*; and at the vault's corners are the four prophets Isaiah, Daniel, Jeremiah, and Ezekiel (Pl. 69). There is a monochrome roundel of the *Holy Trinity* on the church's choir-wall. In all, Tiepolo's frescoed complex is a magnificent pictorial ensemble, linking Venetian patriotism with Judeo-Christian narrative, Catholic devotions, Roman traditions, and Dominican spirituality.

Tiepolo's organization of the nave ceiling, the most complex part of the cycle, is like other painted ceilings in Venice and yet fundamentally different from all of them. Its similarity consists in its subdivision into separate geometric components, an organizational solution that had dominated the decoration of Venetian ceilings since the fifteenth century.[46] One particularly useful and apt Renaissance prototype for Tiepolo must have been the ceiling of the Chapel of the Rosary in SS Giovanni e Paolo, which was begun in 1575 and which contained three main scenes of events connected with the Rosary.[47] But the ties linking the Gesuati and Rosary ceilings were, as I shall discuss below, more specifically iconographic in kind rather than compositional. In the complication of its elegant pattern, the Gesuati ceiling follows the more elaborate ceilings of the Ducal Palace. Tiepolo's design of sixteen small fields of varying shape to surround the three principal scenes lined up to emphasize a longitudinal axis, brings to mind, I suggest, Antonio da Ponte's framing of Veronese's paintings in the ceiling of the Sala del Collegio

---

[43] Cf. Niero, *Tre artisti*, pp. 28ff. The documents themselves specify that Tiepolo received his first payment in Feb. 1738, 'a conto delle piture a Fresco da farsi nel soffito della Chiesa'; this is repeated in June. In Sept. he is paid 'a conto delle Pitture che va facendo'; payments continue in Nov., then in Jan., May, and Aug. 1739. In Sept. of that year, he is paid 'per resto e saldo di tutte le pitture a Fresco del soffitto della Chiesa': cf. ASV, 'Mani Morte, Convento Dei PP. Domenicani ai Gesuati, b. 59: Esito della fabbrica della nuova chiesa dal anno MDCCXXV Sino MDCCXLII.'

[44] The scene was first identified by Don Niero in his guide to

the church: *Tre artisti*, p. 116.

[45] There are stars, candles, dogs, and lilies, all references to Dominic, as well as roses, pastoral hats, tiaras, crosiers, and books.

[46] Cf. J. Schulz, 'The Revival of Antique Vault Decoration', in *The Renaissance and Mannerism*. (*Studies in Western Art: Acts of the Twentieth International Congress of the History of Art*, Princeton, 1963), 90ff.; and id., *Venetian Painted Ceilings of the Renaissance* (Berkeley, 1968), *passim*.

[47] See Rambaldi, *La chiesa dei SS Gio. e Paolo*; R. Pallucchini and Rossi, *Tintoretto*, i. 262; and Schulz, *Venetian Painted Ceilings*, pp. 130–1, no. 72.

(Fig. 3).[48] In particular, Tiepolo created four grisailles along the sides of the Gesuati vault whose lobes extend towards the ceiling's centre in the same way that Da Ponte placed four rectangles that protruded from the ceiling's sides into the middle. There are also similarities in the two ceilings' four corners. But in rethinking Da Ponte's work to suit S. Maria del Rosario's large and spacious setting, Tiepolo had to adapt the design to fit a vault. Some of the compartments had to conform to a bowing surface, and, as a result, many of the forms expand, swelling as it were to meet the ceiling's curvature.

Tiepolo's departure from the traditional Venetian ceiling can be seen in his painting medium, in the shift from oil to fresco. Used infrequently in Venice during the seventeenth century, the fresco technique had been mostly ignored by native painters who, when faced with decorative commissions, usually preferred to work in oil on canvas: witness Fumiani's ceiling for S. Pantaleon, Sebastiano Ricci's for S. Marziale and the Seminario Patriarcale, and Piazzetta's for the Chapel of St Dominic in SS Giovanni e Paolo, to name only a few.[49] Tiepolo, in contrast, had begun to paint in fresco early in his career, and his success in the medium was unique at the time. One wonders whether, apart from considerations of speed, Tiepolo's decision to work in that rarely practised technique was influenced by its noble connotations in Venice, in particular with the murals of Giorgione and Titian. Was fresco another artistic challenge he imposed upon himself in order to meet the heroic pictorial legacy left by the cinquecento?

Tiepolo's accomplishments on the Gesuati nave ceiling can be readily appreciated if the work is compared with another Venetian ceiling, that in S. Maria Assunta, the Jesuit church called the Gesuiti. A comparison of the two frescos is apposite because, apart from their contemporaneity, the Gesuati and the Gesuiti vault systems are also almost identical in size, shape, and structure (Pls. 70, 71).[50] The final results, however, could not be more different. At the Gesuiti, lavish stucco-work covers every possible surface.[51] Only two fields in the centre of the ceiling were left free for narrative, and in these Fontebasso depicted *Abraham and the Three Angels* and *Elijah Carried into Heaven*, two Old Testament subjects. These paintings are not intended to serve as metaphors for the Venetian State and its people, however; indeed, given the tense historical relations between the Jesuits and the local government, the possibility that this Order would even consider extolling the Serenissima seems unlikely. In fact, the two paintings are representations of fundamental Catholic belief in the Trinity and the Ascension of Christ into heaven.[52] In other words,

---

[48] Other examples can be found in the Sala dei Pregadi and the Sala del Maggior Consiglio as well as in the Church of S. Sebastiano. Tintoretto's second-storey ceiling at the Scuola di S. Rocco, although containing more painted fields than Tiepolo's at the Gesuati, follows the same arrangement. See Schulz, *Venetian Painted Ceilings*, pp. 104–7, no. 41.

[49] Non-Venetians like the Roman Girolamo Pellegrini and the Frenchman Louis Dorigny were successful in fresco, however, and Ricci had used it outside Venice.

[50] The Gesuiti was built by Domenico Rossi between 1715 and 1729: cf. Lewis, *Churches of Venice*, p. 81. According to Lewis, p. 255, Fontebasso's frescos in the Gesuiti can be dated to *c.*1745.

[51] Abbondio Stazio was the stuccoist, the best in Venice at the time, and his designs for the Gesuiti include a wealth of scrolls, garlands, mouldings, volutes, etc., all of them painted in a variety of colours. For Stazio, see B. Aikema, 'Patronage in Late Baroque Venice: The Zenobia', *Mededelingen van het Nederlands Instituut te Rome*, 41 (1979), 213ff.; G. Mariacher, 'L'arte dello stucco a Venezia nel '700: Il Palazzo Sagredo a Santa Sofia', *Il giornale economico*, 4 (1961), 399–408; and id., 'Stuccatori ticinesi a Venezia tra la fine del '600 e la metà del '700', *Arte e artisti dei laghi lombardi*, 2 (1964), 79–91. Over the Gesuiti's crossing is the *Triumph of the Name of Jesus*, and a *Concert of Angels* and the *Holy Trinity* appear over the high altar area; they were all executed by Dorigny.

[52] The banners in the two scenes explain them: that ornamenting *Abraham and the Three Angels* reads 'Tres vidit et unam adoravit' and refers to the Trinity; whereas the one around *Elijah Carried into Heaven* has 'Sanctus, Sanctus' written on it, reminding us of Elijah's ascent to heaven in a fiery chariot.

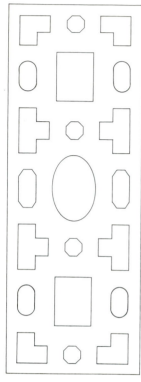

FIG. 3. Diagram of the ceiling of the Sala del Collegio, Ducal Palace, Venice

70. G. B. Tiepolo, *Ceiling of S. Maria del Rosario* (fresco)

71. F. Fontebasso, Ceiling of S. Maria Assunta (fresco)

the Gesuiti ceiling is a plain-speaking exposition of Christian salvation enclosed within an ornate framework.

The Gesuati ceiling contrasts sharply with this. Its ornamentation is simple; plain mouldings define the vaults, marking the springing from the cornice up to the rectangular framework in the ceiling's centre, which is elegantly curved to give shape to the three frescos exalting the Virgin and St Dominic. Through these mouldings, the apparent structure of the vault and the decorative shapes of the central scenes are brought into agreeable harmony. Within the central rectangular frame, each of the pictorial fields is emphasized by its own strongly three-dimensional moulding; those encircling the grisailles, however, are more delicate. The purpose of these mouldings is not to embellish but to assert the ceiling's structure and to render the individual scenes legible and comprehensible. The scroll-work is slightly more ornate than the mouldings, but it is used sparingly. Elegant forms around the medallions fasten them like lockets on to the vault surface; intertwined within the central oblong are ribbons and flowers, roses recalling the Rosary and pairs of lilies symbolizing St Dominic's chastity. Painted a warm beige several tones deeper than the neutral colour of the vault itself, the stucco-work complements the grisailles in value.

Tiepolo's use of monochrome in the Gesuati's subsidiary scenes was a brilliant decorative idea which can be traced back to such Roman prototypes as Michelangelo's ceiling in the Sistine Chapel. The grisailles not only help to achieve pictorial conformity across the nave vault and throughout the fresco cycle, but they also modulate beautifully the bright light from the exterior. The largest number of grisailles represent the fifteen mysteries of the Rosary; they were a clever answer on Tiepolo's part to the problems imposed on him by the Gesuati vault and its irregular shapes. Perhaps they were also meant to facilitate prayer; it will be remembered that the *Agonizzanti* recited the Rosary at the Gesuati throughout the day and night.[53] The solution was suggested by the Rosary's own pictorial tradition, by a work such as Lorenzo Lotto's Cingoli altar-piece.[54] Tiepolo, like Lotto, offers the mysteries of the Rosary while at the same time depicting its gift to the world.

Over the church's inner doorway, another monochrome, *Pope Pius V's Vision of the Battle of Lepanto*, recounts historical truths concerning the Rosary and its earthly efficacy. The tondo, flanked by papal keys, recalls the Christian destruction of the Turkish fleet in 1571, and reminds viewers of Pius's encyclical recognizing the benefits of the Dominican Rosary.[55] The scene's relevance to a Venetian church is self-evident; the Serenissima's ships formed the largest segment of the victorious fleet, and the Senate itself acknowledged Mary's responsibility for the Christian triumph. Tiepolo's positioning of the grisaille cleverly turned churchgoers towards the Giudecca Canal; in other words, to the south-

---

[53] There are five joyous, sorrowful, and glorious mysteries. They are the Annunciation, Visitation, Nativity, Presentation in the Temple, and Christ among the Doctors; the Agony in the Garden, the Flagellation, the Crowning with Thorns, the Way to Calvary, and the Crucifixion; and the Resurrection, the Ascension, Pentecost, the Assumption, and the Coronation of the Virgin. Hinnenbusch, *Dominican Spirituality*, p. 13, wrote: 'Focusing attention on the principal mysteries of our Lord's life, the Rosary in a sense epitomizes Dominican spirituality.'

[54] Cf. B. Aikema, 'La pala di Cingoli', in P. Zampetti and V. Sgarbi (eds.), *Lorenzo Lotto (Atti del Convegno Internazionale di Studi per il V Centenario della Nascita)* (Treviso, 1981), 443–56. For works in the Marches that follow Lotto's example, see P. Dal Poggetto and P. Zampetti, *Lorenzo Lotto nelle Marche: Il suo tempo, il suo influsso* (exh. cat., the Gesù and S. Francesco alle Scale, Ancona, 1981 (Florence)), nos. 92, 118, 143, 148, 157, 165.

[55] See Bianchi dei Predicatori, 'Il Rosario e i Papi', p. 204.

west and thence to Lepanto, helping them to reflect upon the State's geographical security and the Rosary's historic role in achieving this.

Monochromatic, too, are the apocalyptic symbols of the four Evangelists over the high altar, and the prophets Ezekiel, Isaiah, Jeremiah, and Daniel painted on the vault over the choir. Their presence has never been explained, and none of them carries specific verses from his Book, but it would seem likely that they refer to the Virgin, the patroness of the Gesuati. They surround *King David Playing the Harp*, a visual reference to the 150 psalms that are an Old Testament analogue for the numeric repetition of the angelic salutation contained in the Marian Rosary.[56] Also in the choir, and again in monochrome, is the *Trinity and the Crucified Christ*, which is flanked by the eucharistic symbols of grapes and wheat, imagery for the Dominican brothers to concentrate upon while reciting Mary's Rosary. By using tempered decorative shapes and a narrow range of colours throughout the church, Tiepolo achieved a narrative clarity which, in contrast to the earlier tradition of Baroque ceiling-painting and to the later Gesuiti vault, appears almost neo-classical in style.[57] The nave's warm beige-coloured plaster and its pearl-toned grisailles further the visual projection of the three central scenes which, with their bright ultramarine blue, cadmium red, and Prussian green, glorify the Dominicans and their devotion to Mary and her Rosary.

Upon entering the church, the viewer sees the *Glory of St Dominic* directly overhead, with the *Virgin Appearing to St Dominic* further down on the nave ceiling, in front of the altar area. These two secondary frescos extend the narrative continuity of the ceiling's central painting, the *Institution of the Rosary*, which is the thematic linchpin of the cycle. Tiepolo's formulation of this subject, the largest in the history of Italian art, rests upon two iconographic traditions: the *Rosenkranzbild*; and the dramatization of the Rosary's efficacy on earth. Of the two, the former was more important for Tiepolo.

The *Rosenkranzbild* had developed in the late fifteenth and early sixteenth centuries as a pictorial expression of confraternal dedication to the Rosary. Dürer's 1506 altar-piece, now in the National Gallery in Prague but executed for S. Bartolomeo in Venice and its resident community of Germans, is one of the earliest painted *Rosenkranzbilder*. In its centre, Mary is seated before a cloth of majesty as two angels crown her Queen of Heaven; laymen and clergy led by the Emperor and Pontiff receive garlands of roses from the Virgin and Christ-child. Dürer's painting, like all early *Rosenkranzbilder*, presents 'the idea of a universal brotherhood of Christianity' under the leadership of Mary.[58] But although Venetian in origin, it was probably unknown to Tiepolo, for it had left the city *c*.1600.

[56] The prophets' relevance to Marian devotion may be found in references such as God's words to Ezekiel 44:2: 'This gate shall be shut, it shall not be opened, and no man shall enter in by it, therefore it shall be shut'; or to Isaiah 29:12, where there is mention of a book that is 'sealed and could not be read.' And cf. Orlandi, *Libro del Rosario*, p. 72: 'La devozione del Rosario ha il suo lontano fondamento nel Salterio davidico ... Il Salterio di David, formato di 150 Salmi, per il suo contenuto profetico, adombra la figura di Cristo.' For the importance of choral chant to the Dominicans, see Padre Pietro Lippini, OP, *La spiritualità domenicana* (Florence, 1953), 42–3.

[57] One need only compare the Gesuati ceiling with Pozzo's in Sant'Ignazio, Rome, or with Fumiani's in San Pantaleon, Venice, to realize how much Tiepolo has eased the viewer's task; Baroque ceilings ordinarily require immense visual acumen and strong powers of mental concentration.

[58] Some of these *Rosenkranzbilder* were only simple woodcuts. For Dürer's painting, see especially E. Panofsky, *The Life and Art of Albrecht Dürer* (Princeton, 1955), 107 ff.; regarding the painting and Venice, see *Giorgione a Venezia* (exh. cat., Gallerie dell'Accademia, Venice, 1978 (Milan)), 83–91, fig. 70. For a listing of nearly 200 *Rosenkranzbilder*, see A. Pigler, *Barockthemen*, i (Budapest, 1956), 512–18. The Sculpturengalerie, Berlin-Dahlem, possesses a *Rosenkranzpende* (inv. no. 1382) referring to the Battle of Lepanto and showing St Dominic, Pius V, Philip II, and the Venetian Doge.

Giambattista was familiar, though, with other Rosary imagery, such as the series of paintings within the coffered ceiling of the Chapel of the Rosary in SS Giovanni e Paolo. Executed at the end of the sixteenth century, shortly after Gregory XIII's creation of the feast of the Rosary, the canvases existed *in situ* until their destruction by fire in 1867. The cycle consisted of three principal works: Tintoretto's *Virgin Giving the Rosary to St Dominic, St Catherine of Siena, Justice, and Christendom*; Palma Giovane's *St Dominic Receiving Indulgences for the Rosary from the Pope*; and Leonardo Corona's *St Dominic Preaching the Rosary before the Papal Court, the Emperor, and the Doge*.[59] These works provided Tiepolo with an important precedent of celebrating the Rosary within a painted ceiling ensemble.

One work that especially influenced Tiepolo in his formulation of the *Institution of the Rosary* was the large *Madonna del Rosario* (Pl. 77), painted by Veronese and his studio for a Rosary confraternity at S. Pietro Martire.[60] Contemporaneous with the SS Giovanni e Paolo ceiling, it furnished Tiepolo with a motif rare in the *Rosenkranz* tradition: it is St Dominic, not the Virgin and Christ-child, who offers the Rosary to the gathered officials—Emperor, Pope, Doge—and their Court. Veronese thereby emphasized the Dominican role in the Rosary's diffusion throughout the Catholic world.[61] Tiepolo reiterated the idea on the Gesuati ceiling, positioning it in the centre as its most dramatic action. Opposite Dominic's arm, Tiepolo painted one covered with a gold mantle: it is the Doge's, seen directly below the Deity and above the halberd representative of military force. The ducal hand is, in effect, a metaphor for the arm of the State, for the Serenissima's responsibility to safeguard its citizens from corruption. Indeed, sin itself appears in the group of figures hurtling forth from the bottom of the painting. The expulsion of evil from the world was often depicted in Catholic art by showing such figures (and/or serpents) being crushed by the Blessed Virgin and the Saviour. Such a meaning is conveyed here through the painting's principal vertical axis that links the cascading figures with both Mary and the Christ-child.[62] Tiepolo's positioning of the tumbling figures directly below the halberdier and his powerfully muscled companion and in line with the saint and the Rosary, also calls to mind the Cathar heresy against which Dominic and his followers struggled in the first years of the thirteenth century. Their military campaign

[59] Cf. Schulz, *Venetian Painted Ceilings*, no. 72. Tintoretto's work was in the ceiling's centre; the other two, octagonal in format, were on either side of Tintoretto's. There were smaller canvases as well with the four evangelists, four Dominican saints, and angels with flowers. In the chancel's ceiling was Palma's *Coronation of the Virgin*.

[60] Cf. T. Pignatti, *Veronese* (Venice, 1976), i, no. A214; and *Venezia e la difesa del Levante; Da Lepanto a Candia 1570–1670* (exh. cat., Ducal Palace, Venice, 1986), no. 16.

[61] Caravaggio's *Madonna del Rosario* (Vienna, Kunsthistorisches Museum), *c*.1606, repeats this. W. Friedländer incorrectly noted that Caravaggio's Dominic was unique in Rosary imagery; cf. his *Caravaggio Studies* (New York, 1969), 198–202, no. 29; cf. also A. Ottino della Chiesa, *L'opera completa del Caravaggio* (Milan, 1968), no. 72; and H. Hibbard, *Caravaggio* (New York, 1983), no. 118. Tiepolo repeated Caravaggio's device of calling our attention to the saint with a bare arm and shoulder that reach up to the Rosary. Cavaliere d'Arpino also painted a Rosary altar-piece, datable to 1601, in which a group of lay people gather to supplicate a crown of roses from the Virgin and Child and St

Dominic: cf. H. Röttgen, *Il Cavalier d'Arpino* (exh. cat., Palazzo Venezia, Rome, 1973), no. 28. In still later representations of the subject, such as Guercino's painting of the mid-1630s for S. Domenico in Turin, lay congregations become less and less important: cf. D. Mahon, *Il Guercino* (exh. cat., Palazzo dell'Archiginnasio, Bologna, 1968), no. 68.

[62] Like all such illusorily cascading monsters, these are meant to be understood not as falling into the church where the faithful worship but into hell itself; the type can be found in Gaulli's Gesù ceiling in Rome and in Tiepolo's own stair-well ceiling in the Arcivescovado in Udine. A more specific reference to the Virgin stamping out evil in Counter-Reformatory Italian art is Caravaggio's *Madonna del Serpe*, now in the Borghese Gallery, Rome. Tiepolo's demons may also symbolize specific vices, such as usury: cf. Niero, *Tre artisti*, p. 130. Usury was a topic of debate at the time (in 1744 Scipione Maffei published his *Dell'impiego del denaro*), especially how much interest could be allowed on loans and whether the same rates should be applied to both the poor and the rich.

72. G. B. Tiepolo, *Glory of St Dominic* (fresco, 350 × 450 cm.)

73. G. B. Tiepolo, *Virgin Appearing to St Dominic* (fresco, 350 × 450 cm.)

74. G. B. Tiepolo, *Institution of the Rosary* (fresco, 1400 × 450 cm.)

75. G. B. Tiepolo, Oil sketch for the *Institution of the Rosary* (oil on canvas, 98 × 49 cm.)

76 (*above right*). F. Lorenzi, Study for the *Institution of the Rosary* (pen and wash over black chalk on white paper, 950 × 445 mm.), after G. B. Tiepolo

77. P. Veronese (and assistants), *Madonna del Rosario* (oil on canvas, 175 × 318 cm.)

made them so famous that the Dominicans were nicknamed the 'domini cani', 'the hounds of the Lord', an association tellingly expressed on the Gesuati ceiling by the greyhound who watches the falling heretics from the left.

By intersecting the fresco's vertical axis, which promises salvation from evil, with a horizontal emphasis upon ducal and governmental responsibility, Tiepolo affirmed the Rosary's ability to rid the world of evil. He followed an iconographic tradition expounded by such works as Domenichino's *Madonna del Rosario*, in which the Virgin and Child appear on clouds surrounded by symbols of the fifteen joyous, sorrowful, and glorious mysteries; holding the Rosary, St Dominic is pointing to Christ and Mary.[63] The composition's lower half is filled with dramatic incidents that vouch for the efficacy of the Marian beads. The *Institution of the Rosary* reaffirms this belief, monumentalizing it across the Gesuati ceiling. For Tiepolo created a third axis that begins with the roundel over the entrance depicting Pius V and the Battle of Lepanto, passes through the altar area and the choir where the Rosary is chanted, and concludes on the choir-wall in the monochrome of the crucified Christ and the Trinity. Reading the entire cycle from beginning to end, above them and around them, the faithful in the Gesuati saw Dominican piety as a means of attaining Christian perfection—and as an instrument of the Venetian State.

Tiepolo's artistic sources for the Gesuati frescos are as local in origin as the entire cycle's theme. For instance, both the *Glory of St Dominic* and the *Virgin Appearing to St Dominic* owe a debt to paintings by Piazzetta. For his sharply foreshortened saint in the former painting, Tiepolo used Piazzetta's St Dominic from the ceiling-canvas in SS Giovanni e Paolo to create a similarly joyous and ecstatic figure with outstretched arms.[64] Tiepolo turned to Piazzetta's Fava altar-piece, the *Virgin and Child Appearing to St Philip Neri* (Pl. 98), for the *Virgin Appearing to St Dominic*, repeating the formula of Mary's triumphant descent on a cloud above an altar, her cloak opening before a golden glory with a saint humbling himself in adoration. Giambattista represented Christ's mother as the Madonna della Misericordia, who enfolds a group of blessed Dominicans within her mantle.[65]

There are two oil-sketches and a drawing that can be associated with the ceiling's central scene: the drawing, in the Art Institute of Chicago, is exactly the same as the oil-sketch in Milan (private collection) apart from one variation; the other sketch belonged to the Gemäldegalerie in Berlin but was destroyed at the end of World War Two (Pls. 76, 75).[66] Studying the two preparatory works together, one notes first of all a significant alteration in the architectural rostrum from which Dominic hands the Rosary to the world. In the Berlin oil-sketch, Dominic stands on a small step on top of a platform

[63] Cf. R. Spear, *Domenichino* (New Haven, 1982), i. no. 62, and ii. pl. 228.

[64] Three Tiepolo drawings in the Pierpont Morgan Library can be associated with Dominic, and they clearly demonstrate that Giambattista turned to Piazzetta's Dominic only after considerable thought: cf. J. Bean and F. Stampfle, *Drawings from New York Collections, III: The Eighteenth Century in Italy* (exh. cat., Metropolitan Museum of Art, New York, 1971), nos. 65, 66, and 67. Tiepolo's oil-sketch for the *Glory* is in the Philadelphia Museum of Art: cf. *Catalogue of Italian Paintings: John G. Johnson Collection* (Philadelphia, 1966), no. 286. A drawing by Tiepolo measuring 420 by 275 mm. and showing the *Madonna della Miseri-*cordia with St Dominic and other Dominican Saints* was sold at Parke-Bernet on 3 June 1980.

[65] This Marian image could be associated with various cults of the Virgin, of course; for example, Moretto's *Madonna del Carmelo* in the Accademia: cf. G. Gombosi, *Moretto Da Brescia* (Basel, 1943), fig. 54.

[66] G. Knox, *Tiepolo: A Bicentenary 1770–1970* (exh. cat., Fogg Art Museum, Harvard Univ., Cambridge, 1970), no. 29, attributes the drawing to Francesco Lorenzi; for the Milan sketch, cf. Morassi, *A Complete Catalogue*, fig. 89. M. Levey, *Giambattista Tiepolo* (New Haven and London, 1986), 85, has also compared the finished fresco with the two oil-sketches.

formed by a series of broad steps that rise from a ledge resting on consoles. Behind and to the right of Dominic there is an elevation of columns supporting a classical entablature with a balustrade above. In the Chicago drawing, and in the Milan oil-sketch, the building has been shifted to the left, opposite the saint, and the ledge has been pushed down in the composition, below the re-entrant division of the lobe from which the figures of heresy fall. Dominic himself has been elevated on to another series of steps leading up from the left, so that he is on a great height *vis-à-vis* the crowd directly in front of him. Tiepolo has thus monumentalized the gift of the Rosary, and has done away with the somewhat empty gesture of oratory in the Berlin oil-sketch, which clearly preceded the Milan image in date.

The pictorial sources for the great architectural armature on which St Dominic presides are to be found, I believe, in Veronese's, Palma Giovane's, and Tintoretto's allegorical ceiling-paintings for the Sala del Maggior Consiglio in the Ducal Palace.[67] Palma's *Venice Enthroned above her Conquered Provinces* (Pl. 78) appears to have been Tiepolo's starting-point for the Berlin sketch, certainly suggesting the ledge at the bottom of the composition upon which several figures sit, turn, and twist.[68] The ledge, although changed in type, cuts horizontally across the bottom part of the composition. The same broad steps lead vertically up to St Dominic, whose outstretched arm makes a similar gesture to that of Palma's figure crowning Venice. A flag unfurls on the left, and below it, silhouetted against the white steps, is a staff held by an arm that reproduces exactly—although in reverse—Palma's formulation for his central soldier. All of these elements appear in the early (Berlin) sketch. Moreover, the architectural background which Tiepolo used to aggrandize St Dominic follows Palma's great canopy and column raised behind the personification of Venice.

Tiepolo's second (Milan) oil-sketch and its copy in Chicago reformulate these first ideas after consideration of Veronese's and Tintoretto's canvases in the Sala del Maggior Consiglio. Tintoretto's *Doge Niccolò da Ponte Receiving the Palm and Laurel from Venice* (Pl. 79) suggested the new architectural unit of steps with a superimposed platform on top; only its direction has been reversed. This system allowed Tiepolo to raise St Dominic above the crowd and to create a zig-zagging, vertical movement that carries our focus high into the heavens and towards the Virgin and Christ. He then accentuated this in the fresco by pushing the soldiers on the ledge further to the left, by regulating more finely the pattern of shadows on the flight of steps, and by adjusting only slightly the position of the columnar architecture in the background. Our glance quickly catches the Doge's outstretched arms amidst a pictorial nexus of military force, Dominican generosity, and heavenly salvation.

Tiepolo took a number of details from Veronese's *Apotheosis of Venice* (Pl. 80), including

---

[67] The pictorial format of Tiepolo's *Institution of the Rosary* may be related to Gaulli's ceiling in the Gesù, Rome, which is also a rectangle finishing in half-circles at both of the short ends; and to Pietro da Cortona's *Miracle of St Philip Neri* on the ceiling of the Chiesa Nuova, Rome, itself based on Venetian types such as Veronese's *Adoration of the Magi*, a canvas originally in the ceiling of S. Nicolò ai Frari but now in the reconstructed Chapel of the Rosary in SS Giovanni e Paolo.

[68] Palma's painting was picked out for special praise by De Brosses when Tiepolo was working in the Gesuati: cf. S. Mason Rinaldi, *Palma Il Giovane* (Milan, 1984), 140. Note the similarity between the old man in the exact centre of Palma's ledge and the turbaned and bearded man in the Berlin sketch; this figure disappears from the Milan sketch and the fresco.

78. Palma Giovane, *Venice Enthroned above her Conquered Provinces* (oil on canvas, 904 × 580 cm.)

79. J. Tintoretto, *Doge Niccolò da Ponte Receiving the Palm and Laurel from Venice* (oil on canvas, 1030 × 650 cm.)

80. P. Veronese, *Apotheosis of Venice* (oil on canvas, 904 × 580 cm.)

the architectural elevation from the painting's second plane, behind the great spiral columns.[69] Veronese's dog, too, furnished Tiepolo with an important motif that he copied almost exactly in the Berlin oil-sketch; although excluded from the Milan–Chicago version, this detail reappears in the fresco, but its position has been rethought.[70] Tiepolo was also struck by Veronese's halberd, which is silhouetted against the lion of St Mark at the bottom of the painting and is pointing up to the figure of Venice. He introduced the bellicose motif into the second sketch, then straightened its direction in the fresco to pull our glance along the vertical axis towards Dominic and the Doge. This motif of ducal primacy came, I think, from the furled flag on the bottom steps in Tintoretto's work.

Tiepolo's use of compositional and figural ideas by Palma, Tintoretto, and Veronese would not have been as linear an exercise as I have presented here; he would have moved from one source to another, reconsidering and rearranging pictorial motifs by all three of the cinquecento masters. Evidence of this constant manipulation is to be seen in the two figures and the dog on the bottom ledge, forms that clearly originated with Palma and Veronese. Their appearance in the Milan–Chicago preparatory works and in the fresco is an amalgam of the lower sections of all three sixteenth-century canvases: the halberd is from Veronese; the soldier who holds it is based upon both the figure in Tintoretto's bottom left-hand corner and Palma's recumbent nude; and the muscular back reflects the same forms by Palma and Veronese. Tiepolo must have been attracted by these three great state paintings not only because of their grand rhetoric but also because they, like the *Institution of the Rosary*, were meant to be both narrative and devotional in function. They seek to explain the honours accrued to, and the achievements attained by the Republic, and thus to inspire in viewers a personal consecration to the Venetian Republic. The objectives are the same in Tiepolo's fresco: to describe the rewards of the Rosary and to urge the pious on towards Christian salvation through Dominican devotions.

Tiepolo's *Institution of the Rosary* is the fulcrum upon which the entire Gesuati cycle rests; each of the subsidiary frescos elucidates the Dominican beads of prayer. Moreover, the Gesuati cycle affirms the political nature of public art in the Serenissima, particularly when it is viewed within the special web of Church and State that pertained there; Tiepolo's contemporaries would have understood the frescos' *venezianità*, both artistic and governmental. Entangling the contextual skein even further were elements of partisan polemics that erupted during the 1720s and 1730s between the Reformed Congregation at the Zattere and their Order's principal theologian in nearby Padua. Behind Tiepolo's commission there smouldered, I suggest, a bitter Dominican debate.

In his guide to the Gesuati, Don Niero briefly states that the Gesuati's 'iconographic plan' is anti-Quietist in sentiment.[71] I would suggest, however, that Tiepolo's Rosary

---

[69] Similar forms can also be found in Veronese's painting of *The Banishment of Vashti* on the ceiling of S. Sebastiano.

[70] Another element that appeared in the Berlin sketch, was then dropped from the Milan–Chicago version, but was reinserted in the fresco is the star over St Dominic's head. According to tradition, the star had appeared during Dominic's baptism,

while the dog holding a torch lighting up the world had been seen by the saint's mother during a dream: cf. A. Walz, 'Domenico', *Enciclopedia cattolica*, iv (Rome, 1950), col. 1825.

[71] Niero, *Tre artisti*, p. 78: 'In tutto il piano iconografico poi, possiamo individuare una sottile polemica antiquietista.'

cycle expresses a Dominican rebuttal not to Quietism but to Jansenism. Although the two rested on similar theological ground regarding the worthlessness of mankind's will before God and the uselessness of outward forms such as the Rosary to manifest Christian belief, Quietism was not a burning issue in Venice during the early eighteenth century; Jansenism was.[72] Indeed, we know that during the key decades of the 1720s and 1730s—while the Gesuati was under construction and just before Tiepolo worked there—there was friction between the Reformed Congregation and Jacques Hyacinth Serry (1659–1738), the Dominican theologian in Padua, whose publications were thought by his Order, the Venetian government, and the Roman hierarchy to harbour Jansenist heresy and anti-papal ideas. I submit that it was through Tiepolo's painted complex glorifying the Rosary, the Virgin Mary, and the papal privileges extended to both that the Dominicans at the Zattere sought to impugn Serry's dangerous beliefs.

Briefly, Jansenism descended from the writings of Cornelius Jansen, Bishop of Ypres, who died in 1638, a full century before Tiepolo painted his frescos in the Gesuati. In his posthumously published *Augustinus* (1640), Jansen held that God alone determines who may be saved, that man can do little or nothing to influence God, and that the victory of spirit over flesh will come about only if man is in a state of grace.[73] Such ideas stirred up the Church's anguished memories of the Protestant revolt, especially since Jansen claimed to base his views on the writings of St Augustine, one of the Church's doctors. Jansen's followers complicated the issue even further by employing citations from St Paul in their arguments. Several seventeenth-century Popes condemned the *Augustinus*, and discussions on its many points were totally forbidden.

None the less, the doctrine raised its head again in the early eighteenth century, and it was this settecento manifestation of Jansenism that rankled with the Dominicans at the Gesuati. In the late seventeenth century, Pasquier Quesnel of the Congregation of the Oratory had published in Paris 101 propositions on the New Testament: *Nouveau Testament en français avec des réflexions morales sur chaque verset*, a work judged as prolonging the Jansenist polemic.[74] Quesnel's work was severely criticized, and its publication was forbidden by Louis XIV. The aged Louis, worried by what was by then a leitmotiv in Jansenist thinking—the refusal to accept any authority save that specified by Holy Scripture—looked to Clement XI for an official church condemnation of Quesnel's *Réflexions morales*. At the same time, Louis watched the Church's hierarchy in France split into factions over Jansenism; his monarchy appeared to weaken through lack of proper ecclesiastical support. In 1709, Louis ordered the demolition of the Convent of Port-Royal, the centre of Jansenist activity in Paris. He continued to exert pressure on Rome for a denunciation of Quesnel's work, which was finally granted to him on 18 September 1713 when

---

[72] Cf. M. Petrocchi, *Il Quietismo italiano del Seicento* (Rome, 1948), 127: 'Quietismo e giansenismo ebbero una medesima posizione di partenza, nell'accentuare su un piano teologico la visione della miseria dell'uomo e della quasi-nullità della sua volontà . . .'. They were directly opposed to each other, however, in their beliefs concerning human perfection, the former accepting it as possible and the latter finding it inconceivable; Quietists and Jansenists were mortal enemies in the eighteenth century: see R. A. Knox, *Enthusiasm: A Chapter in the History of Religion*

(Oxford, 1962), published in Italian as *Illuminati e carismatici* (Bologna, 1970).

[73] The literature on Jansenism is immense: cf. L. Cognet, *Le Jansénisme* (Paris, 1964); the basic work on the situation in Italy is A. C. Jemolo, *Il Giansenismo in Italia prima della rivoluzione* (Bari, 1928). Other literature on the subject will appear in subsequent footnotes.

[74] O. Chadwick, *The Popes and European Revolution* (Oxford, 1981), 279ff.

Clement XI published his Bull *Unigenitus*, in which Quesnel's propositions were condemned and censured.[75] For the next quarter of a century, the very word *Unigenitus* developed into a battle-cry *vis-à-vis* the questions of divine grace and the freedom of religious conscience.

In Italy the struggle over Jansenism and *Unigenitus* caused fewer ripples than it did in France, where prelates and theologians saw the Vatican as a threat to the Gallican Church's traditional independence.[76] Nevertheless, Jansenist doctrine received strong support on the Italian peninsula, particularly in the north.[77] Venice and Padua were epicentres of the 'disturbance', a phenomenon which can be explained by the Venetian State's traditional anti-papal stance and by the city's wealth of publishers.[78] Jansenist beliefs were particularly well known in Venetian theological circles during the 1730s. As elsewhere, these beliefs were cause for partisan politics. But while Venice gave Jansenism its voice in the Veneto, the doctrine's 'dangerous' ideas and intellectual platform actually originated in Padua. Its seat was S. Giustina, a Benedictine monastery and Serry's home.

Serry, born in Toulon in 1659, had entered the Dominican Order in Marseilles.[79] In 1690 he left for Italy, where he worked in the Holy Office in Rome, the very heart of Catholic power, under the powerful Cardinal Altieri. In 1697, Serry was appointed to the important Chair of Theology at the University of Padua. There, under the eyes of the traditionally minded Venetian government, his French background and his interest in the Gallican Church's problems with the papacy catapulted him into the centre of the Jansenist dispute.[80] His first publication in Padua expressed beliefs that at the time were considered to be Jansenist in tone; and Serry found himself accused of having associated with Quesnel during the very years in which Louis XIV sought the Church's condemnation of that troublesome heretic.

Very simply put, Serry supported St Augustine's views on predestination, that God alone saves. This was the Dominicans' own stance, but it was also, as I have stated above,

[75] For the strong anti-papal tone of Jansenism, see Jemolo, *Il Giansenismo in Italia*, p. 91; and M. Vaussard, 'Le Jansénisme vénitien à la fin du xviiie siècle: Giuseppe-Maria Pujati', *Revue historique*, 227 (1962), 418.

[76] During the regency of the Duc d'Orléans (1715–21), Jansenist thinkers received unofficial support from the Court for their opposition to the Jesuits, who were not only very much disliked by the Regent but were also staunch supporters of the papal decree: cf. Pastor, *History of the Popes*, xxxiii, p. 255.

[77] E. Préclin and E. Jarry, *Le lotte politiche e dottrinali nei secoli XVII e XVIII 1648–1789* (Turin, 1974), i. 413.

[78] See H. F. Brown, *The Venetian Printing Press 1469–1800* (Amsterdam, 1969; reprint of London, 1891), 1972, where it is estimated that there were 77 presses in the city in 1752; and cf. M. Infelise, 'L'editoria', in *Il Settecento* (*Storia della cultura Veneta*, v¹), 91–111. Almost every author dealing with Jansenism in Italy refers to Venice's leading position in the publication of relevant material: Jemolo, *Il Giansenismo in Italia*, p. 126; Préclin and Jarry, *Le lotte politiche*, p. 419; A. Vecchi, 'La vita spirituale', in V. Branca (ed.), *Storia della civiltà veneziana: Dall'età barocca all'Italia contemporanea*, iii (Florence, 1979), 185; and M. Petrocchi, *Il tramonto della repubblica di Venezia e l'assolutismo illuminato* (Venice,

1950), 47. Jemolo (pp. 393–4) wrote that the ideas of Jansenism were ignored in Venice, even though they originated there. More recent research has shown this not to be the case; see below, p. 133, and n. 88. For further bibliography on the subject, cf. M. Berengo, *La società veneta alla fine del Settecento* (Florence, 1956), 230 n. 1.

[79] See 'Serry, François-Jacques-Hyacinthe', in *Dictionnaire de théologie catholique*, xiv² (Paris, 1942), 1,957 ff.; and D. Fiorot's very important 'Nota sul Giansenismo veneto nei primi decenni del secolo XVIII', *Nuova rivista storica*, 35 (1951), *passim*, but especially p. 216.

[80] It is ironic that Serry had originally been appointed to the Chair of Theology in Padua instead of Scipione Maffei, whose nomination was refused because his ideas were considered 'poco ortodosse'; cf. M. L. Soppelsa, 'Le scienze teoriche e sperimentali tra Sei e Settecento', in *Il Settecento*, v², 321. Serry's *Historia congregationum de auxiliis divinae gratiae*, prepared in Rome, was published in Padua in 1700 under the pseudonym of Augustin le Blanc, a reference to St Augustine. The treatise attacks the supporters of Molinism, who believed that man can indeed influence his own salvation: cf. *Dictionnaire de théologie catholique*, xiv², p. 1959; and Fiorot, 'Nota sul Giansenismo', p. 217.

a corner-stone of Jansenist belief. However, this ran counter to Jesuit teaching, which stated that man, through his earthly acts, is able to sway God and influence his personal salvation. Serry, like all Dominicans, found himself delicately balanced between his Augustinian training on one side, and the politico-theological dispute between Jansenists and Jesuits on the other.[81] The theologian found himself forced either to retract his ideas and submit to papal and Jesuit coercion, thus compromising his Dominican education, or to stand his ground and provoke stinging criticism from Rome, where, ironically, he had formerly held a position of importance.

Serry's brothers in the Order sought a compromise with the Society of Jesus.[82] The General of the Dominican Order agreed to sit on the papal commission that promulgated *Unigenitus*, thus calming Jesuit anxiety about the sincerity of the Dominican's allegiance to the papacy, and the Jesuits in turn sought to separate Augustine's teachings from their more recent association with Jansenist beliefs. Serry, however, did little to reconcile himself with the Roman hierarchy, and in the 1720s his position worsened as both the Roman and Venetian governments tried to isolate him.[83]

The immediate stimulus for this appears to have been the election to the papacy in 1724 of the Venetian-educated Dominican friar, Vincenzo Maria Orsini.[84] As Benedict XIII, Orsini was anxious to settle disputes within the Church, and he exhorted his brother Dominicans to obey the Holy See; he designated the Order *tout court* as an enemy of the Jansenists, and he praised *Unigenitus* for its rightful thinking.[85] But Serry would not fall into line. In 1726 he published his *Theologia supplex*, in which he inquired whether *Unigenitus* had not unjustly censured Augustinian teachings at the same time as condemning Quesnel's propositions.[86] Rome soon rejected the *Theologia* just as it had Serry's *Historia congregationum* (1700) and his *Exercitationes historicae criticae, polemicae de Christo ejiusque Vergine Matre* (1719). In this last work, Serry had examined the cult of Mary, refuting the legends surrounding Christ's mother and complaining about the devotional excesses that had accrued to her figure. The Holy See also condemned Serry's *De*

[81] For the Jansenist–Jesuit battle, cf. Jemolo, *Il Giansenismo in Italia*, p. x. Serry's *Historiae congregationum* attacked the Jesuits and their position *vis-à-vis* the papacy.

[82] Cf. Jemolo, *Il Giansenismo in Italia*, pp. 72 ff. For Dominican manoeuvring between Jansenists and Jesuits, see also Préclin and Jarry, *Le lotte politiche*, p. 488.

[83] A. Vecchi, *Correnti religiose nel Sei–Settecento Veneto* (Venice, 1962), 290.

[84] The Dominicans of Venice commemorated Orsini's novitiate there by placing a statue of Benedict, cast in gilt silver, in S. Domenico di Castello, the monastery where he had studied; in response, the Pope sent gifts of silver to S. Domenico: cf. Zorzi, *Venezia scomparsa*, ii. 328. Other papal–Dominican ties are reflected in the presence in the Chapel of S. Domenico in SS Giovanni e Paolo of Benedict's coat of arms: cf. C. Puglisi, 'The Cappella di S. Domenico in SS Giovanni e Paolo, Venice', *Arte veneta*, 40 (1986), 230–8.

[85] On 26 May 1727, Benedict published the Bull *Pretiosus*, in which he confirmed the Holy See's privileges to his Order: cf. Chadwick, *The Popes*, pp. 282–3; and E. Appolis, *Entre Jansénistes et Zelanti: Le 'Tiers Parti' catholique au XVIIIᵉ siècle* (Paris, 1960), 61.

[86] J. Serry, *La Théologie suppliante aux pieds du Souverain Pontife*

pour lui demander l'intelligence & l'explications de la Bulle Unigenitus (Cologne, 1756); for Serry's peaceful intentions, cf. p. 296: 'Si le Souverain Pontife nous fait la grace de répondre aux demandes que nous avons pris la liberté de lui faire, Sa Sainteté rétablira la paix dans les Écoles; les troubles excités à l'occasion de la Bulle Unigenitus cesseront pour toujours . . .'. Serry's refusal to accept *Unigenitus* did not proceed from any maverick tendency or from a whole-hearted espousal of Jansenist beliefs, but because he felt that Quesnel's propositions had not been fairly represented by Clement XI's Bull. At the same time, in Paris, Cardinal De Noailles, First Prelate of France, yielded in his support of Quesnel, as did the Sorbonne itself in 1729: see Jemolo, *Il Giansenismo in Italia*, pp. 56 ff. Those Dominicans who continued to reject *Unigenitus*, asking first Benedict and then Clement XII to reconsider it, were thought to be Jansenists and were called Appellants. One of them supposedly made a retraction of his position in March 1744 ('E noi pur troppo sappiamo, che non pochi de' nostri Frati si sono lasciati sedurre, sino ad alzar bandiera contro le Bolle de' Papi, e dichiararsi Appellanti.'), which was then quoted by L. I. Cocconato in *Ritrazzione solenne di tutte l'ingiurie, bugie, falsificazioni, calumnie . . . contro la venerabile Compagnia di Gesù* (Naples, 1744), 27.

romano pontefice, a work of the early 1730s which placed papal infallibility under close scrutiny.[87]

At the same time, the State Inquisition in Venice was looking into the teaching of Jansenism in Padua. Fearing the spread of heretical doctrine, the Inquisitors wrote to the Podestà of the city to warn him of the ideas 'born in part in the school of Father Serry'.[88] Podestà Loredan's reply was that Serry and his colleagues were merely discussing the works of SS Augustine and Thomas and that their conversations centred only on the subject of God's grace! Alarmed by this piece of calmly delivered information, the Inquisitors immediately tried to bring the matter before the Senate so as to restrain Serry. But the phlegmatic Loredan merely observed that the Holy Office had not made any objections so far, and that Serry's intelligence and obedience would ensure his loyalty and adherence to the precept ('precetto') once it had been clarified to him. Well aware of the scrutiny of the Republic, the cautious Dominican theologian would probably pay attention to Loredan; in 1724, Serry had refused the possibility of an attachment to the schismatic Church of Utrecht on the grounds of the surveillance of the Venetian government.[89]

So, Serry was viewed by both the Serenissima and Mother Church as a contentious theologian; it is not surprising that the Dominicans of Venice looked askance at him. But their hostile attitude towards Serry was also based on issues that only they found especially sensitive. Vecchi explained Dominican anger against Serry by pointing to his *De monachatu S. Thomae Aquinatis . . . antequam ad Dominicanum praedicatorum ordinem se transferret* (1724), in which the theologian speculated that St Thomas might have been a Benedictine monk before he became a Dominican.[90] Dominicans everywhere lamented Serry's work; one of

---

[87] For Serry's anti-papal stance, cf. Jemolo, *Il Giansenismo in Italia*, pp. 238, 250; and Vecchi, *Correnti religiose*, pp. 292–3. One should keep in mind that anyone in Italy challenging the traditional legends was considered a Jansenist; even Archbishop Lambertini of Bologna was considered pro-Jansenist on the eve of the papal conclave from which he emerged as Benedict XIV: cf. F. Callaey, 'La Critique historique et le courant pro-Janséniste à Rome au XVIIIᵉ siècle', in *Nuove ricerche storiche sul Giansenismo (Studi presentati nella sezione di storia ecclesiastica del Congresso Internazionale per il IV Centenario della Pontificia Università Gregoriana)* (Rome, 1954), 189.

[88] As cited by Fiorot, 'Nota sul Giansenismo', p. 205. This same accusation has been repeated in our own century: cf. E. Codignola, *Illuministi, Giansenisti e Giacobini nell'Italia del Settecento* (Florence, 1947), 207: 'Il Giansenismo nel Veneto ebbe inizio, fin dai primi anni del Settecento, per opera del P. Serry . . .'. S. Giustina, where several of the *cattedratici* of the University lived, seems to have been the trouble spot: cf. R. Mazzetti, 'Giuseppe Maria Puiati a Scipione de' Ricci', *Bollettino storico pistoiese* (1933), 143: 'A Padova, in un primo tempo, solo focolare giansenistico fu il convento di S. Giustina . . .'. It is amusing to read in our own century how the smell of Jansenism is still attached to S. Giustina: see D. Ruperto Pepi, *L'abbazia di Santa Giustina in Padova* (Padua, 1966), 58: 'Secondo la corrente comune ai benedettini del tempo, c'è nell'ambiente un aleggiare di giansenismo; ma di quel giansenismo all'italiana che non ha perduto completamente il buon senso. Del resto notiamo che i più sfegatati fautori delle nuove idee, se abitavano in Santa Giustina per

ragione della cattedra che tenevano all'Università, non erano di Santa Giustina.' Although it might seem paradoxical that the State Inquisitors in Venice should be so worried about differences of opinion between Venetian residents and the Roman Court, events of the 1720s explain the Republic's newly acquired circumspection: the election to the Throne of St Peter of a Venetian-trained friar, and the hotly debated issue of the Patriarchy of Aquileia, for which Venice desperately needed Rome's support against Vienna: cf. Chapter 1, p. 57. The extent to which Jansenism occupied the best of minds during the 1720s and 1730s can be judged by Scipione Maffei's explanation of why he wrote his *Istoria teologica . . . in proposito della divina grazia, del libero arbitrio, e della predestinazione* (Trent, 1742); Maffei notes (pp. ix ff.) that when he arrived in Paris in 1732 people were talking so much about Jansenism and Catholicism that he decided to put everything else aside and turn his thoughts exclusively to this argument. Cf. also D. Hume, 'Of Superstition and Enthusiasm', in D. Wollheim (ed.), *Hume on Religion* (Cleveland and New York, 1964), 250–1.

[89] Fiorot, 'Nota sul Giansenismo', p. 221, remarks that although Serry in fact rejected any official invitation to ally himself with the revolt in Holland, his 'lettera pur concludendo in un rifiuto, mal dissumula la simpatia dell'Autore per i scismatici ultraiettini . . .'. Serry's works were republished in Venice in 1773, just as the Jesuit Order was dissolved by Clement XIV: cf. Fiorot, ibid., p. 224.

[90] Vecchi, *Correnti religiose*, p. 283, and 'La vita spirituale', p. 184.

the Order's greatest figures had been torn from its history and replaced within the context of another spiritual training. From S. Maria del Rosario itself there came an immediate and important rebuttal to the *De monachatu*.[91] But the tensions between Serry and his fellow Dominicans at the Gesuati were not limited to the 1720s and 1730s. Harsh judgements of his philo-Jansenist opinions continued to originate from the monastery on the Zattere even after his death in 1738.[92] The friars at S. Maria del Rosario were furious with Serry for the positions he took on Jansenist doctrine, papal infallibility, and the education of St Thomas, and for his criticisms of the Marian cult.

The picture emerging from Dominican polemics in the Veneto, *c.*1710–40, is not one of friendly collegial debate. In the aftermath of *Unigenitus* and Benedict XIII's subsequent call for his Order's submission to the Bull, the Dominican community of Venice closed its ranks against Serry for his persistent wish to examine it. S. Maria del Rosario responded harshly to Serry, not only through publications, but also, I suggest, by presenting its case visually in the form of a monumental fresco cycle. Most obviously, Tiepolo's exaltation of the Rosary contradicts Serry's adverse judgements of the Marian cult. However, the *Institution of the Rosary* expresses an even more fundamental disagreement between the two parties. In demonstrating the Rosary's efficacy in the expulsion of heresy from the world, the image asserts mankind's power to determine its own salvation. The humble Venetian worshipping in the Gesuati, like his or her pictorial equivalent gathered around St Dominic, saw that Christian perfection was attainable through as simple a measure as the multiple recitation of prayers. The fresco implies that merely the performance of this pious act will bring the faithful closer to Christian redemption.

Serry, however, believed that an individual could not influence his heavenly destiny, that the relationship between God and humanity is not a collaborative partnership. Subscribing to St Augustine's doctrine of predestination, the French theologian condemned the belief in free will. Could the world really be freed of evil and man actually achieve divine grace through a bead-roll? Serry had been battling against such ideas since the 1690s; at first, the Dominicans had even stood ground with him. But after their peace with the Jesuits, and Benedict XIII's official confirmation of *Unigenitus*, Serry's brothers on the Zattere looked at the matter differently. They rallied behind their papal leader, adapting their attitude to conform with his. To their surprise, their theologian in Padua

---

[91] *De Fabula Monachatus Benedictini Divi Thomae Aquinatis . . .* (1724) was written by Bernardo Maria de Rubeis, who dwelt on the subject well into the 1730s; support for de Rubeis' position can be found in some of his correspondence, preserved in BNM, Cod. It. X 50 (6703), fos. 141, 143, 151, and 155. One Frenchman asked de Rubeis (fo. 141, 11 Aug. 1724) why Serry 'se rend inutile à l'un [his Order] et à l'autre [the Church] par de si pitoiables ouvrages?', and: 'Que dira le Pape qui estimait tant le P. Serry d'une conduite si bizarre?' On the Gesuati versus Serry, cf. Vecchi, 'La vita spirituale', pp. 184 ff. Serry was himself very much aware of the Dominican's antagonism towards him: cf. BNM, Cod. It. X 50 (6703), fo. 227, a letter dated 28 Feb. 1723, in which Serry says to de Rubeis that he knows the authorities will not allow him to publish and that he is sad that his ideas 'incontrano così pocca fortuna nel Convento del Rosario, che stentano assai pigliar La strada di collà, ne ardiscono d'andar in mano de suoi Accusatori, e Percusatori'.

[92] In the dedication (n.p.) to his *Della storia del probabilismo e del rigorismo* (Lucca, 1743), Padre Daniele Concina, the Gesuati's most illustrious theologian, called Jansenists: 'i nimici più contumaci della infallibilità Pontificia . . .'; and on p. 4 of vol. i: 'I partitanti di questa setta [Jansenism] imitando il solito inveterato costume di tutti gli altri Eretici de' secoli passati, si travisarono sotto la maschera di zelanti Cattolici.' It should be noted that throughout the Gesuati correspondence preserved in the Biblioteca Marciana, Serry is associated with Jansenists and Quesnellists. For Concina, see Vecchi, *Correnti religiose*, pp. 343 ff.; Eusebio Eramiste (pseudonym for D. Sandrelli), *Vita del Padre Daniello Concina* (Brescia, 1768); A.-T. Volpi, *Della vera idea del Giansenismo*, ii (Bergamo, 1784), 189 ff.; 'Concina Daniel', *Dictionnaire de théologie catholique*, iii (Paris, 1910), 676–707; and 'Concina, Daniele', *Dizionario biografico degli Italiani*, 27 (Rome, 1982), 716–22.

did not follow suit. In fact, he not only questioned Benedict's wisdom concerning *Unigenitus*, he also wrote against the very ideas which in part sustained Dominican piety: the Marian cult, and papal power. While he was doing this, they were dedicating their new church to a Marian feast which had been created, expanded, and ultimately raised to universality by three different Popes. Then, they commissioned a painted ceiling that exalts deference to the Virgin and promotes papal authority. Indeed, on leaving the building, the two points in question are made manifest by the grisaille tondo directly over the inner doorway, which—centred amidst apostolic keys—depicts Pope Pius V angelically inspired to attribute the victory of Lepanto to Mary and her Rosary. Begun at the very moment of Serry's death, Tiepolo's grand painting cycle represents the Dominicans' rebuttal to their 'Jansenist' theologian in Padua.

The Marian devotion and papal prerogative so brilliantly projected by Tiepolo in the Gesuati were the most hotly debated subjects in the settecento Roman Church. The two issues had been building in intensity over the last two hundred years, and they would continue to cause friction between their numerous adherents and detractors for another fifty years to come. The questions of the extent to which papal authority ruled within the Church and Mary's place in salvation were only laid to rest, if indeed that is the right phrase, in the mid-nineteenth century, when Pius IX defined both papal infallibility and the Virgin's Immaculate Conception as Catholic dogma. Pius's pronouncements sought to put an end to the virulent disputes that had emerged specifically during Tiepolo's age. Jacques Serry was not a unique phenomenon in the eighteenth century; many in the Roman hierarchy were sceptical of various aspects of Catholic tradition, and they appealed to the papacy to make fundamental changes in church custom to avoid the potential abuse of papal power and misplaced zeal for the Virgin Mary.

These appeals appeared in the publications of prelates who, although faithful to Catholicism, did not always feel sure of Rome's universal and historic wisdom. For instance, with regard to *Unigenitus*, the Apellants seeking a re-examination of the Bull were really expressing doubts about whether Clement XI and Benedict XIII had the exclusive right to define Jansenist heresy; could the Popes individually and alone determine how Quesnel's writings conflicted with tradition? Those challenges that were made to papal authority tended to undermine the juridical primacy that Popes had enjoyed within the Church since the beginning of the Counter-Reformation. In some quarters, there was even a wish for democratic ecclesiastical processes, whereby policy would be decided by a General Council and not by an autocratic Pope or, worse still, by his favourite nephew.[93]

It was both this desire for reasoned debate and the quest for internal reform that gave rise to the Catholic Enlightenment. This movement, which is important for our

[93] On the question of papal (in)fallibility, see A. C. Jemolo, *Stato e Chiesa negli scrittori politici italiani del Seicento e del Settecento* (Turin, 1914), 133 ff., and Chadwick, *The Popes*, pp. 284 ff. The issue of papal nepotism was no longer a burning one in the eighteenth century, but Clement XI favoured Agostino Steffani (cf. Pastor, *History of the Popes*, xxxiii. 356 ff.), Benedict XIII delegated enormous authority to Niccolò Coscia (cf. ibid. xxxiv. 123 ff.), and Clement XII did indeed promote his nephew Neri Corsini (cf. ibid. 334 ff.).

understanding of Tiepolo's ecclesiastical ceiling-paintings, expressed a strong reaction above all to what many saw as an ungovernable fervour within contemporary Catholicism for the figure of the Virgin Mary.[94] Nowhere can Marian zeal be better examined than in *Le glorie di Maria*, a two-part treatise written during the 1730s and 1740s and published in Naples in 1750 by Alfonso de' Liguori.[95] Part One, over two hundred pages long, concerns the 'Salve Regina'. Part Two is composed of 'Discorsi sulle feste principali di Maria', and is followed by examples of Mary's power. 'Esempio 5', for example, recounts the events that took place in Carcasonne when St Dominic preached before the Albigensian heretics: 'Then St Dominic had the people recite the Rosary, and oh what a marvel! at every Hail Mary many demons in the form of burning coals flew from the body of the tormented [singular], so that when the Rosary was completed he was perfectly free. Witnessing such a deed, many heretics converted . . .'.[96] In its highly dramatic form, this could easily be read as a libretto for Tiepolo's *Institution of the Rosary*.

The Catholic Enlightenment responded to such glorification of the Marian cult in numerous tracts. The most significant of these were by Ludovico Antonio Muratori, a somewhat younger contemporary of Serry, who wrote a series of treatises on Catholic and Marian devotion.[97] In his *Della regolata divozione dei cristiani*, first published in Venice in 1747 and then reprinted many times, Muratori openly condemned the confusion which he thought many Catholics made between veneration for the Mother and worship of the Son. For Muratori, Marian exaltation surpassed what was fitting and proper: 'But it is up to us to remember that Mary is not God . . . We must venerate her as our Advocate, but not begin to believe that she can pardon us our sins or save us . . . Mary's task is to pray to God for us, to intercede for us, but not really to command. *Sancta Maria, ora pro nobis*: this is what the Church teaches us.'[98] Thus, Muratori's position was directly opposed to de' Liguori's. Indeed, their points of view represent the two extremes of Catholic thought on the matter in the mid-eighteenth century.

De' Liguori versus Muratori? Tiepolo's answer to this question, and those of his ecclesiastical patrons, are clearly set forth in his four great ceilings depicting the Virgin Mary. The Gesuati cycle is the earliest of the group chronologically, but although it is devoted to the glorification of a Marian cult, it ennobles the Virgin to a significantly lesser degree than the artist's subsequent ceilings in the Scalzi, the Scuola dei Carmini, and the Pietà. Indeed, the figure of Christ's mother grew in these later paintings to command more

[94] But see P. Hoffer, *La Dévotion à Marie au déclin du XVIIe siècle; Autour de Jansénisme et des 'Avis salutaires de la B. V. Marie à ses Dévots indiscrets'* (Paris, 1938), 27, who wrote that the Marian cult lost ground in the eighteenth century.

[95] For St Alfonso, cf. 'Alfonsus Liguori, St.', *New Catholic Encyclopaedia*, i (Washington DC, 1967), 336–41.

[96] S. Alfonso de' Liguori, *Le glorie di Maria* (Bassano, 1845), 215: 'Indi S. Domenico fece dal popolo recitare il Rosario, ed oh meraviglia! ad ogni *Ave Maria* uscivano dal corpo di quell'infelice molti demoni in forma di carboni ardenti, sicchè terminato il Rosario ne restò affatto libero. A tal fatto si convertirono molti Eretici . . .'.

[97] Muratori was born in 1672, 13 years after Serry, worked throughout his life for the Duke of Modena, and died in that city in 1750, 12 years after Serry in Padua. Muratori's most famous work, of course, is his 25-volume history of Italy.

[98] L. A. Muratori, *Della regolata divozione dei cristiani* (Venice, 1761), 316–7: 'Ma convien ricordarci che Maria non è Dio . . . Dobbiamo venerarla qual'Avvocata nostra, e non già farci a credere, che a Lei appartenga il perdonarci i peccati, il salvarci . . . Uffizio di Maria è il pregar Dio per noi, l'intercedere per noi, e non già il commandare. Sancta Maria, ora pro nobis: questo è quello che la Chiesa c'insegna.' At approximately the same time, but from another critical point of view, Hume wrote: 'The Virgin Mary, ere checked by the reformation, had proceeded, from being merely a good woman, to usurp many attributes of the Almighty . . .': cf. 'The Natural History of Religion' [1749–51], in Wollheim, *Hume on Religion*, p. 58.

pictorial space than she had in the Gesuati, to assume a more hieratic appearance, and to signify ever-deeper Christian meaning.

Of the three ceiling-paintings, the one in the Church of S. Maria di Nazareth—the Scalzi—was completed first. Commissioned in 1743 by the Discalced Carmelites of Venice, Tiepolo began the *Translation of the Holy House* in March 1745 and finished it late that same year.[99] Unfortunately, the ceiling was demolished when the Scalzi was partially destroyed during an air attack on the adjacent railway station in World War I; but there are photographs, two autograph oil-sketches, some fragments of the original, and a twentieth-century copy in oil that can help us to recall the artist's impressive fresco complex.

The *Translation of the Holy House* (Pl. 81) glorified an important Marian relic: the Nazarene home in which, according to tradition, the Angel Gabriel had announced the Incarnation. But destiny did not permit the Holy House to remain in Nazareth, for when the Holy Land was invaded by Saracens in the thirteenth century the Santa Casa was carried by angelic hands first to present-day Yugoslavia and then to the Marches in Italy, where it settled in 1295. There, the town of Loreto was founded, and pilgrimages were made to it in veneration of Mary. Tiepolo's central fresco in the Scalzi depicted the Santa Casa crossing the heavens in its miraculous flight to safety. The Virgin stands on top of the roof like an acroterion on a Greek temple and is sheltering the infant Christ within her robe. On the right, St Joseph adores the Godhead far above, while still further to the right, trumpet-blowing angels herald the Holy House's supernatural journey. Along the vault's sides, within a *trompe-l'œil* framework, six scenes from the Old Testament narrate the story of the Ark of the Covenant.[100] High in the ceiling's empyrean, reign God the Father, crowned by a triangular nimbus, and the Holy Spirit. At the bottom of the fresco, personifications of evil cascade down from the ceiling, creating an illusion similar to those seen over the stair-well in the Arcivescovado (*c.*1726) in Udine and above the Gesuati nave (1738–9).

The *Translation of the Holy House*, like the earlier *Institution of the Rosary*, is a reflection of both the Marian traditions of the Order that commissioned it and Venice's own dedication to the Virgin. There were also historical links tying Venice to the Loretan cult, just as there were connections between the Rosary and the Republic's victory at Lepanto. For example, construction of the Loretan Basilica had been initiated by Pope Paul II, a member of the Venetian Barbo family, as an ex-voto to the Madonna di Loreto.[101] In the sixteenth century, Venetian ambassadors travelling to and from Rome chose 'la via di la Madonna di Loreto' as their usual route. Political ties between the Venetian State and Loreto were established and maintained, with only one interruption, until the fall of the Republic in the 1790s. Throughout the late seventeenth and eighteenth centuries, the city recognized the sanctuary's special status by allowing all goods going there to pass through Venetian territory untaxed: 'because . . . the building of the Holy House of Our Lady of Loreto is a very holy undertaking and its needs must be met'.[102]

---

[99] For fuller discussions on this commission, see G. B. Knox, 'G. B. Tiepolo and the Ceiling of the Scalzi', *Burlington Magazine*, 110 (1968), 394–8; and W. Barcham, 'Giambattista Tiepolo's Ceiling for S. Maria di Nazareth in Venice: Legend, Traditions, and Devotions', *The Art Bulletin*, 61 (1979), 430–47.

[100] For these scenes and the Marian significance of the Ark of the Covenant, see Barcham, 'Giambattista Tiepolo's Ceiling', pp. 440ff.

[101] For this and following historical ties, cf. ibid., pp. 435–6.

[102] P. Davide da Portogruaro, 'Venezia e Loreto', *Rivista di Venezia* (1929), 20ff.

Venice's devotion to the Santa Casa is further attested by the city's two replicas of the holy relic, both of which still stand. The first was constructed during the 1640s in the island church of S. Clemente as the fulfilment of a vow made in 1630 by Francesco Lazzaroni, the Patriarchal Vicar. In 1646, when a sacred image of the Madonna was carried to S. Clemente, the entire city organized a triumphal procession on the lagoon; so great was the devotional fervour, one eyewitness reports, that from across the water shouts were heard of '"Viva, viva Loreto", which made some of our gravest Senators cry with tenderness . . .'.[103] The second Venetian Santa Casa was built in 1744 in the parish church of S. Pantaleon, while Tiepolo was planning the *Translation of the Holy House*. On 25 March 1745, the feast of the Annunciation, a solemn procession carried an image of the Virgin to the new replica in S. Pantaleon; three weeks later, Tiepolo received his first payment for work in the Scalzi.[104] Although there appears to be no direct link between the two, Venice's dedication to Mary's Holy House was clearly made manifest by these events.

The papacy's interest in the Santa Casa in the first half of the eighteenth century matched Venice's own. In 1728, Benedict XIII extended the celebration of the Office and the Mass of the feast-day of the Translation of the Holy House to the Papal States, in whose territory Loreto was situated, and elevated the church built around the Marian shrine to the rank of 'basilica minore'.[105] In the 1730s, a group of antiquarians returning from Palestine where they had seen the Santa Casa's original site at Nazareth, testified before Clement XII to the archaeological correctness of the house, thereby documenting its authenticity. Benedict XIV (1740–58) intensified papal involvement at Loreto. As Archbishop of Bologna, Benedict had visited Mary's house several times, and in his treatise, *Delle feste di Gesù Cristo . . . e della B. Vergine Maria*, written shortly before ascending the Throne of St Peter, he commented extensively on the feast of the Translation and affirmed the legitimacy of the Loretan relic.[106] Benedict was also responsible for a lot of building in Loreto itself: he began renovations in the Piazza della Madonna in front of the basilica, and he commissioned Luigi Vanvitelli to erect the delightful onion-topped campanile that, together with the church's imposing cupola, dominates the surrounding countryside. Finally, as a proclamation of the Santa Casa's authenticity, Benedict organized the most elaborate celebration ever accorded to the shrine in the Loretan basilica in 1751.[107] In sum, Tiepolo's great fresco in the Scalzi celebrated the Santa Casa, while the Church itself was focusing attention on the small wooden structure.

---

[103] Cited in P. Davide, *L'isola di S. Clemente* (Venice, 1934), 28. Another report and history of S. Clemente can be found in BNM, Misc. Apostolo Zeno, MS Cl. It. XI, Cod. LXIII (6794), fos. 128ᵛ–130ᵛ.

[104] Cf. 'Erezione della S. Casa di Loreto', *Memorie della chiesa parrocchiale di S. Pantaleone medico e martire di Nicomedia* (Venice, n.d.), 262 ff.

[105] The feast was also given 'alla piissima Repubblica Veneta'. Cf. V. Murri, *Dissertatione critico-storica sulla identità della Santa Casa di Nazarette ora venerata in Loreto* (Loreto, 1791), 144. In 1732–3, P. V. Martorelli published the *Teatro storico della Santa Casa nazarena*, the greatest compendium of material on the Holy House,

and dedicated it to Clement XII. Fundamental for any study of Loreto and the Santa Casa, Martorelli's work gathers together some of the most important histories of the Holy House; it updates papal decrees and statutes concerning the relic and the shrine at Loreto; and it prints the texts for Masses and hymns recited on the feast-day of 10 December.

[106] Benedict XIV, *Delle feste di Gesù Cristo . . . e della B. Vergine Maria* (Venice, 1747), 334–8: 'L'Edificio Lauretano non è la Casa intera . . .', but it was 'una Camera della Casa, quella cioè, in cui la Vergine fu salutata dell'Angelo . . .'.

[107] Cf. P. Arsenio d'Ascoli, *La Santa Casa* (Loreto, 1965), 38.

81. G. B. Tiepolo, *Translation of the Holy House* (fresco)

Glorifying the Loretan relic was, of course, a way to exalt Mary, its sainted inhabitant. In the Scalzi, Tiepolo confirmed the Virgin's unique status in Roman Catholicism by her central position in the *Translation of the Holy House*, her brilliant blue/white cloak, and her grand scale before the enormous sphere of the silver moon. The Virgin's pivotal role in the Christian plan of salvation is also expressed through her unique association with Christ: she alone is permitted to stand alongside the Saviour. The faithful in the church would have understood that redemption could not be attained without her, for she mediates on a longitudinal axis between the Godhead and the darkened figures of evil falling towards hell. The Scalzi fresco, like the *Institution of the Rosary*, also insists upon a horizontal axis, along which the Santa Casa soars through the heavens, its triumphant progression heralded on the right by trumpeting angels. Finally, Tiepolo enriched the central image by framing it within a complex of six Old Testament scenes symbolizing the mother of Christ as the new Ark of the Covenant, a traditional metaphor in Marian veneration.[108]

Just as Tiepolo's ceiling in the Scalzi must be viewed in conjunction with Venetian traditions, papal involvement at Loreto, and contemporary exaltation of the Virgin, so, too, it should be seen in regard to the Catholic Enlightenment. In point of fact, the fresco's completion coincided with the successful conclusion of a campaign launched by a large section of the Church's hierarchy to abolish the feast of the Translation along with other feast-days in the liturgical calendar. The moving force behind this effort to reduce the number of yearly *feste di precetto*, days when workers refrained from labour and attended Mass in their local parishes, was Muratori. He directly associated the poverty of the Italian peasantry with the surfeit of 'holidays of obligation'. Deeply disturbed by the workers' loss of livelihood, Muratori organized a campaign by letter to convince Benedict XIV that the work-force should be returned to full employment: '. . . among the many reasons for so many poor people in Italy is the overwhelming number of feast days, so that poor people get accustomed to the comfortable employment of doing nothing, to games, etc.'.[109]

Many bishops and archbishops remained unconvinced that economic need should outweigh religious duty and opposed Muratori's initiative. They pointed out to the Holy Father that few towns and villages would acquiesce silently in the suppression of their local cults by authorities in distant Rome. Benedict, always open to new ideas but desirous none the less of reconciling innovation with tradition, promulgated the 1745 Bull *Ab eo tempore*, which allowed each archdiocese to reduce its own festivities, pending Rome's final approval.[110] As a result, nearly all of them decided to abolish the holiday of the Translation

[108] In the left octagon, Tiepolo painted *David's Transportation of the Ark* (2 Sam. 6: 3; and 1 Chr. 13: 7) and in the right, he showed *Solomon Kneeling before the Ark during the Consecration of the Temple* (1 Kgs. 8: 10–13; and 2 Chr. 5: 14). The other scenes are *Moses and Aaron*, the *Annunciation to Nathan* (1 Chr. 17: 3), *David Charging Solomon to Build the Temple* (1 Chr. 22: 6), and the *Annunciation to Gad* (1 Chr. 21: 18ff.). For the last scene, cf. Barcham, 'Giambattista Tiepolo's Ceiling', pp. 440–1.

[109] '. . . fra le molte cagioni di tanti poveri che abbiamo in Italia . . . v'entra ancora il soverchio numero delle feste, per le quali si avvezzano le povere genti al comodo mestiere di far nulla,

al giuoco, ecc.'; cited in F. Venturi, *Settecento riformatore: Da Muratori a Beccaria* (Turin, 1969), 139, where this important debate in eighteenth-century Italy is discussed. See also G. F. Scottoni, 'Semi per una buona agricoltura pratica italiana', *Giornale d'Italia spettante alla scienza naturale e principalmente all'agricoltura, alle arti ed al commercio* (1767), in M. Berengo (ed.), *Giornali veneziani del Settecento* (Milan, 1962), 133–8.

[110] *Sanctissimi Domini Nostri Benedicti Papae XIV Bullarium*, i (Rome, 1746), 582–90; the Bull is dated 5 Nov. 1745. Cf. also Muratori, *Della regolata*, pp. 288ff.; and 'Fêtes', *Dictionnaire de théologie catholique*, v². 2183–91.

VIII. G. B. Tiepolo, *Patron Saints of the Crotta Family* (oil on canvas, 195 × 320 cm.)

IX. G. B. Tiepolo, *Virgin and Christ-child Appearing to St John Nepomuk* (oil on canvas, 346 × 145 cm:)

of the Holy House. It was only two weeks after Benedict published the Bull (5 November) that Tiepolo completed his painting in the Scalzi (the final payment is dated 18 November). The fresco was ready, paradoxically, for the feast-day traditionally celebrated on 10 December.[111] Through its pictorial glorification of the Virgin as *victrix* over evil, the *Translation of the Holy House* is a refutation of the attacks made against the Marian relic and its place in Christian salvation.

During the decade in which he worked for the Discalced friars, Tiepolo also executed a ceiling for the lay confraternity linked to Venice's Calced community.[112] In the second-floor Sala Capitolare of the Scuola Grande dei Carmini, just across from the Church of S. Maria ai Carmini, Tiepolo painted the *Virgin of the Carmine and Christ-child Appearing to Simon Stock*, together with eight lateral canvases (Pls. 82, 83, 86–93). Although less ambitious in size than the contemporary Scalzi fresco, the Carmini ceiling took longer to complete. The first documents for the commission are dated 1739, the year Tiepolo finished at the Gesuati, but the project was not concluded until 1749, four years after the unveiling of the *Translation of the Holy House*.[113] This 'Marian period' of 1737–49 is chronologically central to Tiepolo's career: if one calculates from the earlier date of 1737 back to 1716, the beginning of his career, and from the later one of 1749 forward to 1770, his death, two intervals of exactly twenty-one years each result. Coincidental though this timing may be, one can still conclude that Tiepolo's absorption with supernal Marian imagery for ecclesiastical ceilings occurred at a pivotal moment in his life.

Although the Carmini ceiling is contemporaneous with the Gesuati and Scalzi commissions, its imagery and decorative framing are unlike either of them. The whole is painted in oil, not fresco, and its nine canvases are all inserted within lavish stucco mouldings which are both more ornate and more colourful than the surrounds of either the *Institution of the Rosary* or the *Translation of the Holy House*. The Scuola's central image concentrates almost exclusively on the Virgin, who, dressed in brilliant white, hovers full length over the faithful (Pls. 82–3). The Carmini image is physically close to the viewer, making Christ's mother loom immense and imminent; holding her head back in space, her heavy lids lowered, she is one of the most imperial and lofty of Tiepolo's Marys. Seemingly removed from those who adore her, the Carmini Virgin approximates the Venetian ideal of a Byzantine icon.

The Scuola Grande dei Carmini was the most popular Marian confraternity in the city; Don Niero reports that its membership reached the remarkable number of 75,000

---

[111] For the fresco's association with the holiday, cf. L. Livan (ed.), *Notizie d'arte tratte dai notatori e dagli annali del N. H. Pietro Gradenigo* (Venice, 1942), 67, 148, and 167. Tiepolo began work on the ceiling three months after the 450th anniversary of the Santa Casa's arrival in Italy; it may be conjectured that the commission was a timely celebration.

[112] This was the fifth Carmelite commission that the artist had carried out in his native city over a 25-year period; the group includes the Brera *Madonna del Carmelo*, and in the Scalzi the

Apotheosis of St Theresa, Christ in the Garden of Olives, and the *Translation of the Holy House*.

[113] For the documentation, cf. G. M. Urbani de Gheltof, *Tiepolo e la sua famiglia* (Venice, 1879), 104 ff.; C. Guglielmi Faldi, *Tiepolo alla Scuola dei Carmini a Venezia* (Milan, 1960); and A. Niero, 'Giambattista Tiepolo alla Scuola dei Carmini: Precisazioni d'archivio', *Atti dell'Istituto Veneto di Scienze, Lettere, ed Arti*, 135 (1976–7), 373–91.

82. G. B. Tiepolo, *Virgin of the Carmine and Christ-child Appearing to Simon Stock* (oil on canvas, 533 × 342 cm.)

83. Detail of Pl. 82

in the late seventeenth century.[114] With so many citizens belonging to its ranks, the Scuola must have been a wealthy establishment; indeed, the *Forestiere illuminato* of 1740 notes that the Scuola housed the '. . . rich furnishings, silver, and jewels . . . used to ornate the Altar in the Church . . .'.[115] Painted on the ceiling of the building's Sala Capitolare was Padovanino's *Assumption of the Virgin* (1634–8). Clement XII further enriched the Scuola in 1738 by donating a piece of the Virgin's veil, thereby intensifying the celebration of the Marian cult there.[116] The next year, the confraternity's governing board asked Tiepolo to embellish the chapter room's ceiling with secondary scenes, but he refused, explaining that: '. . . from the large Painting in the middle, the Painter must draw his Idea for the laterals . . .', but that '. . . in the large Painting [i.e., Padovanino's] there is no allusion to the Confraternity's Titular Saint [Patron] . . .'.[117] Dated 21 December 1739, this document also furnishes rare evidence of Tiepolo's own religious beliefs, for it notes that the artist 'lives in devotion' to the Virgin of Carmel.

Between the end of 1739 and 19 January 1740, the confraternity changed its plans, probably influenced by Tiepolo's criticisms, and commissioned a new canvas for the ceiling's centre as well as the eight laterals already requested. The contract called for a principal subject that would glorify Mary, the confraternity's protectress, and honour Simon Stock, its founder; it was stated that Tiepolo would depict '. . . the Most Holy Virgin who, revered by the Most Holy Prophets Elijah and Elisha and by bands of Angels, descends from Heaven with the sacred scapular in hand, offering it to St Simon Stock who implores Her in supplication for some sign of her personal Protection'.[118] In other words, the new ceiling for the Sala Capitolare would not repeat the Assumption, Padovanino's theme, but would celebrate the Marian scapular and its power to liberate souls from purgatory.

According to tradition, the Virgin appeared before Simon Stock, an Englishman of the mid-thirteenth century who created the Third Order of the Carmelites and founded convents in Cambridge, Oxford, Paris, and Bologna, and offered special protection to 'the brothers of Carmelus who died piously while wearing the scapular', a brown tunic carried close to the body.[119] A century later, on 3 March 1322, Pope John XXII promulgated the so-called 'bolla sabbatina'; this promised that all those who joined with the Carmelites in wearing the simple, homespun fabric would, on the first Saturday after

[114] The Madonna del Carmelo was the most popular of the Marian cults in Venice, and apart from the confraternity at the Carmini, there were smaller *scuole* to the same devotion at S. Pietro di Castello and S. Aponal: cf. S. Tramontin, 'Il culto dei santi nelle confraternite', *Santità a Venezia*, pp. 44, 50, and 53. For the membership at the Carmini, cf. A. Niero, *La chiesa dei Carmini* (Venice, 1965), 13, who cites seventeenth-century sources. However, Coronelli, *Guida de' forestieri* (1724), p. 351, reports that the Scuola dei Carmini had only 300 'Fratelli'.

[115] *Il forestiere illuminato intorno le cose più rare e curiose della città di Venezia* (Venice, 1740), 236: '. . . le ricche suppellettili, le argenterie, e le gioje, che servono ad ornar l'Altare ch'è nella Chiesa . . .'.

[116] A. Niero, *La Scuola Grande dei Carmini* (Venice, 1963), 20. In 1735, Clement had granted a special indulgence to the

Carmini: see Padre Giuseppe Maria Sardi (Carmelite theologian at the Carmini), *Il giovane dell'ordine della S. Vergine Maria del Carmine dell'antica osservanza* (Venice, 1737), 330.

[117] Urbani de Gheltof, *Tiepolo*, p. 106: 'Che dal Quadro grande nel mezzo, deve il Pittore ritraerne l'Idea per li laterali; che nel Quadro grande non v'è Concetto allusivo alla Titolar della Confraternita . . .'.

[118] Ibid., p. 109: 'La SS. Vergine che cortegiata dalli S.S. Profeti Elia ed Eliseo e da molte schiere d'Angeli scenda dal Cielo col sagro scapulare in mano e lo porga al S. Simeon Stock, mentre questo in atto supplichevole implora da Lei qualche contrassegno del suo particolar Patrocinio.'

[119] R. P. Elisée de La Nativité, OCD., 'La Vie mariale au Carmel', in *Marie: Études sur la sainte Vièrge* (Paris, 1949), 841 ff.

their death, be liberated by the Virgin from their punishments in purgatory.[120] Not surprisingly, scapular devotion increased rapidly as a result, especially after Alexander V confirmed the decree in 1409.

Purgatory, a very old idea in the Christian concept of the universe, is a 'staging-post' for those souls who, although saved, still need purification.[121] After *c.*1560, this otherworldly byway formed an important theological distinction between post-Tridentine Catholicism and Protestantism. Painted images of souls yearning to be freed from their cleansing torments began to appear in Catholic churches towards 1600; Palma Giovane's canvases for the Scuola di S. Maria della Giustizia e di S. Gerolamo, perhaps helpful to Tiepolo when he painted the *Madonna del Carmelo*, date from that very year (Pl. 85). St Gregory the Great, the patron saint of souls in purgatory, was often represented; for example, in altar-pieces by Cerano and Guercino.[122]

During the seventeenth century, the Sacred Congregation of the Inquisition allowed the Carmelites to deliver public sermons specifically on Mary's aid to the souls of the Order's deceased members.[123] The increased number of images of the later seventeenth and early eighteenth centuries showing the Virgin interceding in purgatory must surely be a reflection of this decision.[124] One such work which would certainly have been known to Tiepolo is Luca Giordano's *Madonna del Carmelo* in S. Pietro di Castello in Venice (Pl. 84), in which a Byzantine-looking Mary, supported on clouds by a group of cherubs, is holding the Christ-child and a small scapular while hovering above purgatory, where souls seek their final release. Like Tiepolo's ceiling at the Carmini, this painting was commissioned by a scapular confraternity.

Serious doubts concerning the authenticity of John XXII's Sabbatine Bull arose in the very late seicento, and towards 1700 polemics on the subject became frequent. At the same time, sceptics began questioning the very origins of the Carmelite Order, which, according to tradition, had been founded by Elijah on Mount Carmel following his vision of Mary. Clement XI (1700–21) and Benedict XIII (1724–30), the very same Popes whose acts and pronouncements promoted the Rosary and the Santa Casa, stepped in to quiet the debates raging around both Carmelite history and the Sabbatine Bull. Clement

[120] Cf. 'Carmelitani', *Dizionario degli Istituti di Perfezione*, iii. 507; and P. Ludovico Saggi, O. Carm., 'Il testo della "bolla sabbatina"', *Carmelus*, 13 (1966), 245. There is no trace of John XXII's original document: see J. Smet, *The Carmelites: A History of the Brothers of Our Lady of Mount Carmel* (Darien, Ill., 1976), 223.

[121] Cf. Warner, *Alone of All Her Sex*, chap. 22, 'The Hour of Our Death', pp. 315 ff.; and 'Purgatorio', *Dizionario di erudizione storico-ecclesiastica*, 56 (Venice, 1855), 88–92.

[122] *Saint Gregory the Great: Dialogues*, ed. O. J. Zimmerman (New York, 1959), chap. 57. For Cerano, cf. C. Puglisi, 'The Mass of St. Gregory and Cerano's Varese Altarpiece', *Marsyas*, 19 (1979), 11–15; for Guercino's painting in S. Paolo Maggiore, Bologna, cf. N. Grimaldi, *Il Guercino* (Bologna, n.d.), pl. 157. See also Poggetto and Zampetti, *Lorenzo Lotto*, no. 144, for a painting by Ercole Ramazzini, the *Liberation of Souls from Purgatory* (1586), in which souls are extracted from their punishing fires half-way between Christ in heaven and four kneeling saints, among whom is St Gregory. Cf. G. Pavanello, 'Una pala inedita di Sebastiano Ricci',

Arte veneta, 36 (1982), 228–9, for a painting in which souls in purgatory entreat the crucified Christ.

[123] P. Ludovico Saggi, 'Santa Maria del Carmelo', in *Santi del Carmelo* (Rome, 1972), 110.

[124] Ricci did four such paintings around 1730: cf. J. Daniels, *Sebastiano Ricci* (Hove, 1976), nos. 33, 294, and 460. See also Giuseppe Maria Crespi's *Virgin of Carmel, Simon Stock and St Anthony of Padua* (M. P. Merriman, *Giuseppe Maria Crespi* (Milan, 1980), no. 136), and Gaspare Diziani's *Virgin with Saints and Souls in Purgatory* and *Virgin of Carmel with SS Joseph and Nicholas* (A. P. Zugni-Tauro, *Gaspare Diziani* (Venice, 1971), figs. 32 and 34; the latter is mistakenly called a *Virgin of the Rosary*). For a related work of the seicento, see Guercino's and Benedetto Gennari's *Virgin of the Carmine Offering the Scapular to SS Albert, Francis, and Another Franciscan Saint* in the Pinacoteca, Cento; cf. D. Mahon, *Il Guercino* (exh. cat., Pal. dell'Archiginnasio, Bologna, 1968), no. 7.

sought to authenticate the former by ordering a statue of 'St Elijah' for St Peter's; the Carmelite Order was thus officially transformed into the West's oldest religious community.[125] And to strengthen the Marian foundations of Carmelite devotions, Benedict extended the feast of the 'Beata Vergine del Carmine' and the 'scapolare mariano', celebrated on 16 July, to the Universal Church.[126] In 1722, the Carmelites observed the four hundredth anniversary of John XXII's 'bolla sabbatina'.[127] Throughout these decades and continuing into the 1740s, numerous pamphlets and treatises dealing with Carmelite traditions issued forth from Venetian presses. One of the aims of these publications was, as we shall see below, to focus attention on Simon Stock and the simple piece of homespun that Mary had given him—the scene that Tiepolo depicted on the Carmini ceiling.

Twenty years earlier, in S. Aponal (Pl. 17), Tiepolo had already celebrated the Carmelites' donation of the scapular to the world. On the far left of that broad canvas, souls imprisoned in purgatory are offered release by an angelic messenger, just as the Sabbatine Bull had promised. On the right, Mary bestows the brown scapular on the Blessed Simon, while Christ offers the small scapular to the Blessed Albert.[128] Kneeling close to Albert and adoring the Child is St Theresa, who wrote the Rule of the Discalced Carmelites. On the far right of this encyclopaedic Carmelite image is the hooded figure of the prophet Elijah (Pl. 18). As befits his Old Testament origin, he lives in a dark, cloud-filled world, behind which looms a distant mountain surely meant to be understood as Mount Carmel. Both the mountain and the prophet confirm Carmelite history. In the larger, Christian context, however, Elijah's presence in the *Madonna del Carmelo* has an even greater significance: his ascension into heaven (2 Kings 2:11–12) was seen in Christian thought as a foreshadowing of Christ's own. Equally powerful is the association between Elijah and the resurrection; in 1 Kings 17: 21–4, the prophet restores life to a dead child after pleas from the supplicating mother. His appearance in the painting not only recalls Carmelite origins, therefore, but it also points to Christian salvation. Indeed, the *Madonna del Carmelo* insists upon this theme through the Infant's swaddling cloth, which reminds the believer of the Saviour's shroud, his crucifixion, and thus mankind's redemption through Christ.

Tiepolo's painting for the Scuola dei Carmini has a more particular focus than the S. Aponal/Brera canvas. The ceiling's hagiographical centre of interest is Simon Stock alone, probably a reflection of the onslaught of Carmelite writings of the 1720s and 1730s which

---

[125] The question of whether Elijah was the founder of the Carmelites was raised in 1688 in the *Acta Sanctorum*: cf. A. A. King, *Liturgies of the Religious Orders* (London, 1955), 235; and E. Mâle, *L'Art religieux après le concile de Trente* (Paris, 1932), 445. Agostino Cornacchini completed *Elijah* in 1725 and the work was unveiled in 1727: cf. Padre Saggi, 'Agiografia carmelitana', in *Santi del Carmelo*, p. 78; and R. Enggass, *Early 18th Century Sculpture in Rome* (University Park, Pa., 1976) i. 203–4, ii, fig. 221. The inscription below the statue reads: 'UNIVERSUS CARMELITARUM ORDO/ FUNDATORI SUO S. ELIAE/PROPHETAE EREXIT. A. MDCCXXVII.'

[126] Before 1726 but after Paul V's decree of 1609, the feast had only been observed by the Order itself: cf. Padre Saggi, 'Il testo', p. 256; and E. Campana, *Maria nel culto cattolico*, i (Turin, 1945), 329.

[127] Cf. Padre Sardi's *Il giovane dell'ordine della S. Vergine Maria del Carmine dell'antica osservanza, istruito nella sua regola, ne' suoi obblighi e ne' suoi privilegi* (BMC, under the classification *F 1056*), 63.

[128] Neither Stock nor Albert has ever been officially canonized, but because the latter drew up the Carmelite Rule (*c.*1208), the Order regards him as a saint. The book below Christ can be identified as the Carmelite Rule. I am grateful to George Knox for identifying Albert to me: cf. 'Albert', *Biblioteca Sanctorum*, i (Rome, 1961), cols. 686–90; and 'Alberto', *New Catholic Encyclopaedia*, i (New York, 1967), 258. E. Modigliani, 'Dipinti ignoti o mal noti di Giambattista Tiepolo', *Dedalo*, 13 (1933), 129–47, called the figure St Andrew Corsini.

84. L. Giordano, *Madonna del Carmelo* (oil on canvas, 312 × 129 cm.)

85. Below: Palma Giovane, *Souls in Purgatory*, detail (oil on canvas, 100 × 270 cm.)

recorded Stock's vision of the Virgin and provided exegeses of its meaning for the Order.[129] One of the most important of these tracts, certainly in Venice, was written by the leading theologian at S. Maria ai Carmini, Padre Giuseppe Maria Sardi. Published in 1737, *Il giovane dell'ordine della S. Vergine Maria del Carmine* is a three-hundred-page text that narrates the thirteenth-century miracle before Stock, discusses instructions, rules, and obligations for young Carmelites, and relates them to the cult of Carmel and the history of papal favours to the Order.[130] A long section of the work lists the indulgences and benefits owed to those who wear the scapular.

Other treatises similar both in subject and tone preceded and followed Sardi's. Padre Simone Grassi (d. 1723) wrote at least two, in one of which he explained that the scapular was a '. . . powerful shield of protection and defence against the many dangers of our present life . . .', and a '. . . happy omen of predestination and health . . .'.[131] In 1739, Padre Giuseppe di Gesù published an *Istruzione intorno al sacro abitino di Maria Vergine del Carmine*, in which no less an authority than the Virgin herself was 'quoted' as saying that the scapular is '. . . the sign of health, an escape from dangers, the obligation of peace and of an eternal accord'.[132] Padre Giuseppe's text then continues for more than a hundred pages with an explication of the above categories (health, dangers, etc.) and both actual and hypothetical examples of the scapular's power to protect; such diverse perils as falling into a well and encountering the Devil are cited. The Scuola dei Carmini would have been familiar with these various tracts, and from the very beginning of their dealings with Tiepolo, the confraternity expected that the scapular's prophylactic functions would be incorporated into the iconographic and decorative plan of their new ceiling.

The contract of 1740 listed two *pensieri* for the lateral canvases which were to surround the *Virgin of the Carmine Appearing to Simon Stock*. The first proposed a series of paintings to glorify the scapular and demonstrate its achievements: (1) the closing of hell's gates; (2) souls lifted out of purgatory by rescuing angels; (3) souls saved by their brothers' prayers and suffrages; (4) a guardian angel preventing a young man wearing the scapular from falling to his death; (5) angels carrying scapulars; (6) others displaying papal bulls and indulgences, including John XXII's Sabbatine Bull; (7) confraternal abstinence represented by a woman covering her mouth; and (8) celibacy or matrimonial chastity portrayed by a woman dressed in white holding various symbolic objects.[133] The second

[129] Such works must be read as necessary explanations, a priori and post factum, of the feast of Our Lady of Carmel that Benedict XIII extended to the Universal Church in 1726. According to tradition, Mary said to the Englishman: 'Hoc tibi et tuis privilegium: in hoc moriens salvabitur.' These words can be found in Bartholomaeus Xiberta's *De visione S. Simonis Stock* (republished Rome, 1950), 102; and in Padre Saggi's 'Santa Maria del Carmelo', p. 131.

[130] Cf. above, n. 128.

[131] I have found Grassi's works in nineteenth-century editions: *Compendiosa narrazione dell'indulgenze, privilegi, e grazie concesse all'ordine, confraternite, e chiese della gloriosissima Madre di Dio Maria Vergine del Carmine* (Rome, 1830); *Origine privilegi doveri e indulgenze del Santo Scapolare di Maria SS del Carmelo* (Venice, 1884), 9: 'possente scudo di protezione e difesa nei molteplici pericoli della presente vita'; and 'il felice presagio di predestinazione e salute . . .'.

[132] P. Giuseppe di Gesù, *Istruzione intorno al sacro abitino di Maria Vergine del Carmine* (Perugia, 1752), 6: 'Ecco il segno di salute, lo scampo ne' pericoli, la convenzione di pace, e di patto sempiterno.' There were, of course, contemporary criticisms of the scapular and the cult of purgatory. In Italy, Muratori commented on them in *Della regolata divozione*, pp. 353–60, and Hume wrote bitingly in 'The Natural History of Religion', p. 61: 'Take two bits of cloth, say the Roman Catholics, about an inch or an inch and a half square, join them by the corners with two strings . . ., throw this over your head, and make one of the bits of cloth lie upon your breast, and the other upon your back, keeping them next to your skin: There is not a better secret for recommending yourself to that infinite Being, who exists from eternity to eternity.'

[133] Cf. Urbani De Gheltof, *Tiepolo*, pp. 109ff. Padre Giuseppe di Gesù's book of 1739 creates just such a classification. For the closing of hell's gates as one of the scapular's functions, cf. 'Scapular', *The Catholic Encyclopaedia*, 13 (London, 1912), 511.

pensiero suggested instead that the eight surrounding canvases should display the 'heroic virtues that adorn the Most Holy Virgin here on earth . . .', those that the confraternity sought most to imitate.[134] Seventeen Virtues are enumerated and their personifications described.

The final result is a fusion of elements from both *pensieri*, with Tiepolo indicating the different schemes in the ceiling's programme by employing canvases of two different shapes positioned in two different ways. 'Shaped rectangles' arranged along the four sides of the *Virgin of the Carmine Appearing to Simon Stock* illustrate numbers 2, 4, 5, and 6 from the first *pensiero* (Pls. 86–9, and see Plan A in the key to Fig. 4);[135] while 'half lunettes' over the room's four corners show eleven personifications, not the seventeen called for in the second (see Plan B). The three Theological Virtues, *Hope, Charity*, and *Faith* (as they appear from left to right in Pl. 90) are on the side of the room nearest to the street, to the right when looking from the staircase landing. Above the diagonally opposite corner, to the right of the altar, are two of the four Cardinal Virtues: *Justice*, with the Holy Spirit hovering overhead—thus 'Divine Justice'—and *Fortitude*, with a column and accompanied by both the lion of St Mark and a cherub with an olive branch (Pl. 91). To the altar's left are *Prudence* and *Temperance*, the other Cardinal Virtues, with *Purity*, a Beatitude, between them (Pl. 92).[136] Don Niero has identified the last three personifications diagonally opposite these as *Humility, Meekness* and *Truth* (Pl. 93).[137] *Humility*, indeed, is present but in the centre of the group and is holding a lamb and crushing a crown and sceptre under her foot. Her two 'sisters' are *Patience*, with a crucifix and a thorny branch held overhead by a cherub ('Christian Forbearance in Affliction'), and *Chastity*, who holds a sieve at arm's length but turns away from it.[138]

[134] Urbani De Gheltof, *Tiepolo*, pp. 111 ff.: 'Per secondo un pensiere più specioso e proporcionato al sito medesimo sul riflesso che la maggior devocione de' Confratelli, tenendo all'imitacione di queste eroiche virtù che adornano la S.ma Vergine qui in terra, sarà benfatto, che disposte queste con loro geroglifici istoriati od altro servono d'adornamento e Corona al quadro principale, e di specchio dove possano i Confratelli stessi con devocione osservarli, perciò potrà rappresentarsi.' The 'heroic virtues' are listed and briefly delineated, although Tiepolo rarely followed the description provided. In sequence, the seventeen are (1) Faith, Hope and Charity; (2) Prudence and Justice; (3) Fortitude and Temperance; (4) Chastity and Poverty; (5) Obedience and Piety; (6) Humility and Meekness; (7) Purity and Modesty; (8) Patience and Perseverance.

[135] No. 2, 'Varij Angeli che levano Anime dal Purgatorio, le trasferiscono al Cielo'; no. 4, 'Un'Angelo tutelare in atto di sostenere un giovine che precipita vestito dal S. Scapolare'; no. 5, 'Altri Angioli, che con veneracione ed allegrezza portano e custodiscono li S. Scapulari'; and no. 6, 'Altri Angioli che portando varie bolle et indulgenza, una tra l'altre ne mostrino più speciosa indicante la Sabatina'.

[136] *Temperance* is described differently in the second *pensiero* ('un Ramo di Palma in mano nella destra e con un freno nella sinistra'), although C. Ripa, *Iconologia* (Rome, 1603, 480ff.) notes that she pours water on hot pincers. The figure could be read as *Penitence*, however; Ripa, p. 389, writes that she is a woman 'fermandosi col pensiero alla contemplatione del fonte, che è la gratia, la quale da lui scaturisce per lavarla nel fonte . . .'. For the Beatitudes, cf. 'Béatitudes', *Dictionnaire de spiritualité*, i (Paris,

1937), cols. 1298–1310.

[137] Niero, *La Scuola Grande dei Carmini*, pp. 35–6.

[138] Although *Humility* in Plan B is 'una donna vestita di bianco con gli occhi bassi ed un Agnello in braccio', Ripa (*Iconologia*, p. 37) describes *Meekness* thus: 'in atto di accarezzare un piccolo, & mansueto agnello . . .'. On p. 40, he notes that the Persecuted (a Beatitude) is holding a cross. Tiepolo's figure of *Chastity* is impossible to reconcile with the description in Plan B ('vestita d'oro, con una corona in testa, sopra alla quale vi sia una colomba circondata da splendore'), but the sieve as *Chastity*'s attribute is found in Ripa (*Iconologia*, p. 66), and in G. De Tervarent, *Attributs et symbols dans l'art profane 1450–1600* (Geneva, 1958), 370; cf. especially H.-F. Gravelot and C.-N. Cochin, *Iconologie par figures* (repr. Geneva, 1972) i, no. 57, who describe *Chastity* as the Vestal Virgin Tutia who looks away while pouring water into a sieve. Several preparatory works can be associated with the Carmini 'Virtues': for *Faith, Hope, and Charity*, an oil-sketch (46.5 by 39 cm.) appeared at Christie's, London, in Dec. 1980; another (18 by 18 cm.) was on the art market in Venice (cf. *Burlington Magazine*, 111 (1969), p. xxxviii); and a third belongs to the Museum in Brussels. Two more entitled *Humility and Meekness* and *Prudence, Innocence, and Grace* were on view in the exhibition *La Peinture italienne au XVIIIe siècle* (exh. cat., Palais des Beaux-Arts (Petit Palais), Paris, 1960, nos. 394–5). For Tiepolo's delivery of the lateral canvases before 16 Jan. 1743, cf. Niero, 'Giambattista Tiepolo alla Scuola dei Carmini', 380–4; and for the artist's membership in the confraternity, cf. Zanetti, 'Memorie per servire', p. 137.

86. G. B. Tiepolo, *Souls in Purgatory and Angel with Scapular* (oil on canvas, 116 × 337 cm.)

87. G. B. Tiepolo, *Angel Saving a Falling Worker* (oil on canvas, 116 × 337 cm.)

88. G. B. Tiepolo, *Angels with Scapular and Lilies* (oil on canvas, 164 × 280 cm.)

89. G. B. Tiepolo, *Angels with Indulgences and Papal Bull* (oil on canvas, 164 × 280 cm.)

90. G. B. Tiepolo, *Hope, Charity, and Faith* (oil on canvas, 235 × 240 cm.)

91. G. B. Tiepolo, *Justice and Fortitude* (oil on canvas, 235 × 240 cm.)

92. G. B. Tiepolo, *Prudence, Purity, and Temperance* (oil on canvas, 235 × 240 cm.)

93. G. B. Tiepolo, *Patience, Humility, and Chastity* (oil on canvas, 235 × 240 cm.)

Such groupings of Virtues and Beatitudes are not infrequent in Christian art; Palma Giovane's ceiling in S. Zulian in Venice, which was also composed of numerous canvases painted in oil and organized around a central image (the *Glory of S. Zulian*), showed them as Christian exemplars, too. Tiepolo's eight lateral compartments respond specifically to the treatises of the early eighteenth century explaining the responsibilities and privileges of the scapular; they thus present a sweeping panorama of Carmelite spirituality. The confraternity's response to these images is well known; upon their delivery, Tiepolo was unanimously voted a brother member.

Tiepolo completed the ceiling's central canvas in 1749, but it does not comply with the specification of the 1740 contract, which called for the Virgin to be accompanied by 'SS Profeti Elia ed Eliseo'.[139] Their absence from the ceiling's iconographic plan is at first puzzling, and it makes an important distinction between the Carmini cycle and both the Gesuati and Scalzi ceilings, where Old Testament figures are used to 'support' the Marian cult. David singing the psalms above the Gesuati's choir accompanies the monks' chanting the Rosary below, while four scenes narrating the building and transportation of the Ark furnish a biblical precedent for the translation of the Holy House. But when he removed Elijah and Elisha from the Carmini ceiling, Tiepolo did not provide the proper Old Testament foundation upon which to 'sustain' the Virgin of the Scapular. Their disappearance must have been partly due to compositional and spatial considerations: the central canvas is simply not large enough to include them alongside the Virgin, Simon Stock, and 'many bands of Angels', and yet still create an imposing effect in a room measuring only approximately ten metres in width by twenty in length and whose ceiling is less than ten metres away. A comparison of the finished paintings and preparatory oil-sketches for the *Institution of the Rosary* and the *Translation of the Holy House* demonstrates that, when he worked for the Dominicans and Discalced Carmelites, Tiepolo was in the ideal position of having to expand his compositions; in both cases, space has been increased and figures added. But this was not so for the Carmini; space was not extended from *bozzetto* (Pl. IV) to final image, and only one important new element was inserted—the imposing angel hovering on the canvas's left side.

Although Tiepolo removed Elijah and Elisha from his composition, he did not lose their significance, however. In Tiepolo's oil-sketch for the painting, Simon appears alone.[140] The subsequent addition in the ceiling of the shadowed angel holding the Marian tunic so that it falls directly on to Stock's white Carmelite robe is a reference to the legacy of the two Old Testament prophets that was claimed by the Carmelites. When Elijah ascended to heaven on a chariot of fire pulled by horses of fire (2 Kings 2:14–15), Elisha his follower '. . . took the mantle of Elijah that had fallen . . . and struck the water saying, "Where is the Lord, the God of Elijah?" And when he had struck the water, the water was parted to the one side and to the other; and Elisha went over. Now when the sons of the prophets . . . saw him . . . they said "The spirit of Elijah rests on Elisha"'. The

---

[139] Cf. Niero, 'Giambattista Tiepolo alla Scuola dei Carmini', pp. 380ff.

[140] The sketch which measures 65 by 41 cm, belonged to a Parisian private collection before passing to the Louvre in the 1970s; cf. *Venise au XVIIIe siècle* (exh. cat., Musée de l'Orangerie, Paris, 1971), no. 234. For a drawing of the Virgin and Child attributed to Domenico, cf. Knox, *Tiepolo: A Bicentenary*, no. 45. Pietro Liberi's version of the *Virgin Appearing to Simon Stock* (1666) in the nearby S. Maria ai Carmini is different from Tiepolo's: cf. R. Pallucchini, *La pittura veneziana del Seicento*, ii, fig. 646.

scapular thus stood for the spirit that descended from Elijah, to Elisha, and then on to the sons of Carmel.

A second modification between sketch and finished work can be seen in Mary's position. In the *modelletto* she turns towards the kneeling Stock, but in the Sala Capitolare she faces forward, peering down at the confraternal brothers. Psychologically dissociated from the scapular's donation, the mother of Christ appears aloof and removed (Pl. 83). Transformed from an earthly participant into a timeless, seemingly suspended vision, Mary is *sine macula*, that is, free from original sin, a state already hinted at in the oil-sketch by her white dress. Mary's immaculacy is, in fact, included in the Carmelites' canon of beliefs; she is their patron, the Virgin of the Scapular, and the *Immacolata*.[141] So, both of the major changes that Tiepolo introduced into the finished work increased the Carmelite content of his painting and its Marian exaltation.

By portraying Mary as both the Virgin of the Scapular and the *Immacolata*, Tiepolo was endorsing the Marian devotions of the Sala Capitolare's altar-statue by Bernardino Falcone (active 1659–94), which shows the Virgin on the quarter-moon holding both the Christ-child and the scapular. When one enters the room and looks up to the right, Tiepolo's Mary appears on the ceiling; below and to the left, Falcone's stands over the altar. A sympathetic chord sounds silently between the two figures. In a sense, the confraternal brother was, and still is, locked between them.

Tiepolo's nine canvases, framed in wood, are surrounded by six zones of stuccoed mouldings that are fancifully designed and elegantly coloured: they contain decorative urns and wreaths painted gold and set against a pastel pink background, each of them further ornamented with gold, light green, and touches of bright ochre. Between and around both these exquisite forms and the oil-paintings is further stucco-work consisting of cherubs, draperies, and roses painted white, all of which contrast with the stair-well's earlier decorated vault.[142] The latter's lavish encrustation of figures, fruits, and scroll-work in thick and luxuriant white forms seen against a gold background provides a stately approach to the Sala's delicate, pastel surfaces. The staircase's decorative opulence recalls the *scala d'oro* in the Ducal Palace, and suggests that the ascent to the Scuola's second floor was often accompanied by ceremonial display.

Beautiful though the Sala's eighteenth-century stuccoed forms are, they are unexpected, for the decorative combination of oil-paintings and stucco-work was new in the history of Venetian ceiling design. Stuccoed mouldings should surround frescos, as in the Gesuati, and canvases painted in oil should be set into wooden coffers, as in S. Zulian. In mixing these conventionally independent media, the ceiling in the chapter room makes use of two separate traditions. But the reasons for the new union are not immediately clear. The fact that the ceiling is flat and that it had been adorned with canvases before, certainly meant that it made sense to do the same again. That stucco should be the intermediary

[141] P. Saggi comments in 'Santa Maria del Carmelo', p. 110, that his Order regards Mary in these three 'states'; cf. also King, *Liturgies*, p. 262, who notes that 4 Marian invocations were added to the Carmelite breviary of 1672: 'Mater decor Carmeli'; 'Virgo flos Carmeli'; 'Patrona Carmelitarum'; and 'Spes omnium Carmelitarum'. This last title is meant to be meditated upon by

Carmelites through the contemplation of the Order's white habit in contrast with the brown scapular: cf. P. di Gesù, *Istruzione intorno*, p. 38.

[142] For the documentation, see Niero, 'Giambattista Tiepolo alla Scuola dei Carmini', pp. 373 ff.

accompaniment to oil-paintings is surprising, however. The most plausible explanation for this rests on the certain knowledge that Padovanino's ensemble contained other canvases apart from the *Assumption of the Virgin*.[143] Their exact number is unknown, but they could conceivably have covered a good part of the ceiling. After Tiepolo's new design and iconographic scheme had been settled upon and the old paintings removed in mid-1740, several areas might have appeared bare, and it may then have been decided that filling the intermediary spaces with decorative designs in stucco was both easy and tasteful.[144] Moreover, the combination of pink, pale green, gold, and white not only offered a beautiful contrast to the 'purgatorial' shadows and deep colouring of Tiepolo's oil-paintings, but it also provided a splendid surround for the radiant Virgin.

The brilliance of Tiepolo's art in the Carmini is evident not only in the elegance of his ceiling's decorative plan, but also in the paintings' relationship to the Sala Capitolare's space. The pictorial complex was conceived so that the visitor would be able to see every figure in all the canvases from the top of the staircase; in other words, the entire ceiling can be understood from one spot and in one short span of time (Fig. 4). The five personifications on the altar side of the *sala* are directed towards the staircase-landing, as are the six at the opposite end. This is true, too, of the figures in the four smaller paintings that flank the *Virgin of the Carmine Appearing to Simon Stock*: the angels with books and scapulars, those with the falling worker, and the souls in purgatory looking at the scapular. Most importantly, the Virgin herself looks towards the confraternity's members as they arrive in the room. In the oil-sketch, Mary had turned to Simon Stock, but in the ceiling-painting she acknowledges the laity instead. On looking up, the Carmini brother realizes that he is the counterpart to the Blessed Simon; like Stock, he is meant to defer to Christ's mother and accept her offer of salvation.

Tiepolo painted the Virgin *sine macula* on the Carmini ceiling only a few years after he had depicted the *Immacolata* in the Scalzi.[145] The conflation of both the Virgin of the Scapular and the Virgin of Loreto with the Immaculate Virgin is not coincidental. That Christ's mother should be identified on two Carmelite ceilings in the same way is not surprising, however, for the Order had supported the immaculist position in the Church's debate over Mary's freedom from sin since the fifteenth century, continuing to do so right into the seventeenth and eighteenth.[146] I would suggest that the timing of the *Translation*

[143] Apart from the description in A. M. Zanetti, *Descrizione di tutte le pubbliche pitture della città di Venezia* (Venice, 1733), 353 ('Nella sala di sopra il soffitto con la Santissima Trinità, la Vergine, S. Gioseppe, ed altro [*sic*] è del Padoanino.'), there are the documents themselves; for which cf. Niero, 'Giambattista Tiepolo alla Scuola dei Carmini', p. 374 n. 5.

[144] As I have noted above, the material also covered the stair-well's vaulting; in using it in the intermediary spaces of the ceiling in the Sala Capitolare as well, a decorative continuum was created. Furthermore, Venice at that time could boast of many brilliant stuccoists, although they mainly seem to have been engaged in secular commissions, such as in the Albrizzi and Sagredo Palaces. It would be helpful to have a survey of the decorative schemes of the period.

[145] For Mary as the Immaculate Virgin on the Scalzi ceiling, cf. Barcham, 'Giambattista Tiepolo's Ceiling', p. 444.

[146] The Franciscans and the Carmelites had traditionally been the doctrine's strongest supporters. Cf. P. Claudio Catena, OC, 'Il culto dell'Immacolata Concezione nel Carmelo', and 'La dottrina immacolista negli autori carmelitani', *Carmelus*, 1 (1954), 290–321, and 2 (1955), 132–215; 'Immacolata Concezione', *Enciclopedia cattolica*, vi, p. 1656; and King, *Liturgies*, pp. 276–7, who also notes that the title 'Immaculate Conception' can be found in the Carmelite Missal of 1733, 'an unusual designation prior to the definition of the dogma in 1854'. Conversely, the Dominicans were the historic opponents of the belief in Mary's immaculacy, and the Gesuati's *Institution of the Rosary* therefore contains no pictorial reference to it. The Dominicans' St Thomas had been opposed to the Immaculate Conception; how could Mary be redeemed if she was free from original sin? Cf. King, *Liturgies*, pp. 362–3.

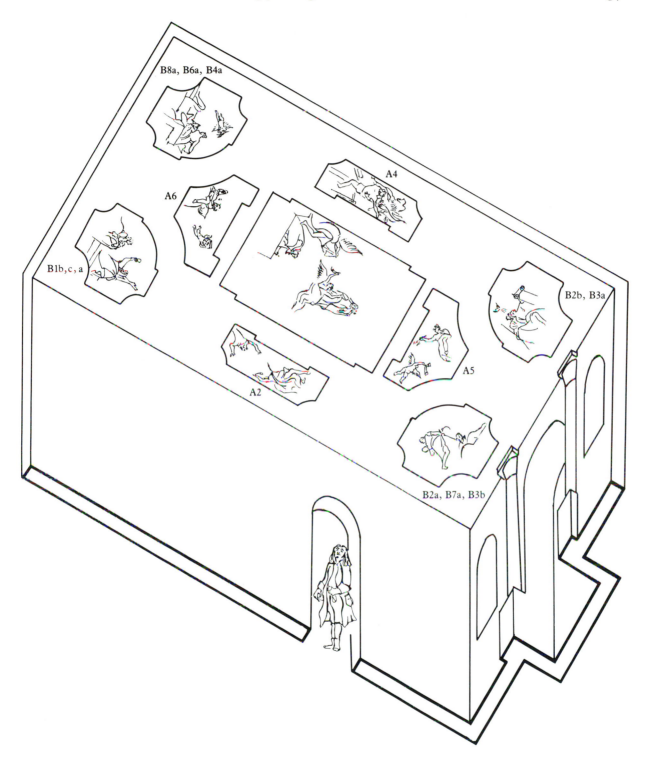

FIG. 4. Axonometric rendering of the Sala Capitolare, Scuola
Grande dei Carmini, Venice (see Pls. 86–93)

PLAN A (cf. p. 148, bottom, and n. 135):
A2 = Souls lifted out of purgatory by rescuing angels
A4 = A guardian angel preventing a young man wearing
 the scapular from falling to his death
A5 = Angels carrying scapulars
A6 = Angels displaying papal bulls and indulgences,
 including John XXII's Sabbatine Bull

PLAN B (cf. n. 134):
B1a = Faith; b = Hope; c = Charity
B2a = Prudence; b = Justice
B3a = Fortitude; b = Temperance
B4a = Chastity
B6a = Humility
B7a = Purity   B8a = Patience

of the Holy House and the *Virgin of the Carmine Appearing to Simon Stock* is also relevant here. Both of them were executed within the same decade, a period rife with argument about the Immaculate Conception.

Mid-eighteenth-century polemics on the subject stemmed in part from Benedict XIV's position on the issue. As Archbishop of Bologna before 1740, Lambertini had been open to new ideas; a well-read and intelligent man (able, too, to savour the culinary pleasures of his native city and as fond of good food as he was of good books), he enjoyed cordial relations with the most open-minded of Catholic thinkers. His election to the papacy fulfilled the hopes of enlightened Catholic thinkers and offered promise of a new epoch in church history. Great reforms were expected. But Benedict was cautious, even orthodox in his Christianity, as his publication on the calendar's Christological and Marian feasts helps to show. He was also perspicacious enough to realize that a sixty-five-year-old man did not have the time to alter ancient ecclesiastical traditions. His leadership did unlock doors, but they were left slightly ajar rather than wide open. This is apparent in the question of the Immaculate Conception.[147]

In 1740, the same year in which Benedict became Pope, Muratori published his *De superstitione vitanda sive censura voti sanguinarii* in Venice.[148] In it, he inveighed against the inordinate role given to the Virgin and her relics in Christian salvation, and criticized especially the so-called 'blood vow' with which many devout Catholics swore to defend to the death their belief in Mary's freedom from original sin. Muratori denied that the Immaculate Conception could be absolute truth, arguing that its proof could not be found in either Holy Scripture or in ancient tradition, and that until such proof was made available, the doctrine was not definable.[149] Benedict found himself in the uncomfortable position of having to respond to his old friend, because Rome was pushing him to censure Muratori's publications on the blood vow.[150] Mounting tension around the church debate on the Immaculate Conception placed Benedict under siege in the papal court, where many people were trying to have the doctrine declared dogma. The Jesuit Andrea Budrioli prepared documentation to prove to the Pope that the belief was undeniable, and by citing past Bulls and briefs in which the matter had been clearly addressed, the Jesuit amassed evidence on the Church's traditional attachment to the Immaculate Conception.

On 24 August 1742, Budrioli presented Benedict with a treatise on the subject; three more publications on the same material were issued in the next ten years.[151] Benedict's

[147] Padre Tacchi Venturi, SJ, 'Per la storia del domma dell' Immacolata Concezione ai tempi di Benedetto XIV', *Civiltà cattolica*, 56 (1905), 673–4, observed that Pius IX's Bull, *Ineffabilis Deus*, which confirmed the Immaculate Conception as dogma was really prepared for by Benedict's pontificate.

[148] Published under the pseudonym Antonio Lampridi, the work was already circulating in the 1730s: see P. Julien Stricher, *Le Voeu de sang en faveur de l'Immaculée Conception: Histoire et bilan théologique d'une controverse* (Rome, 1959) i. 38; and A. Vecchi, 'I modi della devozione', in V. Branca (ed.), *Sensibilità e Razionalità nel Settecento* (Venice, 1967), 95–124.

[149] On the subject, cf. W. Sebastian, OFM, 'The Controversy after Scotus to 1900', in E. D. O'Connor (ed.), *The Dogma of the Immaculate Conception* (Notre Dame, 1958), 238–70, and the almost contemporary response to Muratori's *De Superstitione*: *Lettere al*

signor Antonio Lampridio intorno al suo libro nuovamente pubblicato (Palermo, 1742), a copy of which exists in the Biblioteca Marciana under *122.C.47*.

[150] For the long friendship between Muratori and Lambertini, cf. Stricher, *Le Voeu de sang*, i. 137: in the autumn of 1731 '. . . il ne se passe un jour . . . sans que les deux amis n'échangeassent à plusiers reprises baisers et embrassades'; and see Chadwick, *The Popes*, pp. 398ff.

[151] Cf. Padre Tacchi Venturi, 'Per la storia del domma', pp. 513–27; and R. Laurentin, 'The Role of the Papal Magisterium in the Development of the Dogma', in O'Connor (ed.), *The Dogma of the Immaculate Conception*, pp. 271–324. Contemporary with this debate was Benedict's project—never completed—to revise the Roman breviary. On 21 Nov. 1741, a panel began to consider Marian feast-days. The Purification,

reaction to all this was cautious; although willing to admit that Mary herself was immaculate, he could not agree to call her conception such. He wrote that although he venerated the mystery, the Church 'could not be a facile dispenser of its treasures'.[152] Finally, urged on by vociferous proponents and persuaded by his own heart, Benedict consented to celebrate and perpetuate the feast of the Immaculate Conception on 8 December in S. Maria Maggiore, Rome. Budrioli and his circle believed they had obtained their much-desired official recognition. During these years of argument, the Carmelites of Venice had supported the immaculist position through Tiepolo's great ceilings.

In 1750, Tiepolo went to Würzburg to work for Prince Bishop Karl Philipp von Greiffenclau, whose patronage of the artist owed more to his princely pretensions in Franconia than it did to his spiritual responsibilities. The artist's German period is famous, in fact, for its secular frescos, not for its religious paintings.[153] However, the apotheoses that Tiepolo painted across metres of ceiling over both the Residenz stairway and the rose, silver, and gold Kaisersaal in order to perpetuate the Prince's fame and lineage were to have important pictorial consequences for the artist's last ecclesiastical ceiling in Venice, the *Triumph of the Faith* in the Church of the Pietà, or S. Maria della Visitazione (Pl. 94).

Tiepolo signed the contract for this great Marian painting on 15 April 1754. In the late 1970s, Diana Kaley published many of the relevant documents, and since then Deborah Howard has written an excellent study of the church and its painted decoration, including Tiepolo's great fresco.[154] Howard has argued convincingly that the Pietà oval depends pictorially upon Piazzetta's *Glory of St Dominic* in SS Giovanni e Paolo. She suggests that Tiepolo's reconsideration of the Dominican ceiling must have been due both to his regard for the older artist (who had just died in May 1754), and to his appreciation of the need for visual harmony in the church, all of whose altar-pieces were assigned to Piazzetta's students and followers. The Pietà fresco is, indeed, notably different from Tiepolo's earlier ecclesiastical ceilings. The use of colour is attenuated; and, furthermore, the artist avoided any of the architectural armatures he had employed in the Gesuati, Scalzi, and Carmini paintings. In the Gesuati, a great flight of stairs and a large podium are the setting for Dominic's donation of the Rosary to the world. In the Scalzi, the Santa Casa provides a support for Mary and Christ; and, even more to the point, Mengozzi-Colonna's surrounding framework and its feigned coffers provide a tight structure for the *Translation*. In the Carmini, both the plinth upon which Simon Stock kneels and the height of the nearby temple offer contrasting weight and pictorial tension to the hovering

Annunciation, Assumption, and Nativity of Our Lady were readily accepted into the revised breviary; the Visitation and Conception were retained—but with much discussion. To be deleted from the liturgical calendar, however, were the feasts of the Rosary, the Lady of Mt Carmel, and the Translation of the Holy House. Cf. P. Batiffol, *History of the Roman Breviary* (London, 1912), 252–3. Catena, 'Il culto', p. 314, notes that a breviary published in Venice in 1749 contains the words 'Immaculata Conceptio gloriosae V. Mariae' for 8 Dec.

[152] Padre Tacchi Venturi, 'Per la storia del domma', pp. 665–9. Benedict's words read: '. . . non intendiamo di concederla: non per difetto di venerazione al mistero; ma per non voler essere troppo facili dispensatori, per non dire dissipatori, del tesoro della Chiesa con una troppo abbondante applicazione del medesimo'.

[153] For Tiepolo's *Assumption of the Virgin* and *Fall of the Rebel Angels* for the Bishop's Chapel, cf. Morassi, *A Complete Catalogue*, figs. 107 and 224. For Greiffenclau's less than enlightened outlook on the world, cf. Chadwick, *The Popes*, p. 9, concerning the 1749 trial for witchcraft in Würzburg.

[154] Cf. D. Kaley, *The Church of the Pietà* (Venice, 1980); and D. Howard, 'Giambattista Tiepolo's Frescos for the Church of the Pietà in Venice', *Oxford Art Journal*, 9 (1986), 11–28.

figure of the Immaculate Virgin. Tiepolo's decision not to preserve this earlier concept in the Pietà ceiling must have been prompted, Howard suggests, by Piazzetta's example, but it was also a product of his own achievements in Würzburg. The stair-well fresco in the Residenz represents void overwhelming substance, space expanding rather than contracting, Apollo soaring amidst the clouds, and gravity prevailing only at the ceiling's outer border. Tiepolo repeated this identical pattern in the Pietà, but reduced it in scale.

In the past, the *Triumph of Faith* has been called an *Assumption* and/or a *Coronation of the Virgin*.[155] Tiepolo's Mary does in fact soar in the heavens, but there are no disciples reacting to the discovery of an empty sepulchre. God the Father does indeed offer the Virgin a crown, but she is not close enough to receive it, nor does she acknowledge his presence and universal authority.[156] Telling a story was not Tiepolo's aim, and the Assumption and the Coronation are narratives, even if they do take place in heaven. Nor did Tiepolo depict measurable space in the Pietà; he declared time and space ineffable in the Catholic firmament.

The *Triumph of Faith* is a painting about hierarchy and doctrine. Each zone in the Pietà's celestial and spiritual 'skyway' carries specific meaning, and each has been qualified by the artist for that purpose. The music-making angels at the edge of the painting define the mediating zone between the earthly church and the heavenly vision beyond; their harmonies echo the actual music that was played by young women hidden in the Pietà's singing galleries.[157] Sitting in a shadowy space where they are held in check by gravity's force and made to follow the rules of a world governed by time, the angelic musicians deputize for the earthly worshippers below. Peering beyond the celestial choir, the pious see a universe immeasurable as well as eternal. Mary does not ascend or look up; she gazes down at the faithful, who understand that she, the *Immacolata* in white, is a Christian exemplar. Above her, Christ carries the cross, not to tell the story of the crucifixion but to represent the ideal of sacrifice. God the Father holds up a crown—a sign of Mary's triumph, yes—but, more importantly, of his own celestial majesty and his perpetual prerogative to confer victory. Finally, looking into the furthest distance, the believer sees the Holy Spirit enlightening the world. This Christian heaven is absolute; neither structure, nor time, nor incident limits it.

Tiepolo's *Translation of the Holy House*, *Virgin of the Carmine Appearing to Simon Stock*, and *Triumph of Faith* were the most beautiful statements made in the mid-eighteenth-century debate on the Immaculate Conception. And, together with the *Institution of the Rosary*, they were also a fitting response to those in the Catholic Enlightenment who, like Serry and Muratori, questioned Mary's unique role, her relics, and her special signs of favour. Tiepolo's ceilings in the Gesuati, the Scalzi, the Scuola dei Carmini, and the Pietà continued the Venetian tradition of identifying Venice as an inviolate and chaste body politic, one that '. . . knew how to conserve uncontaminated for all time the flower of its

[155] Cf. Kaley, *The Church of the Pietà*, p. 29; Howard, 'Giambattista Tiepolo's Frescos', p. 18; and G. Knox, *Giambattista and Domenico Tiepolo: A Study and Catalogue Raisonné of the Chalk Drawings* (Oxford, 1980), i. 335. Morassi, *A Complete Catalogue*, p. 57; and A. Pallucchini, *L'opera completa*, p. 119, refer to it as the *Triumph of Faith*, however.

[156] Titian narrated both events perfectly in the Frari *Assunta*; and although Mary is not next to God there, her entire attitude reveals her preparation for God and her subsequent coronation.

[157] Howard, 'Giambattista Tiepolo's Frescos', p. 21.

94. G. B. Tiepolo, *Triumph of the Faith* (fresco, 320 × 200 cm.)

eternal Virginity'.[158] Elaborate and sumptuous confirmations of Mary's celestial majesty, each painting is displayed in its respective hall of worship like a crown, offered on the one hand to the Queen of Heaven herself and on the other to those seeking Christian salvation.

[158] BNM, MS It., Cl. VII, 9141 (1774), cited in J. Georgelin, *Venise au siècle des lumières* (Paris, 1978), 948 n. 172: '. . . sebbe [*for* seppe] custodire illibato in ogni tempo il fiore della sua perenne Virginità'.

3

THE SAINTLY ALTAR-PIECE

IN 1749, the year that the *Virgin of the Carmine Appearing to Simon Stock* was unveiled, David Hume began writing his *Natural History of Religion*. Comparing theism with idolatry and deeply cynical of traditional religion, Hume feared '. . . that the corruption of the best things gives rise to the worst'.[1] On Roman Catholicism he wrote that:

The heroes in paganism correspond exactly to the saints in popery . . . The place of HERCULES, THESEUS, HECTOR, ROMULUS, is now supplied by DOMINIC, FRANCIS, ANTHONY, AND BENEDICT . . . whippings and fastings, cowardice and humility, abject submission and slavish obedience, are become the means of obtaining celestial honours among mankind.[2]

A quarter of a century later, in a similar but milder tone, Edward Gibbon commented that: 'in the long period of twelve hundred years, which elapsed between the reign of Constantine and the reformation of Luther, the worship of saints and relics corrupted the pure and perfect simplicity of the Christian model'.[3] In the same chapter of his *Decline and Fall of the Roman Empire*, which was published only a few years after Tiepolo's death in 1770, Gibbon wrote: 'The sublime and simple theology of the primitive Christians was gradually corrupted; and the MONARCHY of heaven, already clouded by metaphysical subtleties, was degraded by the introduction of a popular mythology which tended to restore the reign of polytheism.'[4]

Hume's and Gibbon's opinions would not have found many supporters on the Italian peninsula; the 'worship of saints', as the British would have termed it, was a corner-stone of Catholic Counter-Reformation spirituality.[5] During the eighteenth century, saintly veneration was stressed even more than before; between 1700 and 1799 twenty-nine new saints were canonized, the greater percentage of which took place during Tiepolo's lifetime. The reasons why the Roman Church glorified so many of its servants are perhaps as varied as the actual figures who underwent saintly apotheosis, but one explanation can surely be found in the ever-growing influence of many religious orders, 'the irreplaceable lungs of ecclesiastical life'.[6] A number of them believed that their strength in the Church would be considerably increased if men and women from their own ranks were exalted into sainthood; fraternal affirmation was their goal. The new saints also

[1] D. Hume, 'The Natural History of Religion', in R. Wollheim (ed.), *Hume on Religion* (Cleveland and New York, 1964), 68.

[2] Ibid.

[3] E. Gibbon, *The Decline and Fall of the Roman Empire* (New York, n.d., The Modern Library), ii. 66. F. Manuel, *The Eighteenth Century Confronts the Gods* (Cambridge, 1959), 22, notes that Protestant condemnation of Catholicism in England was as much a political response as a religious one.

[4] Gibbon, *Decline and Fall*, p. 69.

[5] In his *Della regolata divozione dei cristiani* (Venice, 1761), 262–85, Muratori differentiates between pious devotion to saints and old-fashioned superstition, writing that the former leads to the love of God and not to a request for rain or good health.

[6] A phrase taken from A. Vecchi, 'I modi della devozione', in V. Branca (ed.), *Sensibilità e Razionalità nel Settecento* (Venice, 1967), 110.

supplied continuing evidence of Christian perfection, and, like the older saints who stand beside the throne of God in innumerable works of art, they furnished links to heavenly salvation. Venetian altar-paintings of the settecento continued to present them to the faithful in this way. If Gibbon had seen such images, he would certainly have condemned them as proof of 'polytheism'. He would probably have reserved his severest criticism for Tiepolo's altar-pieces, for they were the most persuasive pictorial statement in northern Italian art of traditional Catholic attitudes. They were also the last great exemplars in the history of Italian art of the *sacra conversazione*.

Tiepolo's leading position in Venetian settecento religious art was achieved through a unique blend of the actual with the supernatural. An example of this is his *Madonna and Child with SS Catherine of Siena, Rose of Lima, and Agnes of Montepulciano* (Pl. 95), painted for the Gesuati in 1748. In the centre, St Rose, identified by her flower, is presenting the Infant to the devout; becoming the vessel through which Christ is offered to the world, she displays the saintly bliss bestowed on those who receive Christian grace. Tiepolo implies that such a gift is both real and mystical. Using a solid-looking architectural setting and volumetric figures, he transforms the holy gathering into a tangible and monumental event. But, at the same time, the celestial cloud that serves as the Madonna's throne and the spiritual ecstasy that overcomes the three saints create a fitting magical sphere for the carrying aloft of the holy sacrament, Christ himself.[7] Tiepolo's resolution of the contradictions between the ponderable and the arcane created a type of religious imagery quite unlike that of his contemporaries Ricci and Piazzetta, as we shall see.

This fundamental difference may explain the surprising fact that Tiepolo did not receive any major commissions for 'saintly altar-pieces' in Venice during the 1720s; any orders he did secure for such work were almost always for churches in the provinces.[8] Yet, evidence suggests that Tiepolo did try to obtain commissions. An examination of the compositions and style of two small oil-paintings that were probably sketches for larger works, of two early drawings, and of his *pala d'altare* for Piove di Sacco (Padua) (formerly dated to the late 1730s but proposed here as a work of the late 1720s), will help to explain why the greatest religious artist in Europe in the eighteenth century did not paint a major altar-piece before he reached the age of thirty-five.

The two works in oil are the *Virgin and Child with a Rosary, Angels, and Cherubs* and the *Glory of S. Luigi Gonzaga* (Pl. 96; Pl. V), both from the Princes Gate Collection and now in the Courtauld Institute Galleries. Both of them are small paintings, and their similar, very loose brushwork suggests that they were prepared as *modelli* and that they were also contemporary in date, *c*.1725–6.[9] Such dating rests in part upon events in the Church: the canonization of Gonzaga and the extension of the Feast of the Rosary to the Universal

---

[7] See Don Niero's very beautiful discussion of this painting in *Tre artisti per un tempio: S. Maria del Rosario—Gesuati, Venezia* (Padua, 1979), 84 ff.

[8] Da Canal does mention in his *Vita di Gregorio Lazzarini* (Venice, 1809), p. xxxv, that Tiepolo's *St Francis Receiving the Stigmata* was in S. Ternita (S. Trinità) and that *SS John and Luke* was in S. Antonin; the two paintings are now lost. Two of Tiepolo's early provincial works are the *Resurrection* for the cathedral in

Udine (A. Pallucchini, *L'opera completa del Tiepolo* (Milan, 1968), no. 49) and a *Madonna and Child with Saints* in Pirano, Istria (ibid., no. 54), although the latter does not seem a totally convincing attribution judging from a photograph.

[9] H. Braham, *The Princes Gate Collection* (London, 1981), 73, nos. 106–7. The first measures 44.2 by 23.9 cm.; the second is 58 by 44.7 cm.

95. G. B. Tiepolo, *Madonna and Child with SS Catherine of Siena, Rose of Lima, and Agnes of Montepulciano* (oil on canvas, 340 × 168 cm.)

96. G. B. Tiepolo, *Virgin and Child* (oil on canvas, 45 × 25 cm.)

97. G. B. Tiepolo, Oil-sketch for a ceiling in the Palazzo Sandi, Venice, of the *Allegory of the Power of Eloquence* (oil on canvas, 50 × 70 cm.)

Church both took place in 1726.[10] But the stylistic evidence is even more convincing. The figural types in the two works are typical of the mid-1720s; there is very little difference, for example, between S. Luigi and the two angels who assist in his glorification, and the cast of characters in the Palazzo Sandi *bozzetto* (Pl. 97).[11] The winged angel in the *Virgin and Child* is very like Jacob in *Jacob and Esau* in Udine; compare their necks, the bulbous heels, and the expressive gestures of the left hands.[12] Both the Sandi and the Udine frescos were painted in the years 1725–7. The two Courtauld sketches show further links to Tiepolo's youthful style in their insistence on dark hues and tonally conceived shadows that are juxtaposed against areas of bright white or pure red. Deep blues are placed next to muddy browns, making each of them deeper and muddier. In the *Glory of S. Luigi* these dark shades are contrasted with S. Luigi's white surplice, while in the *Virgin and Child* they are pitted against the Virgin's red gown.

If, as is probable, these works did serve as *pensieri* for large altar-pieces, then one can deduce that the young Tiepolo conceived of devotional imagery in terms of three-dimensional settings; in each painting, the holy figures are seen against monumentalizing architectural backgrounds. S. Luigi and his angelic host hover on a cloud in a hallway defined by an oversized column and an archway, not very different from some scenes by Titian and Veronese.[13] In the second work, the Virgin and Child appear within a golden apse reminiscent of those in Giovanni Bellini's altar-pieces for S. Giobbe, the Frari sacristy, and S. Zaccaria; even more specifically, it is like Sebastiano del Piombo's two magical niches painted on the organ shutters of S. Bartolomeo al Rialto.

In these two early paintings, Tiepolo is referring back to paradigms of Venetian cinquecento art, creating solutions clearly at variance with those of his contemporaries. Three representative altar-paintings by Piazzetta, Pittoni, and Ricci may be compared with the London sketches. Piazzetta's *Virgin and Child Appearing to St Philip Neri* (Pl. 98), completed in late 1726 for the Church of the Fava, resembles Tiepolo's *Glory of S. Luigi Gonzaga* in its diagonal, zigzag composition and in the extent to which spiritual ecstasy overcomes the two protagonists; note, too, the clasped hands of both Luigi and Philip. It is different, however, in that Piazzetta portrays a space burst asunder; Mary, Christ, and their angelic companions shatter the three-dimensional reality around Neri. Similar in concept, and contemporary in date, is Pittoni's *SS Jerome, Peter of Alcantara, and another Franciscan* (Pl. 99), painted for S. Maria dei Miracoli.[14] As in Piazzetta's painting, a platform and altar are visible, but they too are overwhelmed by a celestial presence. Lastly, Ricci's *bozzetto* for the *Vision of St Benedict, with SS Jerome, Paul, Scolastica, Roch, and Peter* (Pl. 100) also shows a saintly gathering within an incomplete architectural background.[15] So, all of these altar-

[10] Two altar-pieces featuring Luigi Gonzaga were painted in Venice in the late 1720s: Balestra's *Madonna and Child with SS Stanislaus Kostka, Francis Borgia, and Luigi Gonzaga* for the Gesuiti, and Piazzetta's *Guardian Angel with SS Anthony of Padua and Luigi Gonzaga* for S. Vidal (cf. R. Pallucchini, *La pittura veneziana del Settecento* (Venice, 1960), figs. 119, 157).

[11] Braham, *The Princes Gate Collection*, no. 105. Compare them, too, with the angel in the San Diego *Rest on the Flight*, pl. 23.

[12] For *Jacob and Esau*, cf. Rizzi, *Tiepolo a Udine* (Udine, 1971), 41.

[13] Although not identical by any means, both Titian's setting for his *St Catherine of Alexandria* in the Museum of Fine Arts, Boston, and Veronese's for the *Annunciation* in the Thyssen Collection, Lugano, are similarly structured.

[14] F. Zava Boccazzi, *Pittoni* (Venice, 1979), 128, no. 59, dates the work to *c.*1725. See, however, H. Brigstocke, *Italian and Spanish Paintings in the National Gallery of Scotland* (Edinburgh, 1978), 99ff., who dates the painting 'not long before 1733'.

[15] The work is now missing or was never completed: J. Daniels, *Sebastiano Ricci* (Hove, 1976), no. 539, dated it to *c.*1720.

pieces picture their saintly visions in the same kind of way; their sources, however, are not to be found in sixteenth-century Venetian art, but in seventeenth-century Roman and Emilian prototypes, in the altar-paintings of Reni, Lanfranco, and Guercino.[16] In sum, within the Venetian pictorial context of the 1720s, Tiepolo's ideas for an altar-piece would have appeared unorthodox and even somewhat odd.

Two early drawings by Tiepolo executed for an altar-piece dedicated to the Santa Casa of Loreto show another of the artist's solutions for a *sacra conversazione* (Pl. 102). The Virgin and Child and the Holy House are seen in the top centre of both sheets, while three male saints, identical in type and age in both drawings, respond to the miraculous vision overhead; in each case, the setting is an open space on a gentle hillock, a lone tree to the left and mountains in the far distance.[17] Also completed in the 1720s, but a little later in the decade, is the *Madonna del Carmelo with SS Catherine of Alexandria and Michael* (Pl. 101) in the Duomo of Piove di Sacco. In the past, the painting has been dated to the second half of the 1730s, a thesis not tenable when the work is looked at *in situ* in the small Veneto town.[18] Such a dating would make the work contemporary with *Pope Clement Adoring the Trinity*, in the Alte Pinakothek, Munich, and—*mirabile dictu*—with the ceiling frescos of the Gesuati! Instead, the beautiful painting in Piove di Sacco should be seen in the artistic context of the late 1720s. Small details like the rubberiness of St Michael's index finger and larger areas like the muscular back of the Devil are typical of Tiepolo's brushwork and figures at that time. Michael's elongated body and small head repeat the figural canon of Sebastiano Ricci, who died in 1734; did Tiepolo ever execute such a form after that date? Note, too, the sensitively rendered landscape with the brightly lit classical temple, similar to the distant view in the *Capture of Carthage*, which was painted for the Dolfin in the late 1720s.[19] Finally, the composition in Piove di Sacco reminds one of much older works, like Annibale Carracci's *Madonna of S. Ludovico* and *Madonna of St Luke*.[20] In other words, the Piove di Sacco painting is old-fashioned, too much so to have been executed by Tiepolo in the late 1730s when he was forty. But this would not have been true of a work done ten years earlier. Lazzarini had used the formula, and he did not die until 1730; a small *sacra conversazione* by him (Pl. 103) shows a similar Carraccesque composition, with a St Catherine very like the one in Piove di Sacco. In conclusion therefore, the evidence suggests that the young Tiepolo's conceptions of saintly gatherings were derived from the cinquecento, both Venetian and Bolognese, with the latter being transmitted to him by his teacher. Both of these traditions show miraculous events taking place in spatially tangible settings, but neither was called upon by Piazzetta, Pittoni, or Ricci.

[16] Amigoni's *SS Andrew and Catherine* (cf. R. Pallucchini, *La pittura veneziana*, fig. 49), Balestra's *St Oswald in Glory*, and Bambini's *Madonna and Child with SS Lorenzo Giustinian, Francis, and Anthony Abbot* (cf. E. Martini, *La pittura veneziana del Settecento* (Venice, 1964), pl. 13 and fig. 9)—all done for S. Stae, *c.*1715—follow the same pattern. Ricci's Veronesesque altar-piece for S. Giorgio Maggiore (Pl. 47), 1708, was an exception to the general trend in the early years of the century.

[17] Cf. A. Bettagno, *Disegni di una collezione veneziana del Settecento* (exh. cat., Fondazione Cini, Venice, 1966 (Vicenza)), 79, nos. 97, 98. The landscapes are close in type to a drawing in the Museo Civico, Udine, showing three male nudes (cf. A. Rizzi, *Disegni del Tiepolo* (Udine, 1965), no. 4), and to the background in *Rachel Hiding the Idols of Laban* in the Archbishop's Gallery in Udine (Pl. 37).

[18] Cf. A. Morassi, *A Complete Catalogue of the Paintings of G. B. Tiepolo* (London, 1962), 45: '*c.*1735–40'; and A. Pallucchini, *L'opera completa*, no. 113: '1736–7'.

[19] The fallen soldier in the Metropolitan Museum painting is close, too, to the Devil in Piove di Sacco.

[20] D. Posner, *Annibale Carracci*, ii (London, 1971), pls. 41a and 67a.

98. G. B. Piazzetta, *Virgin and Child Appearing to St Philip Neri* (oil on canvas, 367 × 200 cm.)

100. S. Ricci, Oil-sketch for the *Vision of St Benedict* (oil on canvas, 53 × 31 cm.)

99. G. B. Pittoni, *SS Jerome, Peter of Alcantara, and Another Franciscan* (oil on canvas, 275 × 143 cm.)

101. G. B. Tiepolo,
Madonna del Carmelo
with SS Catherine of
Alexandria and Michael
(oil on canvas,
262 × 128 cm.)

102. G. B. Tiepolo (attributed), Drawing for an altar-piece of the *Virgin and Christ-child with the Holy House and Saints* (pen and ink with brown wash on white paper, 285 × 185 mm.)

103. G. Lazzarini, *Trinity, Virgin, and Saints* (oil on canvas, 113 × 48.2 cm.)

Perceiving the differences between Giambattista's formulations for a saintly altar-piece and those of his slightly older contemporaries helps us to understand Venetian settecento art better, but it does not explain why one pictorial conception should have been preferred to another. The question persists: why were Tiepolo's ideas not acceptable to the patrons and religious orders of the moment? To answer this question, we have to pose another one. How many large-scale religious altar-pieces were commissioned in Venice during the 1720s? Not very many, it would seem, for Piazzetta painted only two altar-pieces (in the Fava and S. Vidal), Pittoni one (S. Maria dei Miracoli, mentioned above), and Ricci perhaps not even that many![21] After 1730, however, the numbers increased. So, the problem may have been less Tiepolo's than Venice's.

This situation, which still needs further study, leads one to reflect upon the city's lack of hard currency between 1720 and 1730, a decade which saw a general decline in prices with a concomitant economic depression. This phenomenon appears to have been connected to the Turkish War of 1714–18, but there were also climatic factors that either sparked off too much agricultural production or permitted too little of it. In the first case, an over-abundance of grain on the market sent prices plummeting.[22] It would be reasonable to suppose, therefore, that when a patron did appear in the 1720s, ready to enrich an altar with a painting, he would be far more likely to entrust his money to an established master than to a less experienced artist. Ricci, Piazzetta, and Pittoni were all over or nearly forty, and in a conservative society such as Venice's, age mattered. One may conclude, in sum, that Venetian attitudes, contemporary economics, a junior position in the artistic community, and pictorial ideas not consonant with prevailing taste all mitigated against Tiepolo obtaining a commission for a major altar-piece before 1730.

In 1732, Tiepolo painted his first important altar-piece in Venice, the *Education of the Virgin* (Pl. 104) for S. Maria della Consolazione.[23] The Church of the Fava, as it is called, was one of the city's new settecento buildings, and by 1730 its interior could already boast of Piazzetta's *Virgin and Child Appearing to St Philip Neri*. Neri's veneration at the Fava is explained by the residency there of the Oratorians, the order which he founded. Tiepolo's subject was determined by the church's possession of a relic of St Anne, which was mentioned in the 1724 *Guida de' forestieri*.[24] In 1733, when it received its first mention in print, the *Education of the Virgin* was hailed as an 'illustrious work'.[25]

Three oil-sketches and two drawings by Tiepolo have been associated with the Fava altar-piece.[26] The sketch in the Musée des Beaux-Arts, Dijon, (Pl. 105) appears to be the

[21] These statistics are based on the relevant monographs by Mariuz, Zava Boccazzi, and Daniels. During these years, Piazzetta, Pittoni, and Ricci all executed works for other cities in the Veneto—Vicenza, Bergamo, Padua, and Verona.

[22] For the general problem, cf. L. Einaudi, 'L'economia pubblica veneziana dal 1736 al 1755', *La riforma sociale*, 14 (1904), 177–96, 261–82, 429–50, and 509–37; and J. Georgelin, *Venise au siècle des lumières* (Paris, 1978), 273–82.

[23] A. M. Zanetti, *Descrizione di tutte le pubbliche pitture della città di Venezia* (Venice, 1733), 190.

[24] V. Coronelli, *Guida de' forestieri ... per la città di Venezia*

(Venice, 1724), 202; (1744) 157: 'Una Reliquia di S. Anna, la di cui F. si celebra con pompa solenne in detta Ch. li 26 Lugl.'

[25] Zanetti, *Descrizione*, p. 190: 'L'altra [tavola] dirimpetto con S. Anna, la V. fanciulla e S. Gioachino è opera insigne di Giovambatista Tiepolo.'

[26] The Fava canvas is 362 by 200 cm. The painting in the Musée des Beaux-Arts, Dijon, measures 48 by 27 cm.; the version in the Cini collection is 50 by 28 cm.; and the oval in the Kaufmann–Schlageter donation to the Louvre is 78 by 62 cm. For the work in Dijon, cf. *Venise au dix-huitième siècle*, no. 230. For the two drawings, see n. 29 below.

earliest of the group in date. The angel is so close in form and colour to those in the Brera *Madonna del Carmelo* and the San Diego *Rest on the Flight* (Pls. 17, 23), both of which were executed in the 1720s, that its contemporaneity with them seems unquestionable.[27] So, it is possible that the Fava commission, completed in 1732, may have been contracted a decade earlier but was delayed for several years. Given that St Anne's relic was already in the church by 1724 and that seven of the building's altars were completed by then, this possibility could even be called a likelihood.[28] Perhaps, as I suggested above, it was only lack of money that prevented both Tiepolo and the enterprise from moving forward. Of course, the Dijon sketch could have been independently conceived; whatever the conclusion, there is no doubt that the Fava altar-piece reflects the sketch of the 1720s.

The second of the three versions in date belongs to the Cini Collection (Pl. 106).[29] Mary and Anne are in the same positions as they are in the Dijon sketch, but the composition is closer to that of the Fava canvas, and the brushwork is of the same period, *c*.1731–2. Joachim has been shifted to the right, which is where he appears in the final work. This change, in effect the only major figural alteration from the *pensiero* in Dijon, makes one think that when he made this oil-sketch Tiepolo knew the precise altar over which the painting would finally be hung, namely, the first to the right. If Tiepolo had simply repeated the Dijon composition, then Joachim would have played as important a role in the scene as Anne and Mary; indeed, with the low garden wall curving up towards his shoulder and then leading the viewer's glance to the monumental column behind, Anne's father would have been the painting's most powerful figure. But the proper focus for a devotional work commemorating a holy relic of St Anne and housed within a temple dedicated to the Virgin, is those two women; by shifting Joachim to the right, Tiepolo successfully directed the faithful's attention away from him and on to his wife and daughter.

One may plausibly suggest, then, that about 1730 Tiepolo received—or competed for—a commission to paint the *Education of the Virgin* above the first altar to the right in

[27] The angel is also very like the nude woman standing next to a tree-trunk on the far right of the Accademia *Apollo and Marsyas*.

[28] Cf. C. D. Lewis, *The Late Baroque Churches of Venice* (New York and London, 1979), 329 n. 24; on p. 76 he notes that Mass was celebrated in the Fava as early as 1715.

[29] No. 58 in A. Pallucchini, *L'opera completa*. P. Rosenberg, *Catalogue de la donation Othon Kaufmann et François Schlageter au Département des Peintures, Musée du Louvre* (Paris, 1984), 124, is wrong, I believe, to doubt this work's authenticity ('est-elle de la main de Tiepolo?'). The handling in the Cini canvas is close to that in the Archinto sketches, particularly to *Apollo and the Chariot of the Sun* in the Akademie der bildenden Künste in Vienna. For the Vienna sketch, cf. H. Hutter and R. Trnek, *Führer durch die Schausammlung der Gemäldegalerie der Akademie der bildenden Künste in Wien* (Vienna, 1983), photograph on p. 43. Note how similar the Cini Joachim is to the hermit on the far right in the Vienna canvas. Knox does not believe that this latter work 'need . . . be described as a sketch for the Archinto ceiling, to which it bears only a very general resemblance' (G. Knox, *Catalogue of the Tiepolo Drawings in the Victoria and Albert Museum* (London, 1975) 12). The similarity between the sketch and the ceiling makes the relationship more than likely, however; but even if the Vienna sketch pre-dates 1731 (before Tiepolo actually saw the room he was to paint in), its organizational sophistication does not allow it to be placed as far back as the mid-1720s. P. L. Sohm, 'Giambattista Tiepolo at the Palazzo Archinto in Milan', *Arte lombarda*, 68–9 (1984), 70–8, has recently published evidence to suggest that the Archinto commission was begun in 1730, 'almost a full year earlier than hitherto thought', and the Vienna sketch, therefore, could well have been conceived at that time or even slightly earlier, in 1729. Sohm, like Knox, believes that the Vienna sketch is not necessarily connected with the Archinto ceiling, but see *Schilderkunst uit de eerste hand: Olieverfschetsen van Tintoretto tot Goya* (exh. cat., Museum Boymans-van-Beuningen, Rotterdam, 1983), 170–3. The two drawings associated with the Fava commission are in New York and Stuttgart; the first (cf. Rizzi, *Disegni del Tiepolo*, no. 22ʳ) provides the intermediary link between the Dijon and Cini versions. Even though the angel hovers above and to the right of Joachim, as in the Dijon sketch, the drawing's technique, the position of the angel's limbs, and the direction of the figures' glances all tie the *idea* to the Cini canvas. For the second drawing, cf. G. Knox and C. Thiem, *Tiepolo: Zeichnungen von Giambattista, Domenico und Lorenzo Tiepolo aus der graphischen Sammlung der Staatsgalerie Stuttgart* (exh. cat., Staatsgalerie, Stuttgart, 1970), no. 8.

104. G. B. Tiepolo, *Education of the Virgin* (oil on canvas, 362 × 200 cm.)

105. Above, left: G. B. Tiepolo,
Oil-sketch for the *Education of the
Virgin* (oil on canvas, 48 × 27 cm.)

106. Above, right: G. B. Tiepolo,
Oil-sketch for the *Education of the
Virgin* (oil on canvas, 50 × 28 cm.)

107. G. B. Tiepolo, *Education of the
Virgin* (oil on canvas, 78 × 62 cm.)

the Oratorian church; and that he returned to his early sketch of the subject (Dijon) and slightly changed its architectural background and composition to accord with one's view of the painting when entering the Fava. If this suggestion is correct, then the Cini canvas was probably Tiepolo's submission piece, perhaps presented to the Oratorians even before he travelled to Milan. The Kaufmann-Schlageter painting (Pl. 107), which is substantially larger than the two in Dijon or Venice, must have been quite close to the Cini canvas chronologically. Indeed, except for the omission of the heavenly figures above, it is an exact compositional replica. Its surface is more finished, however, and its format is oval. It was conceived, I would suggest, as a private devotional work for someone who wanted a copy of the Cini sketch.

When he executed the final, eleven-foot-high canvas for the Fava altar, Tiepolo wrought still further changes. Apart from the angelic figures, one fundamental alteration involved Anne's relationship with Mary. In the three small versions, Anne's body was directed to the left, but her head was turned forward towards her daughter, who sits in profile facing to the right. In the altar-piece, Anne is shifted into profile and Mary faces the devout at prayer. Mary is elevated on a small stool so that she rises like a column above a pedestal. Dressed in brilliant white, with a celestial blue robe draped over her left shoulder, she is offered to the faithful as the Virgin of the Immaculate Conception. She is enclosed within a heavenly glory, and seraphim support the holy book so that she and her mother need not. These various alterations were made to diminish Anne's importance and to glorify the young Virgin. Thus, the altar-piece differs significantly from the three small paintings that can be associated with it. It does not merely 'narrate' the *Education of the Virgin*. The painting supports church doctrine that Mary, although born of Anne and Joachim, was not at all like them: she had been conceived without original sin.

In proceeding from sketch to finished painting, Tiepolo altered the architectural surround as well as the figures within it. In the Dijon version, a giant column rising from the level of Joachim's shoulder and disappearing above the canvas's upper limit defines the left-hand side of the composition. The column's size and position monumentalize Joachim, focusing our attention on him as if he were a protagonist.[30] In the Cini sketch, the column has been shifted to the centre, but it is somewhat masked by the angel and cherubs that hover in front of it. And in the Fava canvas, the column has become a pilaster, now located behind Joachim and topped with an Ionic capital. Its elegant form echoes that of the beautiful stool on which Mary is standing; the floor, too, is enhanced with a chequered design. But this architectural setting, although sturdy and definable, has been overwhelmed by two groups of heavenly figures, angels above and seraphim below, who are joined by a golden glory that isolates Joachim in a shadowed space and separates him from his wife and daughter. In the Dijon composition, the celestial figures hover in their own sphere, respecting the space of the family below and not intruding upon the architectural surround. In the Cini sketch, executed later, Tiepolo moved towards a less stratified, more integrated gathering; there is an angel on the left, next to Anne, and, as noted above, others partially mask the column behind. The aim of the

---

[30] This is similar to what Ricci does for the figure of St Benedict in his sketch of the saint's vision (Pl. 100). Note, also, the simi- larities between Tiepolo's Joachim and Ricci's SS Benedict and Peter.

altar-piece remains the same, even though its composition has been altered: the setting is intruded upon, and the architecture diminishes in importance as the earthly is overcome by the heavenly.[31]

This shift away from the spatial solution of the Dijon sketch was an important one, representing, I believe, an accommodation on Tiepolo's part to the prevailing fashion in Venetian altar-pieces—Pittoni's for S. Maria dei Miracoli, datable to *c*.1725–30 (Pl. 99), and Piazzetta's for the Fava (Pl. 98) and S. Vidal. That is, specificity of place has been cut by the descending celestial figures. Did Tiepolo, in fact, adjust the *Education of the Virgin* to accord with Piazzetta's *Virgin Appearing to St Philip Neri*, which already sat on the left of the Fava's nave? The answer must be in the affirmative, for in comparing the *Education of the Virgin* with the Dijon and Cini sketches on the one hand, and with the *Virgin Appearing to St Philip Neri* on the other, one discerns new and telling ideas very like several of Piazzetta's. Apart from the golden glory in the two visions—and it should be noted that there is no such device in Tiepolo's *modelli*—there is the detail of Joachim's clasped hands, clearly similar to Philip's. More importantly, the diagonal, zigzag composition in the *Education of the Virgin* has been articulated with an intentional angularity that is not apparent in either of the two sketches but is very like Piazzetta's.[32] But, even if Tiepolo did adjust his style to the pictorial solutions of his older contemporaries, he did not in any way compromise it. The architectural setting of the *Education of the Virgin*, although partially hidden by clouds, remains solid and decipherable.

The Fava canvas was an impressive début. Tiepolo followed it immediately with a series of equally striking altar-pieces, including the *Adoration of the Christ-child*, now in the Sacristy of the Canons in St Mark's Cathedral (Pl. 108), and *St Joseph with the Christ-child, SS Anne, Francis of Paola, Anthony of Padua, and Peter of Alcantara* in the Accademia (Pl. 109). The *Adoration* celebrates the Saviour's birth, and was first exhibited, in fact, during the Christmas season of 1732–3 in the Church of S. Zulian. As I have noted in Chapter 2, the white cloth held by St Joseph enfolds the sleeping Infant as if it were his shroud, foreshadowing the death of Christ and his deposition from the cross. The Accademia painting, which originally belonged to S. Prosdocimo, a convent of Benedictine nuns in Padua, exalts St Francis of Paola (1416–1507), who had created the Order of the Minims.[33] A book lying open at St Francis's feet may be understood to represent the Order's Rule. St Francis's reputation was considerable in the late seventeenth and early eighteenth centuries, having grown ever since his posthumous canonization in 1519. One biography of the saint had been through a dozen impressions by 1712.[34] Bossuet, in

[31] This differs from the *Glory of S. Luigi Gonzaga* (Pl. V), where Tiepolo defines the foreground, middle ground, and far distance very definitely; although the church interior has been invaded by a celestial group anxious to carry S. Luigi to heaven, the building's architectural definition has been retained.

[32] The relationship of Tiepolo's art to Piazzetta's with regard to 'un'intonazione chiaroscurale più accentuata', *c*.1732–3, has been noted by R. Pallucchini in *La pittura veneziana*, p. 72.

[33] Zanetti, *Descrizione*, p. 486, noted that the first painting was on view in S. Zulian 'in questi giorni' (the date of the book's

dedication was 1 Jan. 1733); the second work was recorded by G. B. Rossetti, *Descrizione delle pitture, sculture, ed architetture di Padova* (Padua, 1765), 243; and by P. Brandolese, *Pitture, sculture, architetture ed altre cose notabili di Padova* (Padua, 1795), 161. Cf. also S. Moschini Marconi, *Gallerie dell'Accademia: Opere d'arte dei secoli XVII, XVIII, XIX* (Rome, 1970), 109. S. Prosdocimo and its convent no longer exist.

[34] P. Fr. Isidoro Toscano di Paola, *Della vita, virtù, miracoli, e dell'istituto di S. Francesco di Paola fondatore dell'ordine de' Minimi* (Venice, 1712).

108. G. B. Tiepolo, *Adoration of the Christ-child* (oil on canvas, 220 × 155 cm.)

109. G. B. Tiepolo, *Christ-child with SS Joseph, Anne, and Francis of Paola* (oil on canvas, 210 × 116 cm.)

particular, was devoted to Francis and wrote a series of orations on his life, stressing how he had maintained strict Christian devotion during his childhood and his old age, times at which the flesh is both weak and needy.[35] This assertion may account for Francis's association in the Accademia/Prosdocimo canvas with the Infant Christ and the elderly SS Joseph and Anne.

The Fava, S. Zulian, and S. Prosdocimo altar-pieces were all executed within the same two-year period.[36] Among the several similarities that can be noticed in the three works are the facial types and the heavy shadows out of which the figures emerge. The woman who 'plays' St Anne at the Fava has the same role in the S. Prosdocimo painting; her husband Joachim reappears as St Joseph and St Francis; the two angels from the Fava flank the Virgin in the *Adoration*; and the seraphic heads supporting the Bible at the Fava are seen again both in the *Adoration* and as Christ's own in the Prosdocimo work.[37] There is the same insistence in each of the paintings upon a strong, vertical, architectural element to define the position of a male saint. Having found his formula for the *Education of the Virgin* satisfactory, Tiepolo repeated it at S. Zulian and S. Prosdocimo, and in a number of other altar-pieces executed in the first half of the 1730s.[38]

Only slightly later in date than these Venetian 'saintly works' is the *Virgin in Glory with Apostles and Saints* (Pl. 110), which was painted in 1734 for the high altar of the Chiesa di Ognissanti in Rovetta, a village twenty-three miles to the north-east of Bergamo; the altar-piece is still *in situ*. As Morassi astutely noted a quarter of a century ago, the Rovetta *pala* was the most ambitious altar-painting of Tiepolo's first maturity.[39] The *Virgin in Glory* is also evidence of Tiepolo's readiness, even as he became famous, to serve the most humble of provincial localities. The work was exactly contemporary with his portrayal of noble allegorical themes in the Villa Loschi fresco cycle.[40] The two very different types of patronage which these two commissions epitomize show Tiepolo's remarkable ability to fulfil the devotional needs of the smallest rural centres, such as Rovetta, Folzano, Rampazzo, or Noventa Vicentina, while at the same time satisfying the most sophisticated of aristocrats and intellectuals.

Two years before submitting the *Virgin in Glory* in 1734, Tiepolo was frescoing in the Cappella Colleoni in Bergamo; and it is likely that he received the Rovetta commission then.[41] Such a date would indeed be acceptable for its oil-sketch (Pl. 111; Pl. VI), since

[35] [G. B. Bossuet], *Orazioni panegiriche di Mons. G. B. Bossuet Vescovo di Meaux in onore di S. Francesco da Paola* (Rome, 1898).

[36] Zanetti's note that the S. Zulian painting was on view 'in questi giorni' (1 Jan. 1733) is contained in an addition to the main text of his *Descrizione* (1733), thus tying the *Adoration* to the last months of 1732. The Fava painting was already in the text; the S. Prosdocimo canvas has been dated by A. Pallucchini, *L'opera completa*, no. 87, to 1734; and by Morassi, *A Complete Catalogue*, p. 54, to c.1730–5.

[37] All of these types are also seen in *Abraham and the Angels* and *Hagar and Ishmael*, contemporary works done for the Scuola Grande di S. Rocco.

[38] Amongst which can be mentioned a small sketch catalogued by Morassi, *A Complete Catalogue*, p. 28 and fig. 100, and A. Pallucchini, *L'opera completa*, no. 63, as in a private collection in Milan. The canvas carries the date 1731 on its verso; not all authorities are agreed upon the attribution to Tiepolo, but from

recent photographs it does appear to be autograph. Also contemporary are the small altar-piece in the Pushkin Museum in Moscow (A. Pallucchini, *L'opera completa*, no. 94, and O. Lavrova, 'Le tele di Giambattista Tiepolo nel Museo Statale delle Belle Arti A. S. Pushkin (Mosca)', *Atti del Congresso Internazionale di Studi sul Tiepolo* (Venice, 1972), photograph on p. 126), and the beautiful *Madonna and Child with SS Hyacinth and Dominic* in the Art Institute of Chicago.

[39] Morassi, *A Complete Catalogue*, p. 46; cf. A. Pinetti, *Inventario degli oggetti d'arte d'Italia: Provincia di Bergamo* (Rome, 1931), 386. The painting is no. 390 in the exhibition catalogue *La Peinture italienne au XVIIIe siècle* (Petit Palais, Paris, 1960).

[40] Cf. A. Pallucchini, *L'opera completa*, no. 90.

[41] One possible artistic connection between Bergamo and Rovetta was Andrea Fantoni (d. 1734), whose wood-carving shop seems to have been responsible for many of the splendid early eighteenth-century altar-tabernacles in the area, among them the

the compositional and architectural formulas that characterize it are close to aspects of the S. Zulian and S. Prosdocimo canvases. The middle distance is determined by a fluted column, and, as in the Paduan painting, the figures are raised on steps and on a platform; the bishop saint kneeling in the foreground repeats St Anne's reverential position. However, distinguishing the Rovetta *bozzetto* from the altar-pieces of the early 1730s is its greater spatial breadth, its chromatic luminescence, and the splendidly hieratic figure of St Peter addressing the parishioners in Rovetta.

A comparison of the *bozzetto* with the completed altar-piece shows that although the composition is very similar, the subject-matter is different. The altar-piece, commissioned for the Ognissanti's high altar, was originally conceived in the oil-sketch as a work glorifying saintly consecration. One recognizes on the left the Roman Church's two protectors, Peter and Paul; in the centre foreground, a member of the ecclesiastical hierarchy kneels in obeisance to heavenly truth, and in the background on the right, SS John the Baptist, Lawrence, and Francis gaze with others towards heaven. The palm-fronds and crowns below the three intersecting circles in the upper centre of the painting imply that martyrdom and saintly dedication serve as earthly corroboration of the celestial Trinity. The brightly illuminated, fluted column linking the two worlds embodies their spiritual union; firmly rooted amidst the human gathering but disappearing into the heavens, the column affirms that it is human devotion that safeguards and sustains divine omnipotence. The column's function, therefore, is not only pictorial, aggrandizing the small *modelletto*, but also spiritually powerful.

When the completed canvas, almost twelve and a half feet high and more than four feet wide, arrived in Rovetta, the authorities saw a painting that was almost identical in appearance to the oil-sketch but extended in meaning. No longer glorifying only sainthood and its dedication to the Trinity, the altar-piece exalts the Virgin.[42] The dazzlingly white figure of Mary rising over a column, whose flutings in contrast are deeply shadowed, suggests the Immaculate Conception, an interpretation that is supported by the fact that her brilliant white robes are partially covered by a celestial blue cloak and there is a golden veil over her head.[43] Although Tiepolo did not repeat the sketch's trinitarian symbol, he did insist upon the painting's ultimate focus on God, and Mary expectantly opens her arms and looks towards a golden glory.

The local authorities gave the new subject an iconographically fitting decorative surround. A figure of the Virgin in stucco sits above the painting, her arms opened wide as in Tiepolo's canvas but facing the congregation. Her feet rest on a banner inscribed with the words VENITE AD ME OMNES, and tiny quarter-moons flank her at knee-level on either side. Further to the right and left, directly above the two projecting

---

rich frame of the *Virgin in Glory*. Fantoni's *bottega* produced settings for altar-pieces by Ricci in both Bergamo and in Clusone: cf. Daniels, *Sebastiano Ricci*, nos. 32, 36. Rovetta is a *frazione* of Clusone.

[42] One cannot exclude the possibility, of course, that there was a second sketch for the commission and that it included the Virgin.

[43] See Chapter 2 for other examples of this in Tiepolo's art;

the *Immaculate Conception*, executed for the Church of the Aracoeli in Vicenza, is nearly contemporary with the Rovetta altar-piece. Mary can tentatively be associated here with the *Madonna del Pilar*, a Spanish iconographical tradition very popular in the seventeenth century: cf. S. Stratton, 'The Immaculate Conception in Spanish Renaissance and Baroque Art', Ph.D. diss. (New York, 1983).

110. G. B. Tiepolo, *Virgin in Glory with Apostles and Saints* (oil on canvas, 378 × 134 cm.)

111. G. B. Tiepolo, Oil-sketch for the *Virgin in Glory with Apostles and Saints* (oil on canvas, 47 × 29 cm.)

112. B. Montagna, *St Peter Blessing and a Donor* (panel, 60.5 × 39.5 cm.)

columns that enclose the frame, there are figures holding an anchor and carrying a cross and chalice who represent Hope and Faith. Thus, Mary welcomes the faithful as they approach the altar; at the same time, from within Tiepolo's painting she passes through a golden glory towards the Deity, who is represented twice in frescos over the altar—as the Holy Spirit on the apse dome and as the Sacrificial Lamb on the chancel vault.[44]

Brilliant colour reinforces the triumphant tone of the Ognissanti *pala*: St Peter wears a chrome/lemon cloak draped over a cobalt blue tunic; behind him and to the right, St Paul, St Lawrence and King David, the latter kneeling in the painting's bottom right-hand corner, wear robes of cadmium red and warm rose. These reds and Peter's yellow, joined in the painting's centre·foreground, are repeated in more resonant tones in the richly patterned brocade of the bishop's vestment. From beneath this dark carmine and gold design, a white satin undergarment falls forward over a step towards a book whose cover is a warm golden ochre. Freed from shadow and chromatic intensity, this union of white and gold recurs in the painting's brilliant upper half, where Mary in a silver luminescence enters a golden empyrean.[45] This splendour marks a new era in Tiepolo's religious oil-paintings. Although he had used some of the same rich reds and warm golden yellows in the Fava and S. Zulian altar-pieces, the *pala* at Rovetta is strikingly different. In the *Education of the Virgin* and the *Adoration of the Christ-child*, the artist had juxtaposed dark hues and had intensified their opacity through the addition of murky shadows. Within the space of dimly lit churches, the mood created by this generalized darkness helped contemplation and deep reverie. The Rovetta altar-piece, however, is characterized by brilliant sunlight, and, unlike the sombre images of the Fava, S. Zulian, and S. Prosdocimo canvases, the *Virgin in Glory* is radiant and exultant in tone, heralding much of Tiepolo's later religious art.

An important and particularly noteworthy aspect of the *Virgin in Glory* is the figure of St Peter. His frontal stance and foreground position associate him directly with the devout praying in the church. He points upward to heavenly truth as he steps down into our world, a bold movement that was not developed in the oil-sketch. Peter's stern, patriarchal countenance accords with his powerful gesture, and he forms a contrast to the other saints, who appear either moved or awed by the Virgin's miraculous ascent. This force can be better appreciated by a comparison with Pittoni's St Paul, who is standing in a similar position in the S. Corona altar-piece in Vicenza which was painted a decade earlier; although beautifully composed, Pittoni's Paul is but a weak pedagogue.[46] He looks down, his face hidden from the viewer; his body arches without significance, and his raised hand points generally upwards without specifically indicating the Virgin and Child. Finally, his sword is held so that it wields no power. Peter's role in the *Virgin in Glory* is altogether more eloquent, implying a silent but powerful oration to the faithful.

---

[44] On the chancel's two side walls, over the organ on the left and the choir-loft on the right, there are six reliefs of King David, including the *Transportation of the Ark* and the *Death of Goliath*. In Tiepolo's sketch and altar-piece, the brightly lit figure wearing a golden crown, a red robe, and a white cloak who is kneeling to

the right of St John the Baptist must represent David.

[45] Tiepolo's control over tonal values at Rovetta is so masterful that it is even communicated in black and white photographs.

[46] Cf. Zava Boccazzi, *Pittoni*, fig. 45.

At first glance, his physical separation and psychological independence from his brother and sister saints would appear to violate the composition's unity, but in fact it strengthens the altar-piece's impact and deepens its meaning. In the sketch, Peter is standing still, his key dangling in the shadows, but in the finished work he is raising it to the sky, thus emphasizing his role as guardian of the gates of heaven, possessor of the key that will open them.

Peter's hieratic and authoritarian posture is new in Tiepolo's devotional imagery, which until now had emphasized figures overwhelmed by visions rather than discoursing on them to the public. Although similar poses can be found in Baroque painting, I believe that there are several figures in Venetian late Gothic art which provide more telling comparisons: Bartolomeo Montagna's saint in *St Peter Blessing and a Donor* (Pl. 112), for instance, stands exactly like Tiepolo's isolated saint in the Poldi-Pezzoli sketch.[47] The Rovetta Peter, although somewhat altered, may well be derived from this prototype. Of course, we do not know whether Tiepolo had this specific figure by Montagna in mind, but far more important than the precise source is the surprising realization that Tiepolo would have made use of a fifteenth-century figural type. He did so because he recognized that through the art of Montagna, or perhaps of Vivarini, whose saints still recall the Byzantine artistic past, he could achieve an image of hieratic force.[48]

By the mid-1730s, Tiepolo's religious art began to receive the great recognition it deserved, although his activity remained geographically more restricted in this sphere than in his secular patronage. However, the number of church commissions increased, as did the pace with which he received them, which is especially impressive if one remembers how bare similar terrain had been for him a decade before. In these new altar-pieces, the pictorial space increases, the architecture grows in size and complexity, and the compositions expand accordingly. In other words, beginning *c*.1736 one sees in Tiepolo's art a definite course towards monumental imagery, leading ultimately to the great altar-paintings of the 1740s.

An indication of Tiepolo's artistic goals at this point can be found in his *Vision of S. Gaetano* (Pl. 113), an altar-piece which, because it is comparatively small, is a good example of how the artist sought to aggrandize his religious iconography.[49] The painting originally decorated the palace chapel of the Labia family and honours their patron saint. A local figure, born in 1480 in Thiene, near Vicenza, Gaetano, or Cajetan in English,

---

[47] For Montagna's painting, a late fifteenth-century panel now in the Accademia, cf. L. Puppi, *Bartolomeo Montagna* (Venice, 1962), 50, 117; id., *Dopo Mantegna: Arte a Padova e nel territorio nei secoli XV e XVI* (exh. cat., Padua, 1976 (Milan)), 51; and *Giorgione a Venezia* (exh. cat., Gallerie dell'Accademia, Venice, 1978), 41–9. A possible Baroque source for Tiepolo could have been Poussin's Christ in *Ordination*, one of the Seven Sacraments painted for Chantelou in the 1640s; the painting, now in Edinburgh in the National Gallery of Scotland, belonged to the Orléans Collection in Paris during the 1730s, but had been engraved by Jean Pesne *c*.1680–94 as well as by others: cf. G. Wildenstein, 'Les Graveurs de Poussin au XVII siècle', *Gazette des Beaux-Arts*, 46 (1955), 237,

no. 102. Poussin's Christ is an archaistic figure like Tiepolo's Peter, and is standing in a similar position, but his physiognomy is totally different.

[48] See for instance the enthroned saint in the Vivarini St Mark altar-piece in the Frari: R. Pallucchini, *I Vivarini* (Venice, 1961), fig. 169. Another discoursing saint by Tiepolo appeared in the 1740s in the St Patrick altar-piece executed for the Convent of S. Giovanni di Verdara in Padua: cf. C. Whistler, 'Tiepolo's St Patrick Altarpiece', *Irish Arts Review* (1985), 32–5.

[49] The painting is 129 by 73 cm.: cf. Moschini Marconi, *Gallerie dell'Accademia*, p. 93.

founded the Order of the Theatines, the *chierici regolari*. He died in 1547 and was canonized in 1671. The altar-piece records a unique Marian vision experienced by Gaetano in S. Maria Maggiore in Rome.

Dated to the period *c.*1736 by both Morassi and Anna Pallucchini, it is the architecture of the *Vision of S. Gaetano* that reveals its chronological proximity to the slightly earlier Fava *Education of the Virgin*, the *Adoration of the Christ-child* for S. Zulian, the *Christ-child with Saints* for S. Prosdocimo, and the Rovetta *Virgin in Glory* (Pls. 104, 108–10).[50] Repeating the same fluted column, once again used to monumentalize a male saint, the foreground of the painting is defined by a chequered pavement, which is closed in the rear by a balustrade extending horizontally across the canvas, exactly as one finds at the Fava. Space is far deeper in the *Vision of S. Gaetano*, however; a platform marking the specific area of Gaetano's vision both deepens and broadens the mystical sphere. Enlarging the pictorial space even further are the fluted column and the pier that create a background dimension far behind the protagonists; in the Fava, S. Zulian, S. Prosdocimo, and Rovetta paintings, the architecture stands directly at the back of the figures, closing space rather than opening it.

The figural composition of the ex-Labia altar-piece is also grand. Tiepolo arranged the figures along a zigzagging diagonal, which begins with Gaetano's lily in the lower left-hand corner and climbs upwards and across to the angel in the top left-hand corner whose wing and staff—the latter belonging to St Joseph—stress further oblique movement. Such a pictorial solution had been used, of course, in both the *Education of the Virgin* and the *Adoration of the Christ-child*. What is new in the *Vision of S. Gaetano* is the lack of crowding; apart from the Christ-child, each figure occupies his or her own space and each is allowed to act individually. Tiepolo's clouds swirl around the protagonists, isolating them and buoyantly lifting them up. There is no similar pictorial device in either the Fava, S. Zulian, S. Prosdocimo, or Rovetta paintings, apart from the grey vapour that supports the Virgin in the last work.

The *Vision of S. Gaetano* recalls Piazzetta's Venetian altar-pieces of the same period: the *Virgin Appearing to St Philip Neri* for the Fava (1725–6; Pl. 98), the *Guardian Angel with SS Anthony of Padua and Luigi Gonzaga* for S. Vidal (*c.*1727–30), and *SS Vincenzo Ferreri, Giacinto, and Ludovico Bertrando* for the Gesuati (1737–8; Pl. 114). The similarities between them are the zigzagging diagonal compositions, the device of a figure on a cloud, and Gaetano's pose, which is very like that of Luigi Gonzaga's in S. Vidal, although such attitudes of saintly ecstasy were neither exclusively Venetian nor eighteenth-century in origin of course. But in spite of any apparent similarities, Tiepolo's religious imagery does not at all conform to Piazzetta's as a comparison of the Labia painting with the Gesuati *SS Vincenzo Ferreri, Giacinto, and Ludovico Bertrando* demonstrates irrefutably. The saintly figures in both works, which are almost contemporary in date, more or less follow the same arrangement—each zigzag begins with an object lying on the ground and concludes with an angel at the top—and the palette in both paintings is bright; but the artistic results

---

[50] Morassi, *A Complete Catalogue*, p. 54, *c.*1735–40; and A. Pallucchini, *L'opera completa*, no. 109, 1735–6.

113. G. B. Tiepolo, *Vision of S. Gaetano* (oil on canvas, 129 × 73 cm.)

114. G. B. Piazzetta, *SS Vincenzo Ferreri, Giacinto, and Ludovico Bertrando* (oil on canvas, 345 × 172 cm.)

115. G. B. Tiepolo, *Virgin and Child Appearing to a Group of Saints*
(oil on canvas, 52.7 × 32.8 cm.)

are not at all alike.[51] Piazzetta eschews an architectural surround whereas Tiepolo insists upon building a real world. Piazzetta's Counter-Reformation saints, while compositionally linked, are physically and emotionally unaware of one another, each one entirely absorbed by an individual revelation. Because the three saints possess no common narrative, they cannot be dramatically integrated.[52] Tiepolo's visionary experience, however, is a unified dramatic event. Of course, the subject of the Labia work is an alleged conversation between Mary and Gaetano, but even in a painting where there is no narrative, Tiepolo linked his protagonists in one spiritual moment. (A good example of this, and one contemporary with the *Vision of S. Gaetano*, is the beautiful small sketch of the *Virgin and Child Appearing to a Group of Saints* in the National Gallery, London (Pl. 115).[53] Apart from St Francis, all of the figures are turned towards Mary and Christ, and even Francis's body acknowledges the holy vision.)

In 1726, Padre Gaetano Maria Magenis of the *chierici regolari* published his *Nuova, e più copiosa storia dell'ammirabile, ed apostolica vita di S. Gaetano Thiene* in Venice.[54] More than five hundred pages long, the book recounts the life, devotions, and miracles of S. Gaetano, who was born into the rich and noble Thiene family. Before his birth, Gaetano's mother heard a heavenly voice telling her that her son wanted to be an 'Imitator of Christ, wanting to be born poor, humble, and abject'. Leaving her comfortable bedroom, she delivered Gaetano in the stables so that his birth would imitate Christ's own.[55] As an adult, Gaetano also tried to emulate the Saviour's life, preserving 'the beautiful treasure of his virginity'. So famed was the saint for this that when a young Venetian woman was raped, she prayed to Gaetano on his birthday and, according to tradition, she found that her virginity was restored![56]

In 1517, Gaetano went to Rome and visited S. Maria Maggiore where he was moved to tears by the cradle in which—so it was told—Mary had placed the Christ-child after his birth. Returning there often, Gaetano underwent a remarkable visionary experience on Christmas night 1517:

Seized by the divine beauty of the Mother, and of the Son, Gaetano could no longer withstand the violence that love created in him, so that he burned, anxiously showing that he was not happy just seeing such beauty but desired something further; but he did not dare ask for what he felt within him . . . So encouraged by St Jerome, and given yet more confidence by St Joseph, Gaetano approached the Throne of the Queen, Christ's Mother, and took to his breast her most sweet Child, whom she gave to him as a gift with her own hands.[57]

---

[51] The colours are different too, of course. Piazzetta's beiges and greys turning to browns and blacks are well known. Tiepolo's painting is less chromatically neutral: Mary is dressed in the traditional red and blue, and Joseph's robes create a warm zone around the Christ-child of golden yellow, sandlewood, and dark brown.

[52] Cf. Niero, *Tre artisti*, pp. 97 ff.; and A. Mariuz, *L'opera completa del Piazzetta* (Milan, 1982), no. 65, for the iconography.

[53] M. Levey, *National Gallery Catalogues: The Seventeenth- and Eighteenth-century Italian Schools* (London, 1971), 221 ff., dates this painting to *c.*1733; but because of its architectural setting, composition, and colour and handling, I believe it ought to be dated *c.*1735–6.

[54] The book may be found in the Biblioteca Apostolica Vaticana under *Ferraioli IV 2607*.

[55] Padre Gaetano Maria Magenis, *Nuova, e più copiosa storia dell'ammirabile, ed apostolica vita di S. Gaetano Thiene* (Venice, 1726), 6.

[56] Ibid., pp. 20–6.

[57] Ibid., p. 52: 'Gaetano rapito da quelle divine bellezze della Madre, e del Figlio, non poteva più sostenere la violenza, che gli faceva l'amore, onde ardeva, ansiava, e mostrava non esser contento di solo vederle, bramando ottenere qualche cosa di più; ma non ardiva di chiedere quel che sentivasi tanto a sospirare . . . Così incoraggito Gaetano da S. Girolamo, e fattagli confidenza ancora da S. Giuseppe s'accosta al Trono della Regina Madre, la quale subito facendogli dono del suo amabilissimo Bambino colle sue stesse mani glielo deposita in seno.'

Tiepolo's painting re-creates Gaetano's vision. Obviously, a few changes from the book have been made: Jerome is not present and Gaetano receives the Christ-child from Joseph rather than Mary. Joseph, in fact, is more important in the painting than he is in the book; his presence is underscored by his miraculously flowering rod in the top left-hand corner that extends the long diagonal joining the two male saints. But, in spite of these modifications, Tiepolo is remarkably faithful to Magenis's narrative. A cloth of majesty indicates Mary's throne; the saint himself is overwhelmed by the divine apparition; and, most importantly, a grand ecclesiastical enclosure provides the setting for the miraculous event.[58] Finally, the Child, whom Tiepolo placed almost exactly in the painting's centre, is the fulcrum around which events move. In this, Tiepolo followed the full sense of the account, if not the actual description. For Magenis emphasizes that the saint received the Lord '. . . not just in appearance, as was represented in the feigned *presepio*, but in Person, the living, and true Son of God'.[59] Tiepolo painted Christ stepping towards Gaetano with his arms outstretched, offering himself to the ecstatic saint as the Crucified Saviour.

The altar-pieces for the Fava and S. Zulian in Venice, for S. Prosdocimo in Padua, the Chiesa di Ognissanti in Rovetta, and the Palazzo Labia demonstrate the wide range of Tiepolo's religious patronage during the first part of the 1730s: respectively, a religious order, a parish church, a convent of nuns, a rural church in the hills above Bergamo, and a wealthy noble family with a palace facing on to the Grand Canal. Looked at as a group, these five paintings also reveal the changing character of Tiepolo's art, its increasing grandeur and brightening tonalities, as well as providing evidence of the artist's ability to transform traditional Christian subject-matter into profound meditations on religious teachings. Asked to paint the *Education of the Virgin*, Tiepolo endowed the scene with praise for the Immaculate Virgin; the *Adoration of the Christ-child* is enriched in his hands to become a pictorial reverie on the death of the Saviour; and, in presenting a dramatic narrative of saintly ecstasy, Tiepolo conceived the *Vision of S. Gaetano* as a re-enactment of Christian submission before the mystery of faith.

The late 1730s saw Tiepolo's religious imagery increase in scale, formalize in character, and deepen in emotional intensity, as the Gesuati ceiling of 1738–9 and the contemporary triptych for S. Alvise, a huge and overwhelmingly impressive narrative of Christ's torments, demonstrate.[60] An altar-piece which can also be dated to this period, or only shortly before, is *Pope Clement Adoring the Trinity*, painted for Clement August, Prince Elector of Cologne; sixteen feet in height, the work is grandiose in its size, in the architecture depicted within it, and in the depth of Clement's mystical experience.[61]

---

[58] For the placement of the *culla di Gesù* within S. Maria Maggiore, see *Rione I—Monti*, iii (*Guide Rionali di Roma*), ed. L. Barroero (Rome, 1982), 102. The Oratory of the Presepe is now below the Cappella Sistina, from which it can be reached by a stairway; a statue of S. Gaetano attributed to N. Cordier stands in the stairwell. During Gaetano's lifetime, the oratory was at the end of the church's nave.

[59] Magenis, *Nuova, e più copiosa*, p. 53: '. . . dalle mani della Vergine l'amabile suo Bambino, non già in figura, come rappresentavasi nel finto Presepio, ma in Persona, il vivo, e vero Figlio di Dio'.

[60] The work has recently been cleaned and now fully reveals its splendid melodrama; for its dating, cf. A. Pallucchini, *L'opera completa*, no. 128.

[61] Cf. M. Levey, 'The Modello for Tiepolo's Altar-piece at Nymphenburg', *Burlington Magazine*, 99 (1957), 256–61; and A. Morassi, 'I quadri veneti del Settecento nella riaperta "Alte Pinakothek" di Monaco ed una nuova pala del Tiepolo', *Arte veneta*, 11 (1957), 173–80.

During the years 1735–40 Tiepolo painted several 'saintly gatherings' like *Pope Clement Adoring the Trinity* that take place inside large halls or before altar-tables, and they testify not only to the increasing grandeur of his art but also to his concern to unite the pictorial image with the sacred Mass that is celebrated in front of it.[62]

The most interesting of these works, partly because of its patronage and partly because of its specifically Venetian ideals, is the altar-piece Tiepolo painted for S. Salvador. The documents published by Giovanni Mariacher reveal that the commission came in 1737 from the Cornaro family.[63] The Cornaro traced their history back to the ancient and noble Roman Cornelii; they had participated in some of Venice's famous historical events, and they had given the Republic one of its most gracious citizens, Caterina Cornaro, the widow of Giacomo II Lusignano, King of Cyprus, Jerusalem, and Armenia. In an act which came to be interpreted as one of great patriotism, Caterina ceded the Island of Cyprus to the Republic after her husband's death.[64] She was also, along with other members of the family, an important patron of art. Tiepolo himself had enjoyed more recent Cornaro favour; one could even say that his career had been launched by them.[65]

The eighteenth-century Cornaro commission in S. Salvador focused on the right arm of the church's transept and involved more than the one work requested of Tiepolo. He was to paint an altar-piece for the transept's right-hand altar, and Fontebasso was asked to do the one on the left, opposite Tiepolo's. The *tagliapietra* Marco Fassina was employed to redo the two altars over which the new paintings would be inserted, as well as 'a Tomb, and part of the pavement of the floor between the two said altars . . .'; Fassina's altars were to resemble the one dedicated to S. Lorenzo, near the baptismal font in the church's left transept.[66] The commission, a unified decorative plan completed within a couple of years, was an expression of piety on the part of one family.

The reason for the project is easy to explain: both the left and right arms of S. Salvador's transept were Cornaro spaces. Occupying all of the short wall of the left arm—that is, the side of the church flanking the Mercerie—is a monument dedicated to Cardinals Marco, Francesco, and Andrea Cornaro; and opposite, over the entire wall of the

[62] Apart from those already mentioned elsewhere, i.e., the *Madonna and Child with SS Hyacinth and Dominic* in the Art Institute, Chicago, and the *Madonna and Child with Saints* in the National Gallery, London, there are a number of drawings with such compositions; see for instance the sheet in the Hyde Collection, Glens Falls, New York (G. Knox, *Tiepolo: A Bicentenary Exhibition 1770–1970* (exh. cat., Fogg Art Museum, Harvard University, Cambridge, 1970), no. 12); and the two in the Robert Lehman Collection, Metropolitan Museum of Art, and the Janos Scholz Collection (J. Bean and F. Stampfle, *Drawings from New York Collections, iii: The Eighteenth Century in Italy* (exh. cat., Metropolitan Museum of Art, New York, 1971), nos. 70, 71). Most of these compositions rely on ideas from Veronese.

[63] G. Mariacher, 'Per la datazione di un'opera perduta di Giambattista Tiepolo', *Arte veneta*, 13–14 (1959–60), 237 ff.; money came from Andrea and Federico Cornaro, and from the branches of the family in S. Maurizio and S. Polo, who were direct descendants of Caterina Cornaro, Queen of Cyprus. Further bibliography on the S. Salvador painting includes two important contributions by M. Levey: 'Tiepolo's Altar-piece for San Salvatore at Venice', *Burlington Magazine*, 97 (1955), 116–20; and s.v. 1193: 'SS. Augustine, Louis of France, John the Evangelist

and a Bishop Saint', in the 1971 edition of the *National Gallery Catalogue*, 218 ff.; also Knox, *Giambattista and Domenico*, i. 236–7, no. M.207. In 1736, Tiepolo had worked for the Cornaros of S. Maurizio in their villa at Merlengo: cf. A. Pallucchini, *L'opera completa*, no. 112; O. Sirén, *Dessins et tableaux de la Renaissance italienne dans les collections de Suède* (Stockholm, 1902), 107–8, publishes Tessin's letter of 16 June 1736, that notes 'Comme il est actuellement occupé chez le noble Cornaro pour 5 à 6 mois . . .'.

[64] BNM, MSS It. Cl. VII, Cod. XVIII (8307) (G. A. Cappellari, 'Il campidoglio veneto', I), fos. 321ʳ ff.

[65] It will be remembered that his very first important private commissions came from Doge Giovanni II Cornaro (cf. Chapter 1, p. 14); the young Tiepolo had also prepared the drawing from which Zucchi executed the print of Bassano's *Rout of the Imperial Troops of Giorgio Cornaro and Bartolomeo d'Alviano* that appeared in Lovisa's *Gran teatro* (Pl. 10).

[66] Cf. Mariacher, 'Per la datazione', p. 238; and ASV, 'Monasterio di San Salvatore', b. 44. Carol Burns, whose work on the church will soon be completed, kindly offered me transcripts of all relevant documentation. For the history and bibliography on the church, cf. M. Tafuri, *Venezia e il Rinascimento: Religione, scienza, architettura* (Turin, 1985), 24 ff.

transept's right arm and around a doorway leading into S. Salvador's sacristy and monastery, is a cenotaph built to commemorate Caterina Cornaro.[67] The body of the Queen of Cyprus had been brought to the church from its original resting-place, the Cappella Cornaro in SS Apostoli, in the late sixteenth century and was placed in the floor below the monument (Pl. 118).[68] Directly over the doorway leading into the sacristy, a relief *alla* Tullio Lombardo depicts Caterina offering her crown to Agostino Barbarigo (Doge, 1485–1501).[69] The Cornaro commitment to S. Salvador's transept was historic, therefore, and the reasons for family pride in its right half are self-evident. Their decision to embellish its altars and repave its floor in the late 1730s was determined by the church's second consecration in 1739.[70]

Although it has not survived, Tiepolo's S. Salvador altar-piece is remembered through two works, a drawing and an oil-sketch (Pls. 116, 117; Pl. VII). The question of which of these is the most accurate representation of the lost altar-piece will be discussed below, but the same figures appear in both: St Augustine, St John the Evangelist, St Louis of France, and a bishop saint. Augustine's identification was made in the eighteenth century, in a catalogue entry by Giannantonio Selva for a small work belonging to the collection of Francesco Algarotti.[71] The brothers of S. Salvador (*canonici regolari*) lived under Augustine's rule, and a panel painted by Lazzaro Bastiani and showing the saint enthroned, hieratically positioned, with three *frati* on either side, had once adorned the same altar given to Tiepolo. The canons' desire to repeat the honour to Augustine was probably due to the nearby doorway, within Caterina Cornaro's cenotaph, that connects S. Salvador with its monastery; the *frati* walked through that space and by those altars daily.[72] The

[67] F. Sansovino, *Venetia città nobilissima* (Venice, 1581), 48; cf. also the later editions by G. Stringa (1603), 93ʳ–94ᵛ; and G. Martinioni (1663; ed. L. Moretti, Venice, 1968), 121–2. Marco was created Cardinal by Alexander VI, Francesco by Clement VII, and Andrea by Paul III.

[68] Sansovino, Stringa, and Martinioni use the words 'All'incontro di questi [the three cardinals], si mette in opera il sepolcro di Caterina Cornaro, Regina di Cipro'; cf. the respective editions, pp. 48, 94ᵛ, and 121. F. Corner, a member of Caterina's family, notes in his *Notizie storiche delle chiese e monasteri di Venezia e Torcello* (Padua, 1758), 231: 'Giace sepolta in questa Chiesa vicino alla porta, che conduce alla Libreria [sacristy, or monastery library?] Caterina Cornaro, Regina di Cipro . . .'. The discoloured marbles on Caterina's monument were meant, no doubt, to be covered with sculpted figures. The inscription on the S. Salvador floor-slab reads: 'D.O.M. | Catharinae Corneliae | Cypri, Hierosolymorum | Ac Armeniae Reginae | Cineres'. For the removal of Caterina's remains from SS Apostoli, cf. BMC, MS Gradenigo 60 ('Trattato di Cattarina Cornelia | Regina di Cipro | E Delle Antichità D'Asolo | Di Cui Ella Fu | Signora'), fo. 55ᵛ.

[69] I am grateful to Sarah Blake McHam for discussing this material with me, as well as that of the architecture and sculpture of the Cornaro Chapel in SS Apostoli.

[70] The *consacrazione semplice* of 1739 was led by Patriarch Francesco Antonio Correr; it was followed in 1743 by a *consacrazione solenne*. For the first, cf. BMC, MS Gradenigo 175 ('Chiese. Tomi Tre . . . che tengono notizie d'ogni genere intorno alle chiese e parrocchie di Venezia', II), fo. 339ᵛ, and G. Tassini, *Iscrizioni della chiesa e convento di S. Salvatore di Venezia* (Venice, 1895), 11; cf. G. Zanetti, 'Memorie per servire all'istoria della inclita città di Venezia', ed. F. Stefani, *Archivio veneto*, 29 (1885), 126 (entry for

13 May 1743): 'Si solennizò dai Canonici di S. Salvatore la consacrazione della Chiesa loro fatta dell'anno 1739, come vedesi dalla iscrizione posta nell'andito per cui si va in sacristia.'

[71] G. A. Selva, *Catalogo dei quadri dei disegni e dei libri che trattano dell'arte del disegno della galleria del fu sig. conte Algarotti in Venezia* (Venice, 1780), p. xxiii. See Mariacher, 'Per la datazione', *passim*; and Levey, *National Gallery Catalogue*, pp. 218–21, for which of today's versions belonged to Algarotti. There are three versions of the oil-sketch: in the Art Gallery, York; in the Musée des Beaux-Arts, Lille (attributed now to Giandomenico rather than to Giambattista); and in the Musée des Beaux-Arts, Rennes. A larger version of the Munich drawing is now in a private collection in Venice; done in pencil it measures 500 × 270 mm. and once belonged to the Bossi Bayerlen collection.

[72] For the *canonici regolari*, cf. Tassini, *Iscrizioni*, p. 5, and Tafuri, *Venezia e il Rinascimento*, p. 31. Bastiani's painting is described by M. Boschini, *Le ricche minere della pittura veneziana* (Venice, 1674), 104–5: 'vi sono cinque partimenti, nel mezzo S. Agostino, con molti Frati inginocchiati attorno, con libro in mano, e nel di sopra in Frontespicio, Christo morto, sostenuto da gli Angeli; & à basso, varie figure, di Lazaro Sebastiani'. L. Planiscig identified this work with one on the Viennese art-market: cf. 'La tavola di Sant'Agostino opera di Lazzaro Bastiani', *Rivista di Venezia*, 8 (1929), 257–60. Planiscig noted that the painting was mentioned in Sansovino, *Venetia* (1581); in Boschini, *Le ricche minere*; and in Zanetti's 1733 edition of Boschini (p. 186), but is not referred to in the 1740 *Forestiere illuminato*. Zanetti writes that Bastiani's St Augustine altar-piece faced Francesco Vecellio's fresco of St Leonard. Tiepolo's and Fontebasso's paintings repeat these same figures.

117. G. B. Tiepolo, Oil-sketch for the destroyed altar-piece in S. Salvador, Venice, of *SS Augustine, John the Evangelist, Magno, and Louis of France* (oil on canvas, 58.1 × 33 cm.)

116. G. B. Tiepolo (attributed), Drawing for the destroyed altar-piece in S. Salvador, Venice, of *SS Augustine, John the Evangelist, Magno, and Louis of France* (black chalk on white paper, 500 × 270 mm.)

Munich drawing shows Augustine standing with a flaming heart, symbol of his religious fervour and piety, in his left hand; he is holding a quill-pen in his right. In the London oil-sketch, he is sitting on a throne, with the heart in his right hand and his Rule and pen in the left.

St John the Evangelist appears on the right in both the drawing and the oil-sketch, standing and gazing at Augustine in the former and sitting on a cushion, his eagle behind him, in the latter. He must be interpreted, I think, as a biblical 'footnote' or 'source' for Augustine, for in both compositions Tiepolo very carefully made John's quill-pen visible and absolutely parallel with Augustine's, implying that St Augustine, Father of the Church, wrote while inspired and supported by Gospel.[73] Standing in front of John in the drawing, and behind him in the oil-sketch, is an unidentified bishop, simply called 'a Bishop Saint who reads . . .' in Algarotti's catalogue.[74] I believe that this figure is S. Magno, little known today but important in Venetian hagiography, who was one of the city's patron saints, ranking alongside such figures as SS Hermagoras and Fortunatus, Anthony of Padua, and Roch.[75] Magno is thought to have been responsible for the founding of eight of Venice's earliest churches, including SS Apostoli and S. Salvador, both of which contained Cornaro family altars.[76] At S. Salvador, festivities on his feast-day (6 October) included a solemn Mass, the exposition of the host, vespers, a special benediction and hymn, and a sermon.[77]

Magno's inclusion in Tiepolo's altar-piece is also confirmed by his proximity to a mitre and a crosier in both the Munich drawing and the London sketch.[78] These are both historically symbolic of S. Salvador. In 1177, Pope Alexander III (1159–81) made a historic visit to Venice to meet Federico Barbarossa. While he was there, he consecrated the Church of S. Salvador (29 August) and confirmed on its monastery all the privileges and prerogatives previously given it, granting to Prior Vincenzo Fioravante and all his successors the use of the mitre and the crosier. Tiepolo's Magno records S. Salvador's foundation, and the mitre and crosier commemorate the church's first consecration.[79] Thus, one may conclude that the centre and right half of Tiepolo's altar-piece, in either the Munich drawing or the London *modello*, embody biblical authority (St John), S. Salvador's foundation (S. Magno), its monastic rule (St Augustine), and its twelfth-century consecration (the mitre and pastoral). This ensemble properly expressed the Cornaro's devotion to S. Salvador, and it also recorded the church's most important

---

[73] St John's Gospel says that Christ is the 'Logos', the word made flesh, a belief developed in the early Church and associated with Augustine's *De vera religione*.

[74] Selva, *Catalogo dei quadri*, p. xxiii: 'un Santo Vescovo che legge . . .'.

[75] Cf. A. Niero, 'I santi patroni', in S. Tramontin (ed.), *Culto dei santi a Venezia* (Venice, 1965), 78; and Tafuri, *Venezia e il Rinascimento*, pp. 27–8.

[76] The 1724 edition of Coronelli's guide notes (p. 190) that S. Salvador was built by the Galetazzi and Caresi families 'per rivelazioni di s. Magno . . .'; and Tassini also writes (*Iscrizioni*, p. 5) that the church was founded by S. Magno, the first Bishop of Oderzo and Eraclea, who came to Venice around 633.

[77] Cf. P. Contarini, *Venezia religiosa: Guida per tutte le sacre*

funzioni che si praticano nelle chiese di Venezia (Venice, 1853), 333.

[78] Magno could be represented wearing a cope and mitre and holding a church; cf. S. Tramontin, 'I santi dei mosaici marciani', in *Culto dei santi*, p. 140. Although the church is not in either of Tiepolo's images, the cope is especially noticeable because its heavy folds and rich embroidery are so obviously emphasized. The mitre is at Magno's feet in the Munich drawing; in the London oil-sketch, it is associated with him even though it sits on St Augustine's pedestal. Magno can also be found in St Mark's atrium, below the Moses cupola and above the *Crossing of the Red Sea*, in a roundel next to St Augustine; he appears as well as a witness to *Christ and Doubting Thomas* in Cima da Conegliano's painting in the Accademia.

[79] Cf. Tassini, *Iscrizioni*, p. 5.

119. F. Fontebasso, *Pala di S. Leonardo* (oil on canvas)

118. Cornaro Funeral Monument

historical moments for all those passing through the transept's right arm just when Patriarch Correr was about to reconsecrate it in 1739.

On the left of Tiepolo's altar-piece, St Louis stood alone. Selva did not specify whether 'S. Ludovico' was Louis IX of France or Bishop Louis of Toulouse, but the royal garments and staff identify him as the King (1214–70).[80] St Louis was famous for having carried the Crusader's Cross to the Holy Land, where 'he took possession of the Relics [Christ's crown of thorns] that had been pledged to the Venetians by Baudouin II, Emperor of Constantinople'; Louis fulfilled Baudouin's promise by giving the Serenissima four of the thorns from Christ's crown.[81] The relics are in S. Marco. Louis' journey to the East, his saintly devotion, and his honesty were expressions of his humble character, emphasized by Tiepolo by his placing of Louis' crown at his feet (a crown that is a princely coronet and not that of a monarch). Ripa's description of 'Humility' is particularly useful in this context: 'Placing a golden crown underfoot demonstrates that humility does not prize great and rich things; rather, it shows a disregard for them . . . and as a proof of this rare virtue Baudouin first King of Jerusalem humbled himself, saying when he refused the golden crown let God forbid that I wear such a crown when my Saviour wore one of thorns.'[82]

Louis IX of France was a pictorial metaphor for royal submission before Christian piety, and as such, his inclusion in Tiepolo's altar-piece was a reference to Caterina Cornaro, whose tomb and cenotaph dominate S. Salvador's right transept. The subject of Fontebasso's facing work, the *Pala di S. Leonardo* (Pl. 119), which is still *in situ*, is consistent with this interpretation. Leonard, a converted Frankish noble, refused a bishopric, abandoned his life at Court, and went to live in a forest near Limoges.[83] Caterina, one recalls, had donated her Cypriot lands to the Venetian Republic and had subsequently established herself in Asolo, a humble town in the Veneto. When looking at Caterina's cenotaph (Pl. 118), it should be noted that the relief showing her patriotic act of abdication is on a line with her tomb and ashes below, and is placed in relation to Fontebasso's and Tiepolo's paintings. Thus the Cornaro associated the Queen of Cyprus's monument with St Louis IX, a celebrated Christian monarch, and with St Leonard, a patrician turned hermit. The project to renovate S. Salvador's right transept may be read, then, both as a timely solemnization of the church's consecration and as a pictorial

[80] Selva, *Catalogo dei quadri*, p. xxiii: 'Sul piano evvi S. Ludovico . . .'. For Louis IX, cf. 'Luigi IX', in *Bibliotheca Sanctorum*, viii (Rome, 1967), cols. 320–38.

[81] Cf. Corner, *Notizie storiche*, p. 195: 'Quattro spine dalla corona del Signore donate già alla Repubblica da San Luigi di Questo nome IX. Re di Francia, allorchè ricuperò le Reliquie impegnate à Veneziani da Balduino II. Imperador di Costantinopoli.' In fact, Baudouin, the last Latin Emperor of Constantinople (Porphyrogenetos, 1217–73), had given the crown of thorns in surety to Venice; Louis IX bought the relic in 1239 and placed it in Ste Chapelle, Paris.

[82] C. Ripa, *Iconologia* (Rome, 1603), 215–16: 'Il tener la corona d'oro sotto il piede, dimostra, che l'humiltà non pregia le grandezze, e ricchezze, anzi è dispregio d'esse . . . & per dimostratione di questa rara virtù Baldouino primo Rè di Hierusalem si rese humile, dicendo nel refutare la corona d'oro tolga Dio da me che io porti corona d'oro la dove il mio Redentore la portò di spine.'

Louis is not wearing a crown in either the drawing or the oil-sketch; Ricci shows him wearing the monarch's crown in *St Louis Showing the Crown of Thorns* (Turin, Basilica of Superga) of 1729: cf. Daniels, *Sebastiano Ricci*, p. 122 and fig. 283. There is confusion around the name Baudouin. Christ's crown of thorns had been sold to Louis by Baudouin II, son of the Count of Flanders who was a leader of the Fourth Crusade and who as Baudouin I (1172–1205) became the first Latin Emperor of Constantinople. Ripa associates the crown of thorns instead with the King of Jerusalem (1058?–1118) who was the son of the Count of Boulogne. This all becomes a little clearer when one realizes that it was from the Jerusalem line that the kingship of Jerusalem and Cyprus eventually passed to Giacomo II Lusignano, husband of Caterina Cornaro.

[83] For Leonard, cf. D. H. Farmer, *The Oxford Dictionary of Saints* (Oxford, 1982), 244; and 'Leonardo di Nobiliacum', in *Bibliotheca Sanctorum*, vii (Rome, 1966), cols. 1198–1208.

mémoire of the glory accrued to the Cornaro by the selfless act of their ancestor: '"fama et honore" privati'.[84]

Sadly, Tiepolo's S. Salvador altar-piece no longer exists but was consumed by fire.[85] One is left to decide, therefore, whether it is the Munich drawing or the London oil-sketch that is most like the lost painting. Knox suggests that the Munich composition was used for the altar-piece that was destroyed in a fire in 1741, after which Tiepolo reworked the composition, and the London version replaced the original (or was meant to), and was copied in 1746 by Franz Martin Kuen.[86] It is unlikely, however, that an image like the one in Munich ever hung in S. Salvador; moreover, Tiepolo's original painting— looking very much like the London oil-sketch, as I shall argue below—may have survived until nearly 1770.

The original documents show that in late 1736 Marco Fassina undertook to make 'in the arm towards the Sacristy two Altars similar to that of S. Lorenzo in the opposite arm, towards the Baptistery'.[87] In other words, the new altars, and perhaps the paintings' frames too, were to be modelled on sixteenth-century forms already in the building, and this stipulation preceded any payment made for the paintings to either Tiepolo or Fontebasso. Fassina's 'Altari' are Renaissance rather than Baroque in style (Pl. 119), closely following S. Salvador's own classicizing architecture. Moreover, both his altar-front and wall-unit are decorated with circular inserts of *verde antico*. Examining the real architecture in terms of the two compositions in Munich and London, one realizes that not only is the groined vaulting under which St Augustine stands in the former completely unrelated to the frame itself, but it is also at odds with S. Salvador's own architectural system. The London *bozzetto*, on the other hand, 'fits' beautifully. The moulding on the feigned arch crowning Augustine copies the real one, and the painted piers and cornices are closely linked to Fassina's columns and pilasters. Furthermore, if a visitor to S. Salvador stands in front of the actual altar with a photograph of the London oil-sketch in his hand and then takes a few steps to the right, he will see that the painted architecture in the photograph and the real bays in the church are in perfect agreement. To conclude, one can also see how Tiepolo unified his image with the altar-table in front of it. The floor in the London sketch contains rounded green inserts that match both the colour and design of Fassina's inlaid *verde antico*. Especially noteworthy is the fact that the circle in front of St John's left foot, directly on the painting's central axis and below Augustine, would have coincided with the green roundel at the bottom of the frame. The hallowed pictorial space in the London *bozzetto* was deliberately co-ordinated with the real altar at S. Salvador.

Could Tiepolo—one of the greatest pictorial decorators in the history of Western art, a man who had ten years earlier completed the extraordinary cycle in the Arcivescovado

[84] Tafuri, *Venezia e il Rinascimento*, p. 3. The visitor to S. Salvador will see the Cornaro coat of arms topped by a crown on the socles below the columns that flank the two altar-paintings.

[85] Selva, *Catalogo dei quadri*, pp. 121–2, wrote that the *modello* in the Algarotti Collection 'servì . . . per una Tavola d'Altare eseguita dall'Autore [Tiepolo] nella Chiesa di San Salvatore di

Venezia, e che ora è consunta'.

[86] Cf. Knox, *Giambattista and Domenico*, i. 23; Levey, *National Gallery Catalogue*, p. 219, provides information on Kuen.

[87] Mariacher, 'Per la datazione', p. 238: 'Doverà far detti due Altari in detta Chiesa nel braccio verso la Sagrestia simili a quelo di San Lorenzo nel braccio oposto verso il Batisterio.'

in Udine, and who at the same time as he was painting for S. Salvador was also frescoing the Gesuati ceiling—could he possibly have intended the Munich composition for the S. Salvador altar, once the latter was designed? The answer has to be no. The Munich drawing must be regarded instead as Tiepolo's first *pensiero* for the Cornaro commission, made before arrangements with Fassina had been concluded.[88] It clearly pre-dates the London oil-sketch, for, as Knox himself observed, the reverse sequence 'would represent an entirely retrograde development . . .'.[89] The Munich sheet presents a less interesting composition and a less monumental and dramatically potent 'saintly gathering' than the small canvas in the National Gallery.

If a painting based on the London oil-sketch adorned the Cornaro altar from the beginning, i.e., from 1738, as I suggest that it did, and was then copied by Kuen in 1746, then it had to have survived the fire of 1741 which, according to Tassini, 'destroyed the choir with the marble cornices of the two altars below (the choir and altars were not redone) as well as the lanterns of the first two cupolas'.[90] He does not mention the transept, or any damage near the sacristy, nor was Titian's *Annunciation*, which stands on the right side of the church, threatened. And if a blaze had raged out of control into the transept, it would surely have consumed Fontebasso's canvas as well as Tiepolo's. A later, more localized, fire must have been responsible for the loss; there were certainly plenty of them in the crowded city of Venice and one need not ponder too seriously on which it could have been. However, Mariacher very plausibly suggests that it must have taken place after 1765, since the *Forestiere illuminato* of that year still mentions Tiepolo's painting *in situ*, but before 1772, when a new edition of the same guidebook does not mention the work.[91] This would explain why Tiepolo, who had left for Spain in 1762, did not replace the lost painting with a new one.

The loss of the S. Salvador altar-piece is a great one, not only for those who admire Tiepolo's art, but also for all those who appreciate the Venetian pictorial tradition. Tiepolo's 'London St Augustine' is the direct descendant of a long line of enthroned saints in Venetian art who speak *ex cathedra* to a gathering of holy brethren: Bartolomeo Vivarini's St Augustine in a triptych in SS Giovanni e Paolo, for example, or his St Mark in the altar-piece of that name for the Frari, or Alvise Vivarini's and Marco Basaiti's St Ambrose, also in the Frari.[92] Tiepolo's Augustine, like St Ambrose, sits within an architectural bay so that a throne of majesty, to use Sinding-Larsen's phrase, is created through the formal, architectonic setting.[93] Tiepolo's pictorial architecture, moreover, reflects the painting's real framework, recalling for any *amateur* of Venetian art Giovanni Bellini's brilliant solution for the S. Giobbe altar-piece, before which the faithful attending

---

[88] Knox is tentative in his attribution of the Munich drawing: cf. *Giambattista and Domenico*, i. 236–7. If it is not autograph, it copies what must have been Tiepolo's first idea.   [89] Ibid.

[90] Tassini, *Iscrizioni*, p. 7: 'che distrusse il coro coi cornicioni marmorei dei due altari sottoposti, (coro ed altari non più rifatti) nonchè le lanterne delle due prime cupole'. See also BMC, MS Gradenigo 175 ('Chiese. Tomi Tre . . . tengono notizie d'ogni genere intorno alle chiese e parrocchie di Venezia' II), fo. 339': '1741. 15 8brᵉ Fuoco orribile in S. Salvador.'

[91] Mariacher, 'Per la datazione', p. 238.

[92] A similar figure can be found in sculpture, too, in the relief of St Gregory who looks out on to the Grand Canal from the exterior of the ex-monastery dedicated to him; he is just to the right of the Salute *pontile*.

[93] S. Sinding-Larsen, 'Titian's Triumph of Faith, and the Medieval Tradition of the Glory of Christ', in *Institutum Romanum Norvegiae: Acta*, vi (Rome, 1975), 326.

Mass became one with the holy world on the other side of the frame.[94] To conclude, Tiepolo's feigned bay is such a convincing re-creation of a part of S. Salvador that the holy gathering in the painting appears to take place within the building itself, an apt pictorial metaphor for an image celebrating the church's founding and consecration.

One final thought about the altar-piece: St Augustine's turn to the left (again, in the London version) might be thought to be a little awkward, for his knees and entire body are not facing towards the faithful arriving from the church's crossing. But Tiepolo was neither confused nor ill-informed about the canvas's position when he devised this; the fact that he understood the relationship between the image and its setting is clearly demonstrated by the lighting emanating from the upper left of the painting, which corresponds to the real light source from the window above Caterina Cornaro's monument (note the draping curtains in Pl. 118). Tiepolo positioned Augustine so that his Rule would greet the *frati* when they entered the transept from the corridor behind the Cornaro cenotaph.

The St Augustine altar-piece meant that the forty-two-year-old Tiepolo had finally placed a major work in an old Venetian church. This 'saintly gathering' does not look like the ones he did in the 1730s, nor does it resemble any of Piazzetta's, although there are links between Tiepolo's painting and Ricci's *Pius V and SS Thomas Aquinas and Peter Martyr* (1732–4) in the Gesuati.[95] One may even postulate that the younger man was influenced by the older's enthroned figure of Pius and by the loggia that defines the background space. Tiepolo's is a far more solemn image, however; the two bishop saints, unlike Ricci's trio, are deeply thoughtful. Tiepolo's architectural bay charges the scene with ceremony, as opposed to Ricci's blue sky and long-limbed flying angels, one of whom undecorously displays his bottom over St Thomas's bald head! The S. Salvador painting is grave in tone, and in this respect the London oil-sketch is even more poignant and moving than the Munich drawing. The image's seriousness was increased with the deletion of the cherubim heads above St Augustine and of the smiling angel at S. Magno's feet. Lastly, Tiepolo placed winged figures in the two distant spandrels, allusions to the Christian victory over death.

About a decade later, *c.*1748, Tiepolo worked for the Cornaro family again, creating one of his most moving images, the *Last Communion of St Lucy* (Pl. 120), for their funerary chapel in SS Apostoli.[96] The chapel had been added to the church's right flank in the late fifteenth century; Caterina Cornaro was buried there when she died in 1510, as were her father Marco (d. 1511) and her brother Giorgio (d. 1540).[97] Sometime early in the sixteenth century, that is around the time that Caterina and Marco died, Benedetto

---

[94] A specific link can even be proposed between the Tiepolo atelier and Bellini's art; the saint whom I have identified as S. Magno and who appears in a Tiepolo drawing now in Weimar is very close in type to the old priest in Bellini's *Presentation in the Temple*, a painting Giandomenico copied in a drawing: cf. Knox, *Giambattista and Domenico*, ii, pl. 71.

[95] Cf. Daniels, *Sebastiano Ricci*, fig. 302.

[96] Cf. Morassi, *A Complete Catalogue*, p. 55: '*c.*1740–45'; and A.

Pallucchini, *L'opera completa*, no. 171: '1745–46'. See below, p. 206, for a discussion of the work's probable date.

[97] G. Orlandini, *La Cappella Corner nella chiesa dei Santi Apostoli in Venezia* (Venice, 1914), 13. SS Apostoli, like S. Salvador, was 'fondata per revelatione di san Magno . . .'; cf. Sansovino, *Venetia* (1581), p. 54. For inscriptions in the chapel, cf. BNM, MS Lat. Cl. X, Cod. CXLIX (3657) (G. G. Palferius, 'Monumenta Memorabilia Venetiarum'), fo. 118r.

Diana (b. 1460–5, d. 1525) painted a *Last Communion of St Lucy* for the chapel's altar. The altar-piece is mentioned *in situ* in 1581 by Sansovino, and this is confirmed right through the seventeenth century and into the mid-eighteenth.[98] The subject of Diana's painting was an appropriate choice for a funerary chapel, especially one which had twelve wheat stalks shooting forth from a vase sculpted on one of its column bases, as well as pelicans feeding their young by piercing their own breasts.[99] Lucy's last communion was chosen instead of the equally well-known and similar events from the lives of St Jerome or the Magdalene (both penitent saints), because she is one of SS Apostoli's titular saints, along with the twelve disciples.[100]

In the later sixteenth century, when SS Apostoli was rebuilt because of structural problems, the sepulchre of the Queen of Cyprus—as I have noted above—was moved to S. Salvador.[101] But Diana's painting remained in the Cornaro Chapel until at least 1740, when the *Forestiere illuminato* mentions it as still *in situ*.[102] But by the end of that decade, sometime before the autumn of 1750 when Tiepolo left Venice for Würzburg, his version of the *Last Communion of St Lucy* must have been in place. A suggested *terminus post quem* for the execution of the small *pala* would be 1748–9. The reasons are stylistic, iconographic, and circumstantial. First, the painting's profoundly moving drama betokens Tiepolo's full maturity. His economy of gesture is remarkable, as is the quiet stateliness of the composition. Lucy herself, both in the simplicity of her movement and in the pictorial power of her bowed head, is very like the Scuola dei Carmini's Simon Stock (Pl. 82), painted towards 1749.

Secondly, the stimulus to the Cornaro to replace the old fifteenth-century painting with a new version was probably provided by events in SS Apostoli, *c.*1748, which substantially confirm a dating of the *pala* to just before the artist's trip to Würzburg. Gradenigo wrote in his diary that the church's roof was ruined by 1748 and that the *pievano*, or parish priest, had it repaired and repainted. The priest, Angelo Maria Ropelli,

[98] Sansovino, *Venetia* (1581), p. 54; (1603, ed. Stringa) p. 141ᵛ; (1663, ed. Martinioni) i. 143; Boschini, *Le ricche minere*, p. 21 ('Nella Capella di Casa Cornara, la Tavola con S. Lucia, e due altri Santi . . .'); C. Ridolfi, *Le maraviglie dell'arte* (Venice, 1648), i. 41; Zanetti, *Descrizione*, p. 389; *Forestiere illuminato*, p. 160 (but without specifying the subject of Diana's work); and Fra' Pacifico, *Cronica veneta* (1751), p. 145 ('Benedetto Diana vi fece la pala di S. Lucia con altri adornamenti . . .').

[99] The symbols appear on the base of the right column as one enters the chapel; for the image of the pelican, cf. Ripa, *Iconologia*, p. 18, 'Amor del prossimo'. A lily and cross sprout out of one of the wheat-stalks.

[100] Contarini, *Venezia religiosa*, p. 384, notes that a solemn Mass and vespers were celebrated on the saint's feast-day, 13 Dec., both there and in S. Lucia. Corner, *Notizie storiche*, pp. 267–8, records that the chapel was dedicated 'alla Vergine e Martire Santa Lucia dalla pietà della nobil Famiglia Cornara . . .'. For Lucy's relics in SS Apostoli, cf. A. Niero, *Sta Lucia Vergine e Martire* (Venice, 1965), 37. In addition, there are special ties linking Lucy to Caterina Cornaro, and the family may have decided to build upon them: both Lucy and Caterina were praised as virtuous females deeply devoted to their families, and both were reported to have gone through severe trials that tested their Christian faith. Lucy's devotion to her mother is almost always cited in her narrative, and her horrible torture by oxen did not sway her from her faith. Caterina, too, maintained deep ties with her family throughout her life; she survived widowhood, the loss of her State (twice, one could say), and the death of her child. For the last, cf. BMC, MS Gradenigo 60 ('Trattato di Cattarina Cornelia/Regina di Cipro'), fo. 27ᵛ, where the author speaks of Caterina's tears after her infant's death, plaintively asking whether the Queen would ever see 'la Chiara luce del Sole' again. Finally, it should be noted that the name Lucy was quite often given to female Cornaro babies; perusing the files of family wills in the Archivio di Stato, I have found six of them dating to the fifteenth century. Cappellari mentions (BNM, MSS It. Cl. VII, Cod. XVIII [8307], 'Il campidoglio veneto', I, fo. 323ᵛ) that in the late fourteenth century there was a famous 'Lucia q. Pietro Cornaro da S. Apostolo' who had generously given money to Venice.

[101] Sansovino, *Venetia* (1663, ed. Martinioni) i. 143, noted: 'disfacendo il Tempio per murarlo di nuovo, [the Queen of Cyprus] fu portata à San Salvador'.

[102] Cf. n. 98 above. Pacifico's *Cronica veneta* (1751), p. 146, also cites it as in the chapel—but this may be an error, like the reference to Varottari's ceiling as still being *in situ*, even though it had been replaced by Fabio Canal's.

120. G. B. Tiepolo, *Last Communion of St Lucy* (oil on canvas,
222 × 101 cm.)

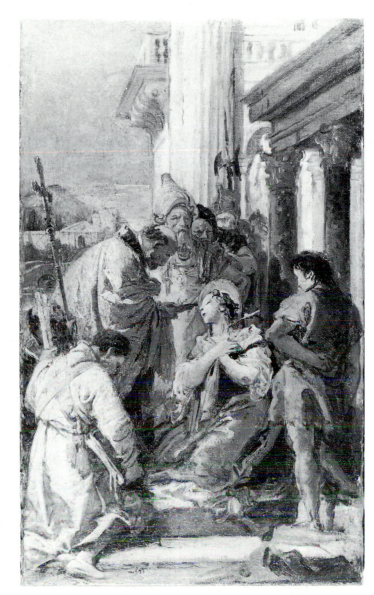

121. G. B. Tiepolo, Oil-sketch
for the *Last Communion of St Lucy*
(oil on canvas, 56 × 35 cm.)

122. Below: P. Veronese,
*Martyrdom and Last Communion of
St Lucy* (oil on canvas,
137 × 173 cm.)

was only appointed to his position in 1748, and the renovation project he began continued under his direction for several years.[103] Zanotti informs us that the architect Pedolo was still working on SS Apostoli's roof in 1752, and a year later (21 June 1753) Gradenigo noted that the ceiling, painted in fresco by Fabio Canal, had just been unveiled to the public.[104] Although one cannot be certain, the *Last Communion of St Lucy* was probably contemporary with Ropelli's assumption of parishional responsibilities, and reflects his concern (conveyed to the Cornaro family) to dress up the building's interior with new altar-pieces as well as to modernize the fabric with a new roof and ceiling.

There is also an iconographic link between Canal's ceiling and Tiepolo's altar-piece. Zanetti's 1733 guide described SS Apostoli's old ceiling very carefully:

In the ceiling, the architecture, ornamentation etc. are by Antonio Dolabella, student of Aliense. The two octagons, one with the Holy Spirit Descending onto the Apostles and its pendant, are by Montemezzano. The four works near the cornice, in the ceiling's central zones [the *mezzarie*, that is, along the middle of each side], are by Dario Varottari . . . and contain the life, and miracles of the Holy Apostles. The central painting, in which Christ ascends into Heaven, is by Aliense with the help of his assistant Dolabella.[105]

The old ceiling's emphasis was on post-Crucifixion events: from the centrally placed *Ascension*, one looked towards an octagon with the *Descent of the Holy Spirit on to the Apostles*, and, from there, to smaller scenes showing the apostles' lives and miracles. Canal's ceiling, in contrast, emphasizes a pre-Crucifixion narrative: the Holy Spirit radiates above Christ as he administers Holy Communion to the apostles at the Last Supper. This new iconography was reinforced only a few years later, in 1756, when a new altar was consecrated which carries a relief of the Last Supper.[106] Given the church's structural alterations in the middle of the century, and given, too, Tiepolo's departure from Venice in late 1750, it would seem reasonable to conclude that, perhaps with a gentle nudge from Ropelli, the Cornaro decided to refurbish their family chapel with a new altar-piece, purposely retaining Diana's subject because of its obvious connection with the church's new iconographic insistence upon Communion. If this is correct, then the *Last Communion of St Lucy* can be dated, as I suggested above, to 1748–9.

Tiepolo's preparatory sketch for the painting (Pl. 121) differs in some small but important ways from the finished *pala*. In the *bozzetto*, a dagger, poised mystically in the air,

[103] L. Livan (ed.), *Notizie d'arte tratte dai notatori e dagli annali del N. H. Pietro Gradenigo* (Venice, 1942), 98 (entry dated 10 Apr. 1763); and BMC, MS Gradenigo 175 ('Chiese. Tomi Tre', II), fos. 200, 203: 'Oratione recitata dal . . . Angelo Ropelli Nell'occasione d'esser eletto Pievano di S.S. Apostoli . . . 1748.'

[104] F. Zanotto, *Tavola cronologica della storia veneta* (Venice, 1859), 128; and Livan, *Gradenigo*, p. 98 (10 Apr. 1763): Ropelli 'lo [the ceiling] fece ripristinare e dipingere. Per la qual cosa riportò molta lode, ed applausi dalla contrada, che assai lo amava'; and p. 9 of the same publication (21 June 1753): 'Fù reso visibile il nuovo Soffitto della Chiesa di S. Apostoli, nel quale dipinse a fresco Fabio Canal con molta sua lode.'

[105] Zanetti, *Descrizione*, pp. 389–90: 'Nel soffitto poi l'ar-

chitettura, ornamenti, ed altro sono di mano di Antonio Dolabella allievo dell'Aliense. Li due ottagoni ove nell'uno è lo Spirito Santo, che discende sugl'Apostoli, e l'altro corrispondente sono di mano di Montemezzano; li quattro quadri nelle mezzarie del soffitto vicini al corniccione sono di mano Dario Varottari padre d'Alessandro, e contengono la vita, e miracoli de' SS Apostoli. Il quadrone di mezzo dove Cristo ascende al Cielo è di mano dell'Aliense coadiuvato però dal discepolo Dolabella.'

[106] Canal's 'Communion' is visually co-ordinated with the church's altar. For the relief decorating that altar, made of Carrara marble, cf. Livan, *Gradenigo*, p. 20, entry dated 1 Feb. 1755, but *more veneto* (Feb. 1756).

pierces Lucy's throat and reminds us of her martyrdom.[107] In alluding to her death simultaneously with her Communion, Tiepolo's oil-sketch brings to mind Veronese's painting of the same subject (Pl. 122).[108] Tiepolo's version is far less dramatic than Veronese's, however, since the act of murder is not graphically enacted. A work that probably intermediated between the two was Sebastiano Ricci's enormous painting of the subject, painted for the Church of S. Lucia in Parma.[109] Like Veronese, Ricci indicates how Lucy would die: blood drips from her throat while an executioner in the background replaces his sword in its scabbard. But Ricci made the saint's Communion the principal action of the painting, thus offering a contemporary example to Tiepolo. Further evidence that Ricci's work was a link between Veronese and Tiepolo is the presence of a kneeling youth holding a double taper; Ricci placed him on the right of his scene as Veronese had done, but balanced him with a standing figure on the far left.[110] Tiepolo used the pair in reverse in the oil-sketch as a compositional framing device for Lucy and her priest.

In the finished painting, Tiepolo replaced the standing youth with several kneeling figures. Among them is an elderly lady, probably Lucy's mother. Often cited in the old hagiographical literature on Lucy, Eutichia played a fundamental role in her daughter's saintly narrative, and before Tiepolo, pictorial tradition called for her presence at Lucy's death.[111] She appeared in Lucy's funeral procession in a fourteenth-century fresco cycle in the Oratory of St George in Padua; and in an anonymous seventeenth-century painting in the Church of SS Geremia e Lucia, Venice, Eutichia assists Lucy at her death and last Communion.[112]

Another important change made from the sketch to the altar-piece includes the removal of the knife from Lucy's neck; but to mark the fatal wound, Tiepolo painted a small red cross which is only visible on close inspection of the canvas. The knife has been transferred to the foreground, along with a platter, which is poised just above the chapel's altar and contains the poor saint's eyes, her traditional symbol. This shift diverts the worshippers' attention away from the anecdotal aspect of murder and on to Communion itself.[113] There were also important modifications to several details of wardrobe. In the *bozzetto*, the priest

[107] According to a few versions of the story, a dagger was used to kill the saint: cf. G. R. Taibbi (ed.), *Vite dei santi Siciliani, ii: Martirio di Santa Lucia* (Palermo, 1959), 17; and G. Cinque, *S. Lucia Vergine e Martire* (Venice, 1981), 38; Latin sources tell us Lucy was 'trafitta alla gola', whereas the Greek tradition reports that she was decapitated.

[108] This great canvas, now in the National Gallery, Washington, DC, was painted during Veronese's maturity. The work once belonged to the Lechi Collection in Brescia, where Tiepolo could possibly have seen it: cf. F. Lechi (ed.), *I quadri delle collezioni Lechi in Brescia* (Florence, 1968), 184, no. 107; and T. Pignatti, *Veronese* (Venice, 1976), no. 279. Both Pignatti and R. Marini (*L'opera completa del Veronese* (Milan, 1968), no. 122) note that there is a copy of Veronese's canvas in the Accademia; this oval version came from the Convent of S. Michele in Murano, where Tiepolo would certainly have seen it. Unlike Tiepolo's, Veronese's painting is horizontal in format and was probably not destined for use as a *pala d'altare*. Rubens produced a very dramatic representation of Lucy's death for the ceiling of the Jesuit church in Antwerp; she was depicted as having been knifed in the throat while tied to a stake and burned. J. R. Martin (*Corpus Rubenianum Ludwig Burchard: The Ceiling Paintings for the Jesuit Church in Antwerp* (Brus-

sels, London, and New York, 1968), 156) notes that there is a copy of Rubens's *modello* (Quimper, Musée des Beaux-Arts) in the Accademia Carrara in Bergamo.

[109] Cf. Daniels, *Sebastiano Ricci*, no. 309 and pl. VIII; the work is signed and dated 1730.

[110] Ricci's Lucy and the priest's hand offering the host are both copied from Veronese.

[111] Lucy travelled from Syracuse to Catania to venerate the body of St Agatha because of her own mother's haemorrhages; Agatha later appeared to Lucy in a dream and suggested a cure for her mother. The saint's subsequent devotion to Christ was in part caused by Eutichia's eventual recovery.

[112] There are several resemblances between Tiepolo's canvas and the work in SS Geremia e Lucia. Apart from the old lady, the offering of the host is represented in the same way; the priest and his brocaded robes are very alike; and a fluted column just behind the saint is common to both images. The painting's pendant in SS Geremia e Lucia is the *Death of St Jerome*.

[113] Lucy's blinding was not part of her martyrdom but helped the illiterate to identify her: in Italian, of course, Lucia is close to *luce*, 'light of the eye'.

is wearing a simple alb or surplice, just as he does in Veronese's and Ricci's two paintings, and his assistant kneeling on our left is dressed in a monk's cowl. In the altar-piece, the priest's garment has become a richly embroidered vestment, of a type usually worn by a celebrant during Mass, and the kneeling monk has been transformed into an assisting deacon. Concomitantly, the figure of the old 'Turk', who is standing immediately behind the holy wafer in both the oil-sketch and the altar-piece, is wearing a turban in the earlier image, but is bareheaded in the Cornaro Chapel, holding his cap in his hands as if he were in church, in fact. The meaning of these substitutions is clear: Tiepolo's clergy and his balding patriarch are dressed to participate in a church ritual. With consonant harmony, then, the painting re-enacts the Communion that would actually take place in front of it during a real Mass for the dead in the Cappella Cornaro.

One very small detail in the painting, which to my knowledge has never been mentioned before and is not present in the *bozzetto*, alludes to the Cornaro themselves. On the far right, painted between the two dark columns just midway along the canvas's vertical axis, are two blue and yellow stripes, superimposed with a crowned rampant lion and a cross. Although inexplicably turned in a horizontal position, they are a copy of Caterina Cornaro's coat of arms, or more specifically, those of her husband, Giacomo Lusignano, King of Cyprus, Jerusalem, and Armenia.[114] This escutcheon, held by a brightly lit youth dressed in sixteenth-century garb (who is perhaps meant to represent a particular family member), carries the same devices as the *stemma* that hangs over the archway leading into the chapel from SS Apostoli's nave.

The two commissions for S. Salvador and SS Apostoli were painted to refurbish old family spaces honouring Caterina Cornaro. In each case, Tiepolo produced a work that represented a milestone in his career: in the 1730s, his first great altar-piece for an ancient Venetian church; and in the 1740s, his first deeply moving and intimate image of saintly rapture. One might ask whether he reached these artistic heights because of the specific patronage: he was, as it were, a Cornaro *creatura*.

Between 1737 and *c.*1748 Tiepolo's secular painting included a series of opulent decorations—the frescos in the *saloni* of the Palazzo Clerici in Milan, the Villa Cordellina outside Vicenza, and the Ca' Labia in Venice—that attest to the increasing nobility of his art and to its heightened splendour of colour. His religious art expresses even more—a passionate seriousness of meaning. The ceilings in the Gesuati, Scalzi, and Carmini, all painted between 1737 and 1749, are proof of this, as are *SS Augustine, John the Evangelist, Magno, and Louis of France* and the *Last Communion of St Lucy*. Another altar-piece of the period that reveals this same intense spiritual fervour is *SS Maximus and Oswald* (Pl. 123). Executed for the high altar of the small Church of S. Massimo in Padua, the painting is one of three altar-pieces that Tiepolo contributed to a project of renovation in the church that was begun in 1742 by Don Cogolo di Thiene, who had been parish priest there for thirty-eight years. The other works are *St John the Baptist*, which is over the left altar, and

---

114 For the Cornaro coat of arms, see BNM, MSS It. Cl. VII, Cod. DCCCCXXVIII ('Il Genealogico Barbaro', III); and   BNM, MSS It. Cl. VII, Cod. XVIII (8307) (G. A. Cappellari, 'Il campidoglio veneto', I), fo. 322.

the *Rest on the Flight into Egypt*, which is over the right.[115] Don Cogolo died in 1745, and one assumes that the new altars and their paintings were finished by then; chronologically, the S. Massimo paintings belong almost exactly half-way between those for S. Salvador and SS Apostoli.

Indeed, there are several motifs in *SS Maximus and Oswald* that link it unmistakably to the two Cornaro paintings. Massimo's crosier is almost exactly the same as Magno's in the Munich drawing (Pl. 116), and Oswald's position is very similar to Louis' in the London sketch (Pl. 117; Pl. VII).[116] With a few variations, the architectural setting for Maximus and Oswald is the same as it was for St Lucy, and the acolyte who is kneeling in front of Maximus holding a book open was a prototype for the young man assisting at Lucy's last rites. A further similarity between *SS Maximus and Oswald* and both the S. Salvador altar-piece and the *Last Communion of St Lucy* is that all the protagonists, apart from Louis of France, are saints from the Church's earliest history.[117] The Paduan altar-piece and the two Cornaro paintings that frame it chronologically are portrayals of historic devotions, expressing the eighteenth century's desire to keep faith with the past. 'Faith' herself appears, in fact, in the niche behind S. Massimo in Padua.

More than six *bozzetti* have been associated with the S. Massimo altar-piece; they are in Zurich, London, Bergamo, Rennes, Champaign (Illinois), New York, and Moscow (Pls. 124, 125).[118] One wonders why Tiepolo produced so many preparatory sketches, if indeed they are all by him. The Zurich version, definitely autograph, was the altar-piece's *modello*, and the two images are almost identical. The few variations between them are evidence of the artist's search for clarification. The statue in the niche, for instance, becomes a figure with specific meaning. Oswald's raven, which is very small and is

[115] I would like to thank Padre Franco Pietrobon of the Ognissanti in Padua for opening S. Massimo and allowing me to spend time there. For the church's three works, cf. L. Grossato, 'I dipinti del Tiepolo della chiesa di San Massimo a Padova', *Atti del Congresso*, 44–50; and Rizzi, *Mostra del Tiepolo*, i, no. 50. *St John the Baptist* sits over the tomb of Giambattista Morgagni (1684–1770), the great anatomist from Livorno. According to oral tradition, the *Rest on the Flight into Egypt* records the Tiepolo family's own summer vacations, or *villeggiatura*, near the Church of S. Massimo, but there is no evidence that Giambattista brought his family there; it is more likely that the subject commemorates S. Massimo's ancient hospice that once stood near the old Portello. Cf. also Rossetti, *Descrizione delle pitture*, p. 234; Brandolese, *Pitture di Padova*, pp. 232–3; and G. Knox, 'A Group of Tiepolo Drawings Owned and Engraved by Pietro Monaco', *Master Drawings*, 3 (1965), 389–97, in which he puts forward 1739 as a *terminus ante quem* for the *Rest on the Flight*. His suggestion is based on the British Museum's copy of Monaco's 1763 edition of the *Raccolta di centododici stampe di pittura della storia sacra*, part i of which is dated 1739 and contains a print of the *Rest on the Flight*. It is difficult to refute such evidence, but the date does not necessarily have to represent each and every image therein; Knox himself wonders 'if they [the dates] can be trusted . . .'.

[116] The 'Munich crosier' can be seen in a drawing that Knox tentatively attributes to Domenico Tiepolo: cf. *Giambattista and Domenico*, ii, pl. 2.

[117] Maximus was the second Bishop of Padua and died around 200; Oswald lived in the seventh century: cf. 'Osvaldo, re di Northumbria', in *Bibliotheca Sanctorum*, ix (Rome, 1967), cols.

1290–6; and Levey, *National Gallery Catalogues*, p. 214. Molmenti wrote (*Tiepolo: La vie et l'œuvre du peintre* (Paris, 1911), 93) that St Maximus was 'Saint Marcien', but the dedication of the church would seem to suggest a simpler and more straightforward explanation.

[118] The London, Bergamo, Rennes, Champaign, and New York sketches are identical. The Zurich canvas (50.5 by 28 cm.) differs in several details, most notably in the architectural surround: cf. *Art vénitien en Suisse et au Liechtenstein* (exh. cat., Seedamm-Kulturzentrum, Zurich, 1978 (Milan)), no. 124; *Schilderkunst uit de eerste hand*, no. 50; and A. Pallucchini, *L'opera completa*, no. 65a. The London sketch measures 58.4 by 32.4 cm.: cf. Levey, *National Gallery Catalogues*, p. 216. The Bergamo canvas is 57 by 32 cm.; the one in Rennes is 58 by 34 cm.; the one in Champaign measures 58.4 by 36.8 cm.; and the one in New York is 57 by 35 cm. The painting in Moscow is 61 by 36 cm. All of the images, apart from those in Rennes and Illinois, can be seen together in Morassi, *A Complete Catalogue*, figs. 137–142; the sketch in Rennes is catalogued on p. 45. For the Moscow painting, cf. Lavrova, 'Le tele di Giambattista Tiepolo', pp. 124–30. The *Bishop Reading*, formerly in the Chiesa Collection, Milan (cf. Morassi, *A Complete Catalogue*, fig. 133; and A. Pallucchini, *L'opera completa*, no. 120a), is a related work, but the bay has been transformed into an apse, whose stuccoed and festooned vault is an exact copy of similar features in Veronese's *SS Gemignano and Severus*, a painting that in Tiepolo's day was still in the Church of S. Gemignano, Venice (it is now in the Galleria Estense, Modena: cf. Pignatti, *Veronese*, ii, fig. 362); a copy of it, made by Manaigo and Zucchi, appeared in Lovisa's 1720 *Gran teatro*.

123. G. B. Tiepolo, *SS Maximus and Oswald* (oil on canvas, 370 × 200 cm.)

124. G. B. Tiepolo, Oil-sketch for *SS Maximus and Oswald* (oil on canvas, 50.6 × 27.8 cm.)

125. G. B. Tiepolo, Oil-sketch for *SS Maximus and Oswald* (oil on canvas, 58 × 32 cm.)

perched gingerly on a finger in the sketch, grows in size and sits solidly on the saint's hand in the finished altar-piece.[119] Oswald himself has been significantly rethought. His crown no longer sits on a cushion at his feet but is on his head. His legs, rather than being angled towards the right, have been directed towards the painting's centre, so that, like Michelangelo's *Moses*, Oswald seems about to rise from a chair; his left knee is pushing forward while his right leg steadies him (the leg and its sandalled foot can be seen next to and below Massimo's great chasuble). Thus, the completed Oswald is almost an exact replica in reverse of the 'London St Louis'.[120]

All of these resemblances make the link between the S. Massimo and S. Salvador commissions explicit, prompting the assumption that it was the earlier altar-piece that was the point of departure, even the pictorial basis, from which Tiepolo developed the Paduan work.[121] Of course, given the chronological proximity of the two paintings, such a conclusion is not surprising. It is, none the less, an especially important observation to make, because it gives us, I believe, a clue towards the resolution of the related question of why so many small canvases are associated with the S. Massimo painting. Was each *bozzetto* really a preparation for the final canvas?

The Moscow painting remains distinct from the larger group because of its obvious dissimilarities. Massimo stands on the left like his counterpart in Padua, but Oswald, instead of sitting, is standing holding a halberd in his left hand. There is no kneeling acolyte on the left. What separates the Moscow work most of all from the Cogolo commission, however, is the architectural surround for the two saints and their acolytes, who are on the right. It is the very same 'church bay', its foreground façade appropriately completed, that encloses SS Augustine, John, Louis, and Magno in the London oil-sketch. Even the victory figures in the pendentives and the rosettes decorating the voussoirs have been reproduced one by one. In sum, the Moscow painting appears to be a direct descendant of the S. Salvador commission.

The architectural bay and its chandelier reappear in the London, Bergamo, Rennes, Champaign, and New York versions—all of which are identical to each other—but the two saints are arranged differently; they repeat the Zurich composition.[122] Oswald,

[119] According to legend, Oswald sent a raven carrying a ring in its mouth as a pledge of faith to his fiancée. Oswald's sceptre is also a usual iconographic detail.

[120] One could object that St Louis is not sitting like Oswald but is kneeling, and that his left leg is not visible because it has been tucked under. However, Louis' height in relation to Magno, who is on the same platform, resolves any perplexity: the figure has merely been abbreviated.

[121] Other similarities linking the S. Massimo altar-piece to the Munich and London images include the pavement design and S. Massimo's robe, which is like Augustine's in the drawing.

[122] These five compositions have sometimes been called *St Proculus with SS Fermus and Rusticus*, but Levey and others have already noted that they should be related to Maximus and Oswald. Levey, *National Gallery Catalogues*, p. 215, explains how the confusion first arose. Fermus and Rusticus are discussed in greater detail below, but one should note here that they were both soldiers who shared their earthly trials as well as their later glory. In the five sketches mentioned above, however, the two figures that flank the so-called Proculus are clearly differentiated: one wears armour, the

other does not; one is mature, the other is very young. Differently dressed, of different ages, and not of equal importance, the two men cannot be Fermus and Rusticus. One has only to look at Ricci's impressive painting for the Duomo at Bergamo, or at Cignaroli's for the same church (or, as we shall see, Tiepolo's own), where the two Veronese martyrs are equitably paired, to realize that the five sketches under consideration cannot possibly represent the same figures. For Ricci's *SS Proculus, Fermus, and Rusticus*, see Daniels, *Sebastiano Ricci*, fig. 30; for Cignaroli's *St Proculus Visiting SS Fermus and Rusticus in Prison*, cf. F. R. Presenti, 'Appunti per Giambettino Cignaroli', *Arte antica e moderna*, 9 (1960), 418–24. See also Pinetti, *Inventario*, pp. 62–3, and F. Zava Boccazzi, 'La documentazione archivistica delle tele settecentesche nel coro del Duomo di Bergamo', *Arte veneta*, 30 (1976), 233–9. A small sketch attributed to Balestra that should be taken to represent the Bishop Proculus with the soldiers Fermus and Rusticus along with S. Grata, is in M. Polazzo, *Antonio Balestra* (Verona, 1978), 187, pl. 77; the work, now in the gallery of the seminary in Rovigo, is identified there as *S. Benedetto, S. Fermo, e S. Apollonio*.

however, is dressed in armour as he is in Moscow. A cherub overhead descends with a crown, slightly reminiscent of the nearly contemporary angel who soars down towards the martyrdom of St John, Bishop of Bergamo, in Tiepolo's painting of 1745 in the cathedral in Bergamo. So, one could devise a scenario in which Tiepolo began to think out the commission for *SS Maximus and Oswald* with the Moscow sketch, continued it with the composition seen in the London, Bergamo, Rennes, Champaign, and New York versions, elaborated it with the work in the Kunsthaus in Zurich, and concluded it, finally, with the altar-piece in Padua. However, this hypothesis presupposes that it took the mature Tiepolo as long as this to arrive at a *sacra conversazione* containing only two figures—a most unsettling thought. Moreover, why did he repeat one of the compositions so many times? Attempting to arrange the seven small *SS Maximus and Oswald* in a precise sequential order is more frustrating than helpful; apart from the canvas in Zurich, it makes far more sense to see them as replicas made after the Paduan commission rather than as sketches made before it.[123]

The *Education of the Virgin* (Pls. 104–7), the many renderings of St Roch, and the several paintings of the *Banquet of Antony and Cleopatra* are just three examples of occasions on which the master and his shop repeated the same image again and again.[124] The production of these multiple versions must have been a result of the artist's fame and of the desire of many contemporary collectors to own one of his works. Da Canal wrote that 'engravers and copiers try to engrave his [Tiepolo's] works, to capture their invention and the cleverness of their thought; and his drawings are already so esteemed that books of them are sent to far away countries'.[125] If that was the case for his drawings *c.*1730, then one may imagine the situation in the 1740s when his paintings were so sought after and his fame was so considerable. By then, too, he was rushing from commission to commission, and his prices had soared.[126] It would have been very difficult to obtain a large-scale canvas from him, making a small copy of an already executed design much easier and cheaper to buy than a large and entirely new work. Furthermore, leaving aside financial reasons, how many of those who appreciated *SS Maximus and Oswald* would have even considered asking for a *sacra conversazione* twelve feet high and more than six feet wide (the actual size of the Paduan work)? The solution for a connoisseur who wanted one of Tiepolo's works but whose purchasing powers were limited was a cabinet painting.

[123] Levey remarked (*National Gallery Catalogues*, p. 217 n. 19), about the Paduan painting that 'the phenomenon of duplication of a design not eventually used for the commission seems common in Tiepolo's œuvre'. The London canvas is squared (over the bishop's mitre and below the chandelier), which does suggest that a larger version might have been planned. As far as authenticity is concerned, the handling of the Rennes canvas is not Tiepolo's, and the painting in Champaign, which I have not seen in person, is also questionable. The work in Moscow is unknown to me except in photographs, but it does appear to be autograph.

[124] For the St Roch paintings, see A. Pallucchini, *L'opera completa*, no. 77. For the *Banquet of Antony and Cleopatra*, there are the fresco in Ca' Labia, the paintings in Melbourne and Moscow, and small versions in the Musée Cognacq-Jay, Paris, and the Art History Institute of the University of Stockholm; see G. Knox's

very interesting 'Anthony and Cleopatra in Russia: A Problem in the Editing of Tiepolo Drawings', in *Editing Illustrated Books* (Papers given at the 15th Annual Conference on Editorial Problems, University of Toronto, 2–3 Nov. 1979; New York and London, 1980), 35–55; see also M. Levey, *Giambattista Tiepolo* (New Haven and London, 1986), 143–66.

[125] Da Canal, *Vita*, p. xxxii: 'intagliatori e copiatori cercano d'intagliarne le opere, di averne le invenzioni e le bizzarrie di pensieri; e già i di lui disegni sono in tanta estimazione, che ne spedì de' libri à più lontani paesi'.

[126] On 29 Aug. 1736, Tessin noted that Tiepolo negotiated the fee for his work in the Royal Palace in Stockholm: 'Voicy une lettre qu'il [Tiepolo] appelle son Ultimatum par laquelle il demande 2000 sequins par an.' The Crown had offered 1500 sequins, and Tessin was angry: cf. Sirèn, *Dessins et tableaux*, p. 111.

Eighteenth-century art contains several examples of painters—Crespi, Watteau, Boucher—who worked for a market that called specifically for small-scale images that were not only less expensive than giant ones but were also better suited physically to most homes.[127] Where Tiepolo is concerned, one could also expect that a painting of such an intimate size would probably be executed with that 'ready and resolute' manner for which he had been famous since his youth.[128]

But the question of why both Maximus and Oswald reappear so often in the architectural bay of the S. Salvador painting still remains. Two answers come to mind. First, the 1737 altar-piece must have been very well known. Tiepolo produced it for the illustrious Cornaro family just before the church's second consecration, and as S. Salvador is very near the Rialto many people would have seen the painting; and also, the architectural type itself recalls an old Venetian tradition that can be traced back to the art of Giovanni Bellini. Secondly, *SS Maximus and Oswald* is a deeply moving image, more so than any photograph can convey. Oswald sits responsively—his face raised, his eyes uplifted, and his mouth open—in a traditional configuration of saintly ecstasy. Maximus, on the other hand, looks within; his mantle encloses his large, upright form, and his deeply contemplative face ponders some phrase from the book in front of him. Tiepolo created an exquisite pictorial and psychological antithesis in this pair of saints. Very simply, the clear definition of two distinctive types—a man of the Church and a ruler, an elderly patriarch and a young warrior, a figure in deep contemplation and one in spiritual rapture—must have touched a responsive chord in those who appreciated Tiepolo's art in the 1740s.

Failure to consider the eighteenth-century historical context of Tiepolo's religious painting results in the forfeiture of all sense of content. Intention is lost, meaning is ignored, and the image itself may be reduced to trivialization, or, worse still, overlooked completely. Such a fate has largely befallen one of the artist's most beautiful mature works, the *Patron Saints of the Crotta Family* (Pl. 126; Pl. VIII). The painting, which now graces the Städelsches Kunstinstitut in Frankfurt, hung in the Palazzo Crotta in Venice until 1902.[129] It is a grand composition, in which monumental architecture provides the setting for the Crotta's heroic ancestors in early Bergamo—SS Lupo and Adelaide on the left, their daughter St Grata stepping towards them in the centre, and the aristocratic figures of SS Fermus and Rusticus looking on, one at the decapitated head of St Alexander in Grata's arms, and the other as a general spectator.[130] Tiepolo has interfused here the

---

[127] Knox has recently pointed out that pastels and 'the small oil paintings of Pietro Longhi' would have been cabinet pieces along with finished drawings: cf. *Piazzetta* (exh. cat., National Gallery of Art, Washington, DC and Cambridge, 1983), 20. There is no reason to exclude Tiepolo's small oil-sketches from the above.

[128] Cf. Da Canal, *Vita*, p. xxx, where the author distinguishes between Lazzarini's style ('maniera diligente') and Tiepolo's ('una spedita e risoluta').

[129] The work was first published by C. Caversazzi, 'Arte retrospettiva: Di alcuni dipinti di G. B. Tiepolo', *Emporium*, 9 (1899),

205–26. The palazzo Calbo-Crotta, the address of which is Cannaregio 122, is near SS. Geremia e Lucia.

[130] The painting's subject is identified for us in a print by Pietro Monaco: 'Sᵗᵃ Grata regina in compagnia dei SS. Fermo e Rustico mostra il reciso capo di S. Alessandro M. ai SS. Lupo e Adelaide Principi di Bergamo suoi genitori . . .'. Giandomenico's print after the painting fails to furnish the names of the protagonists but identifies Giovanni Antonio Crotta as the patron: 'Procerum ex familia Crotta sanctorum icones, quas pater pinxit, obsequ.ᵐᵒ animo Filius incidens Excell.ᵐᵒ Nob. viro 10.ᴵANTO.ᴵᴼCROTTA Q:D: ALEXN.' For the dramatis personae in the painting, cf. G.

contemplation of Bergamo's first Christian martyr with the glorification of the city's earliest Christian rulers.

Originally from Lombardy, the Crotta could trace their ancestry back to Roman times when Roberto Crotta was Consul in Bergamo. Centuries later, the family moved to Belluno and, subsequently, to Venice. They built their fortune in mining, becoming substantial enough to marry into the patrician class. During the War of Candia (1645–99), the Crotta appealed to the Senate for admission into the patriciate, a wish that the Serenissima fulfilled on 13 April 1649.[131] Various members of the family then became senators, and some served the Republic in Bergamo or Brescia. The family fortune increased as investments were directed into the production of peat near Rovigo.[132] One of the illustrious eighteenth-century Crottas was Giovanni Antonio, the great grandson of Francesco, who had brought the family to the Veneto. Giovanni, the son of Alessandro, was born in 1681 and represented Venice as *castellano* in Brescia. It is his name—'io.ᴵanto.ᴵᴼcrotta q:d: alexn.'—that appears as the patron on the print that Domenico Tiepolo made after his father's painting.

The painting dramatizes the confrontation between S. Lupo, grandson of Roberto the Roman Consul, and his daughter Grata, who is showing her father the head of S. Alessandro. This strange narrative records a momentous event in the history of Christian Bergamo.[133] Widowed after her marriage to a German Prince, Grata returned to her native Bergamo. With the aid of her mother Adelaide and her confidante Esteria (two Christian women who were eventually canonized by the Church), she tried to convert her pagan father to the true faith. But Lupo was obstinate of heart, and Grata asked the advice of Alessandro who, when he arrived in Bergamo, predicted 'that in a short time you will see your Father a Christian, a great apostle of the Faith'.[134] Although Alessandro was soon martyred for his refusal to worship before the statue of Pluto, he himself was the cause of Lupo's conversion; for while Grata carried his decapitated head through the city, beautiful flowers blossomed from the drops of blood. Then, appearing before her father, she showed him

. . . the miraculous flowers. She offered them to him [Lupo] to smell their perfume, and with that tender and efficacious persuasion with which she had always succeeded in moving others' hearts, she sought to inspire in him a supreme idea of the infinite Omnipotence of God. . . . The spirit of this Prince wavered between a thousand cruel agitations, nor could he resolve them by embracing the truth which was already well known to him . . . He no longer doubted that the Christian

Swarzenski, 'Giovanni Battista Tiepolo's "Heilige aus dem Hause Grotta" im Städelschen Kunstinstitut zu Frankfurt', *Münchner Jahrbuch der bildenden Kunst*, 4 (1909), 60–5. See also BNM, 'Genealogico Barbaro', III; BNM, Cappellari, 'Il campidoglio veneto', I, fo. 349ᵛ; BMC, MS P. D. 613c/IV ('Origini delle Famiglie aggregate per l'Offerte nella Guerra di Candia nel 1646'), 8; C. Freschot, *La nobiltà veneta* (Venice, 1707), 295–6; and M. A. Tassis, *La vita di S. Grata Vergine Regina nella Germania . . . Principessa di Bergamo e protettrice della medesima città* (Padua, 1723), 7–8.

[131] Cf. BNM, 'Genealogico Barbaro', III.

[132] See the rather pretentious tracts, etymological as well as chemical in character, by G. C. Silvestri, BMC, Cod. Cicogna 3043/14, dated 1769. They were written for Paolo Antonio Crotta, born 1725, who filed wills on both 19 Aug. 1791 and 26 May 1802. I am indebted to Dott.ˢˢᵃ Tiepolo of the Archivio di Stato for opening these sealed documents to me.

[133] Tassis narrates this story (*La vita di S. Grata Vergine*, pp. 7–8), quoting from Luca de Linda's *Relazioni, e descrizioni universali, e particolari del Mondo* (Bologna, 1674).

[134] Cf. Tassis, *La vita di S. Grata Vergine*, p. 47: 'Io v'assicuro, che in breve vederete vostro Padre fatto Cristiano, e divenuto grande amplificator della Fede.'

126. G. B. Tiepolo, *Patron Saints of the Crotta Family* (oil on canvas, 195 × 320 cm.)

Religion was the only road leading each Soul to salvation; but at the same time he felt within his heart great obstacles to his conversion.[135]

Tiepolo portrayed this remarkable father–daughter confrontation in a great hall, with the Crotta coat of arms above the throne. Lupo extends his arm towards the bizarre bouquet his daughter presents, while with a troubled brow he looks up to heaven for guidance. The two protagonists are wearing spectacular and complementary robes: Lupo's is gold, faced with ermine, and around which hang several gold chains; Grata is wearing a gold gown embroidered at the hem with giant pearls, and she is covered with a gleaming white satin cloak. A brightly coloured orange hood frames her head, while a red ducal *berretto* sits on Lupo's. Their pre-eminence, interaction, and radiant colouring draw attention to Alessandro's almost incandescent head.

Next to Lupo, Adelaide is bowing in submission before the divine will, providing a sub-text, as it were, for her husband's imminent conversion to the true faith. On the painting's central vertical axis, where Tiepolo created a caesura between the composition's two halves, a palm-frond and a sword, symbols of martyrdom, point down towards an old woman humbling herself, who is to be identified as Esteria. A family retainer at the canvas's bottom right-hand corner is also kneeling. Grata's cousins, Fermus and Rusticus, stand on her immediate right and left. Although they were not present at the miracle, they are included here both as witnesses of Lupo's conversion, following which all of Bergamo became Christian, and, as I shall discuss below, as evidence of the city's devotion to the two saints' cult.[136] Maria Angela Tassis, a nun in the Bergamasque convent of S. Grata and the author of the fullest account of the saint's life, explained: 'She [Grata] was the cause of S. Lupo's conversion, and by consequence of the entire city, which through Grata was cleansed of its filth from Idols, restored to the grace of God and sanctified.'[137] Thus, Tiepolo's *Patron Saints of the Crotta Family* aspires as much to celebrate Bergamo as it does to honour specific patron saints. Given the degree to which the Crotta family controlled the key offices in this western border area of Venetian territory, the family's desire to re-enact and demonstrate its pivotal role in Lombard history is quite understandable.[138]

The Crotta commission to Tiepolo must also be seen within a larger context. Bergamo and its inhabitants enjoyed a period of great prosperity during the settecento, and local pride in their achievements was manifested in a number of ambitious artistic monuments,

[135] Ead., p. 54: 'Perciò ripiena di fiducia in Dio, portossi dal Padre, seco recando i fiori miracolosi. Glieli porse da odorare, e con quella tenera ed efficace persuasiva, con cui le riuscì già di rendersi padrona de' cuori, si sforzò d'ispirargli un'alta idea dell'infinita Onnipotenza di quel Dio . . .'; and p. 55: 'Ondeggiava lo spirito di questo Principe tra mille crudeli agitazioni, e non sapeva per anche risolversi ad abbracciare la verità da lui abbastanza conosciuta . . . Già egli più non dubitava che la Religion Cristiana non fosse quell'unica strada, che conduce ogni Anima alla salute; ma nel medesimo tempo sentiva dentro il suo cuore grandi ostacoli alla sua conversione.'

[136] Lupo and the fathers of both Fermus and Rusticus were brothers; the ties are explained by Luca de Linda (Tassis, *La vita di S. Grata Vergine*, p. 7).

[137] Tassis, *La vita di S. Grata Vergine*, p. 83: 'Ella fu la cagione della conversion di San Lupo, e per conseguenza anche di tutta la Città di Bergamo; la quale fu da lei purgata dalla sordidezza degli'Idoli, restituita nella grazia di Dio, e santificata.'

[138] Both Giovanni Antonio and his brother Filippo were *castellani* in Brescia; their relative, Francesco Maria, born in 1723, was *podestà* in Bergamo. For the Republic's gratitude to Francesco on the success of his mission, see the letter from Daniel Renier, *vice-doge*, in BMC, Cod. Cicogna 2029/14 ('Memorie venete per la Biblioteca di Monsigr Ill.mo. e Re.mo. Gasparo Negri'), fo. 201.

one of which was Tiepolo's series of frescos in the early 1730s in the Colleoni Chapel (cf. Pl. 66). A short time later, Filippo Juvarra designed a new altar for the Duomo, and its inauguration was celebrated in 1737. The largest artistic commission of all, however, was a group of twelve monumental canvases for the Duomo.[139] But it was only during the 1740s that the majority of them were executed and placed *in situ*. Seven of them, each over eighteen feet in height and with the martyrdom of local saints as their subjects, decorate the choir; Tiepolo himself contributed the very moving *Martyrdom of St John, Bishop of Bergamo* to the project.[140] His *Patron Saints of the Crotta Family* is exactly contemporary in date and may be regarded as the private counterpart to Bergamo's public display of patriotic spirit.

The presence of Fermus and Rusticus in the painting helps to sustain this argument. Contemporaneously with Tiepolo's execution of the work, the two towns of Bergamo and Verona were indulging in a bitter polemic concerning the two martyrs, which they argued out in both literary tracts and ecclesiastical acts. Although they had been born in Bergamo, Fermus and Rusticus were killed in Verona in the late third century. According to most sources, seven men miraculously came from heaven, wrapped their bodies in white linen, and took the saintly remains to Africa in a boat. The corpses were later brought to Trieste but were eventually returned to Verona. It was Bergamo's continued commemoration of the saints' martyrdoms that Verona contested, therefore. The *bergamaschi*, however, would not yield. Indeed, during the settecento, they contentiously sought to exalt veneration for both Fermus and Rusticus, along with their friend Bishop Proculus, in such works as Ricci's great canvas for the Duomo.[141] In 1737, Bergamo honoured the trio during the Duomo's inauguration of Juvarra's new altar.[142] And in 1766, the city commemorated the completion of a precious silver reliquary for the three saints' remains by instituting four days of public festivities: with great pomp and circumstance, Masses were celebrated in the Duomo, in S. Alessandro in Colonna, and in S. Alessandro in Croce.

Verona did not remain silent. In 1727, its prominent citizen Scipione Maffei acted as spokesman for the town when he published documents in his *Istoria diplomatica* with descriptions of the torture and death of Fermus and Rusticus in Verona; in addition, Maffei maintained that the two bodies lay in S. Fermo Maggiore, one of the city's churches.[143] Whether this was the first salvo to be fired from Verona I cannot say, nor do I know exactly when Bergamasque authors entered the battle, but by the 1760s a fully fledged literary fray was engaging the two cities. The central issue was, where did the

---

[139] For the entire group, which was begun early in the century, cf. Pinetti, *Inventario*, pp. 62 ff. One of the first works chronologically was Ricci's *SS Proculus, Fermus, and Rusticus* (1704), which was placed in the church's right transept.

[140] Cf. Zava Boccazzi, 'La documentazione', 233–9.

[141] Cf. above, n. 139; by standing Rusticus on the right (or is he Fermus?), Tiepolo is reproducing in reverse Ricci's handsome young soldier on the left.

[142] B. Belotti, *Storia di Bergamo e dei bergamaschi* (Bergamo, 1959), 305–6. An extensive bibliography on the saints from both Verona and Bergamo can be found in the Biblioteca Vaticana under *Fermo*.

[143] S. Maffei, 'Passio sanctorum Firmi et Rustici', in *Istoria Diplomatica . . . con raccolta de' documenti non ancor divulgati* (Mantua, 1727), 303 ff.; and id., *Verona illustrata*, iv (Milan, 1826; repr. Rome, 1977), part 3, 280. A painting by Jan Liss now in the Wadsworth Atheneum depicts the saints' martyrdom within a Veronese topographical context; Verona's great castle can be seen on the distant hill above and beyond the banks of the River Adige. I am indebted to Linda Horvitz Roth of the Wadsworth Atheneum for pointing this painting out to me.

saints' remains lie?! Had the bodies of Fermus and Rusticus been transferred from Verona, or not? Bergamo, of course, insisted that they had, and that the date could be pinpointed to 1576.[144]

The tone of the polemic was very bitter at times, particularly in publications by the *veronesi*. Domenico Vallarsi, for example, who contributed at least four works supporting their point of view, wrote that the opposition presented 'an accumulation of falsities' and that what Bergamo quoted as historic evidence 'had never even been dreamt of . . . .'.[145] Bergamo, on the other hand, sustained a much calmer rhetoric, with even a certain haughtiness of tone: 'this is not the place where proof must be given, for several of our writers have already produced adequate response . . . .'.[146] The Bergamasque quoted S. Carlo Borromeo's confirmation of the presence of Fermus and Rusticus in their city, and they also recorded that the Sacred Congregation of Rome had given Bergamo a special set of prayers for its liturgical veneration of the saints.[147] The dispute revolved around Verona's insistence on history and Bergamo's insistence on ecclesiastical tradition.

Through a splendidly colourful but solemnly dignified interweaving of figures and signs, Tiepolo's *Patron Saints of the Crotta Family* created a noble image of duty and sacrifice. The unfortunate but miraculous trophy of S. Alessandro's head, which is aligned with the great sword and palm-frond at the painting's centre, conjoins Grata with Lupo, locking them together just as the keystone below 'fastens' the distant arch. The blossoming relic symbolizes heavenly salvation, linking the Christian traditions of saintly martyrdom and conversion with statesmanship and patriotic responsibility. The Crotta painting is an allusion to contemporary political polemics and, simultaneously, a celebration of civic allegiance as well as patrician lineage and patriotic service.

Did the Crotta family commission the proclamation of these sentiments after 1754, when Tiepolo had returned from Würzburg, or just before he left, *c*.1747–50?[148] The question is not only one of import to art historians; I think the answer will explain exactly what it was that made the family hire Venice's most famous painter. Looked at in terms of Tiepolo's artistic accomplishments after his visit to Germany, the Crotta painting seems totally out of place. Not only is the brushwork more careful and more tightly worked than is customary in works of the mid-1750s, but the stable figural composition and the monumental architecture have more in common with commissions of the pre- and mid-Würzburg periods than with those executed after that date. Counterparts to the *Patron*

[144] D. Alessandro Rigamonti, *Ragguaglio della nascita, vita, e morte de' SS Martiri Fermo e Rustico con Alcune notizie ancor di S. Procolo* (Bergamo, 1766), 54.

[145] D. Vallarsi, *Dissertazione seconda sopra la esistenza e identità de' sacri corpi de' santi martiri Fermo e Rustico in Verona* (Trent, 1754), 11: 'Si nella mia primiera Disertazione ho detto, che quanto ha riferito il nostro R. Oppositore [Gaetano Moroni Bergamasco] intorno al furto e all'invenzione de' mentovati sacri Corpi, *è un cumolo di falsità*, non dev'egli offendersene, mentre neppur io mi disdico, anzi torno à più francamente ripeterlo, e a dimostrare com'egli faccia dire à suoi scrittori [of the sixteenth and seventeenth centuries] *quello che di dire giammai si sognarono . . .*'.

[146] G. Finazzi, *Atti dei santi martiri cittadini di Bergamo . . . ed ora novellamente collezionati coi codici della chiesa di Bergamo* (Bergamo,

1852, but written in the eighteenth century), 37: 'Della qual ultima traslazione e autenticità de' nostri venerati depositi *non è qui il luogo da doverne dare le prove; avendole parecchi nostri scrittori già più volte prodotte in appositi scritti . . .*'.

[147] For the first, cf. ibid., pp. 36–7, and for the second, cf. Rigamonti, *Ragguaglio della nascita*, p. 63.

[148] A. Pallucchini, *L'opera completa*, no. 215: *c*.1754–5; vs. Morassi, *A Complete Catalogue*, p. 12: '*c*.1750 (?)'; and Knox, *Giambattista and Domenico Tiepolo*, i. 330, no. X. 26: '1745–50'. Cf. also Knox's 'A Group of Tiepolo Drawings', pp. 389–90, where he notes that a print after the Crotta painting is in Monaco's *Raccolta di centododici stampe*, part ii of which is dated 1745 in the British Museum copy; cf. n. 115 above.

Saints of the Crotta are found in the similarly conceived scenes of the *Banquet of Antony and Cleopatra*, completed in the mid-1740s in Ca' Labia, and the *Marriage of Frederick Barbarossa and Beatrice of Burgundy*, executed in 1752 in the Würzburg Kaisersaal. The monumental architectural surrounds and classical rhythms that characterize these works are rare after 1754. And even when they do reappear, as in the frescos of ancient subject-matter in the Villa Valmarana (1757), they are overpowered by intimate personal dramas; for example, the *Sacrifice of Iphigenia* in the Valmarana itself, in which the heroine forlornly expresses her fate while Agamemnon covers his face, overwhelmed. Strong visual evidence that the Crotta painting does indeed precede 1750 is provided by comparing it with *Esther and Ahasuerus*, a work of the early 1750s which is very similar in many ways but which, through an extended system of gestures, conveys far deeper emotion. The expressiveness of the Crotta painting, by contrast, is strictly controlled.[149]

A date of c.1747–9 would help to explain the Crotta family's decision to glorify their native city and their ancestors. It will be recalled that the family had applied to join the Venetian patriciate during the War of Candia and that they were then *aggregata* in 1649.[150] A century later, in 1749, the Crotta could proudly celebrate their rise in position: the family's financial holdings had increased; their home was a palace on the Grand Canal; and senators, *podestà*, and *castellani* issued from their ranks.[151] Whether commissioned just before or during 1749, Tiepolo's great painting was meant to herald the centenary of the Crotta entry into the Venetian aristocracy. The canvas recalled the family's old and noble origins as well as its continued interest and participation in the affairs of Bergamo.

But why did the Crotta turn to Tiepolo for their painting? Piazzetta, an excellent candidate for the commission, had just completed two monumental paintings of historical subject-matter that should have recommended him to the family.[152] Perhaps Piazzetta's tenebrist style did not please the Crotta, and it would certainly not have given them what Tiepolo's did: an artistic mode that recalled Venice's heroic pictorial tradition—the same manner that he had used so brilliantly at Udine two decades earlier in the *Judgement of Solomon* (Pl. 41; Pl. II). Tiepolo employed it again in the Antony and Cleopatra frescos for Ca' Labia, a commission which was almost contemporary with the *Patron Saints of the Crotta Family*. Unlike the Pisani and the Barbaro, who were Piazzetta's patrons for *Alexander before the Body of Darius* and *Mucius Scævola*, neither the Labia nor the Crotta

[149] Cf. A. Morassi, *G. B. Tiepolo* (London, 1955), pls. 49, VII, and fig. 49, for the *Banquet of Antony and Cleopatra*, the *Marriage of Frederick Barbarossa and Beatrice of Burgundy*, and the *Sacrifice of Iphigenia*; and id., *A Complete Catalogue*, fig. 24, for *Esther and Ahasuerus*. Two works that accord in style with the Crotta painting are the *Reception of Henry III at the Villa Contarini in Mira*, a fresco now in the Musée Jacquemart-André, Paris (cf. Morassi, *A Complete Catalogue*, fig. 317), and the *Portrait of a Venetian Procurator* (cf. A. Pallucchini, *L'opera completa*, pl. XXXIII); both are dated just before 1750.

[150] Cf. n. 130; Freschot, *La nobiltà veneta*, pp. 295–6, wrote in 1707 that 'Radicato con questo impiego [working in the mines] il proprio affetto nelli Stati di questa Serenissima Repubblica, e sviscerata dal Pubblico aggradimento la Fede de' migliori Sudditi, colle fruttuose sue applicationi; diramarono vena copiosissima d'oro à prò dell'erario nell'ultime emergenze, li suoi figlioli, quali con la posterità aggregati l'anno 1649, all'ordine Patritio, riportarono mercede immortale della loro benemerenza.'

[151] I insert here a fragment of Daniel Renier's congratulatory letter to Francesco Crotta which, although written several years later, expresses Venetian gratitude towards the family: 'Li sentimenti da Ella esposti formano un forte motivo di agradimto, e di applauso alle sue direzion; a qta dovuta Lode si aggiungon Le universali voci di tutti quelli del Territorio, et Abitanti della Città di Bergamo affezionati alla virtù del suo Rapresentante.'

[152] For *Alexander before the Body of Darius* and *Mucius Scaevola*, both datable to 1745–6, cf. Mariuz, *L'opera completa*, nos. 121, 123.

could trace their membership in Venice's ruling class back to the sixteenth century.[153] What they needed to cap their positions in Venetian society were 'icons' of the Venetian past. Tiepolo offered images that were 'ancient' and 'patrician' in character; Piazzetta, instead, produced paintings that were—dare one say—'gloomy and mournful'.[154] Turning to Tiepolo to celebrate their achievements, the Crotta got a masterpiece in the heroic and patrician style.

During his three-year sojourn in Würzburg, Tiepolo must have been sorely missed in Venice, not only by his family but also by would-be patrons who, like the Crotta family, required a very specific pictorial style. Following this line of reasoning, Deborah Howard has speculated 'that work on the interior decoration of the Church of the Pietà, suspended between September 1751 and early 1754, may have been held up specifically in order to await Tiepolo's return'.[155] Orlandi probably spoke for many when he wrote so touchingly in the *Abecedario pittorico* (published in 1753) that '. . . as his [Tiepolo's] ability and strength grow from day to day, so does the desire on the part of connoisseurs and amateurs to have his paintings; and so that he may satisfy that desire, it is to be hoped that the bestower of every good thing will allow him a long and prosperous life.'[156]

Arriving home for Christmas 1753, Tiepolo would not have thought that Venice had changed very much. But several events between 1750 and 1754 had deeply affected the ecclesiastical patrons whose employment he depended upon. Even before he had left for Würzburg, the ancient traditions of his city had begun to modify. In 1748, Montesquieu published *L'Esprit des lois* in Geneva, and the book achieved immediate notoriety in Venice. By 1754, critical debate on its merits—or demerits according to some   filled discussions in literary and philosophical circles.[157] Many looked upon the book as an attack upon God and the Church. The always argumentative Concina, for instance, violently criticized Montesquieu's writings in his *Theologia Christiana Dogmatico-Moralis* (1750); other negative opinions followed in 1751 in the *Giornale de' letterati oltramontani*, with further debate appearing in a work written by Giovanni de Cataneo.[158]

Venice's religious establishment had other reasons for alarm, too. Growing ever more audible during the second quarter of the eighteenth century, the dispute between the

---

[153] It cannot be coincidental that the Crotta painting reiterates details from Veronese's *Family of Darius before Alexander* (Pl. 46) then in the Pisani Collection. The similarities between the two works are significant: the two levels of dramatic action in the foreground and middle ground, the architectural system in the distance (note the perspective of Tiepolo's archway and Veronese's closest to the centre), and the trio of protagonists on the right with the secondary figure bending over next to them; note, too, the halberds directly behind both Alexander and Grata. Veronese's *Presentation of the Cuccina Family to the Madonna and Child* (in Modena until 1746 when it went to Dresden), also offers points of comparison with Tiepolo's work.

[154] This is quoted from Mariuz's excellent discussion of *Alexander before the Body of Darius*, *L'opera completa*, no. 121, p. 104: 'un'ispirazione di tono drammatico che volge ormai al tetro e al lugubre'.

[155] Howard, 'Giambattista Tiepolo's Frescos for the Church of the Pietà in Venice', *Oxford Art Journal*, 9 (1986), 13.

[156] P. A. Orlandi, *Abecedario pittorico* (Venice, 1753), 282: '. . . crescendo ogni dì in lui l'Abilità e la forza, e negli intendenti, ed amatori dell'arte la brama d'avere de' suoi dipinti; alla qual brama perchè soddisfare egli possa, è desiderabile, che una lunga e prospera vita dal dator di ogni bene se gli conceda'.

[157] A. Vecchi, *Correnti religiose nel Sei–Settecento veneto* (Venice, 1962), 389, has written that 'L'intellettualità italiana si aggiornò su *l'esprit des lois*, rimanendone commossa fin entro il midollo spinale.'

[158] Berselli Ambri, *L'opera di Montesquieu nel Settecento italiano* (Florence, 1960), 31, 127: Concina attacked Montesquieu's book in vol. vi, calling it 'scandaloso' and writing of the author's honesty that 'La protesta, che vi si inserisce di essere Cristiano, è una maschera troppo ridicola per cuoprire la empietà del suo cuore . . .'.

Republic and the Austrian Empire over the Patriarchy of Aquileia had terrible ecclesi-astical consequences for Venice.[159] In July 1751, Benedict XIV promulgated a Bull that permanently divided the ancient see into two archbishoprics, an Italian one in Udine and a 'German' one in Gorizia; nominations for the two church officials were to come from the Venetian Senate and the Hapsburg throne, respectively. Thus, Venice was deprived of its most ancient link to St Mark, the legendary founder of the Patriarchy of Aquileia, and with this the Serenissima lost its historic and impassioned claims to a national Church.[160]

Whether these crises had a specific and tangible effect on Tiepolo's religious art must remain speculative. But it is not risking too much to say that the altered world the sixty-year-old painter found in Venice, together with Piazzetta's death in the spring of 1754, must have affected him deeply. Although his personal thoughts are unknown, these events and the grandiose pictorial challenges he had recently faced in Würzburg must have been responsible for the innovations he started to make in his religious painting from 1754, when his art reveals a changed sensibility.

The first painting he unveiled in Venice that year was the *Virgin and Child Appearing to St John Nepomuk* (Pl. IX). It was shown on 8 May 1754 in S. Polo, where it can still be seen today, and it presents a striking metamorphosis after his earlier altar-pieces.[161] One need only compare the work to the *Madonna and Child with SS Catherine of Siena, Rose of Lima, and Agnes of Montepulciano* (Pl. 95) of 1748 to notice that in the later work there is only the slightest of architectural references. The figures fill the canvas, and their breadth of form is matched by heavy atmosphere and deep, lustrous colour. Dense clouds and thick air enfold the Virgin and St John; she is dressed in a ruby-red gown and a dark blue robe, and he is wearing a brilliant white surplice with a light blue-grey cloak. At the painting's centre, a radiance emanates from around his head.

In the 1730s and 1740s, Tiepolo had often used architecture to stabilize his compositions, balancing them with artful juxtaposings of tonal values and chromatic fields, but in the *Virgin and Child Appearing to St John Nepomuk* he seems almost to return to his youthful mode of masking architecture within zones of divine light and opposing deeply shadowed areas with bright patches of colour. (One recalls, for instance, the *Glory of S. Luigi Gonzaga* (Pl. V) painted in the 1720s.) But the S. Polo altar-piece was not a throw-back to a ready formula from the past. The architecture, rather than being merely overshadowed, vanishes almost completely, and colour is treated very differently. Opaque tones and muddy shadows disappear, and in the S. Polo painting their place is taken by the luminous incandescence of Nepomuk's white surplice framed by the light blue-grey cloak, the whole seeming to vibrate across the pictorial surface in front of the Virgin's ruby-red gown.[162] The lack of topographical specificity and the 'lightness of being' suggested by the saint's dress are further heightened by Nepomuk's ecstatic response to his mystical vision.

[159] Cf. Chap. 1, pp. 56ff.
[160] Contemporaneously, the government began a campaign to alter the tradition which allowed secular goods to pass into ecclesiastical hands (mainmort). A decree of 7 Sept. 1754 led to legislation that took effect later: cf. Introduction, p. 6.
[161] Cf. Livan, *Gradenigo*, p. 11.

[162] Another painting similar in these aspects and close in date to the S. Polo canvas is the *Glory of S. Gaetano of Thiene* in the parish church in Rampazzo, near Vicenza. Against a golden sky, the saint wears white and bright yellow, with orange drapery waving below him on a cloud. For a black and white photo, see Morassi, *A Complete Catalogue*, fig. 184.

Although he is rather like S. Lupo in the Crotta painting, St John is more dramatically intense, made so by the use of expression and light. The *Virgin and Child Appearing to St John Nepomuk* heralds a new era in Tiepolo's religious art, one in which the sacred transpires in a world deprived of physical weight.

This may be a result of Tiepolo's accomplishments in Würzburg; in the Residenz ceiling-frescos, space assumes an all-encompassing role and architecture plays a relatively minor one. But, as Howard has suggested, Tiepolo may also have been deeply influenced by Piazzetta's work, particularly after the latter's death on 29 April 1754, when it must have seemed to Tiepolo that the long pictorial tradition of Venetian tenebrism had finally ended.[163] Two weeks later, on 8 May, Tiepolo unveiled the S. Polo altar-piece, and while it is not likely that its entire conception and execution could have taken place within fourteen days, it is certainly more than possible that the work was changed after Piazzetta's demise. Indeed, whereas a comparison of the two artists' altar-pieces in the Gesuati reveals how different their art was *c.*1740, a glance at the S. Polo painting alongside *SS Vincenzo Ferreri, Giacinto, and Ludovico Bertrando* (Pl. 114) demonstrates how Tiepolo was redirecting his 'saintly work' of 1754 towards a more Piazzettesque vision. This is confirmed if one looks at the *Virgin and Child Appearing to St John Nepomuk* together with Piazzetta's *Virgin and Child Appearing to St Philip Neri* (Pl. 98): both are of visions in which Mary and Christ emerge miraculously from within a dense, nubilous glory in front of a saint kneeling at prayer.

Strolling past the S. Polo altar-piece today, the casual visitor may wonder why a fourteenth-century saint from Prague appears in an eighteenth-century Venetian painting. The saint's presence is explained by the 1740 donation to the church of a Nepomuk relic by Augustus III, King of Poland and Elector of Saxony. At the time of the gift, eleven years after Nepomuk's canonization by Benedict XIII (19 March 1729), a magnificent new altar was built in S. Polo on a direct axis with the church's principal entrance. A print of the saint's image was offered to the faithful who gathered there for prayer on St John's feast-day, a holiday that was extended to the city of Venice in 1749.[164]

Beautiful and moving as it is, Tiepolo's vision of Mary and Christ was—admittedly—a rather conventional one by the mid-eighteenth century. Holy encounters in which a saint kneels before the veiled Madonna who is standing with the Christ-child in her arms were almost formulaic. The best-known example of the type in Italian art is Raphael's

---

[163] Howard, 'Giambattista Tiepolo's Frescos', p. 22. It should be mentioned that the seventy-year-old Piazzetta had become the most prominent figure in Venetian art (the director of the *scuola del nudo* in the newly created Academy) while Tiepolo was in Germany.

[164] Nepomuk's relevance to Venice may be that he is the patron saint of bridges and 'works' against floods; he studied in Padua in 1383. Cf. 'Giovanni Nepomuceno', in *Bibliotheca Sanctorum*, vi (Rome, 1965), 847–55, and *Johannes von Nepomuk* (exh. cat., Münchner Stadtmuseum, Munich, 1971 (Passau)), *passim*. For S. Polo, cf. F. Corner, *Ecclesiae Venetae antiquis* (Venice, 1749), i. 317; id., *Notizie storiche*, p. 344; and BMC, MS Gradenigo 175 ('Chiese. Tomi Tre', II), fo. 332: '1740. Federico Augusto III. pmogenito del Rè di Polonia regalò alla Chiesa di S. Polo una Reliquia di S. Gio. Nepomuceno. Per questo motivo fù introdotta

una divozione, e si dispensa nel giorno della Festività l'effigie di esso Santo in stampa di Rame, e vi si legge la seguente Inscrizione: *Sanctus Joannes Nepomucenus, Presbiter, et Canonicus Pragensis ob costanter servatem . . . Confessioris sacramentalis Martyr, Anno 1383. die 29 Aprilis . . .'*. Frederick Augustus III had notable ties with Venice and Venetian art: he visited the city three times and later commissioned paintings from Piazzetta, Tiepolo, Rosalba Carriera, and Bernardo Bellotto. Beginning in 1747, he employed the latter in Dresden for more than ten years. Frederick sent the relic of St John Nepomuk to S. Polo in 1740, the year his son the Prince Elector of Saxony visited Venice. Giandomenico Tiepolo painted the *Martirio di S. Giovanni Nepomuceno* (as the saint is known in Italian) for S. Polo *c.*1749; cf. A. Mariuz, *Giandomenico Tiepolo* (Milan, n.d.), 144.

Sistine Madonna (Dresden, Gemäldegalerie), where the Virgin miraculously appears on a cloud and seems to be walking towards the faithful, at whom the Infant Christ gazes. Tiepolo's Mother and Child, although not centred in the composition like Raphael's, follow the Renaissance paradigm rather closely; so closely, in fact, that one is tempted to ask whether Tiepolo could have turned to the famous altar-piece for inspiration. The question may not be as whimsical as it first seems. Tiepolo could have seen Raphael's painting in Piacenza when he was working near there; and even if he did not visit the town, he would certainly have known the image from prints. Moreover, the *Sistine Madonna* was of topical interest in 1754, for it had just been bought by a foreign prince and was leaving Italy for Germany. Travelling through Verona, Innsbruck, and Augsburg (the old Imperial route), the precious cargo was directed towards the Court of Saxony in Dresden.[165] It is conceivable that the similarity between Tiepolo's Madonna and Child and Raphael's was not just generic, but was a meditated act of homage by the Venetian towards the great 'Roman', whose most famous work in northern Italy was about to leave forever. Confirming Tiepolo's purposefulness, I believe, is the little cherub on the left who is holding his hand to his mouth just like his predecessor in Raphael's work who is leaning on his elbow at the bottom of the painting. May I venture to suggest that Tiepolo's unexpected act of subtle reverence in the S. Polo altar-piece is as important a reminder of the Raphaelesque heritage in the eighteenth century as Mengs's classicizing imitation of Raphael's art in the almost contemporary *Parnassus* (1761; Rome, Villa Albani)?

There is another, albeit tentative, connection between the *Virgin and Child Appearing to St John Nepomuk* and the *Sistine Madonna* which hints at the possibility that Tiepolo's 'quotations' from Raphael may have been prompted by more than personal esteem. Tiepolo painted the S. Polo altar-piece to complement the Nepomuk relic in the church: the relic's donor had been Augustus III, who was also the *Sistine Madonna*'s purchaser; the *Sistine Madonna* left Italy in 1754, and the *Virgin and Child Appearing to St John Nepomuk* was painted in 1754. Was the King of Poland the patron of the S. Polo altar-piece? Are the figural similarities linking the two altar-pieces a homage to him as well as to Raphael? Was Francesco Algarotti, who left Dresden in 1753 for Venice (where he remained until 1756), the intermediary between Augustus and Tiepolo? Probably, although one cannot answer these questions with certainty. Ten years earlier, however, a similar script had been acted out with the same dramatis personae: the King of Poland had commissioned Tiepolo through Algarotti to paint *Caesar Contemplating the Severed Head of Pompey*.[166] Given Augustus's commitment to the Nepomuk altar in S. Polo, it is quite possible that he did the same thing again, but with two important modifications: the painting was sacred in nature, and it remained in Tiepolo's native Venice.

The last great altar-piece that Tiepolo painted in Italy was *St Thecla Freeing Este from the Plague* (Pl. 127), an enormous canvas twenty-two feet high by almost thirteen feet wide.

---

[165] This information was courteously given to me by Dr Angelo Walther of the Gemäldegalerie in Dresden.

[166] The painting is lost, but a drawing of the same subject attributed to Tiepolo was sold as Lot 147 at Sotheby-Parke Bernet, New York, on 16 Jan. 1986; the drawing measures 209 × 295 mm. Through Algarotti, Tiepolo had also sold Augustus the *Banquet of Antony and Cleopatra* (Melbourne, National Gallery of Victoria).

It was placed in the presbytery behind the high altar of the Church of S. Tecla in Este on Christmas Eve 1759, and Tiepolo himself was present.[167] The small town of Este, some twenty miles to the south of Padua, can trace its noble history back to the pre-Roman era. Its fortunes declined in the seventeenth century, but during Tiepolo's lifetime the town enjoyed a revitalized economy, with several Venetian families maintaining farming interests there.[168] A group of important artistic commissions in S. Tecla, the town's Duomo, reflect Este's eighteenth-century financial boom: an architectural renovation by Antonio Gaspari, who had been responsible for S. Maria della Fava in Venice; a large canvas by Antonio Zanchi (*estense* by birth) of the *Canonization of Lorenzo Giustinian* (1702); an impressive altar-sculpture by Antonio Corradini (also *estense*) of the *Triumph of the Eucharist* (1725); and a ceiling-canvas by Jacopo Amigoni showing the *Martyrdom of St Thecla* (*c*.1745).[169] Tiepolo's canvas dominates the large Duomo from its apse and was the culmination of this local activity; the painting was commissioned in 1758, ten years after the Duomo's consecration by Carlo Rezzonico, Bishop of Padua, who in that year ascended the Throne of St Peter as Clement XIII.

The painting shows Thecla, the town's patron saint (who lived in the first century and knew St Paul in Asia Minor), praying to God for the plague to end against a background landscape of Este, its Duomo, and the Euganean Hills in the far distance. The efficacy of saintly supplication is indicated by the flight of the personfication of pestilence. The image recalls the terrible scourge that hit Venice and its *terraferma* in 1630. Este, in particular, had been ravaged; and, worse still, the town's first Duomo, an eighth-century structure that had been decaying for centuries, collapsed. Rebuilding the church represented civic reconstruction. Este's commemoration of its salvation from an epidemic 120 years after the event may seem extraordinary today, but in reminding the town of its seventeenth-century devastation, Tiepolo's image was emphasizing the flourishing life of the eighteenth. In 1748, when the new Duomo was consecrated, Zanchi's *Canonization of Lorenzo Giustinian* was removed from the presbytery, probably with the intention of replacing it with an image more representative of Este's history and public spirit. A decade later, the town's patron saint took her rightful place close to the Duomo's high altar, and the *estensi* could proudly contemplate the miraculous rebirth of their *paese*. Showing God the Father on a vertical axis with Este's sunlit bell-tower, his arm stretched forth in a sweeping gesture of peace and comfort to a town hit by disaster, Tiepolo's painting is one of the clearest pictorial celebrations of *campanilismo*, town pride, ever made in Italian art.

The Este altar-piece was also a great deal more than this, for it was the last great plague painting in European art.[170] Four elements reveal Tiepolo's debt to the pictorial tradition that had preceded him: the child seeking the dead mother's breast; the grieving man raising his hands to his head; the figure holding his nose against the stench of death; and the cortège in the middle distance carrying a corpse wrapped in a shroud. Tiepolo

[167] Cf. Morassi, *A Complete Catalogue*, p. 12; A. Pallucchini, *L'opera completa*, no. 248; Rizzi, *Mostra del Tiepolo*, no. 70; and G. Knox, *Tiepolo: Tecnica e immaginazione* (exh. cat., Ducal Palace, Venice, 1979), 100.

[168] Cf. C. Gallana, *Il Duomo di Este* (Este, 1961), 74.

[169] Ibid., *passim*.

[170] The one exception is David's *St Roch Interceding for the Plague-Stricken* (Marseilles, Musée des Beaux-Arts) of 1780. For an incomplete but rich survey of the pictorial 'plague' tradition, see *Venezia e la peste 1348–1797* (exh. cat., Ducal Palace, Venice, 1979), especially S. Mason Rinaldi's essay, 'La peste e le sue immagini nella cultura figurativa veneziana', 209–86.

127. G. B. Tiepolo, *St Thecla Freeing Este from the Plague* (oil on canvas, 675 × 390 cm.)

128. M. Raimondi, *Plague in Phrygia* (engraving after a design by Raphael, 195 × 249 mm.)

130. A. Giarola, *Verona Supplicating at the Feet of the Trinity for the Virgin's Intercession in the Plague of 1630* (oil on canvas, 336 × 272 cm.)

129. G. B. Tiepolo, Oil-sketch for *St Thecla Freeing Este from the Plague* (oil on canvas, 80 × 45 cm.)

would have been familiar with all of these motifs from prints such as Marcantonio Raimondi's *Plague in Phrygia*, based on drawings by Raphael (Pl. 128), Pietro Testa's *Saints Interceding with the Virgin for the Victims of the Plague*, and engravings made after Poussin's *Plague of Ashdod*.[171] It was probably from Poussin's image that Tiepolo took the two men carrying a cadaver; although they are not in his preparatory oil-sketch (Pl. 129), they are included in the final version. But it was Raimondi's print that was the major source for the Este painting. At the far right of the Renaissance engraving, there is a man holding one hand to his nose while with the other he reaches over to a dead mother and her living child; this group appears on the right of the oil-sketch, with only minor alterations.[172] Tiepolo subsequently moved the man to the centre of the painting, and replaced him with another figure from Raimondi's print, the despondent 'father' who expresses desolation at his 'wife's' death by clutching his hands to his head, a detail not usually found in the 'plague pictorial tradition'. Tiepolo also signed his name on a stone slab in the bottom left-hand corner of the canvas, just as Raimondi had acknowledged Raphael on a block in the bottom right-hand corner.

Unlike Poussin's *Plague at Ashdod* and Raimondi's *Plague in Phrygia*, however, the Este altar-piece is a devotional painting rather than a narrative. Following that tradition, Tiepolo created a two-tiered composition, using an imploring female in voluminous drapery to personify the body politic: Antonio Giarola's impressive *Verona Supplicating at the Feet of the Trinity for the Virgin's Intercession in the Plague of 1630* (1636; Pl. 130) could well have been a prime source for this.[173] The Veronese painting shows the Divinity above, with corpses and scenes of civic supplication in an identifiable and plague-stricken town below. In 1700, Ricci painted *St Gregory the Great Interceding with the Virgin and Child against the Plague* (Padua, S. Giustina), monumentalizing St Gregory by placing him on a platform. Then, in order to compose a pictorially dramatic sequence of 'plague events'—infection, death, prayer, and intercession, to be read sequentially from the bottom to the top—Ricci painted a sewer near the dead and below St Gregory; Tiepolo appropriated this same device.[174]

The Este altar-piece is much grander than its individual parts, and not just because of its dimensions; the space intervening between heaven and earth and near and far accounts for much of the painting's effect. God and St Thecla are heroic forms. And colour plays a major role in the altar-piece's power through the Este Duomo. Contrasting with the

---

[171] For the Raimondi, cf. *Venezia e la peste*, p. 238; for Testa, see E. Cropper, *The Ideal of Painting* (Princeton, 1984), fig. 3; and for Poussin's painting, see A. Blunt, *Nicolas Poussin* (Washington, DC, 1967), ii, pl. 64. The last two images, like Tiepolo's, were aftermaths of the 1630 epidemic. The 'nose-holding' motif can be found in Venetian paintings as well, in Zanchi's *The Plague in Venice* (1666) in the Scuola di S. Rocco (Pl. 33).

[172] Mason Rinaldi, 'La peste', p. 239, remarks that Raimondi's 'topoi sulla peste' were 'ripresi e sfruttati nelle figurazioni fino al Tiepolo'. On p. 146 of her review of Levey's *Giambattista Tiepolo* (*Art History*, 11 (1988)), D. Howard notes the similarities between Tiepolo's God the Father and Raphael's in the *Vision of Ezekiel* (Florence, Pitti Palace).

[173] Cf. for instance Domenico Tintoretto's *Venice Supplicating the Virgin and Christ* of 1631 (Venice, S. Francesco della Vigna) in *Venezia e la peste*, p. 261, no. a35; and for Giarola, ibid., p. 270,

no. a45. However, where the local saintly tradition was 'male', as in Bologna, saintly supplication was differently represented; compare Reni's Bolognese *Pala della Peste* (1631; Bologna, Pinacoteca Nazionale), in D. S. Pepper, *Guido Reni* (Oxford, 1984), fig. 164.

[174] Cf. Daniels, *Sebastiano Ricci*, pp. 84–5, fig. 202. Zanchi's *Plague in Venice*, a narrative painting devotional in character, too, includes archways that are Venetian bridges, not underground sewers. Two other 'borrowed' motifs in Tiepolo's painting—the fleeing personification of the plague which recalls Just Le Court's similar figure over the high altar of S. Maria della Salute, and the *macchina* of the globe, angels and swirling clouds, particularly as they appear in the Metropolitan Museum's oil-sketch—can be related to Corradini's *Triumph of the Eucharist* (1725) in the Este Duomo.

neutrals, earth tones, and pale hues of the landscape, the clouds, the town, and the stone platform are two areas of brilliant tonalities. In front of the ochre clouds and the cerulean sky, Tiepolo used a sunlit, chrome-like gold and cobalt blue to define God; and on earth, Thecla is draped in layers of bright gold, rose, and deep vermilion that fall around ample sleeves of radiant white. This fiery image, together with her feverish gaze as she sends her prayers up to God, express the saint's devotional intensity.

Although they did not mention the Este altar-piece, several discerning critics of the period who commented upon Tiepolo's art noted that the expression of true emotion was one of his greatest achievements. Cochin wrote of the *Martyrdom of St Agatha* in S. Antonio in Padua that 'the head of the saint expresses sadness very well . . .'.[175] Algarotti said of the same figure that 'one clearly seems to read the pain of the wound inflicted by the scoundrel blending with the [saint's] happiness at seeing Paradise open'.[176] Bergeret de Grancourt praised the *Way to Calvary* in S. Alvise, saying that it 'could not be better composed, better organized; *the expression is exact throughout . . .*'.[177] And, almost a century later, when Zanotto compared that same painting to Raphael's depiction of the subject (*Lo Spasimo*, in the Prado, Madrid), he said that to appreciate Tiepolo, the 'great composer, learned draughtsman, magical colorist, wise historian, and *profound judge of the passions*', one must go to S. Alvise.[178] St Thecla in Este also conveys deep emotion and pathos; but the elderly artist does not communicate them in the same way as he did when he was younger. In his late religious painting Tiepolo freed his protagonists from crowded figure compositions and ponderous architectural settings; they attain spiritual enlighten-ment and saintly ecstasy while liberated in space before the divine.

During his last years working in Madrid (1762–70), Tiepolo continued to paint images of saints in supplication or conversation with the Deity. Indeed, they dominate his late religious art, as six of the seven altar-pieces he executed for Charles III of Spain in the Church of S. Pascal at Aranjuez demonstrate.[179] This commission included some of the most orthodox of saintly themes in Christian art (i.e. *St Joseph with the Christ-child* and the *Stigmatization of St Francis of Assisi*), consonant with the lifelong conservatism of Tiepolo's sacred subject-matter. Although there is nothing innovatory in the narrative, several of the Aranjuez paintings do reveal something new in his art: a saintly mysticism expressing full relinquishment of the physical self. Achieved in part through expression and pose, this material surrender was also arrived at through an insistence on complementary

[175] C.-N. Cochin, *Voyage d'Italie . . . (1758)*, ed. M. Gault de Saint-Germain and M. Guyot de Fère (Geneva, 1972), 160: 'La tête de la Sainte exprime bien la douleur . . .'.

[176] F. Algarotti, 'Saggio sopra la pittura', in E. Bonora (ed.), *La letteratura italiana: Storia e testi*, xlvi. *Illuministi italiani*, ii. *Opere di Francesco Algarotti e Saverio Bettinelli* (Milan, 1969), 398: 'E nel volto di una santa Polonia [Algarotti's mistaken identification], che dipinta vedesi dal Tiepolo in S. Antonio a Padova, pare che si legga chiaramente *il dolore della ferita fattagli dal manigoldo misto col piacere dal vedersi con ciò aperto il Paradiso*.' Algarotti made this statement in the section of the essay entitled 'Della espressione degli affetti', where he mentions Le Brun and Rubens along with Tiepolo.

[177] M. A. Tornézy (ed.), *Bergeret et Fragonard: Journal inédit d'un voyage en Italie 1773–1774* (Paris, 1895), 388: 'On ne peut rien de mieux composé, de mieux groupé; *l'expression est juste partout . . .*'.

[178] F. Zanotto, *Pinacoteca veneta ossia i migliori dipinti delle chiese di Venezia* (Venice, 1867), no. 34: 'grande compositore, disegnator dotto, magico nel colorito, studioso della Storia, *e profondo conoscitore delle passioni . . .*'. And: 'Ma niuno, che sappiamo, lo espresse, come qui fece il Tiepolo, in mezzo a tanta prostrazione di forze e di dolore . . .'.

[179] For the most recent work on Tiepolo's religious paintings in Spain, cf. C. Whistler, 'Giambattista Tiepolo in Spain: The Late Religious Paintings', Ph.D. thesis (National University of Ireland, 1984); ead., 'A Modello for Tiepolo's Final Commission: The *Allegory of the Immaculate Conception*', *Apollo*, 121 (1985), 172–3; ead., 'G. B. Tiepolo at the Court of Charles III', *Burlington Magazine*, 128 (1986), 199–203. Five of the Aranjuez sketches are in the Princes Gate Collection, the Courtauld Institute Galleries, London, nos. 111–16.

colours of the same luministic intensity, thereby avoiding deep shadows and the illusion of spatial depth.[180] Even in *St Charles Borromeo Meditating on the Crucifix*, the one altar-piece of the group with a specific architectural setting, the pinks and reds of the saint's cope and the orange drapery on the right vibrate feverishly, particularly since they are seen against olive green (the archway) and bright whites (the angel, the column, and Borromeo's gown). All of the Aranjuez scenes appear to float on the canvas surface rather than to recede behind it. The figures, who are positioned close to the picture plane either in complete frontality or very nearly so, complement this modulation of colour so that the images seem to advance towards the viewer. The artistic result is almost hallucinatory, an old-age style comparable to that of Tiepolo's great Venetian predecessor, Titian.

The deep solemnity that imbues Tiepolo's late altar-pieces characterizes all of his religious art in fact. Whether his paintings depict Hebrew narratives or themes from the New Testament, Christian legends and traditions or saints in 'sacred conversation', the tone is invariably earnest. One could say this, of course, about all great religious art—that Tiepolo's is no different. But that is the point! His sacred imagery is no less hallowed than Raphael's or Bernini's, whose own seriousness was only recognized again in this century. But because Tiepolo's Virgin Mary sometimes resembles one of his 'secular' females, for example, his representation is denigrated and the entire context in which she appears is dismissed.

But it is damaging to Tiepolo, as it is to most painters, to interpret either his sacred or his secular scenes by taking one of the figures out of its context. This is the case, for example, with his Danaë in *Jupiter and Danaë* (Stockholm, University Museum) who, in isolation, is a luxuriously carnal figure; but when Tiepolo 'rolls' her over to be seduced by a decrepit, odious, and lecherous King of the Gods amidst the cacophony of a yelping terrier and screeching eagle, the scene loses all sensual appeal and shifts into irony.[181] But Tiepolo never sniggered behind his sacred imagery, not even when he portrayed the elderly Sarah toothlessly grinning in the Gallery at Udine (Pl. 40).[182] Like all Christians, Tiepolo had faith in the omnipotence of God.[183] Like most of his contemporaries, he believed that the world functioned not through impersonal, natural laws—which only a small, educated minority thought at the time—but because the Creator furnished mankind's existence with supernatural guidance.[184] This guidance was made manifest, as it had always been for Christians, through the saints, cults, and devotions that God offered. In his acceptance of Catholicism's fundamental beliefs, at least as he represented them in his painting, Tiepolo did not run counter to his age. Indeed, in depicting such a wide range of them, he embodied the settecento's encyclopaedic outlook towards knowledge and understanding. His art was entirely of its time.

Tiepolo's departure for Spain in 1762 marked the end of great religious painting in

---

[180] This is clear even in black and white photographs in which the complementaries 'cancel' themselves out and the Aranjuez sketches appear grey.

[181] For *Jupiter and Danaë*, cf. A. Pallucchini, *L'opera completa*, pl. xxii.

[182] Cf. Chap. 1, n. 105.

[183] And we know that he lived 'in devotion' to the Virgin of Carmel: cf. Chap. 2, p. 144.

[184] For a recent discussion on the eighteenth century's new views regarding God and natural law versus traditional attitudes, cf. J. Turner, *Without God, without Creed* (Baltimore and London, 1985), chap. 2: 'Enlightenment and Belief, 1690–1790', 35–72.

Venice: Piazzetta had died in 1754; and Pittoni (hardly a serious competitor) only lived until 1767. Nor were there any other contemporary 'religious artists' of significance in Italy. Naples, the only centre on the peninsula that had produced sacred art of a comparable quality to that of Venice, had already lost its most accomplished master, Francesco Solimena, in 1747. And only two painters of some importance survived him there: Corrado Giaquinto and Francesco de Mura. Giaquinto died in 1765, having returned from Madrid in 1762 just as Tiepolo went there; and de Mura, although he lived until 1782, is mostly remembered as an epigone of Solimena. Thus, Tiepolo was the last great Italian artist to portray tender devotion to the message of Christian salvation. He was also the last to express the piety of his native and millennial Republic which, within a generation of his death, was to meet its own demise. Venice's fall in May 1797 meant more than the dismantling of the State and its governmental apparatus. When Napoleon's armies marched into the city, the aristocracy was dissolved, and many of the religious corporations were eventually suppressed. The long and vigorous system of Venetian patronage was dead; Tiepolo's religious painting was, in conclusion, the end of a tradition.

SELECT BIBLIOGRAPHY

I. PRIMARY SOURCES

A. Manuscripts

BMC, MS Gradenigo 175 ('Chiese. Tomi Tre . . . che tengono notizie d'ogni genere intorno alle chiese a parrocchie di Venezia').

BNM, MSS It. Cl. VII, Cod. XVIII (8307) (G. A. Cappellari, 'Il Campidoglio Veneto').

BNM, MSS It. Cl. VII, Cod. DCCCCXXVIII ('Il Genealogico Barbaro').

BNM, MS Lat. Cl. X, Cod. CXLIX (3657) (G. G. Palferius, 'Monumenta Memorabilia Venetiarum').

B. General

ALGAROTTI, F., 'Lettera sopra la pittura', *Opere*, viii (Venice, 1792).

BOSCHINI, M., *Le ricche minere della pittura veneziana* (Venice, 1674).

CORNER, F., *Ecclesiae Venetae antiquis* (Venice, 1749).

——*Notizie storiche delle chiese e monasteri di Venezia e Torcello* (Padua, 1758).

——*Notizie storiche delle apparizioni, e delle immagini più celebri di Maria Vergine Santissima nella città, e dominio di Venezia* (Venice, 1761).

CORONELLI, V., *Guida de' forestieri . . . per la città di Venezia* (Venice, 1724, 1744).

DA CANAL, V., *Vita di Gregorio Lazzarini* (Venice, 1809).

——'Della maniera del dipingere moderno', *Mercurio filosofico, letterario, e poetico* (Venice, 1810).

DE BROSSES, C., *Lettres familières écrites d'Italie en 1739 & 1740* (Paris, 1929).

Forestiere illuminato (Il) intorno le cose più rare e curiose della città di Venezia (Venice, 1740).

FRESCHOT, C., *La nobiltà veneta* (Venice, 1707).

HUME, D., *The Natural History of Religion*, in *Hume on Religion*, ed. R. Wollheim (Cleveland and New York, 1964).

LIVAN, L. (ed.), *Notizie d'arte tratte dai notatori e dagli annali del N. H. Pietro Gradenigo* (Venice, 1942).

LONGHI, A., *Compendio delle vite de' pittori veneziani istorici più rinomati del presente secolo* (Venice, 1762).

ORLANDI, P. A., *Abecedario pittorico . . .* (Venice, 1753).

PACIFICO, P. A., *Cronica veneta, sacra e profana . . .* (Venice, 1697).

RIDOLFI, C., *Le maraviglie dell'arte . . .* (Venice, 1648), ed. D. von Hadeln (Berlin, 1914, 1924).

RIPA, C., *Iconologia* (Rome, 1603).

SANSOVINO, F., *Venetia città nobilissima et singolare* (Venice, 1581), ed. G. Stringa (1603); ed. G. Martinioni (1663).

ZANETTI, A. M., *Descrizione di tutte le pubbliche pitture della città di Venezia . . .* (Venice, 1733).

——*Della pittura veneziana e delle opere pubbliche* (Venice, 1771).

Zanetti, G., 'Memorie per servire all'istoria della inclita città di Venezia', ed. F. Stefani, *Archivio veneto*, 29 (1885), 93–148.

C. Religious Tracts

Benedict XIV, *Delle feste di Gesù Cristo . . . e della B. Vergine Maria* (Venice, 1747).

Da Ferrara, Francesco Antonio, *Orazione panegirica della protezione della Santissima Vergine sopra la città di Venezia . . .* (Venice, 1746).

De' Liguori, A., *Le glorie di Maria* (Bassano, 1845).

Finazzi, G., *Atti dei Santi Martiri Cittadini di Bergamo . . .* (Bergamo, 1852).

di Gesù, P. Giuseppe, *Istruzione intorno al sacro abitino di Maria Vergine del Carmine* (Perugia, 1752).

Grassi, P. Simone, *Compendiosa narrazione dell'indulgenze, privilegi, e grazie concesse all'ordine, confraternite, e chiese della gloriosissima Madre di Dio Maria Vergine del Carmine* (Rome, 1830).

——*Origini privilegi doveri e indulgenze del Santo Scapolare di Maria SS del Carmelo* (Venice, 1884).

Maffei, S., *Istoria teologica delle dottrine e delle opinioni corse ne' cinque primi secoli della Chiesa in proposito della divina grazia, del libero arbitrio, e della predestinazione* (Trent, 1742).

Magenis, P. Gaetano Maria, *Nuova, e più copiosa storia dell'ammirabile, ed apostolica vita di S. Gaetano Thiene . . .* (Venice, 1726).

Muratori, L. A., *Della regolata divozione dei cristiani . . .* (Venice, 1761).

Querini, C., *Relatione dell'immagine Nicopeia . . .* (Venice, 1645).

Raccolta di panegirici sopra tutte le festività di nostro Signore, di Maria Vergine, e de' santi, recitati da più celebri oratori del nostro secolo (Venice, 1760).

Rigamonti, D. Alessandro, *Ragguaglio della nascita, vita, e morte de' SS Martiri Fermo e Rustico con alcune notizie ancor di S. Procolo* (Bergamo, 1766).

Sardi, P. Giuseppe Maria, *Il giovane dell'ordine della S. Vergine Maria di Carmine dell'antica osservanza, istruito nella sua regola, ne' suoi obblighi e ne' suoi privilegi* (Venice, 1737).

Sarnelli, P., *Lezioni scritturali alla mente, ed al cuore sopra l'uno, e l'altro Testamento* (Venice, 1744).

Tassis, M. A., *La vita di S. Grata Vergine Regina nella Germania . . . principessa di Bergamo e protettrice della medesima città* (Padua, 1723).

Tiepolo, G., *Trattato dell'imagine della Gloriosa Vergine dipinta da San Luca* (Venice, 1618).

Tornielli, P. Girolamo, *Raccolta di canzoni in aria marinaresca sopra le festività di Maria sempre Vergine Madre di Dio* (Venice, 1786).

Vallarsi, D., *Dissertazione seconda sopra la esistenza e identità de' sacri corpi de' santi martiri Fermo e Rustico in Verona* (Trent, 1754).

Venezia favorita da Maria: Relazione delle immagini miracolose di Maria conservate in Venezia (Padua, 1758).

Zucconi, F., *Lezioni sacre sopra la divina scrittura . . .* (Venice, 1714).

II. SECONDARY SOURCES

Aikema, B., 'Early Tiepolo Studies, 1. The Ospedaletto Problem', *Mitteilungen des Kunsthistorisches Institutes in Florenz*, 26 (1982), 340–82.

Ambri, P. Berselli, *L'opera di Montesquieu nel Settecento italiano* (Florence, 1960).

ARNALDI, G. and STOCCHI, M. PASTORE (eds.), *Il Settecento* (*Storia della cultura veneta*), v¹⁻², (Vicenza, 1985).

ARSLAN, W., 'Studi sulla pittura del primo settecento veneziano', *Critica d'arte*, 1 (1935–6), 238–50.

BARCHAM, W., 'Giambattista Tiepolo's Ceiling for S. Maria di Nazareth: Legend, Traditions, and Devotions', *Art Bulletin*, 61 (1979), 430–47.

——'Patriarchy and Politics: Tiepolo's "Galleria patriarcale" in Udine Revisited', in D. Rosand (ed.), *Interpretazioni veneziane: Studi di storia dell'arte in onore di Michelangelo Muraro* (Venice, 1984), 427–38.

BATIFFOL, P., *History of the Roman Breviary* (London, 1912).

BEAN, J. and STAMPFLE, F., *Drawings from New York Collections, iii: The Eighteenth Century in Italy* (exh. cat., Metropolitan Museum of Art, New York, 1971).

BERENGO, M., *La società veneta alla fine del Settecento* (Florence, 1956).

BETTAGNO, A., *Disegni di una collezione veneziana del Settecento* (exh. cat., Fondazione Giorgio Cini, Venice, 1966 (Vicenza)).

BETTANINI, A. M., *Benedetto XIV e la repubblica di Venezia: Storia delle trattative diplomatiche per la difesa dei diritti giurisdizionali ecclesiastici* (Milan, 1931).

BOSISIO, A., *La chiesa di S. Maria del Rosario o dei Gesuati* (Venice, 1943).

BRAHAM, H., *The Princes Gate Collection* (London, 1981).

CALLAEY, F. 'La Critique historique et le courant pro-Janséniste à Rome au XVIIIᵉ siècle', in *Nuove ricerche storiche sul Giansenismo (Studi presentati nella sezione di storia ecclesiastica del Congresso Internazionale per il IV Centenario della Pontificia Università Gregoriana)* (Rome, 1954), 185–94.

CAMPANA, E., *Maria nel culto cattolico* (Turin, 1945).

CAVERSAZZI, C., 'Arte retrospettiva: Di alcuni dipinti di G. B. Tiepolo', *Emporium*, 9 (1899), 205–26.

CECCHETTI, B., *La repubblica di Venezia e la corte di Roma* (Venice, 1874).

CESSI, R., *Storia della repubblica di Venezia* (Florence, 1981).

CHADWICK, O., *The Popes and European Revolution* (Oxford, 1981).

CICOGNA, E., *Delle iscrizioni veneziane* (Venice, 1830).

CODIGNOLA, E., *Illuministi, Giansenisti e Giacobini nell'Italia del Settecento* (Florence, 1947).

CONTARINI, P., *Venezia religiosa* (Venice, 1853).

COPE, M., *The Venetian Chapel of the Sacrament in the Sixteenth Century: A Study in the Iconography of the Early Counter-Reformation* (New York and London, 1979).

DANIELS, J., *Sebastiano Ricci* (Hove, 1976).

EINAUDI, L., 'L'economia pubblica veneziana dal 1736 al 1755', *La riforma sociale*, 14 (1904), 177–96, 261–82, 429–50, and 609–37.

FARMER, D. H., *The Oxford Dictionary of Saints* (Oxford, 1982).

FEINBLATT, E., 'More Early Drawings by Giovanni Battista Tiepolo', *Master Drawings*, 5 (1967), 400ff.

FIOCCO, F., 'Aggiunte di Francesco Maria Tassis alla guida di Venezia di Antonio Maria Zanetti', *Rivista di Venezia*, 6 (1927), 141–74.

FIOROT, D., 'Nota sul Giansenismo veneto nei primi decenni del secolo XVIII', *Nuova rivista storica*, 35 (1951), 199–226.

FOGOLARI, G., 'Dipinti giovanili di G. B. Tiepolo', *Bollettino d'arte*, 2 (1923), 49–64.

FRANZOI, U. and DI STEFANO, D., *Le chiese di Venezia* (Venice, 1976).

GEORGELIN, J., *Venise au siècle des lumières* (Paris, 1978).

GROSSATO, L., 'I dipinti del Tiepolo della chiesa di San Massimo di Padova', in *Atti del Congresso Internazionale di Studi sul Tiepolo* (Venice, 1972), 44–50.

HASKELL, F., *Patrons and Painters: Art and Society in Baroque Italy* (New Haven and London, 1980).

HOWARD, D., 'Giambattista Tiepolo's Frescos for the Church of the Pietà in Venice', *Oxford Art Journal*, 9 (1986), 11–28.

JEMOLO, A. C., *Stato e Chiesa negli scrittori politici italiani del Seicento e del Settecento* (Turin, 1914).

——*Il Giansenismo in Italia prima della rivoluzione* (Bari, 1928).

KING, A. A., *Liturgies of the Religious Orders* (London, 1955).

KNOX, G., 'G. B. Tiepolo and the Ceiling of the Scalzi', *Burlington Magazine*, 110 (1968), 394–8.

——*Tiepolo: A Bicentenary Exhibition 1770–1970* (exh. cat., Fogg Art Museum, Harvard University, Cambridge, 1970).

——*Catalogue of the Tiepolo Drawings in the Victoria and Albert Museum* (London, 1975).

——*Tiepolo: Tecnica e immaginazione* (exh. cat., Ducal Palace, Venice, 1979).

——'Giambattista Tiepolo: Queen Zenobia and Ca' Zenobio: "Una delle prime sue fatture"', *Burlington Magazine*, 121 (1979), 409–18.

——*Giambattista and Domenico Tiepolo: A Study and Catalogue Raisonné of the Chalk Drawings* (Oxford, 1980).

——'Piazzetta, Pittoni and Tiepolo at Parma', *Arte veneta*, 39 (1985), 114–24.

——and THIEM, C., *Tiepolo: Zeichnungen von Giambattista, Domenico und Lorenzo Tiepolo aus der graphischen Sammlung der Staatsgalerie Stuttgart* (exh. cat., Staatsgalerie, Stuttgart, 1970).

LANE, F., *Venice: A Maritime Republic* (Baltimore, 1973).

LAVROVA, O., 'Le tele di Giambattista Tiepolo nel Museo Statale delle Belle Arti A. S. Pushkin (Mosca)', *Atti del Congresso Internazionale di Studi sul Tiepolo* (Venice, 1972), 124–30.

LEVEY, M., 'Tiepolo's Altar-piece for San Salvatore at Venice', *Burlington Magazine*, 97 (1955), 116–20.

——*National Gallery Catalogues: The Seventeenth- and Eighteenth-century Italian Schools* (London, 1971).

——*Painting in XVIII Century Venice* (London, 1980).

——*Giambattista Tiepolo* (New Haven and London, 1986).

LEWIS, C. D., *The Late Baroque Churches of Venice* (New York and London, 1979).

MARIACHER, G., 'Per la datazione di un'opera perduta di Giambattista Tiepolo', *Arte veneta*, 13–14 (1959–60), 237–9.

MARIUZ, A., *L'opera completa del Piazzetta* (Milan, 1982).

——and PAVANELLO, G., 'I primi affreschi di Giambattista Tiepolo', *Arte veneta*, 39 (1985), 101–13.

MARTINI, E., *La pittura veneziana del Settecento* (Venice, 1964).

——*La pittura del Settecento veneto* (Udine, 1982).

MASON RINALDI, S., *Palma Il Giovane* (Milan, 1984).

MODIGLIANI, E., 'Dipinti ignoti o mal noti di Giambattista Tiepolo', *Dedalo*, 13 (1933), 129–47.

MOLMENTI, P., *Acque-forti dei Tiepolo* (Venice, 1896).

——*Tiepolo: La Vie et l'œuvre du peintre* (Paris, 1911).

MORASSI, A., *G. B. Tiepolo* (London, 1955).

——*A Complete Catalogue of the Paintings of G. B. Tiepolo* (London, 1962).

MORETTI, L., 'La data degli apostoli della chiesa di San Stae', *Arte veneta*, 27 (1973), 318–20.

——'Notizie e appunti su G. B. Piazzetta, alcuni Piazzetteschi e G. B. Tiepolo', *Atti dell'Istituto Veneto di Scienze, Lettere, ed Arti*, 143 (1984–5), 359–95.

M OSCHINI M ARCONI, S., *Gallerie dell'Accademia: Opere d'arte dei secoli XVII, XVIII, XIX* (Rome, 1970).

M UIR, E., *Civic Ritual in Renaissance Venice* (Princeton, 1981).

M URARO, M., 'Ricerche su Tiepolo giovane', *Atti dell'Accademia di Scienze, Lettere, ed Arti di Udine*, 9 (1970–1), 5–64.

M ROZINSKA, M., *Disegni veneti in Polonia* (exh. cat., Fondazione Giorgio Cini, Venice, 1958).

N IERO, A., *La Scuola Grande dei Carmini* (Venice, 1963).

——'Giambattista Tiepolo alla Scuola dei Carmini: Precisazioni d'archivio', *Atti dell'Istituto Veneto di Scienze, Lettere, ed Arti*, 135 (1976–7), 373–91.

——*Tre artisti per un tempio: S. Maria del Rosario—Gesuati, Venezia* (Padua, 1979).

O'CONNOR, E. (ed.), *The Dogma of the Immaculate Conception* (Notre Dame, 1958).

O RLANDINI, G., *La Cappella Corner nella chiesa dei Santi Apostoli in Venezia* (Venice, 1914).

P ALLUCCHINI, A., *L'opera completa del Tiepolo* (Milan, 1968).

——'Nota tiepolesca', *Studi di storia dell'arte in onore di Antonio Morassi* (Venice, 1971), 303–7.

——'Aggiunte e precisazioni al catalogo delle opere del Tiepolo', *Atti del Congresso Internazionale di Studi sul Tiepolo* (Venice, 1972), 101–4.

P ALLUCCHINI, R., *La pittura veneziana del Settecento* (Venice, 1960).

——*La pittura veneziana del Seicento* (Milan, 1981).

——'Un Tiepolo in più, un Bencovich in meno', *Studi in onore di Giulio Carlo Argan* (Rome, 1984), 367–70.

P ASTOR, L., *History of the Popes*, xxxiv–xxxv (London, 1949).

Peinture italienne (La) au XVIIIe siècle (exh. cat., Palais des Beaux-Arts (Petit Palais), Paris, 1960).

P ETROCCHI, M., *Il Quietismo italiano del Seicento* (Rome, 1948).

——*Il tramonto della repubblica di Venezia e l'assolutismo illuminato* (Venice, 1950).

P ICCHINI, L., 'La repubblica di Venezia e l'Immacolata', *Mater Dei: Rivista mariana*, 5 (1934), 262–6.

P IGNATTI, T., *Veronese* (Venice, 1976).

P RANDI, A., 'Spiritualità e sensibilità', in V. Branca (ed.), *Sensibilità e razionalità nel Settecento* (Venice, 1967), 65–94.

P RÉCLIN, E. and J ARRY, E., *Le lotte politiche e dottrinali nei secoli XVII e XVIII, 1648–1789* (Turin, 1974) (*Storia della Chiesa dalle origini ai nostri giorni*, ed. L. Mezzadri).

R IZZI, A., *Disegni del Tiepolo* (Udine, 1965).

——*Mostra del Tiepolo: Dipinti* (exh. cat., Villa Manin di Passariano, Udine, 1971 (Milan)).

R OSA, M., *Riformatori e ribelli nel '700 religioso italiano* (Bari, 1969).

R OSENBERG, P., *Catalogue de la donation Othon Kaufmann et François Schlageter au Département des Peintures, Musée du Louvre* (Paris, 1984).

S ACK, E., *Giambattista und Domenico Tiepolo: Ihr Leben und Ihre Werke* (Hamburg, 1910).

Schilderkunst uit de eerste hand: Olieverfschetsen van Tintoretto tot Goya (exh. cat., Museum Boymans-van-Beuningen, Rotterdam, 1983).

S CHULZ, J., *Venetian Painted Ceilings of the Renaissance* (Berkeley, 1968).

S EMENZATO, C., 'Venezia religiosa nell'arte del Seicento', *Studi veneziani*, 14 (1972), 185–93.

S INDING-L ARSEN, S., *Christ in the Council Hall: Studies in the Religious Iconography of the Venetian Republic* (*Acta ad Archaeologiam et Artium Historiam Pertinentia*, 5; Institutum Romanum Norvegiae, Rome, 1974).

Sirèn, O., *Dessins et tableaux de la Renaissance italienne dans les collections de Suède* (Stockholm, 1902).

Sohm, P. L., 'Giambattista Tiepolo at the Palazzo Archinto in Milan', *Arte lombarda*, 68–9 (1984), 70–8.

Stella, A., *Chiesa e Stato nelle relazioni dei nunzi pontifici a Venezia: Ricerche sul giurisdizionalismo veneziano dal XVI al XVIII secolo* (Vatican City, 1964).

Swarzenski, G., 'Giovanni Battista Tiepolo's "Heilige aus dem Hause Grotta" im Städelschen Kunstinstitut zu Frankfurt', *Münchner Jahrbuch der bildenden Kunst*, 4 (1909), 60–5.

Tassini, G., *Iscrizioni della chiesa e convento di S. Salvatore di Venezia* (Venice, 1895).

Tramontin, S. (ed.), *Culto dei santi a Venezia* (Venice, 1965).

Vecchi, A., *Correnti religiose nel Sei–Settecento veneto* (Venice, 1962).

——'I modi della devozione', in V. Branca (ed.), *Sensibilità e razionalità nel Settecento* (Venice, 1967), 95–124.

Venezia e la peste, 1348–1797 (exh. cat., Ducal Palace, Venice, 1979).

Venise au XVIII siècle (exh. cat., Musée de l'Orangerie, Paris, 1971).

Venturi, F., *Settecento riformatore: Da Muratori a Beccaria* (Turin, 1969).

Urbani De Gheltof, G. M., *Tiepolo e la sua famiglia* (Venice, 1879).

Voss, H., 'Un taccuino di disegni del Tiepolo giovane', *Saggi e memorie di storia dell'arte*, 2 (1958–9), 317–22.

Warner, M., *Alone of All Her Sex* (New York, 1983).

Zampetti, P., *Dal Ricci al Tiepolo: I pittori di figure del Settecento a Venezia* (exh. cat., Ducal Palace, Venice, 1969).

Zanotto, F., *Tavola cronologica della storia veneta* (Venice, 1859).

——*Pinacoteca veneta ossia i migliori dipinti delle chiese di Venezia* (Venice, 1867).

——*Storia della predicazione nei secoli della letteratura italiana* (Modena, 1899).

Zava Boccazzi, F., *Pittoni* (Venice, 1979).

Zorzi, A., *Venezia scomparsa* (Milan, 1977).

GENERAL INDEX

(Arabic numbers in *italics* refer to pages with illustrations;
Roman numerals refer to colour plates.)

INDEX OF WORKS BY G. B. TIEPOLO

(Arabic numbers in *italics* refer to pages with illustrations;
Roman numerals refer to colour plates.)